The *Shari'a* State

Set against the backdrop of the Arab Spring, *The Shari'a State* examines the Islamist concept of political order. This order is based on a new interpretation of *shari'a* and has been dubbed 'the Islamic state' by Islamists. The concept of 'the Islamic state' has been elevated to a political agenda, and it is this agenda that is examined here.

In contrast to the prevailing view which sees the Arab Spring as a revolution, this book argues that the phenomenon has been neither a spring, nor a revolution. The term 'Arab Spring' connotes a just rebellion that led to toppling dictators and authoritarian rulers, yet in *The Shari'a State*, Bassam Tibi challenges the unchecked assumption that the seizure of leadership by Islamists is a part of the democratization of the Middle East.

Providing a new perspective on the relationship between the Arab Spring and democratization, this book is an essential read for students and scholars of Middle Eastern Studies, Islamic Studies and Politics.

Bassam Tibi is a Professor Emeritus of International Relations. Between 1973 and 2009 he taught at the University of Göttingen, and he was A. D. White Professor-at-Large at Cornell University until 2010. Between 1982 and 2000 Professor Tibi was, in parallel to his appointment at Göttingen, at Harvard University in a variety of affiliations, the latest of which was as the Bosch Fellow of Harvard. His work has been translated into 16 languages, and he has published a great number of books including *Islamism and Islam* (Yale University Press, 2012), *Islam's Predicament with Modernity* (Routledge, 2009) and *Islam, World Politics and Europe* (Routledge, 2008). In 1995 the president of Germany, Roman Herzog, presented him with the *Bundesverdienstkreuz*, Germany's highest federal decoration, for his 'bridging between Islam and the West'.

The *Shari'a* State
Arab Spring and Democratization

Bassam Tibi

Routledge
Taylor & Francis Group

LONDON AND NEW YORK

First published 2013
by Routledge
2 Park Square, Milton Park, Abingdon, Oxon OX14 4RN

Simultaneously published in the USA and Canada
by Routledge
711 Third Avenue, New York, NY 10017

Routledge is an imprint of the Taylor & Francis Group, an informa business

British Library Cataloguing in Publication Data
A catalogue record for this book is available from the British Library

Library of Congress Cataloging in Publication Data
Tibi, Bassam.
   The Shari'a state : Arab Spring and democratization / Bassam Tibi.
   p. cm.
   Includes bibliographical references and index.
   1. Islam and state–Arab countries. 2. Arab Spring, 2010–
   3. Islamic law–Political aspects. 4. Democracy–Arab countries. I. Title.
   BP173.6.T53 2013
   320.55'709174927–dc23
   2012039844

ISBN: 978–0–415–66216–1 (hbk)
ISBN: 978–0–415–66217–8 (pbk)
ISBN: 978–0–203–38555–5 (ebk)

Typeset in Times New Roman
by Swales & Willis Ltd, Exeter, Devon

Printed and bound in Great Britain by
TJ International Ltd, Padstow, Cornwall

Contents

Preface

Finally, a miracle happened at the beginning of 2011 in the Arab world, when a rebellion occurred toppling a series of ruling autocrats. The Middle East and North Africa (MENA) region seemed to join post-bipolar world history and its drive toward a global democratization. In the West two terms were generally indiscriminately used by scholars, journalists and Western politicians alike to dub the just and long overdue uprising in the Arab core of Islamic civilization: 'spring' and 'revolution'.

Two years after this uprising there seems to have been neither a spring nor a revolution. Throughout the six chapters of the present book I deplore the lack of accuracy in the use of these terms. Nonetheless – and simply for convenience – I do use the term 'Arab Spring', as a technical term for describing the uprising or rebellion of 2011–2012. The uprising resulted from the endless exasperations the Arab people had to endure for decades under ruthless dictatorship. The core questions this book poses are: Will the new regimes fulfil the needs that generated the uprising? Will there be a redeeming of the promise of an Arab Spring to bring freedom and prosperity? Will this spring deliver what the name 'spring' promises? Will there be a genuine democratization (let us not fool ourselves: democracy is much more than just elections) after all of these years of suffering? Will the exasperation of Arab people come to an end? These questions compelled me to write this book and they determine the scope of the present inquiry.

Among the slogans that spread in the aftermath of the breakdown of communism and after the end of the East–West conflict ('post-bipolarity') was the formula of a 'third wave of democratization'. Notions such as 'global democracy' and the 'globalization of civil society' followed and became promptly established in the public debate. Honest and more realistic students of the MENA region reserved judgement or simply expressed caution and scepticism about what they saw as the naive optimism of some opinion leaders. The views of scholars of the prevailing narrative were not supported by facts on the ground. Underlying the sceptical attitude is the fact that Arab-Islamic societies have not joined yet the global trend of democratization. Therefore the MENA region seemed to stand outside global history. Will the unexpected rebellion in the MENA counties, dubbed the 'Arab Spring', bring a real wind of change and make a difference? The uprising was an indication of a sea change, and it entailed a promise. But what kind of sea change was it, and what has been the outcome?

The core beneficiaries of the Arab Spring are the Islamist movements, not the people who took to the streets in rebellion. Islamists were the best organized opposition in the MENA region. The Arab Spring was not of their making, but they were in a position to incrementally take over and be in charge of all affairs and at all levels. Their professed plan for change is based on an envisioned replacement of the secular order of the sovereign nation-state by a *'nizam islami'*/'Islamic system' based on what they believe to be *'shari'a'*, which is not the traditional one. The question that arises in this context is: Will this drive lead to democratization? I wrote this book to provide an answer to this question. I felt this to be a duty, for reasons that I will elaborate upon.

In the past decades I have been fortunate to acquire a constituency of readers of my books. Those who consulted my most recent book, *Islamism and Islam*, published in 2012 by Yale University Press, are aware of my decision to leave the stage after a rich 40 years of activity. Hence my decision, expressed in that book, to view it as my final one. In Chapter 4 of the present book I shall explain and provide a justification for the reconsideration that led to the writing of this book. The Arab Spring has been the incentive.

Parallel to the Arab Spring there has been a most perplexing and intriguing sea change in the West itself in regard to the matters under discussion. Earlier, when the dictatorial, authoritarian regimes persecuted the Islamist movements, the West basically applauded them as it viewed Islamism through the lens of counter-terrorism. In a way, the West gave the authoritarian regimes credit for fighting Islamism. Today, the same people in the West move from maligning what is named 'radical Islam' to a highly naive exoneration of Islamism. Torn between these extremes, this book seeks to provide a critical study of the Islamist *shari'a* state. It is most important to dissociate this book from all kinds of thinking devoid of distinctions and nuances. True, I criticize Islamism, but it is alien to my thinking to engage in a polarization that is based on binaries. Only skimming reviewers fail to discern my elaborations on these distinctions and nuances, attacking my work. My books not only account for distinctions within Islam, but within Islamism as well.So, I refuse to join those who replace the 'bogeyman' of communism with the 'bogeyman' of Islamism in the spirit of a Cold War waged by the West (see Chapter 3).

The frame of reference of the reasoning developed in this book is the direction within Islamdom that my Moroccan fellow-Muslim Abdou Filali-Ansary identifies as 'enlightened Muslim thought'. As will be shown in Chapters 1 to 3, there are many authoritative Muslim sources on which this thought rests. The work of Ali Abdelraziq is the first. Abdelraziq argues on solid grounds that traditional Islamic *shari'a* has never been an order of the state. Islam is a religious faith, not an ideology for a political order. I combine this line of reasoning with the tradition of humanism in Islam to look critically on this basis at the *shari'a* state that Islamists wrongly bill as an Islamic democracy. Another Muslim authority on which the present inquiry draws is the late Mohammed Abed al-Jabri. His work is appreciated in an article that appeared in parallel to the completion of this book. I am grateful to the editor of the US journal *Soundings*, John Kelsay, who published my article 'Islamic Humanism vs. Islamism' (see below, note 14 to the Introduction), in which I highlight the significance of the work of al-Jabri in the context of the Arab Spring. His pursuit of the revival of the tradition of Islamic humanism (see the first section to Chapter 3) should be combined with the work of Abdelraziq, and this is what I do. In short, the critique of the Islamist *shari'a* state is inspired by Muslim sources, not by Western ones.

As a student of value conflicts who recognizes the tensions between religious and secular concepts of order, I adopt from Mark Juergensmeyer the notion of a 'new Cold War' – actually hit upon earlier by Islamists themselves in their coinage '*harb al-afkar*', the Arabic word for the same notion. However, I do not share the spirit of continuation of the old Cold War against communism in the shape of a new war against Islamism. Some – for instance at the Hoover Institution – do this as a pretext for justifying *Pax Americana*. I do not share this sentiment, which could never be the spirit that drives the undertaking of a critique of the Islamist *shari'a* state endeavoured in this book.

Two historical events, the Arab Spring of 2011 and earlier the 9/11 attacks in 2001, have contributed to a polarization between what is viewed as 'left' and 'right'. The left, including liberals, upgrades Islamism to a drive for Islamic democracy, while the right (e.g. the Hoover Institution's Working Group on Islamism and the International Order led by Charles Hill and Fouad Ajami) fights a new Cold War on Islamism in favour of *Pax Americana*. I disagree with both directions and go 'beyond left and right' (Anthony Giddens) in a commitment to a democratic world peace as an order based on pluralism, not on US American hegemony. I criticize Islamists because their *shari'a* state is not a contribution to a genuine democracy, and also because I believe that their rejection of *Pax Americana* would be reasonable if it were not contaminated by an antisemitic anti-Americanism. These nuances and differentiations are not only not shared by the mainstream in the West; they are simply ignored. Therefore, and despite my location as a European citizen in the West, I prefer to look at the Arab Spring and at the Islamist *shari'a* state through the lens of enlightened Muslim thought. Nonetheless, I have never been a follower of Edward Said's 'Orientalism in reverse'. The implicit (never spoken) conclusion of Said is that only Middle Easterners could have accurate insights into their region. In contrast to this, I honestly appreciate the work of bright-minded Western scholars and do not accuse them of Orientalism. Their contributions – examples are the work of Marshall G. Hodgson and Maxime Rodinson in the past and John Kelsay in the present – are among my sources.

There is a sentiment of Eurocentrism, enhanced to West-centrism, which is often at work when Islam is the issue. This notion could have a variety of meanings, the most popular of which is a self-centric imposition of Western views on the non-Western other. In the context of the theme of this book I suggest also seeing in the West-centred mindset a focusing by Westerners on the self in complete ignorance of what others think. Often it is a 'language' barrier that separates the two parties. Since the fall of the Berlin Wall, the most common view in the West has been that the greatest obstacle to democracy has fallen. The inference has been a belief in the global triumph of democracy. The hoped-for democratic peace rests on the institutions of the sovereign nation-state combined with democratic governance. This positive thinking was interrupted for a decade following the 9/11 attacks of 2001. The debate became diverted towards what was then named 'Islamic extremism' or, worse, 'radical Islam'. That focus ended abruptly with Arab Spring, when it moved from one extreme to the other. Suddenly a debate on 'moderation' and the 'inclusion' of Islamist movements has replaced the debate on 'countering terrorism'. These movements were classified earlier in a defamatory and erroneous way by the vague notion of 'radical Islam'. Today, the same movements have become champions of democratization in the context of the Arab Spring. Whom should one believe?

The reality on the ground often differs completely from prevailing Western views and perceptions. The post-bipolar age of 'global democratization' did not materialize. The Arab world that constitutes the cultural core of Islamic civilization continued to be ruled by ruthless authoritarian regimes. These regimes were not very well understood, not even by some established academic experts. The core opposition to these regimes was formed by the Islamist movements. They wanted to replace existing dictatorships by their vision of a *shari'a* state, not by democracy. It is not I who impute this to them. This is what they themselves state, in their own sources. I only cite what they say. These Islamist opposition movements were not properly understood either. The present book begins in its first chapter by taking issue with the prevailing misinterpretations and misconceptions in a sober analysis of the envisioned *shari'a* state as a political order that Islamists themselves are fighting for.

The present book aims to fulfil two tasks: first, it takes issue with the Western prevailing narrative about Islamism, and, second, it screens the Islamist project of a *shari'a* state on the basis of changing assumptions. To put it another way: this book deals with the political thought of Islamism, specifically with the assumption that the core political idea of Islamism is the *shari'a* state. I claim to be a democrat, but do not claim to be impartial. I therefore acknowledge my adherence to the 'enlightened Muslim thought' (the 'enlightened turn') outlined above, which will be discussed in more detail in the first section of Chapter 3.

In looking comparatively beyond the world of Islam, I reject the comparison of the Arab Spring with the successful post-communist democratization in Eastern Europe following the fall of the Berlin Wall in 1989 that led to the breakdown of communism. This comparison is baseless on all counts; it is often made by people who lack knowledge of facts on the ground, whether with regard to Eastern Europe or to the MENA counties. Underlying this rejection is a solid analysis of Islamism. Islamist movements are not comparable with the Polish Solidarność, because their concept of political order does not reflect a genuine democratic rule. The Islamist ideology of the *shari'a* state is not in line with the basics of democracy.

That said, Islamists should nonetheless be given a chance and engaged with; their movements should be allowed to participate – on condition that they really change their agenda. If they really do this, then there will be a post-Islamism. If not, we should be prepared for a new tyranny, this time in the garb of a political religion. Muslims like Abdou Filali-Ansary (he of the 'enlightened turn') would be unhappy to see their tolerant religious faith being abused to legitimate the new intolerance of a religion-based authoritarianism replacing the secular one in the garb of an 'Islamic *shari'a* democracy'.

This book was completed at the University of Göttingen, where I served as Georgia-Augusta Professor of International Relations from 1973 onwards until I retired in 2009. This book project was supported by a new centre established at this university by the acclaimed and renowned scholar of democracy, Professor Franz Walter. His Institute for the Study of Democracy provided a grant to cover the extremely valuable research assistance provided by Thorsten Hasche. I am also grateful to Professor Walter for providing a forum for the discussion of the research findings included in this book, in the community of researchers and fellows of his institute. Thorsten and I were given the opportunity to present our research in this community. This young scholar Thorsten Hasche has been my close associate at every stage of writing this book. Although his name also appears in the Acknowledgements, I should like to acknowledge in this place the great contribution that Thorsten has made to this book; I am proud to be his advisor and supervisor for the PhD dissertation on Islamism he is in the final stages of completing. I cannot imagine being able to complete this book – as indeed my earlier one with Yale University Press, *Islamism and Islam* – without the invaluable and unfailing assistance Thorsten provided with great commitment at literally every level of the work in this project. My gratitude is unbounded.

In the final chapter of this book I take issue with the culture of policing speech to impose limits on free academic research. I wrote this book as a native Syrian Sunni-Muslim, born in Damascus, who fled his home to Europe to enjoy freedom and all civil rights. I hope that those who dislike my presentation of the Arab Spring and my criticism of the Islamist *shari'a* state will not subject my person and my work to the deplorable culture I criticize in Chapter 6. I not only hope for supportive readers and for a balanced reception of my contribution, but also welcome constructive criticism on the grounds of civility and mutual respect. The US journal *Soundings*, which – as mentioned above – published my first article this year on 'Islamic Humanism vs. Islamism' (presenting a pluralist Islamic humanism as the alternative to the false unity of a *shari'a* state) introduces itself on its first page as a forum that 'encourages scholars to challenge the fragmentation of modern intellectual life', but then cogently adds 'however, our century shows that there are worse things'. These 'worse things' are 'the disguised violence of false unity and forced coherence'. In my view this caveat fits well to characterize the prevailing opinion in Islamic studies. In line with the caveat, the present book argues against the prevailing narrative and contradicts its unchecked assumptions concerning the *shari'a* state. I share *Soundings*' misgivings. There are indeed 'worse things than a fragmented life' caused by dissent. The opening chapter of this book, and equally the concluding one, face squarely the 'disguised violence of false unity and forced coherence', based on the presentation of fresh and different outlooks.

Bassam Tibi
Göttingen, October 2012

Acknowledgements

The basic acknowledgement relates to the place of this book in my personal and academic life as an academic author of Muslim-Arab background (I am a Sunni native of Damascus) as well as a human rights activist. I have endured the dictatorial regimes ruling the Arab world and fled Damascus to take refuge in Europe. A German ambassador reported to me a conversation he had with the late Hafez al-Assad, in the course of which this dictator expressed his wish to twist my neck with his own hands in response to my appearances – as commentator on the German television channel ZDF and to my newspaper articles in the *Frankfurter Allgemeine Zeitung*. These activities were reported to him by the Syrian *mukhabarat/* secret police. Unlike his immature son Bashar, the late senior Assad had a full grip on power, holding all strings. I was advised not to take the risk of attending the funerals of my dear parents in Damascus when they passed away. The risk would have included that of being escorted afterwards to one of the prisons of the *mukhabarat* – there to be tortured. For me personally, therefore, the Arab Spring is most welcome as a promise of freedom, and I greatly applaud it. The yearning for freedom is at the top of Arab-Muslim aspirations. Democracy may not be perfect, but it is the best system for guaranteeing human dignity and therefore it deserves to be universal. Muslims are no exception. I wrote this book to grapple with the question as to whether the Arab Spring brings democracy to the Arab world or not. In my inquiry I draw on earlier research, which constitutes the backbone of this book. The present project has been supported by numerous persons and institutions. These supporters share with me the view that this inquiry into the interrelation between Islamism and democratization stands above chronicles and topicalities. Therefore, this inquiry focuses on the big picture and addresses general questions. The topmost of these questions is the Islamist invention of a political *shari'a* to legitimate a new political order in the process of democratization – a process that is used instrumentally to empower Islamist movements.

In the first place I acknowledge the funding for the research for this study provided by the Institute for the Study of Democracy at the University of Göttingen. The director of this institute, Professor Franz Walter, who has been a great source of support and inspiration, provided funds to cover the expense of the research assistance of Thorsten Hasche. Since 2007 Thorsten has been my associate in the writing of several books. I have many reasons to repeat the acknowledgement made in the Preface that this book would have been utterly impossible without the research assistance provided by Thorsten at all levels, and the same is true for all my books since 2008. Also at the top of the list of institutions that have promoted the thinking unfolded in the ensuing six chapters of this book is the Beirut-based Centre for Arab Unity Studies. This centre honoured me in 1983 with an invitation to join a community of Arab democrats engaged in illuminating 'the crisis of democracy in the Arab world', as well as with the great privilege of co-authoring the book published in Arabic under the same title. Ahead of that project we had in October 1980 the project called 'The Arabs Face Their Destiny/*Les Arabes face à leur destin*', run by the Tunis-based Centre d'Etudes et de Recherches Economiques et Sociales (CERES). The project was possible at that time because it predated the Ben Ali dictatorship. The proceedings of both projects were published in Arabic; the books are referenced and discussed in more detail in Chapter 4. These books have already become historical documents in the history of the introduction of democracy into the Arab world.

There are other institutions that have supported my research on Islam, Islamism and democracy. This research viewed Islamism as just one variety of the global phenomenon of religious fundamentalism, which I studied in several team projects in its interrelation to democracy and in the context of the need for democratization. The persons to whom I owe great debts are numerous. At the top I mention Seymour M. Lipset, who gave me with the honour of writing an extensive entry on 'Fundamentalism' in his four-volume *Encyclopedia of Democracy* (1995), and Professor Mark Bevir for providing the opportunity to do the same in his *Encyclopedia of Political Theory* (2010).

As already stated, no one would be able to form a proper judgement on democracy and the Arab Spring without placing both in an overall context. The themes of this overall context revolve around democracy and the *shari'a* state. In this regard, many earlier research projects have had a great impact on the present study. Concerning the first focus, democracy, two big research projects are to be singled out, which resulted in books to which I had the honour to be a contributor and that are pertinent to the present one.

The first of these is the University of Louvain (Belgium)-based project on 'Democracy and Democratization in Asia' conducted in 1994 and published in 1997. Professor Michèle Schmiegelow, the project's director and the book's editor, refers in her preface to the research findings and notes: 'On this basis it was easy to conclude that liberal democracy . . . is as promising a form of government for Asia as it is for other parts of the world.' From this she concludes a universal validity of liberal democracy. The core of Islamic civilization is based in Asia, as the birth of Islam took place in Arabia. I share Professor Schmiegelow's view, as I demonstrate in my chapter to her volume. That contribution deals with the quest for an Islamic enlightenment that is needed to underpin the introduction of democracy into Islamic civilization in a process of democratization. In this stance I find myself in conflict with the foremost Islamist of our times, Yusuf al-Qaradawi. This Islamist sheykh contends in his book *Hatmiyyat al-Hall al-Islami/The Islamic Solution* that 'the liberal-democratic solution failed' (p. 7) and he then concludes on p. 88

that 'the Islamic (*shari'a*) state is the solution'. He defames Muslims who disagree as 'disbelievers, wrong-doers and truly wicked' – labels used by him for 'liberal Muslims'. For this reason, I learned while writing this book to avoid the now charged label 'liberal', using instead the notion of 'Islamic enlightened thought'. This is a new direction in contemporary Islam, and one to which this book adheres. It is intriguing to find Qaradawi among the authors selected by Charles Kurzman for his reader *Liberal Islam*. Comment is superfluous, but the reference may serve as one of the reasons for avoiding the use of the formula 'liberal Islam'.

The second project on democracy to be acknowledged was conducted on behalf of the Club of Madrid by Professors Leonard Weinberg and Peter Neumann within the framework of a big event, 'The International Summit on Democracy', held in Madrid in March 2005. The completed papers were published in the book *Democratic Responses to Terrorism*, edited by Weinberg. The president of the Club of Madrid, Fernando Henrique Cardoso, formerly the president of Brazil, prefers a focus on democracy to obsessive, security-centred dealing with terrorism. In his Foreword to *Democratic Responses to Terrorism*, he recommends 'fighting terrorism' in the mindset 'of democracy and human rights'. This is the better 'moral imperative' that is 'also a practical one'. My contribution to the book is 'Islam, Islamism and Democracy. The Case of the Arab World'. The mindset of that project guides the present book.

After democracy, the second focus of the present book is the Islamist idea of a *shari'a* state, placed in the overall context of the *shari'a* tradition. My work on *shari'a* is as old as my own study of Islam and its civilization. My 1990 book *Islam and the Cultural Accommodation of Social Change*, completed in Princeton and Harvard, included a major chapter on *shari'a* and social change. On the basis of my research on *shari'a* I was invited to join various projects in which I continued this work. Among the published work on *shari'a* are books that include my contributions. I am grateful to Professor Mashood Baderin for placing a chapter by me in his handbook on *International Law and Islamic Law*, and to Professor Shahram Akbarzadeh for doing the same in his multi-volume *Islam and Globalization*. The Norwegian scholars Tore Lindholm and Kari Vogt included my work in their *Islamic Law Reform and Human Rights*. Earlier, Abdullahi An-Na'im and Francis Deng ran a project on 'Human Rights in Africa' at the Wilson Center in Washington, DC, which I joined. Professor Renata Uitz invited me to Budapest's Central European University to join her School of Law's project on 'Religion in the Public Square'. I presented there a paper on the return of *shari'a*, which will be published soon as an article in a scholarly journal.

During my six years' tenure as A. D. White Professor-at-Large at Cornell University I delivered many lectures on *shari'a* law at the Cornell Law School. The Japanese Association of Comparative Law and Constitutional Law invited me to speak on *shari'a* as an alleged constitutional law at its international conference in Tokyo in 2005. My extensive paper was published in Tokyo in the proceedings volume *Church and State: Toward Protection for Freedom in Religion*, in both English and Japanese. My research background in *shari'a*, which I have documented in the activities and publications listed, informs all the *shari'a* chapters in the present book. Although these rest on the earlier studies that I have cited, all six chapters engage in fresh, new and updated reasoning that relates to the place of Islamism in the new context of the Arab Spring.

After the acknowledged persons and institutions that – in a long-term perspective – were supportive of the research presented in this volume, I need to mention again by name Professor Franz Walter and Thorsten Hasche, the pivotal supporters. In particular Thorsten Hasche's contribution to this book (as to all my earlier three Routledge books and to my Yale book on Islamism) is of great significance. The debt I owe Thorsten is immense and I fail to find the right words to express my deep gratitude for his research assistance and also his practical support in the completion of the manuscript. The next person to whom I owe great gratitude is my editor at Routledge, Joe Whiting. With Joe's unfailing support I have published three major books with Routledge since 2006. I am also grateful to Kersti Wagstaff for careful and sympathetic copy-editing that improved my English prose tremendously and for superb collaboration in finalizing the edited manuscript, as well as to Kat Rylance for her preparation of the manuscript, and to Emma Hudson and Caroline Watson for supervising the production of the book.

I am fully aware of the controversial character of my work, which is guided by a reform Islam and based in 'enlightened Muslim thought'. Knowing the obstacles in my way, I count myself most fortunate to enjoy the support of such great editors as Joe Whiting of Routledge and Bill Frucht of Yale University Press, who not only pay lip service to pluralist academic freedom, but truly practise it and grant it to others. This is a declining virtue in the business of publications in the field, particularly on the subject matter of the present book. My gratitude for this is immense and my appreciation unlimited.

This fourth book I publish with Routledge is exceptional for the following reason. In my 2012 *Islam in Global Politics* (a Routledge book), I announced in the Preface that it would be – alongside my Yale UP book published in parallel – my last one, to 'end my 40-years-long academic career and leave the stage'. I explain the exception I have made to this in Chapter 4, but already ask my readers here for indulgence, both for my personal way of addressing the issues and for their approval of the exception I made in writing this book.

Bassam Tibi
October 2012

Introduction

Will the *shari'a* state be the outcome? The Arab Spring and the hope for democratization

Since the Arab Spring, the region of the Middle East and North Africa has been undergoing a process of radical change. Its direction affects the entire environment of this regional subsystem of the international system, and probably world politics in general as well. This region has three kinds of states: Arab, non-Arab but Muslim (Turkey and Iran), and Israel, a Jewish state with a European orientation. This book links three concerns; all are mentioned in the heading to this Introduction, and they also occur in the title of this book. While this Introduction outlines the trajectory of this book and its contents, it focuses on the core question: Will the changes induced by the Arab Spring bring the long-awaited democracy to the Arab world? For make no mistake: democracy is far more than just the ballot box.

One interpretation of modern history suggests viewing it as composed of three historical 'waves' of democratization. The most recent and last of these waves followed the fall of the Berlin Wall and the related breakdown of communism in Eastern Europe. This wave then spilled over beyond Europe to become global. The authoritarian Arab regimes of the MENA region were an exception, remaining untouched by this development; they succeeded in keeping this pivotal world region out of that third wave. The Arab Spring seems to have changed this blockade. It began with a promise of freedom. The rebelling 'no-hope younger generation' took action in a grassroots leaderless uprising. This revolt was coupled with the hope that the Arab world would join the mainstream of world history. This promise of freedom is the positive point of departure for writing this book. There is, however, also a negative aspect that relates to the hijacking of the Arab Spring by well-organized Islamist movements – who have not only restricted their approval of democracy to approving of elections, but have coupled this with a dismissal of democratic values as Western. This Islamist venture amounts to their viewing democratization as having given them a mandate to establish a state based on *shari'a* billed as an 'Islamic democracy' – a notion to be discussed later in this Introduction.

The evidence for this assertion is the political conduct of the Movement of the Muslim Brothers, the most significant power in the aftermath of the Arab Spring. The leaders of the Muslim Brothers are well known for their practice of double-speak (Chapter 4, note 41), but the empowerment of their movement emboldened them to speak out and acknowledge their agenda, or at least of a part of it. Unlike the AKP (Justice and Development) Islamists of Turkey, the Muslim Brothers of Egypt do not deny that their goal is a state based on *shari'a*. However, for convenience they say that this *shari'a* state is what they see as an Islamic democracy. All this may be read in the election programme of the Egyptian Muslim Brothers party, called the Freedom and Justice Party (FJP). The programme will be cited in more detail in Chapter 4.

Throughout modern history, since Mohammed Ali came to power in Egypt in 1805, Egypt has been the core location for exemplary developments that spill over to the entire region.[1] What happens there is indicative of what may happen later elsewhere in the region, be it modernization (under Mohammed Ali), the introduction of democracy and a multi-party system (under the Wafd party of Saad Zaghlul), or the intervention of the military authorities into politics under the banner of a revolutionary pan-Arabism (under Gamal Abdel Nasser and his fellow 'Free Officers'). The most recent example of Egypt as a place that generates new directions is the Islamist rise to power to establish a 'state . . . based on *shari'a* (Islamic law) as a frame of reference', as the election programme of the Muslim Brothers' FJP states. After all, Islamism was born in Egypt in 1928. The statement gives rise to this question: *Is the Islamist agenda that has been cited compatible with democracy?*

This question is the driver of the analysis laid out in the following six chapters. The Introduction outlines the basic features and the trajectory of this inquiry.

Beyond obsessions and Western wishful thinking

It is not an easy job to provide an inquiry with the scope outlined above, particularly when it is coupled with questions that touch on strongly guarded taboos. The reason for this difficulty is the present politicization of scholarship in Middle Eastern and Islamic studies. Given the resulting polarization, I need to state, in a resolve to avoid any misunderstanding, first that questioning the Islamist commitment to democracy is not about Islam as a religion, and second that my criticism is not guided by any spirit of exclusion. I see no problems related to this religion viewed as faith/*iman*. Moreover, the ethics of Islam could be mobilized as a wellspring for promoting a spirit of true democratization. The problem is Islam*ism*. I operate a strict distinction between Islamism and Islam. The first chapter of the 2012 book with which I hoped to conclude my academic career, *Islamism and Islam* (Yale University Press), bears the heading, 'Why Islamism is not Islam'. This distinction firmly underpins the argument that Islamist *shari'a*tization does not constitute a part of Islamic faith, nor does it promote the democratization process. Although I see problems with Islamism, I argue for engagement, but do not conflate this with empowerment.

To go beyond obsessions and Western wishful thinking one needs to look at the reality of an ongoing process of *shari'a*tization of Islam. This is the defining issue in the current thriving Islamist politics; hence the focus of the present book – on the idea itself of a *shari'a* state. The 'religionized politics' of Islamist movements compel one to distinguish quite clearly between engaging these movements in a democracy and empowering them in a *shari'a* state. The political order represented by a *shari'a* state is an Islamist construction to be analysed in the context of the assumed connection between democratization and the Arab Spring. The distinction already addressed between what is Islamic (relates to faith) and what is Islamist (relates to a political ideology based on religionized politics) is essential to the present analysis. If this basic distinction is ignored or dismissed – as it is by some pundits – then the core argument of the present book will be incomprehensible. Islam as a faith is not only a respected world religion, it can also claim freedom to worship as an entitlement under human rights. Islam is also a world civilization that constitutes an essential part of world history: a fact that can be ignored only by one constrained by a Eurocentric view of the world. Although Islamism draws on both – that is, on faith (the claim of *shari'a* /Islamic revival) and on history (the claim to reverse 'the end of history' in a revival to 'a return of history') – a close examination reveals that novelty is at work in the invention of a tradition.

There is another area of distinction besides the one between Islamism and Islam that needs to be mentioned in order to avoid a potential misunderstanding in the minefield that this book is entering. This is the distinction between engagement and empowerment mentioned above. One may have the right to question whether Islamist movements have a true commitment to democracy, but in a democracy no one has the right to exclude them from politics. All three authoritarian regimes toppled in the course of the Arab Spring – Ben Ali in Tunisia, Mubarak in Egypt, and Qadhafi in Libya – demonized Islamism to legitimate their dictatorial grip. Democratization must entail an end to this evil. Islamist movements could become political parties (as happened in Egypt) that need to be engaged at all levels. The issue is, however, how to do this. First, I repeat that engagement is not to be confused with empowerment. Second, engagement needs to take place on the grounds of democratic rules shared by all, Islamists and non-Islamists alike. Pluralism is also the framework of any democracy and Islamists need to respect this. If the terms of engagement are tampered with by Islamists, then non-Islamist Muslims and minorities have reason to worry about their freedom and also their faith. The *International Journal for Religious Freedom* rightly worries that 'uncertainty and anxieties will remain among minorities . . . (due to) calls for the implementation of Islamic *shari'a* law and the establishment of an Islamic state' and asks 'whether . . . Islamists will grant religious freedom to minorities or will they move toward repression?'[2] For the sake of honesty, it must be stated that not only Islamist *shari'a*, but also traditional *shari'a* does not approve the basic individual right of religious belief.

These preliminary remarks must be properly grasped if the venture of the present book is to be understood. On the basis of an 'enlightened Islamic turn' (Abdou Filali-Ansary's phrase; see notes 8 and 18), I want as a Muslim to go beyond Western obsessions and the related wishful thinking to address the linkage between the three notions contained in the title of this book. Driving the present inquiry is the desire to raise and grapple with some pertinent related questions on the grounds of facts. It is a fact that the region of the Middle East and North Africa was the birthplace of Islam and continues at present to be the centre of its Islamicate civilization. There are collective memories related to these facts that underpin contemporary nostalgia and identity politics. In this book I leave classical history aside, although I keep it constantly in mind to address the present crisis-ridden situation in a historical context. Contemporary history can be characterized as follows: that postcolonial nation-building took place in the development to modern society, but was burdened by failure properly to come to terms with modernity at the political, economic and cultural levels. The resulting failed states are based on authoritarian rule. The watershed event in contemporary history was the shattering Arab defeat in the Six-Day War of 1967. This contributed to a wholesale de-legitimation of all secular ideologies, in particular pan-Arab nationalism. It made clear the need for alternatives. Even then – as today in the course of the Arab Spring – the chief beneficiary of this de-legitimation has been Islamism and its political movements. During the East–West conflict the Arab world was entangled in the related alignments of a global conflict parallel to all the regional dynamics of the Middle Eastern subsystem of the international system. This entanglement has come to an end in favour of an 'unveiling of the heterogeneity of civilizations' (Raymond Aron).

After the 1967 war and its repercussions, the next point of reference for this Introduction is the fall of the Berlin Wall and the ensuing breakdown of communism, combined with the sad recognition that this global historical change barely affected the Arab world. The Middle East and North Africa continued their own imprisonment and did not join the world's third wave of democratization. Authoritarian regimes were successful in suffocating any opposition to their rule. The only opposition they failed to eradicate was the Islamist movements. There were two reasons why these movements succeeded in escaping the grip of secret police surveillance and the related suppression. The first was highly sophisticated and efficient clandestine action in the underground, and the second was the instrumental use of asylum in Europe in an abuse of the Islam diaspora networks. It is a fact that Islamist movements are the core opposition, with considerable organizational power also underpinned by the rich funds at their disposal. This is reason enough to compel every person committed to democracy (as I am) to agree to engage with Islamism. However, the distinction between this and empowerment must be constantly borne in mind. It is as important as distinguishing Islam from Islamism.

Based on these facts, I take a close look at the Arab Spring, beyond Western wishful thinking about a transition to democracy, to ask: Will this uprising launch a process that leads to true democracy? A comparative study of the breakdown of authoritarian regimes compels comparison of this change with the contribution of the fall of the Berlin Wall to the breakdown of communism in Eastern Europe. I was invited to Gdansk, Poland, in 2011 to make this comparison on the occasion of the anniversary of the Solidarność movement. The question I asked then was: Will there be a post-authoritarian (like the post-communist) democratization in the Middle East and North Africa? Given the significance of Islamist movements and their ability to determine political development, one needs to look at their agenda.

It is all about the *shari'a* state. Is this state compatible with democracy? Whether a positive answer can be given to this core question is uncertain, since Solidarność, unlike the Muslim Brothers of Egypt, had a genuinely democratic programme.

Having outlined the trajectory of the present inquiry and its intentions, I turn now to addressing the two points of departure from which this book sets off. The first is the contemporary world-historical situation of a phase that began with the Arab Spring. The toppling of authoritarian regimes in the Middle East and North Africa has often been accompanied with great uncertainty. The second is the way in which Western academics, journalists and politicians perceive this process under the impact of literature published by people considered to be experts on Islamism. This Western literature on Islamism is burdened with two deficiencies: first, the focus on topicalities in an opportunist adjustment to changed circumstances, and, second, a lack of knowledge about what Islamists (in contrast to Western scholars and journalists) really think. One seldom sees original sources being quoted by these pundits. These deficiencies can be demonstrated in what happened after the 9/11 attacks in 2001, and then a decade later after the Arab Spring of 2011. In the aftermath of 9/11 the Western debate focused obsessively on what was called 'jihadist terrorism' or, a little more smoothly, 'radical Islam'. Books were published by serious university presses that carried titles such as: *Knowing the Enemy: Jihadist Ideology and the War on Terror* or *Leaderless Jihad: Terror Networks*.[3] Book titles in this format were the standard in that post-9/11 decade. In that debate two basic distinctions were completely ignored[4]: first, that between Islamism and Islam, and, second, that within Islamism itself, between jihadist and non-violent Islamists. At the beginning of the second decade of the new century, which was shaped by the Arab Spring, the focus of the Western literature on Islamism executed a breathtaking U-turn. From associating Islam indiscriminately with violence in a context of 'countering terrorism', the shift has been a complete reverse, now looking at Islamism in terms of 'inclusion and moderation'. In this perception Islamists who were earlier viewed – without differentiation or nuance – as 'the enemy' have, amazingly, today become the champions of democracy in a believed deradicalization. Today they are honoured in a process of engagement and inclusion, and are protected against criticism by the hurling of accusations of Islamophobia against the critics. It is incredible to see how the Islamists – once defamed as terrorists – have become a force that allegedly promotes democracy in the Arab world.

In contrast to the questionable ways of Western pundits in their pendulum swinging from the evil of maligning to the naivety of exoneration, I prefer to look at the phenomenon itself from inside, as an Arab-Muslim insider. I shall undertake this venture with the assistance of fellow Muslims of 'enlightened Muslim thought' (see note 18). Nonetheless, one is never safe. The presentations of the relations between authoritarian regimes and Islamist movements in Western studies is highly damaging to the democratic cause of those Muslims of the 'enlightened turn', as can be illustrated in the case of my country of origin, Syria. The murderous sectarian Ba'th regime of Syria killed tens of thousands of innocent Sunni civilians, claiming to be waging war against 'Islamic terrorists', as the state's propaganda asserted. The Islamists themselves, in Syria and elsewhere, use the uprising of the Arab Spring to promote their own agenda of a *shari'a* state. If one dares to criticize them, as I do in my book *Islamism and Islam*, one is slapped down at once, as here in a review of that book: 'his [Tibi's] argument should be music to the ears of Bashar al-Assad and his Russian friends'.[5] I ask those Westerners who endorse Islamism: How on earth could an argument based on civil Islam be 'music in the ears' of a murderous dictator like Assad and his even more bloodthirsty father? I can barely find the words to express my indignation about this grotesqueness, but it does illustrate the minefield I am entering with this book.

The binary I deplore in Western commentators is combined with conspicuously fuzzy knowledge about the issues. This makes clear how strong is the need for civility combined with enlightenment based on solid information and robust analysis. I do my best to provide both, but profess the restrictions not only related to my limits, but also to my deep involvement in the process in question. In all honesty, I do not claim to be detached. I cannot. As explained in Chapter 4, in the past I acted jointly with those Muslim-Arab activists who were fighting for democracy and individual human rights in our homeland. And I am a Sunni native of Damascus whose heart bleeds in response to the news of the barbarian shelling of the residential areas of the Sunni majority population by the infantry of the Alawite–Shi'ite Syrian armed forces using children as human shields. The pictures of the ruins in Damascus on television in the last week of July and of Aleppo in August 2012 resemble those of the Warsaw ghetto after the suffocation of the Jewish rebellion by German Nazis. Let me risk this comparison: If the Israeli Defence Force were ever do something like this to rebelling Palestinian civilians in the occupied territories, then there would rightly be a global outrage. But the Israeli Defence Force has never behaved like this despite Hamas's terrorism. I ask myself, why does the world keep silent and idly watch the military force of the Syrian army killing children and abusing women and elderly people while bombing their homes with its attack helicopter gunships imported from Russia? Do human rights apply to us Sunni Syrians? I ask this question with an eye on the Sunni–Alawite tensions that I honestly deplore. With the same honesty I assure my readers that I am not sectarian, and also promise to restrain my emotions as a non-Islamist and a non-sectarian Sunni Muslim and native Damascene. I shall focus on the scholarly analysis. However, in a section on Syria in Chapter 4 I write 'Professions of a Sunni Native Damascene'. There I address problems related to sectarian strife, hoping for the reader's forbearance. Sectarianism is an evil, but it does not wither away merely if one refrains from talking about it out of respect for the rules of political correctness. It must be possible to question these rules when their effects become damaging.

What do Islamists want? Epistemology employed in the search for an answer

The thinking unfolded in the present book reflects a commitment to rationalism that not only claims to be universal, but also to have roots in the classical heritage of Islamic civilization in its Averroist *falsafa* tradition. I have already referred to the Moroccan writer Abdou Filali-Ansary and his notion of 'enlightened Muslim thought'. I share the mindset of those Muslims committed to this school of thought and join them in this line of reasoning. Thus, I count myself among those Muslims who engage in the pursuit of an enlightenment and who are normatively committed to a civil Islam. With them I argue against Islamism not as an outsider, but rather from this enlightened Islamic perspective and then ask: What is Islamism all about and what do Islamists want? Why do some Westerners legitimate and defend them while they sideline and defame 'enlightened' Muslims?

The founder of Islamism, Hasan al-Banna, was clear about the goal: Islamism is about *din-wa-dawla*/unity between religion and state order in the pursuit of a *nizam islami*/Islamic system for a *shari'a* state.[6] Today, Yusuf al-Qaradawi acts as the guardian of al-Banna's heritage. In his book on Islamic law, Qaradawi states unambiguously that *shari'a* is not just a morality, as revealed in the Qur'an, but a 'law' legislated by Allah, and that therefore 'the Muslim must abide by the *shari'a*'.[7] But the history of Islamic law compels us to ask: which *shari'a*? Those Muslims who fail to comply with what Islamists want them to do run the risk of being excommunicated from the *umma*/universal community of Muslim believers 'as disbelievers, wrongdoers, and truly wicked'. This is Qaradawi's labelling of Muslim dissidents who refuse to share his Islamist views.

Shari'a is for Islamists the constitution of an Islamic state in which rights are obligations. Obedience in a *shari'a* state is one of these obligations. Qaradawi and his Saudi sponsor and publisher do not admit rights as entitlements, as does the civil–liberal Islam that inspires this book. The Muslims who took to the streets in Cairo and Tunis were fighting for rights, not for an obligation to obey, whatever the rulers. Qaradawi's Islam of a *shari'a* state resembles a prison in which people are expected to obey their rulers in the name of submission to God. Otherwise, they would be (in the phrasing of Qaradawi) 'disbelievers, wrongdoers and truly wicked'. It is beyond comprehension to see a text by this most authoritarian figure included in a Western reader on 'Liberal Islam'.[8] Qaradawi was once received with all honours and hosted by the British Labour politician Ken Livingstone, at that time mayor of London. In that most questionable European 'welcome' Qaradawi was accepted as the representative of Islam. As a founding member of the Arab Organization for Human Rights and the founder of the concept of Euro-Islam that rests on the mindset of the community of 'enlightened Muslim thought', I can only shake my head, dumbfounded.

Qaradawi dismisses all 'critics of the *shari'a*' and accuses them of 'an inability to grasp it as a complete and comprehensive system of law'. We shall see in Chapter 1 that highly respected academic Muslim authorities disagree. On the basis of solid knowledge, these Muslim scholars refer to the Qur'an to demonstrate that *shari'a* exists there in the sense of a morality, not a law. In addition, these respected Muslim scholars present strong evidence for the argument that in Islam there is no 'complete and comprehensive system of law', the latter being constructed by *fiqh*/Islamic jurisprudential orthodoxy and by Islamists in a variety of ways. Are these enlightened Muslims 'disbelievers, wrong doers and truly wicked'? Is this defamation by Qaradawi an example of the way Islamists deal with Muslims who claim a right to dissent/*haq fi al-ikhtilaf* within the framework of pluralism?

When it comes to political order, most Islamists no longer speak today of the caliphate. In following al-Banna they prefer to adopt the new notion he once introduced to his movement, namely the *nizam islami*/Islamic system. In the history of ideas of Islamism, the foremost authority is Sayyid Qutb. As there can be no Marxism without Marx, there can be, in a similar vein, no Islamist ideology without the writings of Qutb. Despite all talk about moderation, Qutb continues to be the major source of Islamism. In his *Signposts along the Road* Qutb states unequivocally: After the bankruptcy of democracy, it is now time to establish the *shari'a* state, viewed as the very alternative to democracy.[9] The democracy–Islamism binary is not an allegation made by me, but rather a reflection of Qutb thinking, the core source of inspiration for Islamist movements. Similar to Leninists who reduce Marxism to a class struggle in the pursuit of the dictatorship of the Proletariat, Qutb reduces Islam to *jihad* against unbelievers in the pursuit of the *shari'a* state. This is a tradition continued today in the writings of Yusuf al-Qaradawi, particularly in his trilogy *Hatmiyyat al-Hall al-Islami/The Islamic Solution*.[10] In line with al-Banna and Qutb, Qaradawi too states: The solution is the *shari'a* state; and the state that he outlines as chief architect is authoritarian. Qaradawi is by no means a representative of 'Liberal Islam', but rather exactly the opposite. Today, he is the foremost living respected authority of Islamism in our time. He spoke on Tahrir Square in Cairo next to the new Islamist president Mohammed Morsi.

In the light of the cited three basic authorities that refer to what Islamists want, two indisputable facts can be stated:

1   Islamism is not about violence, but rather about the order of the state.
2   The writings of most Western writers on Islamism reveal great ignorance about what Islamism is all about. They discuss theoretical models, but not the subject matter itself.

My work on Islamism highlights these facts and aims to go beyond the deficiencies to be identified in Chapter 1. In the main I discuss what Islamists themselves want: namely the *shari'a* state, not the wishful thinking of Western pundits. Islamists say they want the *shari'a* state, but some Westerners, despite all odds, impute to them a drive to democracy. I do not construct this Islamist agenda, I merely quote it. For this reason this book deals primarily with the Islamist concept of political order and operates on the assumption that the order of the *shari'a* state is not a democracy. The Islamist *shari'a* state is an order based on a new, highly politicized interpretation of *shari'a* in an invention of tradition. This concept has been elevated to the highest good in the Islamist political agenda. The *shari'a* state is placed here in the contemporary historical context of the 2011 uprising against authoritarian regimes commonly referred to as the Arab Spring. The unchecked assumption is that the seizure of leadership by Islamists in the Arab Spring is a part of the democratization process of the Middle East. Though I agree to the engagement of the Islamists, I do not share the belief in a moderation of Islamism that amounts to compatibility of the *shari'a* state with democracy. I doubt this unchecked assumption, and guess it is wrong. In a combination of doubt and conjecture in the mindset of rational epistemology, I prefer to check the unchecked assumption rather than take it for granted merely to indicate naive good will.

The present book follows a trilogy by myself on Islamism (political Islam) published between 1998 and 2012.[11] Parallel to my retirement, I viewed that publication as conclusive and final both for the subject matter and for my own academic life. Unexpectedly the Arab Spring happened in 2011; expectedly, however, it was hijacked by Islamism. This is the context in which I decided to write the present book, in which I place the political reality and relate it to the Islamist agenda of a *shari'a* state that predates the Arab Spring. This is a new and an original contribution, not a rehash of earlier research. In Chapter 4 I give a detailed explanation for my return to the stage.

The core question asked is whether the project of democratization forms a single complement of Islamism, or whether there are two different visions for the future of the Middle East that are at odds with one another. I know how controversial these issues are and how mined is this field of inquiry, but hope to share this epistemological position with all: if one agrees to the procedure that facts, not a preconception (worse: wishful thinking) should be the point of departure, then one can on this basis admit freedom to interpret these facts in different ways, but not the freedom to contend one's own facts. One can discuss the context of these facts in different way, and also the notions coined to conceptualize them (such as 'inclusion', 'moderation'), but one should not wrangle about the validity of facts themselves. This is the point of departure of the present inquiry that draws a strict distinction between facts, narratives, and wishful thinking.

Among the facts is the wreckage caused by still existing or fallen authoritarian regimes in states and societies of the Arab core of Islamic civilization. The wrecks are a home-made reality. It is too simple to attribute existing ills to a colonial legacy, or to blame external powers in a litany of complaints about the results of globalization. If the thinking to which this book is committed, namely to go beyond putting the blame on others in blame games, were not correct, why is India a rising power? The heavy and burdensome colonial past of India is well known, as are the negative effects of globalization. Nevertheless, India is more developed than any other Arab-Muslim country. The fact of home-made wreckage on all levels also relates to the fact that all postcolonial experiments, ranging from liberal democracy to the 'development regimes' of the modern military, have failed in the Arab world. As a result, all of the related ideologies, from liberalism to Islamic modernism and secular pan-Arab nationalism, have been de-legitimated. The one exception is the traditional tribal monarchies in Saudi Arabia and the Gulf region that persist through the disruptive change with the help of their petrodollar-based power. All other postcolonial regimes are unable to survive the failed development in economy, society, and the state. There is a strong need for alternatives, and this has been the driver of the rebellion (not yet a revolution) dubbed the Arab Spring. Many pin high hopes on the change generated 2011. Will these hopes be fulfilled? Is the *shari'a* state the proper institutional framework for the fulfilment?

To answer the questions posed by the Arab Spring properly requires a solid knowledge of Islamism and its project of a *shari'a* state. Although there is great inner diversity within Islamism, one element of Islamist ideology is shared by all: the *shari'a* state. The combination of unity and diversity within Islamism is not well understood in the West. It is outrageous to see politicians of the European Union answering questions with conspicuous ignorance about the *shari'a* state. A representative example is an opinion article by Catherine Ashton, the EU foreign affairs representative, published in the *International Herald Tribune* (the global edition of the *New York Times*) under the heading 'Supporting the Arab Awakening', in which she says: 'I have heard scepticism about whether we can trust . . . various strands of Islamism. I disagree. We have a moral duty . . . to help our neighbours secure democracy and prosperity.'[12] In a conspicuous confusion of epistemology (doubt) and the ethics of responsibility (moral duty), the EU quasi-minister of foreign affairs takes it for granted in this statement that Islamism is not a problem. In this way Western politicians approve the Islamist *shari'a* state they know little about as a means to securing democratization and security. In this book I suggest proceeding otherwise, and begin by checking the underlying assumption instead of taking it for granted.

The political realities of 2012, the year following the Arab Spring, reveal a shift from an 'Arab' to an 'Islamist Awakening' in which the *shari'a* state is presented by Islamism as the foremost solution. This goal seems to stand at the top of the existing and powerful agenda. The alternative to the wreckage caused by the toppled authoritarian regimes seems to be Islamism. There is an other competing alternative, namely a democratization in the spirit of a civil Islam based on a pluralist culture of democracy and on power sharing, alien to the *shari'a* state. Some suggest that these alternatives – that is, democracy and the *shari'a* state – are not competing, but rather are complementary – that is, compatible with one another. Well, that is an opinion, not a fact.

In short, the view that the *shari'a* state and democracy are compatible is no more than an unchecked assumption. The inquiry into the issues related to this assumption shapes the trajectory of the present book. I doubt that the *shari'a* state is compatible with democracy, but acknowledge this is an assumption, too. I restate my commitment to the Cartesian epistemology that solid knowledge emerges from doubt and conjecture.

When one talks about the need for democratization, one has to keep in mind that democracy is much more than just balloting. Democracy is a political culture of participatory politics practised in free pluralist institutions of an open society combined with a civil state of power sharing. If this prerequisite of democracy is missing, regimes that come to power through balloting cannot be viewed as democratic. No one would seriously call the Nazi regime of Hitler a democratic one, merely because Hitler's NSDAP party came to power with the help of the ballot box as an expression of the will of the German people at the time of the Weimar crisis. This is an insight based on comparative politics, not a polemic.

I started this Introduction with a commitment to facts against obsessions and wishful thinking. This approach is also about the nature of knowledge. I profess that I belong to those who view knowledge as universal, and this mindset follows the great tradition of rationalist Muslim medieval philosophers, from Averroes to Ibn Khaldun. Islamic rationalists were committed to a universal epistemology that dismisses cultural particularisms. In contrast to this, the postmodernists of today place restrictions on the validity of knowledge when they impose their ideologically blinkered epistemology. The result is a cultural relativism that limits knowledge of other cultures and practices, thus standing in a kind of an absolutism. This ideology is not only counterproductive but also self-contradictory, pronouncing a relativism while at the same time acting as an absolutism.

There are universal standards of knowledge on which one can determine among many other things the notions one employs in a rational and therefore universal reasoning.[13] Among these is the one of democracy, to make clear what we are talking about. I refer again to the principle of doubt and conjecture viewed as a basis for a universal epistemology that also applies to us Muslims. The famous project of the late Moroccan philosopher Mohammed Abed al-Jabri revives the great Islamic tradition of *falsafa* rationalism and suggests that the universality of reason-based knowledge is to be accepted across cultures.[14] This knowledge stands above all cultural particularisms. In a commitment to this al-Jabri project which documents an 'enlightened turn' in 'enlightened Muslim thought' (see the first section of Chapter 3), I refer to the United Nations Development Programme report on the Arab world, *Building a Knowledge Society*.[15] With this in mind I look at the *shari'a* state and check its ability to generate democratization and development. To conduct this inquiry is the task this book seeks to accomplish.

About this book

Major themes and core assumptions

The major theme of this book relates to the question whether the political order of a *shari'a* state is eligible to meet the needs generated by the Muslim-Arab yearning for freedom and improvement in the social and economic conditions of everyday life. This yearning is the source of the power that led to the rebellion dubbed the Arab Spring. How can the needs underlying this yearning be fulfilled?

It is argued that the best way to fulfil the expectations raised would be democratic rule – a reference to the modern notion of democracy (*al-dimuqratiyya*) that does not exist in any of the languages of Islamdom. A modern Muslim scholar, Sohail Hashmi, asks 'So is there an Islamic conception of democracy?'[16] He answers this question on two levels. First, referring to the Qur'an, he writes, 'The Qur'an provides little guidance regarding the form of government'. Then he turns to traditional Islamic thought and states, 'Medieval political theory . . . left little scope for popular participation in politics'. Well, this participation is what democracy is all about. In this impasse one is compelled to ask: What then is an 'Islamic democracy'? For sure, the notion does not exist – neither implicitly nor explicitly – in the Qur'an. The same applies to traditional Islamic thought. In this regard, intellectual and political history show no precedent (see the final section in Chapter 6). This statement applies both to the past and to the present.

As Hashmi correctly tells us about the past, 'by their virtue of their enforcement of the *shari'a*, the caliph and his ministers were owed obedience'. The present has not been much better, it is the bleak 'choice . . . authoritarianism, either in the name of secular rationalism, or in the name of Islam'. The classical caliphs and contemporary rulers have this feature in common: to oppress their subjects. These solid facts (to be elaborated upon in Chapters 1 and 2) lead the present inquiry. These facts are pertinent to the study of the Arab Spring in a larger historical context.

The point of departure is the insight that acceptance of the need for Islamic legitimacy is required for whatever happens in the Islamicate. Whatever is to be introduced to Islamdom – democracy and democratization are no exceptions – has to be based on Islamic legitimacy. Noah Feldman, with whom I basically disagree, is, therefore, on the one hand right when he cannot 'imagine comparatively secular democracy in the Muslim world', but on the other, he is wrong when he goes to the other extreme of 'imagining some kind of Islamic democracy'.[17] Based on what is stated above one is compelled to ask: What is that, precisely?

The wishy-washy answers Feldman provides do not convince at all. Questioning an 'Islamic state' is never meant to question the compatibility of Islam (not Islamism) with democracy or the need for Islamic legitimacy. At issue is not a system, but rather an ethics of government based in Islam, a task that only reform-oriented and creative Muslims – not the Islamists – could accomplish. I am in full agreement with Hashmi's belief 'that the soundest argument for representative government is to be found in Islamic ethics'. To be sure, and to avoid ambiguity: this government is not tantamount to the constructed '*shari'a* state'.

Among the assumptions on which the present book operates is the idea that Islamism and its solution of a *shari'a* state emerge out of a deep crisis. In this context the *shari'a* state is not to be seen as a revival but rather a recent addition to Islam that functions as a salvation in the existing crisis. This imagined order is not the traditional caliphate and it has no roots in traditional Islam. Of course, wise and intelligent Islamist leaders well know that they cannot impose the *shari'a* order they envision at once. As will be demonstrated on the case of Egypt in Chapter 4, Islamists proceed incrementally and make short-lived compromises. A prominent representative of 'enlightened Muslim thought', Filali-Ansary, does not believe in a moderation of the Islamist movement, nor does he trust the Islamists. He points out that when Islamists accept power sharing, they merely engage in 'grudging tactical concessions'. This has happened in an exemplary manner in Egypt under the Islamist president Mohammed Morsi. Islamists never agree in substance to democratic values as 'matters of principle', in contrast to the mindset of the 'enlightened Muslims'.[18] When Islamists are not powerful enough to push forward their agenda, they tactically agree to share power in short-lived political coalitions. Islamists act in this manner in countries where there are no other options in the preliminary stage (e.g. Lebanon and Tunisia). However, where they enjoy full empowerment (e.g. Hamas in Gaza), they go their own way and deny to others not only power sharing, but also political participation. The Islamist discourse is not based on political ethics, but rather on politicized religion that uses Islam as legitimation for the political order of a *shari'a* state. Few, if any, references are made to economic and social development to solve the crisis. These issues are, however, the core of the existing problems and the source that generated the uprising of the Arab Spring.

Despite my background as a scholar who thinks that 'culture matters' (though with no inclination whatever to 'culturalism'),[19] I know well that the post-authoritarian wreckage in the Arab world embodies a crisis that is not cultural in its nature. It is determined by two core issues: one of them is failed development and the other the weak institutions in states where power is personalized (e.g. Qadhafi's Libya, Assad's Syria, Saddam's Iraq). The consent of the people to authoritarian regimes has been coerced by the security apparatus. Then comes the culture that allows these circumstances. If this outline of the crisis were correct and adequate, how could one see an exit strategy in the Islamist slogan '*al-Islam huwa al-hall*'/'Islam is the solution'? To deal with the existing wreckage Muslim people need concrete policies, not empty promises based on a constructed *shari'a* state as a dream palace for castles built in the air. Let us look at the reality on the ground, and then consider the scholarly insights of two highly respected social scientists investigating the question posed by that slogan.

The 2012 anniversary of the toppling of the authoritarian Ben Ali regime in Tunisia exposed the reality on the ground. On television in January 2012 one could see thousands of demonstrators carrying banners in Arabic with almost exclusively economic slogans, such as 'We want jobs', 'We want a better life'. At the same time there were unconvincible Islamist demonstrators who held to their slogans. They were asking the democratically elected coalition government to implement more *shari'a*-Islam. How can a sick economy embedded in a failed development be cured by *shari'a*, which is a system of duties and prohibitions? Reality is determined by economic and social needs. How could religious tenets provide the solution for economic and social problems of development?

In their book *A Political Economy of the Middle East*, the best experts in the world on this matter, John Waterbury and Alan Richards, refer to the slogan *al-Islam huwa al-hall* in the title of their Chapter 14: 'Is Islam the Solution?' Delving into the issue they emerge at the end of the chapter with the following conclusion, which I fully endorse: 'The answer to this question posed at the beginning of this chapter is no'.[20] This 'no' is persuasive because in the Qur'an *shari'a* is about Islamic conduct and morality, not about political order. In Islamic history *shari'a* was about worship, civil law and the penal code, not about economy, society and the state. Chapter 1 of the present book commences with documenting these facts.

After the economic needs that could not be fulfilled owing to failed development come the legitimacy of power and the weak institutions in state and society. It matters to see how Arabs themselves view this issue. In November 1983, about 70 leading pro-democracy Arab opinion leaders were summoned by the Centre for Arab Unity Studies to engage in deliberations about *'azmat al-dimuqratiyya*

fi al-watan al-arabi/the crisis of democracy in the Arab world. Those Arab opinion leaders planned to meet in Cairo, but the Mubarak government withdrew its
permission under Saudi pressure. The meeting had therefore to take place in a
non-Arab place, in Limassol in Cyprus. However, proceedings were able to be
published in Arabic in an influential book with the same title as the congress.[21]
In Chapter 4 I discuss this venture, which was more political than an academic
conference, at greater length. It was admirable to see how the participants (ranging from S. E. Ibrahim, to Ali E. Hilal, Hichem Djait, Sayyid Yasin, Ali Oumlil,
Burhan Ghalyun, and others) proceeded: first establish the terms used, then see
how Arabs use them, and then move on to the reality and to practices indicating
the Arab predicament with democracy. It was a great fortune and a great honour
for me to be part of that venture, with the invitation to speak on 'the economic and
social underpinning of democracy'.[22]

In short, there exists a common agreement among the Arab opinion leaders that
democracy does not fall from heaven. For the consolidation of a process of democratization, economic and social as well as institutional underpinning is required.
To this day, this requirement continues to be unfulfilled. And here 'culture matters' (see note 19). Enlightened Arab thinkers are clear about the need for cultural
legitimacy for the introduction of democracy into the Arab world. As stated earlier,
there is no doubt about this. These Arabs know that the often-acclaimed *shari'a*
state is the perennial issue, but is not supportive of a real democracy based on
rights, democratic pluralism and power sharing. This insight is unfortunately not
shared by the prevailing narrative in US Islamic studies. Why are these Western
scholars presumably wrong? I shall cautiously address this question in Chapter 1.

It is self-evident that the crisis of contemporary Islamic societies in modern
times underpins the rise of the *shari'a* state as a contemporary addition to Islam.
I want to demonstrate the state of the art of Western knowledge on this subject
matter in an exemplary manner in a dispute and have chosen a book, *The Fall
and Rise of the Islamic State*, written by a Harvard law professor – Noah Feldman, already cited above – and published by Princeton University Press.[23] It is a
book that argues differently, reflecting a different, and I may add utterly wrong,
thinking that is in line with the prevailing Western narrative, not with the facts of
history as well as with those of the present on the ground. The author suggests that
there is a continuity between the fall of the Islamic imperial order of the caliphate and the current rise of the Islamist *shari'a* state. This is wrong on all counts.
Feldman's book lumps together two different historical phenomena in deplorable
confusion. The Islamist call for a *shari'a* state is not a return to or a restoration
of the imperial caliphate, nor is it a revival of a state tradition that ended with the
fall of Islamic empire. In Chapter 3 I try to rectify this error. The Islamist *shari'a*
results from an invention of tradition, and so does the pattern of an order for the
state that is attributed to it.

Over the past 30 years I have had the unpleasant experience, with the prevailing
narrative of majority Islamic studies, that those who disagree are suppressed in a
debate on Islamism that lacks freedom of thought. In the section on 'enlightened
Muslim thought' in Chapter 3 I shall present an (anonymized) example of this

conduct. I deplore this conduct, but refuse to turn the tables on the perpetrator. In contrast to such conduct, I not only give credit to Noah Feldman, but also combine this attitude of respect with a request to respect the historical facts. Western scholars must be confronted with the expectation that they must read properly the Islamist literature published in Arabic. Close examination shows that the *shari'a* state is an Islamist ideology, not a revival of the early Islamic order. To argue otherwise is to give a false presentation of the *shari'a* state – as indeed happens in the prevailing Western narrative. For this reason, I start the opening chapter by taking issue with the dominant ways in which Islamism is dealt with in Western Islamic studies. As I have done in the past, I dissent with these studies and present in contrast to them my study based on the new approach of Islamology.[24] To be clear: this is not the place to explain the new approach, and I ask the reader not to expect this; I have explained it elsewhere and will not now repeat it. Suffice to say that in my understanding Islamology is an international relations approach combined with comparative politics and historical sociology for the study of the realities of Islamicate civilization (religion being viewed as a *fait social* in the tradition of Durkheim). My focus is not the religion of Islam itself as a religious faith. In a way Islamology resembles, as a study of conflict, Sovietology in the times of the East–West conflict, but with one a very great difference: namely that it has the aim of cross-civilizational bridging, not polarization into a Cold War.

Furthermore, I continue the line of reasoning pursued in *Islamism and Islam* (see note 4) to maintain that Islamism is not Islam. In the present book I draw already in Chapter 1 on Marshall Hodgson, not only to elaborate on the distinction between faith and historical realities, but also between the past and the present. Because I do not wish to rehash what has been stated in my trilogy on political Islam (see note 11) (although it is the foundation of my thinking on the matter in hand), the present book presents new research.

The major assumption relates to the Islamist *shari'a* state in the process of the religionization of politics. In this context a state order emerges that attributes to the self a fulfilment of a function of Islamic *shari'a*. This order runs counter to democracy. Why does Islamism, as I have already stated, fail to approve democratic pluralism and power sharing? The answer lies in the core political thought of Islamism, in which Islam is viewed as *din-wa-dawla*. The *dawla*/state that Islamist movements aspire to is the *shari'a* state (a full section is devoted to this in Chapter 3). The contemporary relevance of this thought is demonstrated by the outcome of the uprising known as the Arab Spring. The overall need is for democratization, but the *shari'a* state envisioned is not compatible with democracy. This is why the Arab Spring seems to have been derailed. It has become a dark and frosty winter. Instead of a genuine democracy, major countries of the Middle East and North Africa region are now under the rule of Islamism. In the aftermath of the Arab Spring, Islamists have succeeded in using the ballot box as a means of empowerment to impose a *shari'a* state (see Chapters 4 and 5).

It cannot be repeated often enough that no democracy can ever result from a flawed democratization process that has been reduced simply to balloting, stripped of the political culture of democracy. It must be remembered that the majority of the voters in Islamdom are illiterate. They go to the ballot box unable to read the voting form, and act on the instructions given to them by Islamist preachers in mosques – who misguide them with false promises. This is not the culture of democracy, which is based on pluralism, power sharing and individual human rights being an entitlement of all, and in particular of minorities.

Throughout the years of my research on Islamism I have repeatedly seen how those who do not comply with Islamist views and with the prevailing narrative risk being accused either of *kufr*/heresy (if Muslims) or of Islamophobia (if not Muslims). This accusation can be very harmful, because Islamists are not the kind of tolerant people who accept dissent. Some of the Western pundits who approve the *shari'a* state as an 'Islamic democracy' do not deal with disagreement in a tolerant manner, and are thus no better than the Islamists in their interaction with critics. They largely ignore the fact that the *shari'a* state contradicts all the elementary features of democracy.

Today, Islamists have successfully hijacked the Arab Spring. They have also been successful in presenting themselves both in the world of Islam and in the West as the only viable Islamic alternative. It is noticeable that prevailing opinion in the West qualifies Islamist movements as democratic. For instance, the *New York Times* described the rise of an Islamist, Mohammed Morsi, as president of Egypt in these terms: 'After 84 years as a secret society . . . the Muslim Brotherhood is now . . . building an Islamist democracy in Egypt.'[25] Quite apart from the notion of an 'Islamist democracy' (mooted by Feldman among others, and called into question above), the formulation is a contradiction in terms. One has to wonder about the blindness of the *New York Times* as to the probability of the Muslim Brothers making the transition to a democratic party, when it is structured by all the criteria that Hannah Arendt lists as qualifying a movement as a totalitarian entity. How could the Muslim Brothers move on from secrecy and clandestine action to a democratic party? I shall discuss this in Chapter 4. Despite the criticism, however, I think one should give credit to the *New York Times* for adding to its qualification of this process of so-called democratization as a 'milestone' the adjective 'ambiguous'. This is, at least, an expression of doubt. Ambiguity is among the Islamist tactics.

Well-informed experts and insiders are sceptical about the wishful thinking in the West about democratization of the Middle East and North Africa. This thinking overlooks the fact that Islamist movements have an authoritarian structure based on adherence to a totalitarian ideology, blind obedience based on unquestioning loyalty, and, last but not least, a patriarchical organizational structure that ensures surveillance of the behaviour and political conduct of all members. In a democracy you can join a democratic party and immediately be a full, equal member. Membership in the Muslim Brotherhood, by contrast, is highly restricted, and is controlled by a system of subjecting those who want to join to surveillance before they can be accepted as members. This membership is embedded in a hierarchical structure.

An extremely well-informed and intelligent study by Eric Trager published in *Foreign Affairs* on 'The Unbreakable Muslim Brotherhood: Grim Perspectives for a Liberal Egypt'[26] states the truth about the 'highly selective membership process' in the Freedom and Justice Party that represents the Muslim Brothers. This process reflects a 'careful recruitment procedure'. The aspirant for membership begins as a '*muhib*'/'lover' (meaning obedient follower or sympathizer) of a local *usra*/family. Only after a year of surveillance may the *muhib* be promoted to *mu'ayyid*/supporter. In a further stage he can be elevated to *muntasib*/affiliated. It takes many years to become a fully trusted person who qualifies for full membership of the Muslim Brothers. Thanks to this structure, the Muslim Brothers have in the past been able to act underground, unnoticed and beneath the surveillance of the state police. In this way the Brothers were able to escape persecution. In a democracy such secrecy is no longer needed, but it is a fact that this structure continues today to characterize the Muslim Brothers. If an open society and transparency are the hallmarks of democracy, how can a movement committed to secrecy claim to be engaged in democratization? In 2012 Trager published a new, illuminating article in *Foreign Affairs* that supports these doubts. I discuss it in Chapter 4 in a section on Egypt in the shadow of Islamist empowerment.

The positive assessment of Islamism in prevailing Western opinion is flawed because it ignores revelations and disclosures such as the one by Trager just cited. Let me identify the basic flaws of this prevailing opinion; but first please note how I am able to claim the right to freedom of expression against the prevailing view. In so doing, I draw on J. S. Mill's classic 'On Liberty' in which the 'tyranny of the prevailing opinion'[27] not only is deplored, but is dismissed as an obstacle to true democracy.

A major flaw of the prevailing narrative is its failure to recognize Islamism as a variety of the phenomenon of religious fundamentalism. Thus, it is not a conservatism. To be sure, Islamic conservatism and Islamic fundamentalism are not the same and should not be confused. Furthermore, the *shari'a* state is not a democracy. In Turkey an Islamist party, the AKP (Justice and Development Party), came to power by democratic means. In a way, Turkey's Erdogan resembles Russia's Putin, but here the AKP party, not the person, is what matters. Do Westerners have the legitimacy to judge Turkey's AKP and about Islamism in general in a reasoning based in Western democracy? Islamists, who are neo-absolutists, and Western cultural relativists jointly deny this legitimacy.

In contrast, the present book argues for the validity of universal knowledge based on rationality shared by all. Earlier I referred to a precedent for this thinking in the medieval tradition of Islamic rationalism and its medieval humanism which shared European Hellenism, and I have also mentioned the late al-Jabri and his project of a revival of Islamic humanism, which I list among the sources of 'enlightened Muslim thought'. One of these enlightened Muslims, Ali Allawi, in his book *The Crisis of Islamic Civilization*, ranks al-Jabri as 'the most significant Muslim thinker of our age'. Allawi is critical of what is termed the 'Islamist awakening'. He does not believe that this Islamist awakening contributes to 'the rebirth of an Islamic civilization; it will be another episode in its decline'.[28] In contrast to the unpromising Islamist *shari'a*tization, the al-Jabri project points to an enlightened civil Islam – a genuine revivalism. Compared with the al-Jabri project, the Islamist venture is not, by any means, an Islamic revival.

Structure and outline

At this juncture it must have become abundantly clear that the Islamist option for the order of the state has been elevated by the outcome of the Arab Spring. Hence the structure of this book: it commences with the *shari'a* state ahead of the Arab Spring.

In the recent past the new term 'post-Islamism' was introduced by some to suggest the passing of the phenomenon of Islamism. If this were true then one must ask: Is this study behind the times, since it assumes that Islamism is alive and kicking, and moreover that it has, in the aftermath of the Arab Spring, become a very powerful reality? What has happened to justify the notion of post-Islamism?

Since 9/11 and for a decade, jihadist Islamism was the top theme in Western thinking. The failure of al-Qaeda to record any success worth mentioning led to a decline in jihadism. Jihadism is, however, only one branch of Islamism, and not even the major one. Thus, the decline is not related to Islamism in general. This is why the two seemingly popular notions of 'post-Islamism' (Olivier Roy) and 'the end of Islamism' (Gilles Kepel) are not just utterly wrong, but also myopic: they look at the decline of jihadism and take it for a decline of Islamism.

More important than what is regarded as a decline is the fact that there has been a switch in many Islamist movements from jihadism to institutional Islamism. This is regarded by most Western scholars as a moderation. With this background in mind I pose the following six questions as drivers of the reasoning advanced in the six chapters of this book. These questions are central, mostly pertaining to institutional Islamism, although they do not correspond directly with the six chapters of the book. Behind all six questions is the view that institutional Islamism is the most serious, and now the most powerful direction in Islamism: not only is it the one that is most prevalent, but it has emerged empowered in the post-Arab-Spring developments. It follows that most terrorism-focused research on Islamism is not just out-dated, but also has become virtually trash. These are the six questions:

1   Does the Islamist *shari'a* state have a *sabiqa*/precedent in Islamic heritage and tradition? Is it a revival at all?
2   Is the *shari'a* state an authentic Islamic pattern for an 'Islamic democracy'?
3   Is the change from jihadist to institutional Islamism a sign of moderation?
4   Is it possible to employ tools of Western social science to understand and properly assess Islamism and its project of a *shari'a* state?
5   Is it 'Islamophobia' to subject the *shari'a* state to critical inquiry?
6   Why is the narrative on Islamism that prevails in US Islamic and Middle Eastern studies and in political science flawed? Is 'enlightened Muslim thought' an alternative to it?

These six questions permeate all six of the following chapters; they determine, not the organization of the book, but the scope of the entire inquiry. Chapterwise, the outline of the book is as follows.

In Chapter 1 I establish terms and argue with reference to authoritative Islamic sources that traditional *shari'a* in Islam is not about governance, but rather about the five pillars of Islamic faith and their practice in the form of worship, as well as in the cultural practices of daily life. In contrast, all Islamists contend, in an invention of tradition, that Islam is coupled in its substance with politics, and then conclude that it prescribes an order of the state based on a politicized *shari'a*. Chapter 1 establishes, however, the fact that the political order of a *shari'a* state that Islamists fight for never existed before in Islamic history. It presents facts and addresses issues that will be dealt with at greater length in the ensuing chapters; the aim of touching on them in this opening chapter is to prepare the ground for the question of why the Islamic studies establishment in the US ignores these historical facts. Those who deny the issues I address and the distinctions I make tend to assault my work simply because it does not join forces with those who overlook the reality for which the name Islamism stands. The other question one needs to ask is: Why is the Islamist agenda of a *shari'a* state not well understood in the West? Chapter 1 seeks an answer and claims to provide a convincing one.

Chapter 2 places the religionized politics of Islamism in the context of a crisis that has led to the emergence of a political Islam revolving around a new notion of a politicized *shari'a*. In my research I have coined the new term of a '*shari'a*tization' of politics in contemporary Islam to refer to this new phenomenon. Given the centrality of *shari'a* in the empowerment of Islamism in the course of the Arab Spring, and in view of the fact that Islamist *shari'a* revolves around the order of the state and of the world at large, Chapter 2 looks at Islamism from this angle. It assumes safely without any binary attitude that the envisioned Islamist order alienates Muslims from an international community based on a shared universal understanding of law.

The Westphalian synthesis on which the international system of secular sovereign states rests is the core issue in Chapter 3. In this chapter, the competing views over the order of the world in the new century are analysed and discussed. The return of *shari'a* pertains not only to an order for the state, but also to the one for the world at large, that is, for an envisioned world order based on Islamist *shari'a*. This is supposed to replace the existing Westphalian one. To illuminate the issue, Chapter 3 refers to the decline of the Islamic-imperial order of the caliphate and to its abolition in 1924, as well as to the aftermath of this development. The core feature of this development is the formation of nation-states in the course of the incorporation of the Islamic world into the international system of sovereign states.[29] In this setting, modern secular law was introduced to replace the abolished *shari'a* law. As shown in Chapter 2, the rise of Islamism parallels the return of *shari'a* to the public square. Chapter 3 continues this debate in catching up with the related political claims. On the top of these is the call for a political order for the state and also for the world at large that is based on *shari'a*. The chapter looks at political order at the level both of the state and of the world. There are three competing models of world order: the Westphalian synthesis, the hegemonic policy of *Pax Americana* and the Islamist vision of a *Pax Islamica*. Furthermore, Chapter 3 engages in intra-Islamic distinctions related to the political order. These are the caliphate, Pan-Islamism and the recent *shari'a* state. The analysis defends, from an 'enlightened Muslim thought' point of view, a neutral world order that is based on the Westphalian synthesis but dissociates the latter, not just from its European origin, but also from *Pax Americana*, thus transforming it into a neutral model.

For obvious reasons, the longest chapter of the book is Chapter 4. Some readers may wonder why the issue that led me to write this book – namely the Arab Spring – appears as Chapter 4, not at the beginning. Given, however, that the vision of an Islamist *shari'a* state has become the prevailing prospect in the post-Arab Spring in the context of the need for democratization, it seemed to me to make more sense to deal first with the *shari'a* state in the context of political order, and only after that with the upheaval of the Arab Spring. This upheaval was associated with the promise of democratization: hence the effort to view the *shari'a* state through the lens of democracy. This is also the flashpoint of the present inquiry into the compatibility of the *shari'a* state and the several projects of democratization in the Islamicate. The contemporary phenomenon of the Arab Spring is still too young and much too recent to be studied accurately. Nonetheless, Chapter 4 ventures to provide a preliminary analysis. Although I take pains to fulfil scholarly requirements for the study of contemporary history in an orientation based in historical sociology, I profess in all honesty that the theme of Chapter 4 strained the aim for impersonality beyond its limits. My intimate link to the matter under discussion compels me as a Muslim native of Damascus to take the liberty to express my emotions and at times become personal, and for this I ask the reader's forbearance. The chapter ends by pondering the 'future prospects' of the Middle East and North Africa in the shadow of Islamism.

The ensuing chapter, Chapter 5, begins by catching up with Islamists emboldened in 2012 to publicly demand a policy based on the implementation of Islamist *shari'a*, and then focuses on *shari'a* in the post-Arab-Spring context within an overall historical perspective. The Islamist line is that the return to *shari'a* is a return to normality. A history of *shari'a* reasoning fully determined by the historicity of Islam forms a part of the Islamic version of the intellectual history of Islam. John Kelsay is one of the great scholars in this field and his work on the history of Islam in terms of *shari'a* reasoning stands at the centre of Chapter 5. However, Kelsay overlooks other traditions in Islamic history that are not consonant with *shari'a* reasoning. The conclusion of Chapter 5 is that the intellectual history of Islam is not exclusively about *shari'a*. The Islamic heritage of *falsafa* rationalism is opposed to the tradition of *shari'a* reasoning focused upon in this chapter. *Falsafa* rationalism constitutes a major source for enlightened Muslim thought.

The book concludes with Chapter 6 on the freedom of academic research and on tendentious accusations aimed at establishing a culture that imposes limits to this freedom. I am well aware, in all that is stated in the first five chapters, that I am moving in a minefield and touching on strongly guarded taboos. This is a difficult task and a risky undertaking in the environment of a war of ideas that Islamists and their Western supporters seem to have won. Among the propaganda weapons employed against the critics of Islamism is the defamatory accusation of Islamophobia. This accusation expresses a sentiment shared with Islamists by some Western sympathizers with Islamist movements – a sentiment that features a lack of civility, testimony to a conspicuous decline of the culture of free debate in a society that is supposed to be, not only civil, but also an 'open society' (Karl Popper).

Exposure to the accusation of Islamophobia has in the recent past been a new invective employed to intimidate critics; it not only undermines, but also taints any subjection of Islamism and its *shari'a* state to critical reasoning. Any inquiry that unravels the core Islamist vision of a remaking of the world along what they view as *shari'a* risks drawing down this accusation. In a recent critical study on multiculturalism, in the chapter on Islamophobia, Jens-Martin Eriksen and Frederik Stjernfelt are correct when they say: 'The concept of Islamophobia . . . is used to stigmatize any criticism of Islamism and aspects of Islam that conflict with democracy, human rights, and the constitutional state. . . .' This use of defamatory accusation happens 'in an attempt to limit criticism of Islamic movements. Both valid and unfounded criticisms of various forms of Islam are brushed aside by the argument that they constitute Islamophobia and are thus grouped with racism, antisemitism, homophobia etc.'[30] If this is to prevail, the result will be the end of any scholarly debate on the subject matter. Can it be averted? In Chapter 6 I quote Muslim and Western opinion leaders who share this question and the accompanying misgivings.

In the venture of this book I am stringent in observing the strict distinction between Islamism and Islam, between the religionized politics of Islamism on the one hand and the Islamic faith on the other, and I utterly reject the accusation of Islamophobia as an illiberal effort to limit the freedom of speech, not just in everyday life, but also in scholarship, research and politics. This is a matter not simply of freedom of speech in the West, but also of freedom of speech for those Muslims of the 'enlightened turn' to ponder on the future of their Islamicate civilization (see Chapter 6).

My awareness that the assumptions and the views expressed here are not shared by the majority constitutes an acknowledgement that this book represents a controversial minority position. I accept this description on the basis that dissent, disagreement and controversy are basic features of the political culture of democracy, and, of course, of scholarship in a free civil society as well. In the shadow of the post-Arab Spring one is challenged to read anew Mill's great essay 'On Liberty' and to recognize on these intellectual grounds the high topicality of Mill's thinking. My fellow Muslim, the Moroccan philosopher Ali Oumlil requests a '*haq fi al-ikhtilaf*'/'right to dissent', and this is exactly what I request.[31]

Whether a view is right or wrong does not hinge on its being shared by a majority, but rather by its passing the test of critical free debate. Defamation and namecalling do not feature in such debate. I hope that this book will generate a fruitful debate – not a heated polemical controversy – on the Arab Spring. Only if this debate is free from such evils can it be fruitful. I accept being exposed to such scholarly testing, but in a combination of fairness and civility. With this in view I ask my readers and reviewers to bear with me, to listen to my arguments in reading my book, to refrain from skimming followed by ugly soundbites, and only then, after reading, to decide how plausible are the assumptions upon which my analysis proceeds and whether I have been able to check them in a convincing manner.

However, the facts should not be disputed. One has the right to one's own opinion, but not to one's own facts. My hope is that this book is not dismissed just on the grounds of disagreement.

Lastly (while we are on the subject), I not only reclaim a democratic right for the freedom of thinking and speech in research, and civility as well, but also the right to write in my own personal style, which was formed by my cultural upbringing in the Middle East. So I also have to protect this book against one variant of Western racism! It is the case that I defend and follow a universal epistemology, but nonetheless I do this with an awareness of culturally different styles that extend to writing. We Middle Easterners write in a personal narrative style that is scholarly as well. In my academic life in the West (Germany and the US) I have repeatedly been exposed to some Westerners who deny that my writing in this Middle Eastern style is scholarly. This is nothing but Western racism and ignorance. Period! Apart from this response I have nothing to add to protect myself and my work.

Intended readership and overview of the field

For the sake of fairness and also to comply with the rules of scholarship, I think it is right to provide an overview of the state of the art in Islamic studies that includes a reference to competing books. By and large, the literature on Islamism evades a critical examination of the hot-button issue of the *shari'a* state for the sake of promoting favourable views. At the top of this list is a book I mentioned above, *The Fall and Rise of the Islamic State* by Noah Feldman (see note 23). I make no bones about the fact that the present book collides head-on on all levels with Feldman's book and reaches 100 per cent different conclusions, as will be shown later. Accepting disagreement as a feature of pluralism in academic culture, I nonetheless acknowledge my respect for Feldman's scholarship and for his solid knowledge; what I disagree with entirely is his analysis. Not all scholars who publish on this subject matter possess such respectable knowledge. Their flaws are demonstrated in the overview provided by a significant review article by Jillian Schwedler, published in a major international relations journal under the heading 'Can Islamists Become Moderate?'[32] This review article documents all relevant recent books on the matter in point, and – of course only implicitly – their flaws.

Schwedler's review article is a good basis for characterizing the state of the art in Islamic studies as it documents the great shift in the study of political Islam. Prior to the Arab Spring the study of political Islam revolved around associating or, conversely, dissociating Islam from violence; conspicuously lacking were not only a distinction between what Islam is and what Islamism is, but also of distinctions within Islamism itself. Most Western authors in the first decade of the twenty-first century were obsessed either with a prejudiced maligning or a naïve exoneration of Islam.

There has been a shift, not, unfortunately, for the better, but from one obsession to another. Schwedler tells us in her overview that 'scholarship on political Islam has moved away from abstract debates . . . toward empirical studies'. These studies of reality are, however, not only selective, but also not really empirical as they claim to be. They are obsessed with a preconception. The so-called 'inclusion–moderation hypothesis' serves as a tool for an imposed theoretical modelling of Islamism, which seems to matter more than dealing with the actual reality of Islamist movements. What US scholars think is right is definitely not what Islamists really want, which is the *shari'a* state. Schwedler's review article covers in its notes and bibliography a huge literature on Islamism, but characteristically refers to the *shari'a* only once to mention in passing that Islamists are partly willing to compromise, but acknowledges nonetheless that, for Islamists, issues related to *shari'a* 'are not open for discussion'. This is the top, red-line issue in an ideological roadblock that seems not to be of interest to US scholars, who prefer to deal with 'drawing a distinction between moderates and radicals' and to use the term 'moderate . . . as a synonym for prodemocratic' instead of studying the Islamist literature and the related action to see what order Islamists fight for in a political reality. I strongly deplore the fact that some Western pundits accept complying with the red line imposed by Islamists on the debate. This reality proves Paul Berman right in his misgiving that the 'Islamist movement . . . has succeeded in imposing its own categories . . . over how everyone else tends to think'.[33] *Quod erat demonstrandum.*

As Schwedler's review article tells us, the following view prevails in most of the political-science-based US publications on political Islam: 'Islamism (is) a term used for highly diverse political actors.' This is correct, but it is incorrect that most of the scholars involved draw from the fact of intra-Islamist diversity the wrong conclusion: the conclusion that Islamism does not include a shared agenda, namely the *shari'a* state. It gets worse when added to this ignorance is the accusation of 'lumping together' made by these scholars against better informed ones when the latter discuss Islamist commonalities.

In this review of dozens of publications the term '*shari'a* state' does not occur at all. In accordance with the prevailing definition, Islamists are simply reduced – in disturbingly wishy-washy thinking – to people who 'find the blueprint for social, moral, political and economic reform in the teaching of Islamic faith'. For me as a reform Muslim who has been professionally studying political Islam since 1980, this characterization gives the worst impression one could ever have about the quality of Western scholarship regarding the study of Islam and Islamism. The question that comes to mind is: What kind of reform is the Islamist drive aiming at? Is it replacing the secular nation-state by a *shari'a* state? One is tempted to think that scholars who think this way and avoid hot-button issues do not 'get it'. The reality of Islamism as presented in the 'empirical studies' in the US barely resembles the reality of Islamism on the ground – a reality that revolves around the *shari'a* state, not around moderation and inclusion. This is the major theme of the present, professedly controversial book. It is controversial only for this reason: that I do not share the common beliefs of Western scholars. My study aims to generate a debate on the real issues, a debate hopefully free of defamation. Is not disagreement an essential feature of scholarship?

Finally, I need to address the character of the present book. As already indicated in the Preface, repeated in this Introduction and elaborated upon in Chapter 4, the incentive to write this book has been the Arab Spring. This book is, however, designed as a research monograph on the *shari'a* state, the political order that the Islamist movements seek to establish in the context of their empowerment after a successful hijacking of the Arab Spring. My books published in the past years also address a general audience. People are daily exposed to the flawed media coverage on the Arab Spring and Islamism. In the past 30 years, starting from 1980 when my first book in English, *Arab Nationalism* (Macmillan Press, three editions, and, I am grateful to be able to say, acclaimed as a 'classic'), came out, I have published ten books written directly in English, in addition to my thirty books written in German published between 1969 and 2009. These forty books combine the interest of experts with that of a public audience. The present book is also written for the general reader. The most recent of my books, *Islamism and Islam*, published in 2012, was also designed this way, although published by a prominent Ivy League university press. The same goes for this book as for that one: I present original knowledge for experts, but also reach out to the general educated public.

And finally . . .

I will end this Introduction with a note that combines methodological with personal concerns. In Chapter 4 I shall discuss in more detail why this book does not aim to provide any account of topicalities related to the Arab Spring. Instead, it focuses on the big picture and places details in an overall context. This is a methodology that adheres to the disciplines of historical sociology and comparative politics. However, I cannot fully comply with the intent to produce a purely academic book. Scholars are also human beings with emotions and feelings, but they are expected to keep this out of their scholarly work. This is not always possible.

One case in point touches deeply on my relation to the subject matter: the massacres in my home country Syria and in my most beloved birthplace Damascus. I beg the reader's forbearance with these human lapses. Being a Sunni native of Damascus, I cannot escape the exposure to the daily crimes committed by an Alawi-dominated military force named the Syrian army, and by its security forces. This happens in close cooperation with the Alawi gangs of Shabiha militia in an action against the majority Sunni population. Although I am highly critical of the *shari'a* state and the Muslim Brothers, as I argue with ample evidence against this order that is not to be confused with democracy, I believe this Islamist order would never do anything as evil as the assaults carried out frenziedly by the Assad–Ba'th regime against the Syrian people. If I were exposed to the choice to live either under the rule of the Alawi Assad clan or in a *shari'a* state, I would not hesitate to pick the latter simply for convenience. However, this should not be considered the real choice, because there is a third option, namely a genuine democracy based on the ethics of a civil Islam. This third choice may not be within reach at the present stage. The realist consequence would be that we have to bear with the *shari'a* rule of the Islamists and live under its rule. If this happens, the least one can do is avoid self-deception. We should not listen to the tellers of fairy tales, who deceive us with the tale that this *shari'a* rule 'is democracy'. This book assumes it is not, and takes pains to check this assumption. However, it is a fact, not an assumption, that the people who took to the streets in the context of the Arab Spring did not risk their life for a *shari'a* state.

In the post-Arab-Spring era there are two decisive concerns that will determine the future prospects: political freedom combined with the fulfilment of basic economic and social needs. If the *shari'a* state fails to deal properly with these two concerns, it will lose its legitimacy within a short time. People may then come back to the streets to protest because they have become confident of their power to topple a powerful regime. Clear evidence for this prospect is what happened on September 21, 2012 in Bengazi, Libya. The Arab Spring led to the toppling of the fascist Qadhafi regime, which was much uglier than just an 'authoritarian regime'. Elections took place, and finally a democratically elected government was forged based on an Islamist–tribal coalition. The problem has been that this government is poised to integrate the great number of armed militias that emerged in the Arab Spring. Some of these serve today as 'security forces' (see the section on Libya in Chapter 4). The name of one of these militias is *'ansar al-shari'a*/ Defenders of *shari'a*. On that Friday, September 21, 2012, Libyan people took to the streets to protest the violent intimidations committed by these militias. Then during the night they stormed some of the headquarters of these groups, including that of *'ansar al-shari'a*, to demolish them. Some 30,000 protesters were shouting slogans in Arabic, such as: 'We did not fight and topple the Qadhafi tyranny to replace it with the tyranny of the Islamist militias.' Comment is superfluous, except for this: it shows that people want freedom and food, not a *shari'a* state.

1 The *shari'a* state and Western scholarship

The reality of the Islamist *shari'a*tization of politics that seeks a name

Do Western pundits properly explain to their audience why so many thousands of 'no-hope generation' Arab-Muslim youth took to the streets in the spring of 2011 in a drive to express discontent? Do they properly understand that the Arab Muslims did this in a quest for freedom and for improvement in the material conditions of their lives, not for the implementation of *shari'a*? To answer this requires an examination of the following issues: that in the course of the unfolding of the Arab Spring the Islamists seem to have prevailed, and their professed agenda is the *shari'a* state. This book examines these issues, placing the Islamist state order at the centre of its focus and explaining it in juxtaposition to the needs of democratization combined with the expectations of a better life. Because most Western contributions fail to accomplish this task, I take issue with Western scholarship from the position of 'enlightened Muslim thought'.

This first chapter pursues, on the basis of defined terms, what *shari'a* is in Islam, and then takes issue with Western scholarship on this matter. In doing so, I operate on the following major assumptions: the agenda of a *shari'a* state does not – as is often supposed – follow from the religious faith of Islam. At issue is an envisioned Islamist political order of the state and of the world. Islamism is an internationalist movement that aspires to remake the world order. This vision is wrongly ascribed to Islamic beliefs. In pursuit of this vision, a *shari'a*tization of Islam takes place that ignores the needs of the rebelling people. The related political action does not herald a religious revival, nor is the *shari'a* state a sign of an Islamic awakening.

Moreover, a closer look shows that the envisioned order of a *shari'a* state is not a democracy. If these assumptions that this book proceeds on can be positively checked, verified and prove to be valid, then it must be possible to generate a free debate. An open and free society guarantees free speech. A scholarly community based on this freedom needs to admit the liberty to state facts and to debate on the basis of making assumptions about the prevailing views to confront these with different perspectives to facts.

Why are most of the issues addressed in this book not only taboo (and well guarded at that), but also not well understood in Western scholarship? This is the question with which this opening chapter aims to grapple. The ground will then, hopefully, be open for exploring new avenues for the study of the interrelations between the Arab Spring, democratization and the *shari'a* state.

Terms, confusions and the trajectory of the argument

The terms used in the debate in hand indicate the existence of great confusions, leading to disastrous consequences. These confusions are further complicated by great ignorance about the issues involved. This chapter aims to eliminate these confusions by an effort at clarification on the basis of solid facts. The core assumption on which this study rests is that there is a fundamental distinction between the religion of Islam as a faith/*iman* and the historical reality of an Islamic civilization.

A major source of the existing confusions is the frequent conflation in Islamic studies between the scripture and the historicity of Islam. A pertinent example is the idea of an Islamist *shari'a* state to be subjected to critical reasoning. This idea relates to a *political reality*, not to the religious faith of Islam.

Among the few helpful Western contributions on which my analysis draws is Marshall G. S. Hodgson's magnificent work *The Venture of Islam.*[1] Compared with the outstanding intellectual quality of this work, most other contributions to the theme are shallow; they not only confuse terms, but also different stages in world and Islamic history, ending up in disarray. I believe that Hodgson provides light at the end of this tunnel and I follow him. To illustrate this need I shall refer to the state of the art in Islamic studies.

Another major inspiration comes from the publications of great enlightened Muslim thinkers on which I draw. Chapter 3 devotes a full section to a discussion of enlightened Muslim thought, to which this book adheres; in the course of the present chapter I shall, however, introduce this 'enlightened turn' in contemporary Muslim thought.

Given the great significance of the problems at issue, any prudent analysis has to start an effort at clarification. A setting straight of all historical records must be combined with a clearing up of the terms employed. This task is imperative. It is intriguing to see the extent to which the contemporary scholarly and non-scholarly debate on Islam and the political order is drenched with confusions. These shortcomings inflict tremendous damage on prevailing thinking about matters of crucial concern. It follows that these confusions must be dealt with. One of them pertains to the interrelation of Islam, Islamism and several political orders placed in the context of long historical epochs. The deeper reason for these confusions – apart from deplorable ignorance – is lack of clarity and distinction in the terms used, resulting in an intellectual shambles. In pursuit of the rectifications required, as I have stated, I draw repeatedly on the magisterial history of Islam as a world civilization by Marshall Hodgson. The confusion of what is 'Islamic' with regard to religious faith (first sense) and what is 'Islamic' with regard to 'culture [and politics – B.T.] associated historically with religion' (second sense) is not peculiar to Islamist thought of our present time. Muslims of the past also did this, and so did Western scholars studying Islam and its civilization. In view of this harmful confusion, Hodgson insists on 'a distinction of terms' and views this job as 'rather urgent', because 'the society and culture called Islamic in the second sense are not necessarily Islamic in the first'. As an illustration, Hodgson presents this example: 'one can speak of . . . Islamic despotism, but in such a sequence one is speaking less and less of something that expresses Islam as a faith.' In my view this insight also applies to the example of 'Islamic state': this notion does not '[express] Islam as a faith'.

Next to this most important distinction, there is a need to establish the historicity of Islam in the course of its de-essentialization. Along with Hodgson, I operate on the insight that 'civilization forms a primary unit of reference', and accept Hodgson's definition that 'we may call a civilization any wider grouping of cultures in so far as they share consciously interdependent traditions'. I suggest identifying this backbone of a civilization in the Ibn Khaldunian way as *'asabiyya* (the best Western translation of this term is *esprit de corps*, implying a value system). To ensure that no essentialization is at work, one needs to keep in mind Hodgson's proposition: 'historical change is continuous and all traditions are open and in motion.' This is the historicity of Islam as distinguished from Islamic faith. On these grounds Hodgson introduces new terms, 'Islamdom' and 'Islamicate', which he defines as follows: 'Various peoples among whom Islam has been predominant and have shared cultural traditions distinctively associated with it may be called collectively Islamdom . . . . The distinctive civilization of Islamdom, then may be called Islamicate.'

Hodgson uses Islamdom as a noun and Islamicate as an adjective. I glady adopt his terms, but with a slight adjustment, in that I relate both to the Islamic term *dar al-Islam*/Islamic territoriality, using Hodgson's term 'the Islamicate' to refer to this. Thus, as I use it, the 'Islamicate' becomes a noun meaning the Islamic territoriality of *dar al-Islam*, while 'Islamdom' is the *umma* during one historical era. Most important is Hodgson's distinction between matters that pertain to Islamic faith (Islamic) and realities both in Islamdom and in the Islamicate. This distinction underpins the already addressed historicity of Islam. Faith and history need to be separated from one another. Thus, the conclusion to be drawn from Hodgson's study of the history of Islam is that the political order that unfolded in this context, namely the caliphate, is a historical reality in Islamic civilization not identical with tenets of Islamic faith. This conclusion and the related critical assessment also apply to contemporary history and, obviously, to the claimed order of the *shari'a* state. The latter is not Islamic faith either. Then one needs to establish a further significant distinction: the envisioned *shari'a* state is embedded by Islamism into a concept of world order, a kind of *Pax Islamica*. The nineteenth century's Pan-Islamism is a different issue since, as will be explained, it is not to be equated with Islamist internationalism. In short, the modern Islamist concept of *Pax Islamica* is neither the traditional caliphate nor the nineteenth-century Pan-Islamism.

In addition to the scholarly clarifications made, the work of enlightened intellectual Muslims needs to be taken into consideration. For them, post-Orientalism is not an Orientalism in reverse that moves from maligning Islam to a mindset of exoneration, but rather a critical reasoning based on the premise of a universal knowledge. At the top of the list of these enlightened Muslims is the late Moroccan philosopher Mohammed Abed al-Jabri. In his tradition, Abdou Filali-Ansary, another Moroccan Muslim committed to what he terms the 'enlightened turn', engages in a promising reasoning on Islam and democracy in the context of cultural modernity. Filali-Ansary is of the view (as I think, rightly) that post-Orientalism has to go beyond 'the confusion between a model and a historical system' – a confusion not restricted to Western Islamic studies, but also 'spread among Muslims at a time when they were confronted by the challenge of modern ideas'.[2] This happens in particular with regard to the understanding of *shari'a* in contemporary Islamdom. Filali-Ansary states candidly: '*shari'a* was never a system of law in the sense in which it is understood nowadays.' As will be discussed in more detail in Chapter 3, Ansary dismisses any attempt to relate *shari'a* to a political order. Therefore, he rightly thinks that contemporary enlightened Muslim thought commences with Ali Abdelraziq's dismissal of the caliphate in his book published in 1925 (see note 6).

Some Western scholars discussed by Filali-Ansary seem to have a great difficulty in understanding these complex issues. One is Charles Kurzman, of whom Filali-Ansary says: 'Not only does he reduce all debate . . . to the issue of religious law (*shari'a*) and its relevance for contemporary conditions; he also arbitrarily defines the modes.' These confusions mislead Kurzman to the extent of lumping together truly liberal Muslims with Islamists – e.g. soft Islamists such as Rashid Ghannouchi or hardliners such as Qaradawi – in his reader *Liberal Islam*.[3] Filali-Ansary thinks differently, as he honours those Muslims who are 'closer to modern humanism', to then add this judgement 'Ghannouchi, by contrast, is not'. Why? Because he argues for a *shari'a* state in a confusion based on the contention that original Islam provides the model for a constitutionalism. Filali-Ansary disagrees and refers to the fact that 'Ghannouchy is a main representative of Islamist attitudes and thought'. Then he continues with citing Ghannouchi's call 'for a return of the implicit constitution that Islam is supposed to have provided. . . . These are typically calls . . . to return to the original. . . . Appeals like these seek a purified and more forceful version of Islam. . . . For all their sincerity . . . such appeals . . . can in no way lead to a real democratization of society.' Based on this argumentation, Filali-Ansary proposes an abandonment of the notion of 'liberal Islam' and dismisses the reader that carries this formula as its title. He proposes replacing it with another one,'enlightened Muslim thought', a proposition that I already adopted in the Preface to this book. The issue will be discussed at more length in the first section of Chapter 3.

In contrast to Ghannouchi's Islamism, the work of critical-minded Muslims committed to the 'enlightened turn' (for which Filali-Ansary stands) inspires the reasoning and trajectory of the present analysis that screens the envisioned *shari'a* state. The fact that this kind of critical thinking faces great obstacles compels me to take issue with Western scholarship.

Anyone who engages in a critical study of Islamism and the related introduction of religionized politics into Islamic civilization in the present crisis-ridden world-historical situation runs risks. Among these risks are dismissal and even defamation. If you go a step further and argue that the envisioned Islamist *shari'a* state is not in line with a project of democratization, you expose yourself to much greater peril. This kind of inquiry is therefore a perilous venture that is undertaken on a thorny path. One becomes liable to defamatory accusations of all kinds. The Islamists themselves – not ordinary Muslims – undermine critical analysis and cry 'Islamophobia' to silence critics, while the mainstream in the establishment of Islamic studies in the US and Europe dismisses honest criticism by calling it a variety of names. Therefore I am compelled to rectify: While I take issue with this unfavourable state of affairs, I never deny the unfavourable Western imagery on Islam and Islamism and I am in the boat with all of those who fight prejudice.[4] Therefore, the present critical study of the *shari'a* state dissociates itself vehemently at the very outset by all means from any of the existing biases. For instance, I dissociate my work and critique of Islamism from the approach of the Working Group on Islamism and International Order based at the Hoover Institution (see Chapter 3). My approach differs in substance because it is a critical study of the Islamist ideology of political order from a point of view of a civil Islam, not from that of an apologetics for a *Pax Americana*. I also argue for bridge-building and dismiss Cold War binaries.

The Arab Spring has compelled me to dare to resume my work after retirement to engage in the present venture, which I undertake as a combination of scholar and liberal Muslim. My thinking is driven by the will to establish a compatibility between an 'open Islam' (a term I coined leaning on Popper's 'open society') and real democracy. I am concerned about the perils of a democratization that is reduced to balloting and therefore I feel constrained to warn about Islamism. Nonetheless, I argue on the one hand for an engagement – as distinct from empowerment – of Islamist movements, and on the other I dismiss binary policies on both sides.

In this opening chapter I start with a critical examination of the prevailing views regarding the misconceived *shari'a* state in Western scholarship. I then take issue with the Islamist agenda itself from a standpoint of genuine democracy and real democratization. I start from where I stopped in my two earlier monographs published in 2012, *Islamism and Islam* and *Islam in Global Politics: Conflict and Cross-Civilizational Bridging*,[5] to continue with this inquiry into the Islamist agenda of a *shari'a* state. From the first, I adopt for the present inquiry the distinction between Islam, as a faith, and Islamism, as religionized politics. From the second, I make use of the insight that the statement of conflict should be kept away from the binary thinking of a 'clash of civilizations' to engage instead in cross-cultural bridging. This approach is employed in the understanding of peaceful conflict resolution. The present book continues the inquiry pursued in these earlier contributions, avoiding rehashing and polarization.

On the grounds of the terms outlined and the clarifications made in this section (to be amplified in the next) about *shari'a*, a solid basis is to be established for a dispute with Western scholarship on Islamism. The analysis is driven by four objectives:

1   To establish with the support of Muslim authorities (*ulama* and secular scholars) the meaning of *shari'a* in Muslim faith in contrast to Islamic history.
2   To look at the ways Islamists politicize *shari'a* to use it as a religious undercurrent for the state order they fight for. Some Western scholars adopt the Islamist narrative uncritically; others view Islamism simplistically as terrorism.

3   To review the confusions that prevail primarily among US scholars of Islamic studies.
4   To outline what Islamism is beyond Islamist prevarications and Western wishful thinking.

By and large, these four tasks determine the trajectory of this book and constitute its subject matter. This opening chapter approaches them and illuminates the basic issues involved.

The facts: traditional *shari'a* is not about governance!

In bewildering contradiction to traditional *shari'a*, Islamism revolves around the political order of the state and of the world. Based on a review of Islamist political thought, I maintain that the Islamists envision a political order they call the *shari'a* state, the proper expression of a *nizam Islami*/Islamic order. My contention is that these new notions have no roots in traditional Islam. They are a contemporary addition to Islam. Furthermore, I repeat the assumption made in the Introduction that the *shari'a* state is not compatible with democracy. In clear contrast to Islamism, civil reform Islam provides a political ethics that supports real democracy and a democratization of the polity in the world of Islam. There is no denying that Islam is not apolitical, as it includes an ethics for politics; but it is a faith/*iman*, not a political religion, nor does it entail a concept for a political order for the state.

The bottom line is that *shari'a* in Islam is about faith and worship/*ibadat*, not about governance. To underpin these contentions with facts, let us take a historical journey into the records of Islamic civilization. Among these facts is the consensus among Muslims themselves, shared throughout their history, that Islam is a religion that rests on only five pillars/*arkan*, no more, no less. These are: the profession of faith/*shahada*, prayer/*salat*, fasting/*siyam*, alms for the poor/*zakat* and pilgrimage/*hajj* to Mecca. According to traditional Islam the practice of these pillars as *ibadat*/worship (the practice or living out of the faith) and the faith itself are the substance of the *shari'a*.

Among the records we shall consult are books by three Muslim religious authorities. The first two are a renowned *shaykh* of al-Azhar, the late Mahmud Shaltut, the foremost authority in Sunni Islam, and the late vice-Mufti of Lebanon, Subhi al-Salih.[6] In the chapter on *shari'a* in the authoritative introduction to Islam by Mahmud Shaltut one finds only the five pillars listed above: governance is not mentioned. In al-Salih's authoritative book *Ma'alim al-Shari'a* one finds next to the issue of worship/*ibadat* the area of civil law/*mu'amalat*, but nothing about governance. As a third authority I add to these two the Azhar professor Ali Abdelraziq. A year after the abolition of the caliphate, in 1925, he published an influential book in which he takes issue with political rulers who imposed the notion of governance on the Islamic faith, and then concludes that Islam is basically a religious faith, not about politics. I shall discuss Abdelraziq at greater length in Chapter 3.

All three of these *ulama* base their arguments on the text of the Qur'an, the foremost source of any argument on the Islamic faith. To enhance the evidence I refer to a fourth Muslim authority on the origins of *shari'a* and the place of the term '*shari'a*' in the text of the Qur'an. This is Mohammed Said al-Ashmawi, a specialist in comparative and Islamic law and a fomer judge. He points out that the notion of *shari'a* occurs only once in the Qur'an, namely in *Sura al-Jathiya* (45:18), and adds that the text of the Qur'an does not combine the notion of *shari'a* with any reference to governance. This textual evidence of fact is provided by Ashmawi in his ground-breaking book *Usul al-Shari'a*.[7] Ashmawi combines scholarship in *shari'a* with the capacity of practitioner; he was not only a high-ranking Egyptian judge, but also the president of the Supreme High Court of his country.

After citing authoritative Muslim *ulama*, as religious scholars, and a senior legal practitioner, I go on to draw on Muslim academic scholars to strengthen and enhance the evidence. I have selected a Sunni and a Shi'ite authority to consult alongside the religious *ulama* mentioned above. Most prominent among them is the late Fazlur Rahman. The Moroccan Filali-Ansary lists Fazlur Rahman among the basic authorities of enlightened Muslim thought.

Fazlur Rahman states the fact that the Qur'anic *shari'a* 'is basically concerned with morality . . . not enforceable in any court except that of the human conscience'.[8] It follows that *shari'a* 'is not strictly speaking law since much of it embodies moral and quasi moral concepts'. State law is enforceable in court, but *shari'a* is not a subject for an imposition because it is morality. If this identification of the religion of Islam and the place of *shari'a* in it is appropriate, which it is, then the understanding by contemporary Islamists of *shari'a* as a state law is false. This Islamist understanding runs counter to the Qur'an and to the facts. There is no denying that there is a historical Islam, which is different from the scriptural religious determination outlined, on which the Islamic faith rests. In historical Islam *shari'a* was admitted as a law, and rulers were allowed to legitimate their power as custodians of the *shari'a*. Is this what the Islamists of today have in mind and want to restore? No, it is not! What they want, as the state order they fight for, has never existed before: this is a tradition they have invented.

The story of the abuse of *shari'a* is older than Islamism. Fazlur Rahman takes issue in his book with the Muslim *ulama*: they 'clung tenaciously, besides personal law, to the two segments of *shari'a* law: the five pillars of Islam . . . and to the *hudud*-punishments'. Although traditional Muslim rulers pretended to be custodians of the *shari'a*, they promulgated 'their own laws based on the principles of social necessity and public interest in the absence of any reformulation or rethinking of Islamic law'.

Historians are familiar with the deplorable practice known in classical Islam as *siyasa*/state administration. Traditional Muslim *ulama* set out to provide the autocratic rulers with religious legitimacy on the basis of arbitrary references to *shari'a*. Their legitimating efforts were founded upon confusing *shari'a* with *fiqh* – a malicious practice dealt with in Chapter 2. These *ulama* stood in the service of the caliph-rulers. The false contention that their *fiqh* reflects *shari'a*, understood as a *lex divina* allegedly revealed by Allah, reflects the confusion of faith and politics. In the past, traditional *ulama* acted in this manner as *faqih*s (pl. *fuqaha'*), that is, jurists who claimed to be in charge of *shari'a*. They only intervened in politics when they were compelled to in order to legitimate the exisiting rule. In so doing they mostly provided the ruler *ex eventum* with religious legitimation. At this point I interrupt my recourse to Islamic sources with a reference to the founder of Islamic studies at Harvard, Sir Hamilton Gibb, who in his basic research on this issue draws attention to this fundamental feature of traditional Sunni political thought: 'Sunni political theory was, in fact, only the rationalization of the history . . . All the imposing fabric of interpretation of the sources is merely the *post eventum* justification of the precedents.'[9] This approach determined, as Gibbs argues, the 'development of political thought among the Sunni jurists'.

After Fazlur Rahman my second Muslim academic authority is the late Iranian Muslim Oxford scholar Hamid Enayat. To him, historical facts matter most. The intellectual reality is outlined by Hamid Enayat as follows: 'But one must not forget that despite the *shari'a* grasp of nearly all aspects of individual and social life, there is no such thing as a unified Islamic legal system, enshrined in integrated codes, and accepted and acknowledged unquestionably by all Muslims.'[10] Having mentioned the lack of a cohesive legal body named *shari'a*, Enayat goes on to tell us that all the legal rules made in its name as 'provisions remained as legal fictions'. These were 'never implemented as an integral system'.

In view of these firm facts stated by two great late Muslim scholars, Fazlur Rahman and Hamid Enayat (one is Sunni, the other is Shi'i), one is inclined to ask: Why then the Islamist fuss about the disappearance of *shari'a* as *farida ghaiba*/ neglected duty, and why the call for its return in an initiative that makes claims to be a restoration or revival? Why do some Western scholars take what Islamists say at face value and, in the name of respect, agree to see in their Islamist ideology an 'Islamic awakening'? I shall come back to this contention about an awakening in Chapter 6.

Among the tasks at hand is an inquiry into the belief that the absence of *shari'a* has been the result of what Islamists name *ghazu fikri*/cultural invasion of the world of Islam. The undercurrent of this belief is that *shari'a* is about politics and the order of the state. The background is the abolition of the caliphate in 1924 and, a few years later, also of the *shari'a* in Turkey. It was this confusion that drove Ali Abdelraziq to publish his above-cited ground-breaking book on the caliphate as early as 1925.

The introduction of secular positive law into Islamdom has been defamed as a conspiracy devised by the 'Crusader West'/'*al-gharb al-salibi*'[11] against Islam. I confine myself in this opening chapter to asking this question: What do the Islamists want to restore when they fight for establishing a *shari'a* state? Is it the classical caliphate? The answer is clearly: No. Those who politicize *shari'a* to make it serve as an underpinning for a *nizam Islami*/Islamic system engage in a novelty. Such an order has never existed before in all Islamic history. Therefore, the Islamist agenda does not herald an Islamic revival, but rather an invention of tradition. Throughout this analytical venture into the Islamist quest for a *shari'a* state, the determinative facts presented by the authoritative Islamic scholars cited above must be constantly kept in view.

Throughout this book I shall continue to present more evidence from Islamic writings to reveal that the 'return' of *shari'a* to the public square is not a revival of traditional *shari'a*. The historical origins of the classical *shari'a* must be clearly distinguished from the ongoing *shari'a*tization project pursued by Islamism which has been thriving since the Arab Spring. The structure of this book is determined by this theme. In this pursuit I shall dismantle the Islamist claim to authenticity – a feature that has been wrongly attributed to the constructed *shari'a* state. I pause here to shift focus onto the obstacles put in the way of free inquiry into Islamism: the third task of this chapter. Thereafter, I shall resume in substance the inquiry into the Islamist *shari'a* state. The fourth task will then be to unveil Islamism as the ideology of a *shari'a* state and to deny it to be a 'revival'. I assume in this that the commitment to the Islamist order does not indicate a drive towards democratization.

The prevailing narrative: the distorted understanding of Islamism in US Islamic studies

This chapter began with a definition of terms and an effort at establishing basic facts. This was done by drawing on the academic authority of Hodgson (see note 1) and on enlightened Muslim thought (Filali-Ansary; see note 2). The sources of this thought consist of the work of leading religious authorities (e.g. Ali Abdelraziq) as well as of academic Muslim authorities (e.g. Fazlur Rahman and Hamid Enayat). Two of these authorities are ranked top of the list by Filali-Ansary. All of these sources provide no support for the prevailing narrative in US Islamic studies that goes along with Islamist pretensions.

One of the most ferocious defenders of the prevailing narrative, Daniel Varisco, supplies this stance with the argument – correct in itself – that '[t]he views of Muslims themselves should be respected by those who observe them', that is by Westerners.[12] Does Varisco comply with this prudent advice? We shall see, but let this be stated in advance: there is a conspicuous absence of any reference to enlightened Muslim thought and to its sources. Does the 'respect', so rightly requested, also apply to Muslims of this school of thinking? I shall come back to this question in Chapter 6 in the context of 'false unity and forced coherence'.

The prevailing narrative operates on the questionable distinction often made in mistaken terms in contemporary Islamic studies between what is labelled 'radical Islam' and 'moderate Islam'. This distinction fails to address the real issues. Two points must be made. First, the issue in religionized politics is not Islam, but Islamism. Second, it is not a question of moderation, but of different tactics on the way to power. The driver of the analysis is this question: Is the current switch of Islamist movements from violent jihadism to peaceful institutionalism a sign of moderation? Will the empowerment of Islamist movements in the course of the Arab Spring be a part of the 'struggle to build free societies throughout the world', or not?

Three years ahead of the Arab Spring a book was published that carries in its subtitle the formula cited above, although not put as a question. That book includes a chapter heading asking the question: 'Can the Middle East democratize?' I add to this question the words 'under Islamist rule', but I also quote

Larry Diamond, the book's author, in his deliberations about the role of Islamism in the expected – or hoped for – democratization of the Middle East and North Africa. Diamond believes 'that Arab countries will not achieve democracy without Islamist participation, and possibly some period of Islamist leadership in governance.'[13] He is, however, not naive as other pundits seem to be, as he knows well that 'Islamist movements need to clarify whether they are willing to accept pluralism among Muslims in interpreting Islam. . . . The ambiguity is more acute, as religious dogma hampers political pragmatism. . . . Islamists . . . will have to commit to democratic principles and rules and clarify where they stand on secular freedoms.' This hard-headed assessment makes clear that democracy is based on a political culture of rules and principles and is not simply restricted to balloting.

Such realism is not reflected in the dominating narrative. The wishful thinking of the prevailing narrative will be juxtaposed to historical and contemporary facts. Then, also in this chapter and ahead of moving to the 'return of *shari'a*', I shall illustrate the dispute in point using the example of a US debate on Islamism in order to set the record straight. The *shari'a* state has been elevated in the context of the Arab Spring to a model for a democratic rule in the process of democratization. The present book challenges this unchecked assumption.

Most disturbing in US Islamic studies is the trend or propensity to take what the Islamist project of a '*shari'a* state' pronounces at face value. Facts seem not to matter. Those who engage in misunderstanding Islamism, believing it to be an 'Islamic revival', overlook the fact that Islamists are acting on a constructed *shari'a* order: neither on faith, nor on a spiritual religious renaissance. This order stands on the top of the Islamist agenda. Since its inception in 1928 Islamism has defined itself with the formula that reflects the Islamist belief: Islam is '*din-wa-dawla*'/'unity between religion and state order', with the implication that Islamism is basically about politics. This belief enshrines religionized politics and the *shari'a* state and promotes them to the status of new pillars attributed to Islam. Adopting the terms 'Islamdom' and 'Islamicate' from Hodgson, I distinguish strictly between Islamism (as a reality of contemporary history) and the faith of Islam.[14] I fail to see this most important distinction in the prevailing narrative in Western Islamic studies.

It is not my intention to dissociate Islam fully from politics. There is a political ethics in Islam. This ethics can become a democratic current in a new interpretation to be guided by the will to religious reform and cultural change. But Islamism is, in contrast, an ideology, not an ethics. It replaces democratic enlightenment with totalitarian indoctrination. The *shari'a* state that Islamists attribute to the Islamic faith is stipulated neither in the Qur'an nor in the *hadith* of the Prophet. It cannot be repeated enough that the terms *dawla*/state and *nizam*/system or order and also the notion of *shari'a* state are the outcome of a twentieth-century history related to the rise of Islamism, not part of the Islamic faith, nor of Islamic history.

Islamism, born in 1928, was on the fringe until the Arab defeat in the Six-Day War of 1967. From the 1970s onwards and throughout the turn to the new century, Islamist movements have been thriving as the core political opposition. The turning point was in the year of the Arab Spring, 2011, when well-organized Islamist movements succeeded in hijacking the just rebellion. Western coverage of this development was replete with the formula 'transition to democracy', erroneously adopted from the post-communist transition in Eastern Europe and uncritically applied as an unchecked assumption to the Middle East.

In contrast to the spirit of wishful thinking combined with limits imposed on a free debate on Islamism, this book takes its starting point in reality and questions the Western perception that a moderation of Islamism is taking place, and that Islamist movements are embracing democracy. The fact is that Islamists are poised to establish a political order, and the assumption of this book is that this *shari'a* state contradicts the substance of democracy. Both facts on the ground and the commitment to research based on assumptions (see Introduction) run counter to the contentions of the prevailing narrative.

If the *shari'a* state that does not exist in Islamic scripture is non-negotiable for Islamists, then one cannot talk about a moderation. The fact that Islamists forgo violent *jihad* and move to balloting in the pursuit of establishing a *shari'a* state does not indicate a genuine moderation. Among the sources of the misunderstanding on this is a widespread misinterpretation of the character of the *shari'a* order and the change it involves. The Islamist trading of the bullet for the ballot box is taken to be, not only a moderation, but also a sign of approval of democracy.

In most contributions of US Islamic studies one encounters the notions of 'the new Islamists' and 'democratization' linked together. Democracy cannot be reduced to a procedure of ballot box. It is rather a political culture based on pluralism and power sharing, as well as on the grounds of institutionalized human rights, understood as entitlements. On the top of these comes freedom of belief and of speech. When Islamists go to the ballot box, they do not become democrats overnight. For them, balloting is just a means to the seizure of power. Continuing the work done in my trilogy on Islamism (political Islam is just one variety of the global phenomenon of religious fundamentalism) (see note 14), in the present book I take issue with the Islamist agenda of a constructed '*shari'a* state', as well as with the positive attributes ascribed to it by the mainstream of US Islamic studies. In the recent past, in particular since the changed fortunes and decline of al-Qaeda, Islamist leaders have prudently recognized that jihadism leads to nowhere. They have come to the conclusion that participating in political institutions is more promising for their grab of power. To varying degrees, all of the authoritarian regimes in the Arab world undermine any institution building. The Arab Spring paved the way for the building of such institutions in the course of elections. The Islamists realized that getting on the democracy train would lead to the creation of an institutional set-up that allows power grabbing without violence. Is this the moderation US pundits have in mind?

Outsiders have the privilege of detachment when they make assessments. Nonetheless, one should not look at political and social phenomena in terms imposed on the people involved, but rather combine detachment with closeness to the matter in hand. Contrary to the allegations of some Western scholars who fail to comply with the wisdom of familiarity and closeness to what they study, the term 'Islamism' is not a Western coinage. It was Hasan al-Banna, the founder of the first underground movement to be named 'Islamist', who coined the term. In 1928 al-Banna founded the *Harakat al-Ikhwan al-Muslimun*/The Movement of the Muslim Brothers. His work is the source of the term *al-Islamiyya*. Al-Banna states:

> The best way to describe our *da'wa*/mission (proselytization) is to call it Islamism/*al-Islamiyya*. This notion goes far beyond the common understanding (of religion as faith). We believe that Islam means a total organization of all realms of life. Islam prescribes ways for designing all affairs along the very strict rules of a precise *nizam*/system that determines all aspects.[15]

For al-Banna this system/*nizam* is about politics/*siyasa*, which in his view lies at the core of the religion of Islam. It follows that, in his understanding, the issue is a matter of religionized politics. Although the Muslim Brothers in the early stages were involved in terror and assassinations, their core concern was remaking politics. Specifically, al-Banna wanted to topple the existing political regimes in order to establish *al-nizam al-Islami*. This is the Muslim Brothers' name for the Islamist order which is a *shari'a* state. Make no mistake: the *nizam Islami* is not the traditional caliphate, and it is about politicized *shari'a*, not about democracy. Al-Banna himself states that the *nizam Islami*/Islamic system is nothing else than Islamic governance (*hukuma*) that dismisses any separation between what is public and what is private. For him this is the *shari'a* state. Then he adds: 'Those who think that religion, precisely Islam, does not determine politics . . . are misled . . . Islam is *shari'a* and it is the origin of all. . . . The Islamic state is based on this *da'wa*/mission.'

The religionization of politics by Islamism is not well understood in US Islamic studies in general, nor is the double crisis that is the overall context. One source of crisis is the loss of legitimacy; the other relates to the failure of development. This is a reality that needs a name. It is Islamism (*al-Islamiyya*), as al-Banna himself calls it. This is not about language; rather, there is a real crisis that has given birth to the phenomenon of Islamism. This is not about religious faith but about politics. Islamism is not a revival of Islamic tradition but a reinvention of it. For these reasons Islamism is not Islam, though the two are closely related. The existing great misunderstanding of Islamism in the Middle Eastern and Islamic studies establishment can only be rectified by explaining the distinction between Islamism and Islam in all the detail necessary. In detail, then, the six distinctive, core features of Islamism are:

1   *nizam*/political order;
2   islamization of European antisemitism;
3   institutional participation and the use of democracy;
4   jihadization;
5   *shari'a*tization;
6   (last, but not least) authenticity.

Avoiding so far as possible any rehashing here, I refer the reader to my earlier book *Islamism and Islam*, which includes a chapter on each of these six core features. In general I dissociate Islamism from violence, shifting the focus from the obsession with terrorism to the reality of governance. This dismisses the obsession with al-Qaeda and with 'counterterrorism' from the present discussion.

It is unfortunate that so few US scholars seem to understand Islamism well: namely, that it is a vision for remaking the world. Islamists envision establishing an 'Islamic state' as a first step, and then an 'Islamic world order'. Both are based on the new Islamist *shari'a*. Among the few scholars who have a proper grasp of this issue is John Kelsay. In his book *Arguing the Just War in Islam*,[16] he places the Islamist movements in the tradition of '*shari'a* reasoning', that is basically concerned with governance. He is, however, aware of the clear distinction between the past and the present, and beween revealed *shari'a* and political *shari'a* as an invention of tradition.

The core argument of this chapter is that most Westerners (there are a few exceptions) have largely failed to grasp the historical facts about *shari'a*. I base this statement on a review of the prevailing narrative. To set the record straight, I want to make four points. First, Islamism is not unique; it is only one variety of a global rise in religious fundamentalism. Second, both the scholarly and the policy-making worlds are deeply confused about the nature of Islamism. Third, it is necessary to disassociate the *religion* of Islam from the *political* phenomena of violence and totalitarianism without denying the Islamist references to both. Fourth, we must move beyond our current habits of either exonerating or maligning Islam to reach a more realistic understanding of its influence in the world. This must include the ability to criticize Islamism and Islamist practices, even harshly at times, without being labelled 'Islamophobic', 'self-hating', or 'self-orientalizing'. Without any denial of the existing prejudiced image of Islam in the West, I reject the new notion of Islamophobia because it not only carries the earlier polemics of Orientalism, but also exceeds it and ends up in outlawing any criticism. I deem it advisable to take the accusation of Islamophobia most seriously, however, and therefore end this book with a chapter focused on it.

Misconceptions regarding the return of the sacred to politics

It has been already argued that the rise of Islamism is not unique; it is part of the larger and global phenomenon of the return of religion to the public sphere, which has become an essential feature of our post-bipolar world. However, the internationalist feature of Islamism that not only envisions a remaking of the order of the state but also of the order of the world at large makes this variety a unique one. In this case, the return of *shari'a* in an Islamist shape to the public debate marks the use of Islam as a current to establish a new international political order.

In contrast to the core assumption of the present book that the *shari'a* state is not consonant with democracy, nor with the political ethics of a tolerant civil Islam, the prevailing narrative in contemporary Western Islamic studies – ignoring the Arabic sources – upgrades Islamism. This upgrading is based on a misconception of the return of religion as social fact to politics. Here against the basic distinction between Islamism and Islam is overlooked. In recognition of the need for alternatives I proposed in my 2009 book *Islam's Predicament with Modernity* a new field of study, which I called Islamology.[17] This is a social-science approach, the groundwork for which was laid in my work in the preceding three decades. Islamology is not the theme of the present book and I will not elaborate on it here; I mention it merely to emphasize a different point of view for dealing with Islamism within the context of the global return of religion to the public space as the 'return of the sacred'.

De-secularization entails a politicization of religious precepts, resulting in what I have called 'religionized politics'. The goal of an inquiry inspired by the proposed discipline of Islamology is not only to study the conflict-ridden relations between the Islamic world and the West, but also to study how political–religious tensions in general develop into international conflicts. Religionized politics is different from the 'sacralized politics' described by the Italian historian Emilio Gentile, in that it is based on a real religion, not on turning a secular ideology such as fascism or communism into a sacral one, that is, into a belief system.

The view that Islamism is a religious renaissance compelled me to propose a new discipline because at present there exists no consensus among scholars on how to think about religionized politics – or even what to call it. Some see a religious revival, others see multiple modernities, still others see a rise of political religion but no religious renaissance. There is also a propensity to set religion itself aside and look at religious articulations as mere expressions of politically and socially legitimate grievances. And when it comes to Islam, the debate gets more intense even as the confusion grows. It is not uncommon, for instance, to hear scholars declare that the entire conflict between Muslims and Jews is over the Israeli–Palestinian issue. This view completely ignores the history of Islamist antisemitism, which both predates the founding of the state of Israel and stands far out of proportion to the magnitude of the Israeli–Palestinian conflict. Apart from the above-mentioned methodological flaws, the existing shortcomings result from two sources. One is the politicization of scholarship; the other is a combination of political correctness with an epistemological cultural relativism that prohibits making general assessments about other cultures.

The failure to apply a concept of religionized politics, and the resulting uncertainty over how to deal with a phenomenon like Islamism, are to be seen in this context. This situation permits Islamist ideologues to use the virtue of respect for religious faith instrumentally as a pretext to prevent serious debate. For instance, Turkey's AKP (Justice and Development Party), which has held power since 2002, is without doubt an organization rooted in political Islam;[18] it is an example of the return of religion to the public sphere in the only real secular republic in the Islamic world. The prime minister of Turkey, Recep Tayyip Erdogan, who is also the leader of the AKP, not only denies that his party is Islamist (the AKP bills itself as 'conservative-Islamic'), but also dismisses the use of the notion of Islamism to identify political Islam. Any distinction between Islam and Islamism, he says, is 'offensive and an insult to our religion. There is no moderate or immoderate Islam.

Islam is Islam, and that's it.'[19] The American authors Andrew Bostom and Andrew McArthur, who quote this statement, add that Erdogan is right, and wrongly infer from this that 'Islam is the problem'.[20] This is fuzzy thinking squared. In an earlier book I argue that the distinction between Islam and Islamism – a specific instance of the distinction between religion and religionized politics, and one with very important consequences – is essential for understanding the politics of the modern world. To accuse this thinking of Islamophobia is baseless and heralds mere polemics, not a sober scholarly debate, as will be demonstrated throughout the present book, and in particular in its concluding chapter.

Confusion among scholars: a representative debate

To illustrate the misgivings I have expressed in relation to the prevailing narrative on Islamism, I take the following example. At its 2004 convention, the Middle East Studies Association of North America (MESA) sponsored a panel discussion that was later published under the title *Islamism: Contested Perspectives on Political Islam.*[21] This book provides an illuminating look at the state of knowledge – or the state of incomprehension – in American thinking about Islamism.

In the highly representative debate published in this volume, which includes sixteen contributions by fourteen authors, the reader is exposed to a great disagreement. The editors, Richard C. Martin and Abbas Barzegar, introduce the book by describing the confusion. They recruited two protagonists, one of whom (the anthropologist Daniel Varisco) wants to banish the term 'Islamism' from the scholarly vocabulary. The other (the political scientist Donald K. Emmerson) would admit the notion, but with the barely comprehensible objection that distinctions (e.g. between Islamism and Islam) are invidious; he then provides a largely unhelpful definition of Islamism. It is left to the remaining twelve contributions to wrestle with these protagonists. The authors were asked 'to uncover the implications and clarify the parameters of the term'.[22] Each does this in his or her own way, either rejecting or endorsing the notion of Islamism. The editors note that 'among the sixteen scholars and intellectuals writing in this volume, no two advocate identical understandings. . . .'

Earlier I quoted one of the protagonists of the MESA debate, Varisco, in his essay 'Inventing Islamism: the violence of rhetoric', requesting 'respect' for the 'views of Muslims themselves'. I endorsed him. He, however, dismisses the notion of Islamism altogether. The 'use of Islamism for politicized Islam,' he writes, is a 'danger'. Does Varisco know that the founder of the first Islamist movement in history, the Muslim Brothers, is the source of this concept? That he is the one who coined the term '*al-Islamiyya*'? I fail to find a reference to al-Banna's writings in Varisco's notes, nor to any other substantial Muslim source! Comment is superfluous. Despite this, one should continue to listen to Varisco's argument. He thinks that Islamism is a 'single word that uniquely associates Islam and violence' and adds 'for myself I will cease to use the term in my future writings without drawing attention to why it is the wrong term.'[23] The notion of *fundamentalism* is not better, Varisco thinks: 'both conceptualizations are not worth perpetuating in academic writing.' Scholars who continue to use these terms, he argues, are doing an injustice to Muslims. It turns out that Varisco would forbid not only 'Islamism' and 'fundamentalism', but many other 'isms' applied to the world of Islam (e.g. 'Jihadism is semantic overkill'). It is not clear whether he is aware that modern Arabic is full of 'isms': just as in English, you can turn any Arabic word into an 'ism' by adding the suffix *'iyya'*. Open any Arabic newspaper to find out how replete modern Arabic is with words that end in '. . . *iyya*/ism'.

In their defence of *usul*/the fundamentals, Arabic-speaking Muslim fundamentalists are the ones who turned *Islam* into *Islamiyya*. The reason I say it is unclear whether Varisco knows this is that he starts his chapter with the line 'In Arabic grammar Islam is indeed an ism.' No: It is not. *Al-Islam* in Arabic is not *al-Islamiyya* (Islam with an 'ism'), any more than *jihad*/jihad is *jihadiyya*/jihadism. These terms are used by native Arabic speakers to denote distinct phenomena: Islam (*al-Islam*) as a religion, for instance, as opposed to Islamism (*al-Islamiyya*) in the meaning cited above. The introducer of the term, al-Banna (see note 15), is the father of this political ideology. This is a political fact and not 'a linguistically resurgent Islamism', as Varisco contends.

Sadly, but significantly, *Islamism: Contested Perspectives on Political Islam* symbolically enacts this linguistic uncertainty on the book's own cover. Floating above the title *Islamism* is a word in Arabic script – not *al-Islamiyya* but *al-Islam*. Well, this is wrong Arabic. The confusion starts on the cover of the book: a key point is muddied before one has even broken the cellophane. What, then, is to be expected?

Before moving to the second protagonist, I repeat my earlier question (p. 34 *note 12 cit.*) when I wondered how serious was Varisco's request to 'respect the views of Muslims themselves'. There is a powerful trend in modern Islam called 'enlightened Muslim thought', represented in significant Islamic writings since Ali Abdelraziq in 1925 and consolidated by Abdou Filali-Ansary. Does Varisco know of these Muslims and respect them? Certainly, he quotes none of them. The reader must judge.

The other recruited protagonist in this confused but representative MESA debate, Professor Donald Emmerson of Stanford University, allows some distinctions, saying in his chapter, 'Inclusive Islamism', that 'distinctions can appear invidious . . . yet no analysis is possible without [them]'.[24] But his own distinctions miss the mark. Emmerson provides a definition of *Islamist* that is borrowed from James Piscatori: one can identify as Islamist a Muslim 'who engages in violent political action on behalf of an ostensibly Islamic agenda'. He makes some modifications in this definition, but I do not think they are worth detailed debate. The point is that this understanding of Islamism depends entirely on *violent action* – in this sense Varisco has a valid complaint. The ideology is so vague as to be irrelevant and need not even be sincere. Anyone can drape himself in an *ostensibly* Islamic agenda. Emmerson and Piscatori disregard the very clearly articulated Islamist political goal of establishing an Islamic *shari'a* state as part of a remaking of the world – an agenda that is, indeed, only ostensibly Islamic. By the definition they provide, Islamism is Islam plus political violence.

The MESA debate obscures the true relationship between Islamism and Islam, and also misleadingly identifies Islamism with violence. Every Islamist is a Muslim, but not every Muslim – not even every Muslim who commits violent political acts – is an Islamist. And not every Islamist is violent. My study of Islamism published in three volumes (see note 14) arrives at the research-based conclusion that Islamism is not about violence; rather, it is about the political order of the state, and the world in a venture to religionize politics.

Professor Emmerson is correct when he writes that 'if stereotyping and prejudice toward Muslims are to be reduced, we need to make more not fewer distinctions'. If this mindset were to be taken seriously, then the chapter 'Inclusive Islamism' would have to be dismissed. After all, one would expect in a book entitled *Islamism* to see the distinction between Islam and Islamism discussed at this point, but this does not happen at all. Is Islamism to be considered so inclusive that it embraces all of Islam, so that the two become interchangeable? It is hard to tell. Yet Emmerson does seem to recognize a difference, stating 'The -ist in *Islamist* points toward collective action and ideology, not individual piety. So do the illustrations of social, economic, cultural, and evangelical Islamism . . . involving as they all do the public sphere.' However, this insightful statement does not lead its author to understand what religionized politics is all about.

The twelve other contributors then sort themselves out without always making the sides very clear. They generally sympathize with Varisco in his dismissal of the notion of 'Islamism' but do not agree with his other arguments and conclusions. Most take positions that either are ambiguous or find fault with both his and Emmerson's positions.

Among the contributors is the left-wing Islamist and Muslim philosopher Hasan Hanafi, who criticizes the Western obsession with 'isms'. He views the term *Islamism* as 'a Western invention as well as *fundamentalism*'.[25] But Hanafi does not confuse reality and terminology; instead he suggests that one 'should look for more neutral vocabulary, such as political Islam'. In fact, this is the preferred term used in the Arabic literature.[26] Hanafi himself, however, is the author of the Arabic book *al-Usuliyya al-Islamiyya*[27] published in Cairo, in which he uses the term *usuliyya* (fundamentalism) in speaking positively about political Islam. This is highly intriguing. The title of this book by Hanafi translates as 'Islamic Fundamentalism'. Why does Hanafi use a vocabulary in Arabic that he dismisses when he writes in English? Is this double-speak?

There is a detached quality to many of these essays that are supposed to reflect the 'contested perspectives on political Islam', as the book's subtitle suggests. This quality can be captured with the phrase 'academic word games'. Several of the American authors seem to be mainly concerned with the *term* 'Islamism' and its usefulness, and preoccupied with its relation to violence. The primary injustice that they acknowledge is the misuse of language. To the extent that this misuse tends to associate the religion of Islam with terror and violence, their concerns are well founded, and also shared by myself. But in a volume whose subtitle promises 'contested perspectives on political Islam', one would expect to find more about the nature of Islamism as a political Islam, that is, as a political religion. Hillel

Fradkin (in Martin and Barzegar, see note 21) rightly asks where the reality lies. At issue, he argues, is not a term but 'a distinct historical movement within the contemporary Muslim world to which the term Islamism has been applied . . . Varisco proceeds effectively as if the phenomenon were non-existent altogether. . . . the result is anything but academic.' The insinuation is clear: many academics confuse their use of language with the reality they claim to deal with. As the heading of the present chapter suggests, in Islamdom there is a reality that seeks a name. Islamism is nothing but a name for the contemporary *shari'a*tization of Islam.

The only other author besides Fradkin to break ranks in the debate is M. Zuhdi Jasser, who is described in the contributor list as 'a physician in private practice in Phoenix, Arizona', and who is apparently free of the self-imposed restraints on Islamic studies scholars. Jasser is also among 'the other Muslims, moderate and secular' Zeyno Baran has recruited for her book of that title.[28] Jasser correctly observes that Islamism (*al-Islamiyya*) is not so much about violence and terrorism as about remaking the world order. It is about a 'form of a theocratic Islamic state' and 'has both militant and nonviolent components'.[29] Like many other liberal Muslims, Jasser feels frustrated when some members of 'the jury' in the West prescribe 'at times paternalistically' that he avoid the term 'Islamism'. 'Sweeping terms under the rug,' he reminds us, 'will not change reality . . . . The reality of militant Muslims is that they derive the basis of their program of social change from theocratic interpretations of Islam . . . . Avoiding the term political Islam or Islamism allows the theocrats to remain without critique.' This is exactly what happens in the West. Jasser decries Western scholarship for its silence on Islamism and criticizes 'Varisco's bewildering hodgepodge' of reasons 'for dismissing the term Islamism'.

Jasser is, like myself, someone of Syrian background who 'came to the West seeking religious freedom' and now deplores the fact that some liberal Westerners 'protect from critique' exactly those Islamists who threaten his freedom. As a self-described 'anti-Islamist, or non-Islamist Muslim', Jasser recommends to Westerners that 'one should read the work of Hassan al-Banna . . . and . . . Sayyid Qutb . . . to understand the all encompassing transnational goals of Islamism. . . . Democracy is not only about the ballot box. It is about a system of law.' Westerners who, by refusing to allow things to be called by their proper names, do not allow such an undertaking are 'the greatest obstacle in this critical, important Muslim debate . . . that keeps us Muslims from this debate at all'.

Martin and Barzegar, the editors of this representative example of the Islamism debate, can neither resolve the conflict between the two protagonists nor clear up the disagreement among the ten expert contributorss. They issue a disclaimer in their introduction: 'The reader should be warned that this book does not resolve the debate about Islamism.' The pros and the cons require that 'The reader must decide . . . [this] is the reader's share of responsibility in entering this debate.' If the reader is not an expert and wants to learn what Islamism is or understand its place in contemporary world politics, he or she will find (these are the editors' words) 'little clarity, much less consensus, on the meaning or accuracy of this widely deployed label that is "Islamism."'[30] Not only is there no common view among scholars on what Islamism is and on the compatibility of *shari'a* state with democracy, but also there is no agreement at all that a free debate is needed – including freedom from accusations and defamation. The ignorance so often on view in discussions of democracy and the *shari'a* state is continued in the context of the Arab Spring and the transformation of Islamist opposition into Islamist rule in some countries of North Africa and the Middle East.

Islam, Islamism and violence: the need for a realistic understanding

Among the backlashes of the jihadist 9/11 attacks was a disturbing, indiscriminate and erroneous association not only of Islamism, but also of the religion of Islam, with violence. In view of this charged background I want to give Martin and Barzegar – despite my critical reading of their work – credit for addressing an important concern: namely, to do away with the dreadful demonization of Islam. The entire religion has been tarred with the brush of violence. Martin and Barzegar's opposition to this ugly occurrence is entirely laudable. However, one should beware of moving from one extreme to the other, as from Orientalism to an 'Orientalism in reverse'. The proper response to what is considered 'Islamophobia' is certainly not 'Islamophilia'. To engage in a distinction between Islamism and Islam and to criticize Islamist movements and their ideology is in no way an expression of Islamophobia.

Among the Islamists' victims are the many Muslims who disagree with Islamist views and are therefore defamed as heretical. For this reason the Egyptian historian Abdelazim Ramadan (not to be confused with Tariq Ramadan) rightly identified Islamist movements as *jama'at al-takfir*.[31] The term *takfir* refers to the excommunication of Muslims from the *umma* to legitimate their killing. The Islamists have been successful in their venture both in the Islamic world and the West to claim that Islamism truly speaks for all of Islam. In debates with other Muslims, Islamists acknowledge their commitment to *al-Islamiyya* (Islamism) or *al-Islam al-siyasi* (political Islam), but – in double-speak – when they talk to a Western audience they deny that there is any distinction between this and Islam. They argue for one Islam, which is theirs. I have already quoted the Turkish Islamist leader Recep T. Erdogan as saying, 'Islam is Islam, and that's it'. The corollaries of this view are, first, that jihadism has nothing to do with Islam, and second, that any criticism of Islamism is an expression of Islamophobia.

Both ideas create a sense, embraced by both Islamists and right-wing Westerners, that the West is at war with Islam. Western intellectuals who see in Islamism a revived third worldism[32] are also susceptible to this view. In fact, however, the real battle is among Muslims themselves: between liberal Muslims and illiberal – totalitarian – Islamists. These represent the two major competing models for the future of Islam. This battle is largely unintelligible to those who do not comprehend the difference between the religion of Islam and the religionized politics of Islamism. And if one accepts the Islamists' premises, then a blanket condemnation of Islam as an inherently violent religion becomes difficult to refute.

Those who go to the other extreme, by forbidding any critique of Islamism, also do great disservice to Islam. The replacement of Islamophobia with Islamophilia is no solution. Martin and Barzegar must be given credit for allowing a joint warning by a Muslim, Ziba Mir-Hosseini, and a Westerner, Richard Tapper, against a 'censoring' in Western scholarship.[33] To be sure, the strategy of introducing censorship in the name of respect for Islam is also pursued by the Islamists themselves. This chapter ends with a resumption of this theme and with a discussion of the related perils. Respect for Islam need not be tainted with the forbidding of free research and thinking. There are Muslims who are engaging in religious reform and cultural change. Islamism not only fails to provide a model for these needs, but also creates obstacles to fulfilling them. The identification of the areas where reform is needed requires the admission of critical reasoning into Islamic thought. This requirement is fulfilled in the work of Muslim adherents of enlightened Muslim thought, but they are defamed by Islamists as 'Islamophobic'.

In contemporary Western Islamic studies, Muslim thinkers who engage in rethinking Islam and in introducing critical concepts often find themselves on the sidelines, while Islamists are celebrated in the spirit of third-worldism. This Western mindset indiscriminately prescribes respect in a kind of a romanticization of the Cultural Other. This attitude is often practised in a culture of imposing limits on free thinking. The beneficiary is Islamism, and the victim is 'civil Islam' and the Muslim adherents of enlightened Muslim thought.

Islamism's core issue: the *shari'a* state

The defining issue in Islamism is the *shari'a* state. How can a scholar be serious and speak of post-Islamism when he or she lacks knowledge, not only about today's thriving Islamism, but also about the continued Islamist commitment to a *shari'a* state? The fourth task of this chapter, then, is to address this core theme and identify, beyond double-speak and Islamist prevarications, what Islamism actually is. Having discussed the prevailing Western scholarly confusions about Islamism, a rectification seems advisable. The importance of a proper understanding of the Islamist *shari'a* state is not just an academic affair. Some academics have great influence on how policy-makers and the public think about important issues like the West's relations with the Islamic world. This is why the disarray in the academic study of Islamism is reflected in a lack of orientation in US policy. In the past, some rogue academics contributed to Bush's politics of polarization. Today, under Obama's presidency, there is some improvement, but the indiscriminate engagement of this administration still seems to end up supporting institutional Islamism in the name of promoting inclusion and a moderate Islam. To be sure, this policy too is supported by some questionable academic advisors. They are better than the Bush advisors in only one sense: in moving from maligning to exonerating, they replace malice by naivety. And, yes, naivety is less harmful than malice.

A proper understanding of the nature of Islamism must go beyond dealing with a policy of counterterrorism. It is utterly wrong to equate Islamism with jihadism as a branch of terrorism, not to speak of imputed 'criminal deeds' or a so-called 'insurgency'.[34] This approach overlooks the fact that the jihadist Islamists are only a minority within Islamism. Nonetheless, they do not stand outside of Islam, nor are they merely 'violent extremists' to be brought to justice. They do share with institutional non-violent Islamists the idea of a *shari'a* state. Saying that they have a shared goal is not the same as 'lumping them together'. But jihadism is in decline. The core issue at this stage is not jihadism but Islamism in general – which is thriving.

One of the few US politicians to address the distinction judiciously is Senator Joe Lieberman. In a *Wall Street Journal* commentary article on June 15, 2010 entitled 'Who is the Enemy in the War on Terror?' Lieberman applauds Obama for his attempt to reach out to Muslim peoples, but criticizes his apparent willingness to overlook too much.[35] The Obama administration's new national security strategy, which had just been made public, did not even mention the word 'Islamist'. Deploring this refusal to acknowledge an important reality, Lieberman wrote that 'Muslims . . . understand better than anyone else the enormous difference between their faith and the terrorist political ideology that has exploited it.' Obama's policies, he added, ignore the 'ideological dimensions of the war taking place within Islam'. It is not only about the West and Islam but about tensions among Muslims themselves. Lieberman urged Americans to support 'those Muslims to have the courage to stand' and to acknowledge that non-Islamist Muslims are able to 'see the ideological nature of this struggle. I believe it is disrespectful to suggest they cannot understand these distinctions and act on them.'

But there is a distinction of which even Senator Lieberman seems to be unaware, namely that Islamism is not about terrorism. It is about the order of the state and a remaking of the world. Putting the spotlight on this ideological goal presents a greater challenge than the one posed by the declining jihadist terrorism. That is why it is the core concern of this book. The fact that jihadism has declined in the past years, becoming only one marginal branch of Islamism, does not signal the arrival of post-Islamism, as the French writers Olivier Roy and Gilles Kepel believe. Islamism revolves around the order of the world, and it is in substance not about terror and violence. The ideological struggle that Islamists fight, including peacefully – at times even in elected parliaments – is geared to a *shari'a* state. This is what Islamism is all about. The trajectory of the present book is governed by this.

Throughout the following chapters core distinctions are kept in mind, such as the one between Islamism and Islam, and other distinctions within both. I argue that the Islamic alternative to Islamism is a civil Islam based on the tradition of Islamic humanism. This tradition can be revived against the Islamist war of ideas to serve as a contribution to cross-civilizational bridging. In the past, Islamic humanism was in conflict with the *fiqh* orthodoxy.[36] At present, civil Islam is the alternative to Islamism. Thus a continuation of the old conflict within Islamic civilization between an open civil Islam and *fiqh* orthodoxy is in place. In the past, the religious establishment suffocated enlightened Islamic rationalism. At present Islamism stands in the same tradition.

Conclusions: the need for an Islamic enlightenment against the obstacles impeding a critique of the *shari'a* state

This opening chapter has been written with awareness of the fact that those who think and write critically in public about Islamism and its proposed *shari'a* state run tremendous risks. They face great obstacles and can also be exposed to defamation. The question to which I keep returning in this chapter is: Why is the debate about Islamism and its agenda of the *shari'a* state charged with such confusion? To a large extent, I believe the answer lies not in *what* we think but *how* we think – in particular, the categories by which we arrange our ideas about both Islamism and Islam. This thinking happens in a war of ideas. As Paul Berman has written in his controversial book *The Flight of the Intellectuals: The Controversy Over Islamism and the Press*, 'The Islamist movement, in prospering, has succeeded in imposing its own categories of analysis over how everyone else tends to think . . . Islamist judgements [thus] end up getting adopted by Western and non-Islamist journalists'[37] – and, one may add, by policy-makers and scholars as well. Berman wrote this one year ahead of the Arab Spring. The elevation of Islamist movements to political parties that win elections has greatly intensified the trend that Berman indicates.

The categories employed for making judgements about Islamism exert a subtle but strong influence. If you think primarily in terms of former colonial powers versus the struggle for decolonization, you may well see Islamism in a third-worldist manner as a legitimate part of that struggle. If you think primarily in terms of civilizational conflict, you may see jihadist violence as an integral part of a 'war of ideas' between the Muslim world and the Christian West. If you think primarily in terms of violent versus non-violent Muslims, you may have trouble distinguishing between the ideas of militant Islamists and those of people you consider 'moderates'. If you think primarily in terms of the religious versus the secular, you may have difficulty understanding how a phenomenon like Islamism freely crosses that divide. To free the mind from this intellectual jungle I will take up several fundamentally different sets of categories: Islamism is a variant of the global phenomenon of religious fundamentalism.[38] This phenomenon is not about religious fanaticism, but rather about 'remaking politics, economies and militance'[39] in a venture of religionized politics in which Islamists present the tradition of *shari'a* in an invented tradition to legitimate the order they call the *shari'a* state. This thinking, combined with a political commitment, is shared by all Islamists, jihadists and non-violent alike.

The place of Islamism in the Arab Spring urgently requires a firm and solid assessment of political Islam as it pertains to democratization. It is essential that we debate the nature and implications of Islamism; but this debate has to occur on terms that do not tilt the field against the Enlightenment values of reason, democracy, of an open society that admits pluralism. If we discard postmodernist cultural relativism and maintain loyalty to the universality of the Enlightenment then we can take issue with those Western scholars who deny the existence of a distinction between Islam and Islamism, and who speak of 'inventing Islamism' and thus undermine this much-needed debate. The truth is the reverse. It is not Islamism that has been invented, but the tradition on which the ideology bases its claims of legitimacy.

The core issue is not a dealing with invented terms, but rather with the politicization of religion as a political-cultural reality in the world of Islam – a reality that needs a name. The name for it is Islamism. The entire political project of Islamism is based on an invention of tradition that results in a *shari'a*tization of Islam as an underpinning for the *shari'a* state. The Western debate on Islamism in terms of 'moderation' and 'inclusion' as an underpinning for an assumed deradicalization overlooks the political agenda of the Islamist *shari'a* state completely. It is like looking at the sea and failing to notice that it consists of water. The *defining issue* in Islamism is the political interpretation of Islam as *din-wa-dawla*/Islamocracy, as an expression of a *shari'a* state. Post-Islamism could only occur when the commitment to this political order ends, which would be the end of Islamism. It is unlikely that the moderation of Islamist movements will develop in this direction. There is an alternative to the Islamist *shari'a* state that is not well understood by most US scholars.[40] This alternative is a state based on enlightened Muslim thought.[41]

This book adheres to a civil Islam of the 'enlightened turn'. One of the significant sources of this 'turn' is the work of the famous Islamic al-Jabri enlightenment project that is based on a revival of the heritage of Islamic humanism.[42] This project provides a better option for Islamdom than the one offered by Islamism. The judgement as to who is wrong and who is right depends on where you stand: I stand by enlightenment against anti-enlightenment.[43] These are not merely contemporary options; they have parallels in Islamic history. The medieval conflict between *falsafa* rationalism and *fiqh* orthodoxy in the classical Islamic tradition is a precedent for today's conflict. This is a conflict between the civil Islam for which the al-Jabri project stands and Islamism. Today's Islamic civilization is exposed to these competing choices: civil Islam based on democracy versus the Islamist project of a *shari'a* state. The 'enlightened turn' reflects a partisanship for a civil Islam.

This inquiry is a scholarly contribution to the study of the conflict to which I have just referred. It is committed to an elaboration of the competing options for the future of Islamdom while checking unchecked assumptions. Scholarship presupposes impartiality, but the commitment I have expressed to the 'enlightened turn' in contemporary Islam is a normative positioning. It should be permitted to side with the Islamic tradition of an enlightenment based on the heritage of humanism and its *falsafa* rationalism. This tradition is opposed to the counter-enlightenment of the *fiqh* orthodoxy of the past, as much as to the current one of the Islamist *shari'a*tization of Islam. In our present time, enlightened Muslim thought stands, from its birth with the work of Abdelraziq, against any *shari'a* state; and it provides the basic inspiration for the present study, which rests on two assumptions. The first is that the *shari'a* state is neither a part of religious faith nor does it historically emanate from the heritage of Islamic civilization. The second is that this new pattern of an emerging political hegemony is not compatible with genuine democracy.

If Islamists succeed in hijacking the fruits of the just rebellion dubbed the Arab Spring, there will presumably be no democratization that allows discord and dissent. Replacing authoritarian, dictatorial regimes by a totalitarian *shari'a* state is not the hoped-for introduction of democracy to the Islamicate. The political conduct of the new Islamist president of Egypt, Mohammed Morsi, reinforces the misgiving that this scenario is going to be the case. The new Islamist rule seems to resemble the rule that was toppled (see the opening remarks to Chapter 5 below). There is an alternative to the choice between these two plagues. The alternative to both is a civil Islam in an 'enlightened Islamic turn' that seeks a place for Islamdom in a world based on democratic peace in freedom, prosperity and, above all, diversity bound by the rules of democratic pluralism. Western scholarship should discern this 'enlightened Muslim thought' and respect those Muslims who adhere to it, while acknowledging diversity within Islam.

2   The *shari'a* state is not the faith of Islam

Shari'a and politics

Having defined terms, enumerated the major themes, and determined, not only the issues, but also exactly what we are talking about, we now have solid ground on which to base a robust inquiry. The inquiry we have undertaken relates to the contemporary return of *shari'a* in the context of empowerment of Islamist movements using the Arab Spring to promote their agenda. To keep my promise to place the issue in a broader context, I think it is imperative first to look more closely at *shari'a* in the history of Islam, not only to make clear which *shari'a* we are talking about, but also to provide evidence that the Islamist *shari'a* is an invention of tradition. It is also important to explore the distinctions between the Qur'anic meaning of *shari'a* and its use in Islamic history. This inquiry also needs to demonstrate that historical *shari'a* (traditional *shari'a*) existed in various traditions that are contrary to the current Islamist *shari'a*, which reflects an agenda for a *shari'a* state. This analysis is essential if we are to understand the return of *shari'a* as divine law to the public square in a process of break and continuity.

In Chapter 1, I drew on Muslim authorities ranging from *ulama* to practitioners of *shari'a* and to Muslim academic scholars at Western universities, in order to establish facts about traditional *shari'a* and allow the reader to see that it was – with few exceptions – about faith (*ibadat*), civil law (*mu'amalat*) and the penal code (*hudud*), not about governance. The next step is to focus on defining basic differences between the three meanings of *shari'a* mentioned above: Qur'anic, traditional-historical in the past, and Islamist at present. The focus of this chapter is an analysis of the claims made for a *shari'a* state made by Islamists in the course of the return of the sacred to politics and to public debate. The basic distinctions between revelation and human thinking, between an authoritative authentic tradition and the invention of tradition in a modern context, are the drivers of the analysis to be provided in this second step.

Shari'a between faith and political abuse: the confusion between *shari'a* and *fiqh*

In the course of this inquiry into *shari'a* in Islam I looked at the text of the Qur'an and established as a matter of fact that the notion of *shari'a* occurs only once, namely in *Sura al-Jathiya* (sura 45, verse 18). This happens parallel to two other derivations as a verb, '*shara'a*' and a variant, '*shar'a*' (in *Sura al-Shura* and *Sura al-Ma'ida*). Muslim scholars founded hereafter a system for *ibadat*/worship (the practice of the five pillars of prayer, fasting and alms/*zakat* etc.). Supported by this fact, and drawing on the work of the former Egyptian Supreme Court judge Mohammed Said al-Ashmawi, I continue to argue that there is no tradition of a *shari'a* state in Islamic history. Ashmawi states that 'the notion of *shari'a* – based on a literal reference to the text of the Qur'an – does not mean legislation/*tashri'*, nor law in terms of its language use.'[1] Ashmawi further refers to the distinction between *shari'a* and *fiqh*, to be elaborated upon later on. I share Ashmawi's concern that the deliberate confusion between *shari'a* (revealed by God) and *fiqh* (human thinking about *shari'a*) pursues the ignoble intention of outlawing any criticism as heretical. The *faqih*s/sacral jurists elevate their human thinking to *shari'a* to make it seem infallible.

The distinction between *shari'a* and *fiqh* relates also to a distinction between the language of the scripture of the Qur'an and historical *shari'a* developed by humans, not revealed by God. To complement the references made at the outset of Chapter 1, I refer here in addition to Ashmawi also to the authoritative *Introduction to Islamic Law* written by the best scholar ever on this subject, the Oxford scholar Joseph Schacht. Schacht acknowledges on the very first page of his book that 'Islamic law is the epitome of Islamic thought . . . it is impossible to understand Islam without Islamic law.'[2] Apart from '*shari'a*' there is another term in Islam for the realm of Islamic law: *fiqh*. Schacht translates *shari'a* as 'sacred law' and *fiqh* as 'the science of *shari'a*'. As shown in Chapter 1, the intended difference between the two is that *shari'a* is believed to be revealed by God, while *fiqh* results from human reasoning in the course of interpreting the revealed text. Another scholar of high calibre, John Kelsay, deals with Islamic history in which *shari'a* and *fiqh* have been confused to the extent that the notion '*shari'a* reasoning' is justified despite the apparent contradiction: *shari'a* is a revelation by God, while reasoning is human. It is a fact that *shari'a* in the sense of a Muslim law is a *lex divina* developed by humans, but falsely attributed to God's revelation. According to Kelsay's research, this *shari'a* reasoning determines intellectual history in Islam.[3] In this way, human 'sacred law' was elevated to God's law. The consequences were severe. In this process human *shari'a* reasoning becomes unquestionable to the extent that doubt is equated with *kufr*/heresy. This procedure closes any debate on thinking that has been developed by humans, because the confusion results in attributing *fiqh* thoughts to Allah in order to protect the *faqih-ulama* from criticism. The word for thinking is in Arabic *tafkir*, while denunciation of a Muslim as a heretic is *takfir*. If you confuse the letters *f* and *k* you change the meaning. The late Muslim reformer Nasr Hamid Abu-Zaid wrote an entire book complaining about the defamation of *tafkir* by the accusation of *takfir*.[4]

These references underpin the fact that historical *shari'a* is based on *fiqh*, not on revelation, as it emerged from human reasoning. In this context an intertwining of *shari'a* and politics took place, when Islam was used as a legitimation for the caliph. Yet, this was not a *shari'a* state, just as it was not the faith of Islam. The Muslim scholar Hussein F. al-Najjar argues that, in the religion of Islam, religion and state are not intertwined . . . . There is nothing in [traditional] Islamic *Shari'a* that underpins the intertwining of religion and politics. *Shari'a* does not prescribe governance, as it is an ethical set-up for conduct, including the conduct of the rulers, but there is nothing in it that legitimates a design of the state in the sense of *din-wa-dawla.*[5]

The notion of *din-wa-dawla*, which al-Najjar rejects, expresses belief in a unity of 'religion and state', the political religion of Islamism, which is clearly not Islam. In the past, Muslim rulers drew on *shari'a* as a device for a legitimation, but they never claimed that their caliphate was 'a *shari'a* state'. Since the abolition of the caliphate in 1924, Muslim thinkers such as Ali Abdelraziq and Ashmawi, among others, have strongly questioned the Islamic legitimation of the order of the caliphate. The caliphate was never the rule of a *shari'a* state. Furthermore, it was an imperial entity and not a constitutional state.

In the caliphate order, *shari'a* and politics were separated in a way outlined by Joseph Schacht as follows: in modern Arabic *siyasa* means 'politics', but in classical Arabic it meant state administration. Even though the caliph embraced the fiction that he was the custodian of *shari'a*, he never determined *shari'a* as his focus was on governance. *Siyasa* was the expression of the full power of the caliph, in contrast to the Qadi, who was in charge of *shari'a*. As Schacht puts it, this was 'a double administration . . . one religious and exercised by the Kadi on the basis of *shari'a*, the other secular and exercised by the political authorities.'[6] This is not what Islamists want.

The invention of *shari'a* as a constitution for the Islamic state

No serious student of Islam knowledgeable about its sources – the Qur'an and the hadith – would ever look to *shari'a* as the constitution of a state. In addition is the fact that constitution is a modern notion and so the Arabic word for it, *dustur*, never occurs in the Islamic tradition. Islamists ignore all of this when they contend that *shari'a* is the constitution for the Islamic state. This invention happened in parallel to the foundation of the Movement of the Muslim Brothers by Hasan al-Banna in 1928. At that time, recourse was made to *shari'a*, but in a new, reinvented shape. In contrast to all the authorities cited above, al-Banna states that 'government is an essential part of Islam', and he recommended that 'if people say [in response to this claim of *din-wa-dawla*] this is politics, then you respond no, this is our Islam and we reject any separation [of religion and politics].'[7] Later on al-Banna adds, 'The Islam in which the Muslim Brothers believe establishes governance as one of its pillars.' This is a clear violation of the five pillars/*arkan* of Islamic faith. In the view of al-Banna, Islamic governance rests on *shari'a* 'and the Islamic state is based on it'. All the Muslim authorities cited in Chapter 1 would disagree. Although al-Banna mentions the caliphate positively in passing, his major concern is the *'nizam islami'*/'Islamic system', which is the Islamist *shari'a* state.

In addition to inventing the tradition of *shari'a*, al-Banna also prescribes *'jihad'* in the new meaning of jihadism to be fought in the pursuit of this Islamist state.

The Islamist *jihad* promoted by al-Banna glorifies violence and death in these words:

> Those Muslims who downgrade physical fighting as small-*jihad* in favour of *jihad al-nafs* [struggle against the self] distract Muslims from true violent *jihad* . . . . The gratification for Muslims is to kill, or to be killed on the path of Allah. Oh Brothers, the *umma* that masters the art of death and knows how to die in dignity shall be favoured by Allah. Know then: death is inevitable and it happens only once.

Not only this explicit commitment to violence, but also the history of the Muslim Brothers provide evidence for the jihadist background of their movement. Today, in the aftermath of the Arab Spring, the Muslim Brothers show up as the new Islamists and pretend to have taken the decision to abandon jihadism in favour of an institutional fight for the *shari'a* state as a sign that they approve of democracy. However, they keep al-Banna's legacy. Although they advance *shari'a* to the status of a constitutional law of the *nizam islami* they seek to establish, they have never dissociated themselves from al-Banna and his legacy.

As repeatedly stated, the Islamist recourse to *shari'a*, as the law of their movement, happens in an invention of tradition. This venture alienates Islamism from the modern cross-cultural concept of law being secular with claims to universality across all religions. Today, international law is based on this concept, which gives it a universal legal validity. This international legal standard is challenged by the current return of religion to the public debate demonstrated in the case of the Muslim Brothers. This challenge has been happening globally since the late twentieth century, as a return of the tradition of *lex divina*, but in a novel guise. It follows that a competition between the universality of the existing secular law and the emerging particularisms of sacral-divine law is happening in a crisis-ridden situation and generating a conflict at present. It is imperative to mark that the return of *shari'a* in the shape of a politicized particularism of Islamic law is not shared by all Muslims. Thus, there are two conflicts: one is between *shari'a*tized Islam and international law, and the other is within Islamic civilization among Muslims themselves.

The return of the sacred as an Islamist *shari'a*

The precursor in the current debate on the return of the sacred is the Harvard sociologist Daniel Bell. As early as 1977, Bell contested Max Weber's view of a universal secularization understood in terms of *Entzauberung*/disenchantment. Bell made a prediction sustained by the rise of political movements based on religion for rethinking earlier concepts in view of the contemporary inversion of secularization in a claim to de-secularization. This development underpins Bell's contesting of Max Weber's ideas of secularization viewed as a rationalization in the form of 'disenchantment of the world'.[8] The process of Islamization of law exemplifies how de-secularization leads to conflict.

Across the turn into the new century, the return of the sacred seems to vindicate the hypothesis of global de-secularization. This process has become visible in a most powerful contemporary phenomenon that occurs on all levels, not only locally, but also regionally and in world politics. The return of religion to politics affects existing law. It is, however, not an indication of an increased religiosity so much as it is a return to the public arena, closely allied with strong political claims and a demand for a new order for polity and society to be determined by *lex divina*. This new feature seems not to be well understood in the West. For instance, Jürgen Habermas suggests in his coinage 'post-secular society' that we are seeing a religious revival based on a 'renaissance of religion' (see note 20 below). Empirically, this view is utterly wrong. *Shari'a*tized Islam is not about religious faith, but rather is a political religion linked to a political order in a contestation of cultural modernity. In fact, in its present shape the return of religion to the public square is a novelty. Despite rhetorical references to a 'revival', religionized politics heralds an invention of tradition. I shall not repeat here my earlier analysis of the transformation of Islam to Islamism. I confine myself to those political conflicts that result from the allegation that *shari'a* forbids peace with those classified as enemies of Islam (with the exception of *hudna*/time-limited ceasefire if urgent). An example for this is the Islamists' argument that peace with Israel runs against *shari'a*. The current process of *shari'a*tization of Islam alienates Muslims from non-Muslims and establishes divides within Islam in conflicts that become intractable, because the issues are religionized. When a conflict is religionized, the issues become non-negotiable, because one cannot negotiate faith.

The return of the sacred in Islamdom in the shape of a demand for an Islamist *shari'a* state is at times discussed by some Western scholars in terms of constitutional law in which the Islamist *shari'a* is wrongly viewed as Islamic law reform. The questions bear on highly relevant issues in the context of the return of the sacred as a global return of religion to politics. These includes the rising claim that religious doctrine provides a concept of a *lex divina* or divine law designed for the public space. This claim is also applied by Islamists to constitutional law, but this Islamist venture is not an indication of religious reform.

The foremost concern relates to the Islamist claim that *shari'a* should be the source of any constitutional law designed for all states within the Islamic civilization. These states are viewed as a unity of *dar al-Islam*/the abode of Islam, called – as will be established in Chapter 3 – the Islamicate. The potential for empowerment of Islamism has a bearing on the need for democratization. Well, there are two different understandings of democracy and rule of law at work, and they collide with one another squarely in a war of ideas: one is the Western secular concept of law, while the other is the new Islamist *shari'a*-based world view. Islamist constitutional law claims to be divine, though it is constructed by humans as *fiqh*, thus not revealed by Allah as *shari'a*. The better alternative to this polarization between the secular and the religious is an inter-civilizational bridging of the existing divides. To argue for the universality of the separation between constitutional law and faith is an argument for a global civil society viewed as an international society. I draw on the historical record of medieval Islamic Spain to argue for inter-faith tolerance based on equality in a peace (rather than a war) of ideas. The hypothesis is put forward that there is in fact a conflict between the Salafi-orthodox scriptural understanding of *shari'a* and modern constitutional law with regard to democracy and individual human rights. This conflict can be resolved peacefully and this is what bridging should be all about.[9]

Shari'a Islamism generates tensions that develop and lead to a conflict. However, Islamists do not engage in conflict resolution. Quite the opposite: they exacerbate the conflict-ridden situation inflamed by their *shari'a*tization of law and politics. On the basis of unhappy experience, I am compelled to repeat the distinction I make between *conflict* and *clash*, in order to dissociate my approach from a Huntingtonian essentialism. A conflict can be resolved, whereas a clash smacks of essentializa- tion. Moreover, value conflicts can be peacefully resolved by intercultural dialogue and cross-cultural bridging. The hypothesis of value conflicts requires an inquiry into the historical formation and the substance of Islamic *shari'a* law.

It is a fact that history is also a history of civilizations. Civilizations are often based on religion as a civilizational identity. This fact matters to the understanding of the self-assertive claims of civilizations. These claims include not only the one of having their own legal tradition, but also the claim that this legal particularism shapes the public space. If this claim comes into being in solid form, there can be no international society based on shared, cross-civilizational, universal legal rules, since the existence of such a global civil society presupposes a sharing of 'common values' beyond particularisms. States in the international system are supposed to 'conceive themselves to be bound by a common set of rules in their relations with one another'.[10] This is a precondition for a functioning world order. It cannot be fulfilled by a *shari'a* state. A vision of world order based on *shari'a* is something that non-Muslims cannot share. In Chapter 3 I shall resume this debate on world order and on a constructed *shari'a* in the context of the Islamist drive to remake the world. Islamist *shari'a* contradicts international standards of consti- tutional law. The same happens in many other realms central to democracy. This is why one needs to defend the secular outlook against any *lex divina* aimed at remaking of the world on any religious legal tenets whatever.[11]

Of course, one needs to respect the Islamic faith and an authentic Islamic *shari'a*. However, this respect is restricted to the original Qur'anic meaning of *shari'a* as ethics and as guideline for *ibadat*/worship. However, an Islamist *shari'a* that contradicts a universal notion of law as grounds for an international society cannot be admitted in the name of respect for faith. It is also argued that *shari'a* Islamism (not the faith of Islam) stands in contradiction to basic human rights, most particularly the right to freedom of faith. The political culture of democracy is based on pluralism and power sharing and many other basic democratic values that are in conflict with *shari'a*, old and new. This culture is universal and has the right to veto cultural-religious particularisms.

In the line of reasoning outlined here, the major argument is that the contem- porary *shari'a*tization of polity and society is a source of the inter-civilizational conflict in global politics. As already acknowledged, it is in line with full respect to Islamic faith to accept honouring the notion of '*shari'a*' as it occurs in the text of the Qur'an, namely in the sense of morality (sura 45, verse 18). This applies only to ethics and the practice of religious faith (*ibadat*). I must repeat that in the history of Islam, *shari'a* was developed as *fiqh* by the *ulama-faqih*s, that is by humans. This is not the faith of Islam. But contemporary Islamism elevates *shari'a* to a state law. In this new function, *shari'a* is claimed to be the constitution of the envisioned Islamic state, which is understood as the divine order of *hakimiyyat Allah*/God's rule. In this way, politicized *shari'a* becomes a source of conflict (a) within Islam, (b) between Muslims and non-Muslims (e.g. Turkey) and (c) in world affairs (war of ideas between the secular and the claimed divine one). In all honesty, I maintain that no inter-civilizational bridging can ever be feasible on these grounds, and I find this honesty lacking in the prevailing Western pattern of dialogue with the Islamicate.

The message is that the return of the sacred, in the shape of a return of an invented *shari'a* to politics, represents a deviation from the original Qur'anic meaning of *shari'a* as ethics. Therefore, it is no offence to Muslims to reject this return. The new *shari'a* is coupled with the claim to provide, on these grounds, an Islamist constitutional law on universal grounds. This agenda threatens the pillars of the present world order. The term *dustur*/constitution is alien to traditional *shari'a* reasoning. In addition, *shari'a*tized Islam stands in a contradiction to democracy and alienates Muslims from non-Muslims due to the human-rights-related tensions it arouses. Neither the classical *shari'a* nor the invention of its tradition by Islamism are in line with the need for international standards of law shared by all members as grounds for an international society in a global democratic peace. Later on in this chapter I shall resume this issue of universality of law to quote Muslim voices of the 'enlightened turn' that support it (see note 38).

The Islamic alternative to the Islamist *shari'a*tization project is a revival of the buried tradition of Islamic humanism, which would be a contribution to bridging between the civilizations (see note 41). This tradition is also in line with cross-cultural universal standards. It follows that the conflict in question is also going on within Islamic civilization between *shari'a*tized Islam and a pro-democracy liberal-civil Islam. The return of religion to public debate in Islamic civilization is a return of the sacred to politics as constitutional law. It needs to be stated with a combination of vigour and candour that this *shari'a*tization project impedes the incorporation of Islamic civilization into a society of nations that rests on shared universal values and rules and on a pluralism of cultures and religions.

This candour is found in the early work of the Muslim legal scholar Abdul-lahi an-Na'im. In his book of 1990 he states unequivocally and succinctly: 'The Qur'an does not mention constitutionalism.'[12] The implication is that those who construct an Islamic constitutional law in an effort at de-secularization engage in constructing a post-Qu'ranic legal body. Islamists create their own legal product, but claim for their human thinking a divine law. The early An-Na'im of 1990 argues further that his analysis 'has clearly shown that this [democratic – B.T.] conception of constitutionalism is unattainable under *shari'a*'. Then An-Na'im emphasizes clearly that 'only two options would be open to modern Muslims: either abandon the public law of *shari'a* or disregard constitutionalism'.

It is shocking to read 18 years later in a book by the very same An-Na'im an approval of the return of *shari'a* to the public space (see note 12). This is a deplorable U-turn. Going beyond this individual case, however, the popularity of the *shari'a* as a public choice is conceded. It is therefore necessary to inquire into the underlying reason for the appeal of *shari'a* in the present conflict- and crisis-ridden situation in the world of Islam.

Why is the return of *shari'a* law to politics a challenge?

In the twentieth century, in the aftermath of the abolition of the caliphate in 1924 and in a process of postcolonial state formation and the related superficial secularization, *shari'a* was removed from the public space and replaced by secular positive law. Kemalist Turkey claimed to be in this regard the secular model for Islamic civilization.[13] The birth of Islamism took place in the same decade, but not until our own twenty-first century did it succeed in giving this secular model a blow. Following the electoral seizure of power by the Islamist AKP in 2002 Turkey has become a torn country. Ever since that year, the ruling Islamist AKP has imposed on Turkey a creeping Islamization.[14] In general, one encounters in the post-bipolar era an emerging competition between the religious and the secular. The US scholar Mark Juergensmeyer terms this phenomenon neutrally a 'new Cold War',[15] which – unlike the bipolar Cold War – is a war of ideas. Unlike the Hoover–Ajami–Hill approach pursued in the 'working group on Islamism and international order' that takes this 'Cold War' at face value and even engages it (see Chapter 3), I prefer to go for bridging. I dissociate my work not only from such approaches, but also from singling out Islam. Nonetheless, I acknowledge that in the context of the return of the sacred to public space in post-bipolar politics, Islamism ranks at the top due to its political internationalism. Why is this so?

On the left it was soon suggested that, with the loss of communism, the West lost the intimate enemy that ensured the unity of its civilization, and that therefore NATO had been on the search for a substitute. Islamophobia replaced the earlier anti-communism. I not only deem this thinking untenable, but also hold it for stupidity to argue that the West found this 'new enemy' in Islam. Unfortunately, the left is right when one reads Fouad Ajami and Charles Hill, who seem to continue the old tradition of anti-communism in a new Cold War against Islamism (see Chapter 3). This is, however, exceptional and not the general trend. At any rate, I want to keep my work free from these ideological games to focus instead on the real issue, which is the return of the sacred in a political shape.

There is a core difference between contemporary Islamism and the nineteenth-century Islamic anti-colonial defensive cultural ideology of revivalism (interpreted as *jihad* in response to the imperialism of the West). As I shall explain in Chapter 3, the anti-colonial *jihad* of Afghani is based on a pan-Islamism while Islamism is an internationalism poised to remake the world.[16] Unlike early Islamic revivalists, the Islamists do not restrict their sights to the territory of the Islamicate: they want to lead the entire world along their Islamist precepts, to replace one hegemony with an other one. This claim is already stated in the writings of Sayyid Qutb in the late 1950s and early 1960s. In his *Signposts along the Road* Qutb claims to see humanity on the 'brink'/'*hafat al-hawiya*', revealing 'a crisis of the West and bankruptcy of its democracy'. On the very next page of this book is the proposition that 'only Islam is eligible to lead humanity after the pending breakdown of Western civilization'.[17] This thinking is continued in a further step articulated in an ensuing major book, *World Peace and Islam*. Here Qutb argues that only Islamic dominance under the rule of *shari'a* can guarantee world peace; then he suggests reinterpreting *jihad* anew in viewing it as 'a permanent comprehensive world revolution in order to establish *hakimiyyat Allah*/God's rule to save the entire humanity'.[18] This quotation demonstrates a mix of Islamist and Marxist–Leninist vocabulary.

The Islamist call for a *shari'a* state in the context of the return of *shari'a* to politics predates the end of bipolarity. As we have seen, 1928 is the birth date of Islamism, although this trend did not become a mobilizing ideology until the shattering effects of the Arab defeat in the Six-Day War of 1967. The fall of the Berlin Wall and the end of bipolarity then gave a further boost to Islamism.

In his *Paix et guerre entre les nations* (1962), Raymond Aron compared the artificial division of humanity by bipolarity into blocks with the real division related to a 'heterogeneity of civilizations'.[19] As post-bipolarity unfolded, the return of the sacred became clearly visible as a return of civilizations to world politics. In Islamic civilization, the failure to cope with modernity coupled with the failed development forms the 'back story' of the crisis of the nation-state. Unsuccessful secularization is a part of this story. At the start of the preceding section I drew on Max Weber's views and on Daniel Bell's 1977 lecture on the 'return of the sacred' (see note 8) with the aim of providing a new assessment. What is right? And what is wrong?

In my view, to conclude from the return of religion to the public square that the secular age is at an end would be wrong – mistaken. This misconception is shared by Jürgen Habermas (who prematurely pronounced a 'post-secular society'[20]) and by Charles Taylor. Both these authors respect the particularisms of Islamic civilization and are misled by this to approve of the return of *shari'a* to the public sphere in a new, politicized form. These respected scholars seem, however, not to be knowledgeable about the *shari'a*tization of Islam in the process of the return of the sacred, and thus they lack the familiarity required to analyse this phenomenon properly. The new *shari'a* runs against an international society based on shared values that fundamentally underpin legal concepts of order. These values are challenged by the agenda of a remaking of the world.

It is pertinent to quote here the questions asked by John Kelsay, more knowledgeable by far on this issue than Habermas and Charles Taylor:

> [W]ho will provide the primary definition to world order? Will it be the West
> . . . or will it be Islam? . . . The question for those who envision world order,
> then, is: who determines the shape of order in the new international context?
> The question suggests a competition between cultural traditions with distinctive notions of peace, order and justice.[21]

These questions refer to a conflict embedded in a competition between *shari'a* and democratic cosmopolitan constitutionalism, i.e. between the return of the sacred in a political form and secular law. At issue is a challenge that generates tensions leading to conflicts at all levels.

The scriptural reality that the notion of *shari'a* occurs once only in the Qur'an, and not with a legal meaning, exists alongside the fact that in Islamic history a development of *shari'a* into a legal system took place. The traditional and classical post-Qur'anic efforts to develop a *shari'a* were undertaken by human beings, i.e. by the *ulama* and *faqih*s. With a few exceptions, these efforts were restricted to *shari'a* as civil law and as a penal code.[22] Apart from the legitimation of the caliphate and of its actions *post eventum*, no political *shari'a* existed, and neither did any claim to constitutionalism.

Honesty compels me to mention one significant exception of two medieval Muslim thinkers. Despite the separation between *siyasa* and *shari'a* in medieval Islam referred to earlier in this chapter, Ibn Taimiyya (1263–1328) associated *shari'a* with *siyasa*/state administration.[23] But the order of the state Ibn Taimiyya argued for is not the contemporary Islamist *shari'a* state. Prior to this exception, also, al-Mawardi (974–1058) wrote *Kitab al-Ahkam al-Sultaniyya* to argue for an Islamic governance. In Chapter 3 I shall come back to this mix of religion and politics in the history of ideas in Islam, old and new, to discuss the abuse of religion as a legitimation for a political order. The embedded tensions are addressed by the late Muslim reformer Nasr Hamid Abu Zaid as a context identified in the title of his book, *Scripture: Power and Reality*. The tensions between these three different issues determine the prevailing *al-khitab al-dini*/religious discourse.[24]

Shari'a law and democratic rights

Charles Taylor and Jürgen Habermas view the return of religion to the public space in positive terms. This view fails to grasp the Islamist claim that *shari'a* divine law is comprehensive and that it even constitutes a source for constitutional law for a *shari'a* state. In terms of the Arab Spring, this claim gives rise to the following question: Is a *shari'a* state a democratic alternative to existing authoritarian regimes?

This question is not new, and it was asked long before the Arab Spring. In my keynote address to the Third International Congress for Comparative Constitutional Law in Tokyo (see note 11) I dealt with the context of the return of religion to public space as a *shari'a* understood as Islamic law. As already mentioned, the term *shari'a* occurs in just one verse of the Qur'an (in *Sura al-Jathiya*, sura 45, verse 18), but with the sense of morality, not of law. This provides the context for the argument that what is called 'Islamic law' is nothing but a post-Qur'anic construction by the *ulama* and *faqih*s to underpin their identification of *shari'a* and *fiqh*. Add to this confusion the fact that this *shari'a* was never codified. Traditional *shari'a* is an interpretative law, mostly restricted to civil law and to a penal code. In contrast to this tradition, Islamists call for *shari'a* as a foundation of an Islamic state based on a *shari'a*-inspired constitution. In this invention of tradition

Islamists engage in a politicized *shari'a* that resonates throughout the Islamic world against the background of the politicization of this religion and Islamization of its law. The question asked in Tokyo, as to whether *shari'a* is really a constitutional law, and as to how consonant the call for Islamization of law is, not only with the rule of democracy based on popular sovereignty, but also with the legal foundations of international society, is a question that will burden the world at large for many decades to come.[25]

There is no denying that one has to look at Islamic civilization in the context of diversity that allows different understandings of democracy and the rule of law. However, it must be added that the Islamist understanding of constitutional law in *shari'a* terms is not shared by all Muslims. In fact, there is no common understanding of *shari'a* among Muslims. In addition, *shari'a* understood as a modern constitutional law is in conflict with individual human rights. This can be illustrated in the case of freedom of belief: *shari'a* denies non-Muslims equality with Muslims – despite the recognition of non-Muslims as 'protected minorities'. The idea of pluralism combines the recognition of diversity with the need for basic commonalities, among which are the basic rules of democratic constitutionalism. It follows that diversity of cultures needs to insist on a common, i.e. universal concept of law. The return of the sacred requires a proper understanding of religious legal traditions that have been recently 'revived', but revived in an invention of tradition. However, it must be made clear that only a radical reform of Islamic *shari'a* law would allow the embedding of Islamic civilization in a democratic peace based on the recognition of commonalities in constitutional law.

The insertion of *shari'a* in an invented new shape provides no model for the rule of law in the envisioned process of embedding Islamdom into international society in the sense of this term outlined earlier. The bottom line is: both classical and contemporary Islamist *shari'a* contradict the values and norms of human rights-based constitutionalism.[26] These are the grounds on which the hypothesis is put forward that a conflict exists between *shari'a* law and democratic constitutionalism. If this hypothesis passes the test, then no positive assessment of the return of religion to public space can ever be made. The invented model of *shari'a* law is not an 'Islamic reformation' – as some have claimed – but the opposite. The *shari'a*tization of Islamic politics is not *al-hall*/the solution needed, as the Islamists claim. The return of the sacred in the guise of *shari'a* is an obstacle for the people of Islamic civilization in their crisis and failure to cope hitherto with cultural modernity. The problem relates not only to the community of Islamdom of the territorialized Islamicate, but also to those Muslims who live as minorities throughout the world (e.g. in India) or as migrants in the diaspora (the West). I myself am one of the latter. Not just because I live in Europe, but for the sake of the issue itself, I believe that Islam and Muslims in the European diaspora are the most significant case in point. I am the originator of a new concept of a European Islam (Euro-Islam) that not only abandons the charged tradition of *jihad*, but also *shari'a*, old and new, altogether. This abandonment is required if Muslims living in Europe are to become 'European citizens of the heart', but with an Islamic faith.[27] This faith is not to be confused with politics or with claims to a political order.

The hypothesis of *shari'a*tization of Islam as an obstacle to democratization

To check the hypothesis that *shari'a*tization of Islam is an obstacle to democratization, I again turn to facts. These are: first, that 'divine law' in historical Islam is human *fiqh*, wrongly presented as revealed divine *shari'a. There exists no common understanding among Muslims* of what is meant precisely by the notion of *shari'a.* Second, the term 'constitution', and the perception derived from it of *shari'a* as constitutional law, are in fact recent additions to Islamic civilization. And finally, the recognition of individual human rights, of which the freedom of faith (or belief) is part and parcel, runs counter to the rules of the constructed historical *shari'a.*

Based on these facts, I put forward the assumption that the contemporary Salafist and Islamist *shari'a* reasoning exacerbates Muslims' dealing with their predicament in relation to modernity.[28] The present inquiry deals with selected areas of issues to test the hypothesis put forward. This work requires an account of the distinction between scriptural and historical Islam, that is between faith and the use of religion in politics. In singling out the human right of freedom of faith (belief), it can be stated that a conflict exists between *shari'a* and democratic constitutionalism. The conclusion would be that a *shari'a* state emerging from the Arab Spring will not fulfill the promise of democratization.

The following three points are to be considered in testing this conclusion:

* Non-Muslim monotheists (Jews and Christians) are classified as *dhimmi*s, i.e. people who are allowed to retain their religious beliefs under restrictions, but are not considered to be the equals of Muslims. At this level one can identify a lack of religious pluralism in Islam.
* Non-monotheist religions (all religions apart from Judaism, Christianity and Islam) are considered to be an expression of *kufr*/unbelief and are to be fought against under Qur'anic provisions.
* Muslims who leave Islamic belief either through conversion or through choice (atheists or agnostics) are considered as committing either *riddah*/apostasy or heresy and are therefore to be punished as unbelievers. The *riddah* doctrine clearly indicates the lack of freedom of faith in Islam.

These three different points indicate the existence of three 'categories' pertinent to the case of freedom of belief in the Islamic constitutional understanding of interpretative *shari'a* law. All the facts support the validity of the hypothesis that views *shari'a*tization as contrasted with democratic constitutionalism. Some persons contend that the fact that *shari'a* was never codified makes it a highly flexible legal system. This may apply to the classical *shari'a*, but it does not apply to the new understanding of *shari'a* as referred to in political Islam. There is a contradiction: politicized *shari'a* is understood in a highly dogmatic manner by Islamists, despite the fact that what they are engaging with is an invention. For instance, all of the three categories mentioned above are confused by Islamists, who classify all of those who disagree with their views as *kafirun*/infidels. Their call for *tatbiq al-shari'a*/implementation of *shari'a* is also directed against these *kafirun*, among whom one also finds people of Muslim faith. Thus, the denial of freedom of belief as part of the Islamist violation of human rights touches Muslims and non-Muslims equally. The politicization of *shari'a* (civil law) and its advancement to a constitutional law (*dustur*) equates to an invention of tradition.

The hypothesis includes the assumption that Muslims themselves do not enjoy freedom of belief, which is based on the consideration of two Islamic *shari'a*-related doctrines: first, *riddah*/apostasy, already mentioned, and, second, the admission of *takfir* (declaration of a Muslim as unbeliever) in Islamic legal thought old and new. Freedom of belief conceded to others in Islam applies only to Jews and Christians, but it is a limited freedom. In addition, this freedom is associated with being assigned the legal lower status of 'dhimmitude', i.e. Jewish and Christian believers are viewed as inferior to Muslims. By modern legal standards this is more a violation of human-rights-based freedom of belief than a form of tolerance, as it is commonly seen. The hypothesis includes the normative contention that to change this situation to the extent of establishing freedom of belief in Islam requires an Islamic law reform, for which this book argues on Islamic grounds. The statement of legal differences pertinent to freedom of belief amounts neither to accepting the rhetoric of a clash of civilizations nor to what is wrongly viewed as legal pluralism. At issue is not a negative or positive view of the differences, as both cases suggest, but rather the need for legal reform to facilitate an accommodation in a situation identified as a predicament of Islam in relation to modernity. The return of the sacred in a political shape intensifies this predicament. The inherited confusion of *shari'a* and *fiqh* by Muslim scribes who view *shari'a* as a 'holy given' never questions the prevailing *shari'a* reasoning.[29] One rarely finds Muslim scholars who go beyond this. One positive example is Najib Armanazi in his 1930 book on international law in Islam. Another is Mohammed Said al-Ashmawi.[30]

Contemporary writings by Muslims on this subject mostly belong to one of two categories. First, classical *shari'a* is maintained with some accommodations, albeit superficial, as in the authoritative books of al-Azhar and some Muftis, like the slain Mufti Subhi al-Salih of Lebanon.[31] These contributions make no claim for a *shari'a* state. Second, *shari'a* is reinvented in contemporary Islamism. The writings of al-Banna and Qutb in the past and Qaradawi at present rank at the top of this category.

Candidly stated: in the Western study of *shari'a* one encounters quite poor scholarship. Since the two major books by Joseph Schacht and by N. J. Coulson – which are of a truly unprecedented high standard – no such ground-breaking studies on the *shari'a* have been seen. Most Western publications on *shari'a* are either highly specialized (these deal with very limited small areas of Islamic law, of interest only to a few very specialized legal scholars) or highly apologetical in character, written by Muslim scholars based in the West who pretend to defend *shari'a* in a drive of a kind of identity politics against what they view as Orientalism.

The argument that the Islamist *shari'a*tization of law reflects an invention of tradition does not overlook the reality that the legal system of the *shari'a*/*usul al-*

shari'a has always been based on human interpretation. The Muslim legal scholar and ex-Supreme Court judge Mohammed Said Ashmawi discusses this and infers that the *shari'a* claim to be divine law is one constructed by humans and therefore is not really based on God's revelation (see note 1). Throughout the history of Islam, all Muslim legal scribes, the *ulama*, who constructed the *madhahib*/four schools of Sunni Islamic law, viewed the *shari'a* as civil law of *mu'amalat* for settling matters related to marriage, divorce, inheritance etc. and as a penal code/*hudud*. In fact, this is the substance of the traditional Islamic *shari'a* law, which never included reference to constitutional law, whether in the Hanafi, Shafi'i, Maliki or Hanbali legal schools. Whether the *shari'a* includes freedom of belief or not is an issue that pertains to the *ibadat*/divine matters, not to constitutional law, which does not exist in traditional Islam. All of the *madhahib* schools mentioned are in agreement that no Muslim has the right to leave the Islamic community/*umma*, whether through conversion to another religion or through renouncing belief/*iman* in Islam. Here there is a consensus that any commission of a *kufr*/heresy by a Muslim is subject to physical punishment fixed by the *hudud* law. Abandoning the Islamic faith is seen as a *riddah*/apostasy also punishable by death. In short: in the established *shari'a* there exists no freedom of belief. This is a statement, no longer a hypothesis. However, it is incumbent on the *umma*, not on the state, to execute punishment, since Islamic scribes, being legal scholars, never dealt with the domain we today call constitutional law under state jurisdiction. In general, Islamic *fiqh* is not a state law, because the state/*dawla* was beyond the deliberations of *faqih*s, i.e. the legal scholars in Islam. Earlier I quoted the exception in medieval Islam, Ibn Taimiyya, who coined the term *al-siyasa al-shari'yya*/*shari'a* law politics, but this case continued to be an exception until recent developments. In our age of the return of the sacred, however, at the beginning of the twenty-first century, Islamists – i.e. the exponents of political Islam – and also Salafists took up the call for *tatbiq al-shari'a*, all the while having constitutional law foremost in mind. The example of Egypt, discussed in Chapters 4 and 5, is here again a case in point.

Given the fact that no codified *shari'a* law exists, one is inclined to ask Islamists: Which *shari'a* do they mean? As we have already stated, there is no common understanding of the *shari'a* in Islam. The call for *shari'a*tization opens the door for arbitrary politics in the name of divine law. As an interpretative law, *shari'a* was always subject to both individual and *madhahib*/legal school-related interpretation of the Qur'an and of the *hadith*. In contrast to traditional *shari'a*, contemporary *shari'a*tization prescribes a new understanding of constitutional law with regard to law and order.[32] This is quite a recent development. In the past, involvement of the *shari'a* in politics was mostly restricted to providing the caliphs *post eventum* with legal legitimacy, which amounted to a declaration that the political deeds of the rulers were in line with the provisions of the *shari'a*.[33] The *faqih*s were never independent in their ruling, nor had they any reason to venture into developing constitutional law as a domain of *shari'a*. The Arabic term for constitution '*dustur*', is as recent as the issue itself. So when asking 'Which *shari'a*?' is to be utilized for the envisioned constitutional law, an awareness of three understandings of Islamic *shari'a*, very different from one another, is pertinent. These are:

1   The scriptural understanding of the oft-quoted Qur'anic verse in *sura al-Jathiya* which reads: '*thumma ja'alnaka ala shari'atun min al-amr fa attabi'uha*'/'we have ordained for you a *shari'a* to live in line with it.' The traditional understanding of this *shari'a* is morality, not law. As phrased in the Qur'an, the provision reads: '*al-amr bi al-ma'ruf wa al-nahi an al-munkar*'/ 'to enjoin the good and forbid the evil.' In short, in this understanding *shari'a* as a morality of conduct for *sumum bonum* is clearly not a legal system. At present, there is a need to revive this understanding in a double-track strategy: To refute in Islamic terms the popular call for the *shari'a*tization of law, and to contain any arbitrary legal system that violates human rights.

2   In the course of the eighth century, four Muslim scribes, Abu Hanifa, Ibn Hanbal, al-Shafi'i and Malik Ibn Anas established the four legal schools in Sunni Islam that carry their names. They were and continue to be restricted to civil law, but also cover the faith, i.e. the *ibadat*. At issue is whether there is a freedom of belief (faith) related to these schools: in Islamic law only monotheists (Jews and Christians) enjoy a restricted freedom of belief, but – as previously stated – only in a state of dhimmitude, living under Islamic rule and dominance. Others are denied this freedom.

3   At present – since the development of political Islam resulting from the return of the sacred based on the politicization of religion – *shari'a* has obtained not only a political dimension, but also a new shape.

In conclusion, Islamism is based on an invention of tradition[34] applied to *shari'a*. This process results in a totalizing *shari'a* that clearly legitimates a political rule that is inconsonant with democracy. The return of the *shari'a* to politics is coupled with the idea of a so-called *hakimiyyat Allah*. This is a term used by Islamists for the *shari'a* state.[35] Clearly, this Islamism emerges from a crisis of modernity that promotes a return of the sacred, but this is definitely not the revival of a belief system, nor is it an indication of a religious renaissance. In reality, what is happening is that religion is coming back in political garb to challenge the secular order, and to question secular constitutional law by establishing a *shari'a*tized law.

The result of testing the hypothesis is that Islamist *shari'a*tization does not indicate a process of democratization, nor is it a contribution to the cross-civilizational bridging that is needed. Rather, the Islamist *shari'a*tization generates tensions which will be closely examined in the next section.

Universality of law: the tensions between the *shari'a*tization of Islam and constitutionalism in international law

Earlier in this chapter I argued for the universality of law against cultural particularisms. In civil society, as well as in international society, law has a function: it is a cultural current that serves as a pillar of order. In this understanding, law is a cultural system. Given the existence of cultural diversity, could there be such a thing as a cosmopolitan universal law?

The problem is that culture is by definition always local, and therefore a world culture could never evolve. However, in a globalized world, humanity needs a universal law to order global structures. This law can be shared on the grounds of cross-cultural tenets based on a consensus. If no consensus over a related concept of law is possible, then cultural tensions arise that could lead to conflict.[36] The return of the sacred includes a call for divine law that affects constitutionalism and precludes universality of law. In contemporary Islam, *shari'a* is a pendulum swinging between ethics and politicization. Ethically the Qur'an includes some tenets that have been developed in law. This is the origin of a problem in Islam, namely that *shari'a* becomes, as *fiqh*, a law that regulates all spheres of life, with the claim that this is a divine law, although it is made by humans. Unlike other religions, where religious scholars are basically theologians, in Islam we find learned men of religion (*ulama*/scribes) acting as sacral jurists/*faqihs* (Arabic plural: *fuqaha*), not as theologians (*mutakallimun*). Nonetheless, a religious tradition of *kalam*/theology was developed in medieval Islam. There were those Mutazilite theologians who were 'defenders of reason', but never succeeded in becoming mainstream in Islamic civilization. The *fiqh*/Islamic sacral jurisprudence possessed and continues to possess the monopoly over the interpretation of religious affairs in Islam. These jurists are, in the scholarly terms of the sociology of religion, clearly clerics, but Islamic doctrine rejects the institution of clergy. On the basis of this rejection, the *ulama-faqih*s strongly reject references to them as 'clerics'.

The historical reality is that *shari'a* law determines the religion of Islam in providing provisions for what is *halal*/permitted and what is *haram*/forbidden. In classical *shari'a* these provisions have nothing to do with governance. Islamism changes this situation in a new interpretation of the Qur'anic term of *shari'a* already quoted above (sura 45, verse 18), arguing that the Qur'anic meaning is not only ethical, but also juridical. Islamists then infer the erroneous conclusion that *shari'a* is a legal system suitable to serve as a design for an Islamic governance. The approval by 'enlightened Muslim thought' of a universal law, quoted at the end of this section (see note 38), collides head-on with this Islamist venture.

When *shari'a* is viewed as divine law for Islamic governance, it becomes the source of tensions that generate conflict, since humanity is subdivided into a number of religion-based civilizations, each of which has its own distinct legal traditions. How might this conflict be resolved? Civilizations are composed of a great number of local cultures, and from this follows the existence of cultural diversity within civilizational unity. Today we live in a world with a global system, hence the need for an international law shared by all.

Contemporary Islamdom needs a legal philosophy that undergirds a universality of law, supplemented with general acceptance by all local cultures and their civilizations. True, international law is Western in origin, as is cultural modernity itself. Here I face a similar problem as the one to which my argument for the universality of the Westphalian synthesis is exposed (see Chapter 3). Drawing on the work of Jürgen Habermas, I argue here as there (see Chapter 3, note 35) for dissociating cosmopolitan law (and modernity) from its European origins to 'stylize it into a spatiotemporally neutral model' (Habermas). In my view, this dissociation provides an exit.

Today, the cultural turn is expressed by the return of the sacred, a process in which each civilization revives its own legal traditions and so perceives international law as 'alien instructions'. In this regard, there exists a similarity between law in Islamic civilization and Western law: Muslims regard their *shari'a* as universal as much as Westerners view their positive law as international and universal. In the mutual denying of the claim of the other tradition to universality, an inter-civilizational conflict arises that needs to be addressed and solved to avoid the worst. In Habermas's solution of a neutral model I see an exit out of this impasse.

The overall need for a cross-cultural consensus on a universally accepted notion of law is beyond dispute. Article 1 of the United Nations Charter lays down the settlement of international disputes by peaceful, that is, legal means, intended to be valid for all people and states. The UN is an international organization of all peoples, but international law is – again – in its origin and cultural roots basically European law. Therefore, this law seems to fall short of what is needed for universal legal awareness and acceptance in non-Western civilizations. In our post-bipolar age it needs to be acknowledged that, although there is only one international law, a diversity of legal systems exist in parallel to the diversity of cultures and civilizations. When it comes to placing constitutional law in this context, we see Salafi Muslims and Islamists applying the Western notion of *dustur* to the Qur'an and thereby viewing this revelation as their Islamic constitution, which they consider to be valid for the whole of humanity in line with Islamic universalism. To grasp this conflict-ridden situation, a reference to the Oxford jurist H. L. A. Hart is worthwhile. Hart shows how European-structured law becomes international law, binding for new states:

> It has never been doubted that when a new, independent state emerges into existence . . . it is bound by the general obligations of international law . . . Here the attempt to rest the new state's international obligations on a 'tacit' or 'inferred' consent seems wholly threadbare.[37]

Under the conditions outlined, the return of the sacred to politics in the context of post-bipolarity is no blessing. This return exacerbates the complexity related to the absence of 'consensus' that is needed on universal law. This phenomenon is referred to as a cultural turn (religion is a 'cultural system'; Geertz), and it occurs in all religion-based civilizations associated with cultural attitudes towards reviving legal traditions. In Islam as in most of the non-European civilizations, the return of the sacred predominantly assumes the shape of a return of a religion-based understanding of law and also a 'revolt against the West'.

In religion-based civilizations, law is perceived to be God-given and to be derived interpretatively from Holy Scripture. By contrast, modern lawmakers in democracies are elected parliamentarians who act as legislators in democratic institutions. In the Islamicate, the unelected *ulama* act in their capacity as the interpreters of scripture. They not only claim to be legal scholars, but also claim to determine the law that is revealed by Allah. Thus, one may contrast two competing legal traditions: the legislative democratic vs. the interpretative authoritarian. This competition is coupled with cultural tensions that become political in an inter-civilizational conflict over patterns of law. Despite this tense, polarized situation, we need a democratic global peace based on the universality of law. To make this concept of law acceptable to adherents of all religions, it has to be grounded in secular legislative law.

I conclude this section by quoting one of the champions of the 'enlightened turn' that represents 'enlightened Muslim thought', the Moroccan writer Abdou Filali-Ansary. He adds his voice to the plea for a universal law as follows:

> There can be convergent paths to establishing social and political systems that promote individual freedoms, human rights and social justice . . . It is therefore time to call for a universal rule of law . . . respected for its own sake in a 'Kantian' way . . . some form for a universal rule of law . . . would help to define a framework – political, cultural and economic – that is truly compatible with democratic ideals on the scale of humanity.[38]

Since I could not agree more, I have nothing to add.

A plea for a reformed Islamic *shari'a* law in the pursuit of a universal cosmopolitan law

Honouring the principle of legal–cultural diversity within one humanity has to be made compatible with the need to find a balance between cultural particularisms and the requirements for a cross-culturally based universality. The option of *shari'a*tization to legitimize an Islamization of law works against such a balance, as it insists on a *tatbiq-shari'a*/implementation of *shari'a* which is, unfortunately, a public choice in Islamdom. The future of the world of Islam as an Islamicate seems to be overshadowed by the return of the sacred in political–totalitarian shape. The bottom line is that the Islamist reinvented *shari'a* is not in consonance with international standards of law. This view also relates to the hypothesis that the *shari'a*tization project contradicts any democratic constitutionalism even on local grounds. Can there be a compromise in the context of the Arab Spring? Could the compromise be based on reform? Can *shari'a* be reformed?

A major problem of Muslim legal thought has been addressed by the earlier quoted enlightened Muslim legal scholar Najib al-Armanazi (see note 30). He announced the embarrassing fact that there is a centuries-old dichotomy related to the fact that *shari'a* was not subjected to any updating despite its ultimate incongruence with the realities in which Muslims live. Traditionally, Islamic legal tradition was seldom revised. This reluctance is tied to the argument that divine law is immutable. On these grounds Muslim reformers were repulsed with the accusing question: Are you changing the law of God? The *ulama-faqih*s keep silent about their confusion of *shari'a* with *fiqh*. Contemporary Islamists maintain their *shari'a*tization of Islamic politics with such ostracizing questions. Under these unpromising conditions, intensified by the empowerment of Islamism, the question needs to be revisited as to whether a reform under these circumstances is feasible at all.[39]

Legal reform requires the admission that contemporary *shari'a* is law made by humans; it is thus not based on Allah's revelation, and therefore it can be revised. Any reform of Islamic law cannot be promising if it continues to be restricted to an exegesis of handed-down law; that is, if the redline of scriptural reasoning is not to be crossed. The rethinking by culturally innovative Muslims based on admitting a free philosophy of law is the alternative and is known by the name 'enlightened Muslim thought'.

The necessity for reforming Islamic law gives rise to questions of law and international morality combined with the idea of the universality of rights and human rights for cross-cultural bridging in the age of the return of the sacred. This reality challenges Islam to find an accommodation with cultural modernity along with a modernization to be achieved in new legal reasoning. This cannot be successful without a rethinking of basic Islamic concepts by Muslims themselves. Do they accept this challenge? The answer is yes, and no.[40]

Orthodox-Salafi Muslims dismiss any historicizing of Islam with an essentialist reference to Islamic revelation. Other enlightened Muslims who reject this essentializing of Islam engage and revive an alternative to this orthodoxy. This needed alternative could be the revival of the medieval Islamic rational philosophy, which approves the primacy of reason. Medieval Muslim rationalists integrated ancient Greek philosophy into their classical Islamic thought. The buried tradition of a 'Hellenization of Islam' is relevant for the required rethinking of Islam in an age of politicized *shari'a* poised to de-secularize, and for this reason the project of an Islamic humanist revival is most urgent for coping with the global conflict. This humanism inspires contemporary Muslims such as Mohammed Abed al-Jabri. His project is the best effort in this direction as established in enlightened Muslim thought.[41]

A further Muslim effort against a *shari'a*tized Islam is the admission of a legal philosophy in Islam that allows human reasoning on law. To underpin this argument, the following deliberations are needed. To be sure, *shari'a* law is a Muslim particularism, but a virtual deviation from the norm in practice is not an Islamic peculiarity: it is often the starting point of every process of jurisdiction, and is also undertaken by modern European jurists. In Western legal thought the principle applies, as one scholar states: 'The legal norm has an existence independent of social reality within its fundamental sphere of validity.'[42] This is the way Muslim jurists proceed in believing in a divine revelation named the *shari'a.* To introduce innovations, the Islamic jurist could learn a great deal from European jurists and from their way of dealing with legal norms in a topical discourse and juristic hermeneutics. These could be integrated into a reformed Islamic legal system, and would allow a concept of rights underpinning freedom of belief (faith).

In leaving aside the question of the origin of law (whether secular legislation or divine revelation), I interpret law along the line of thought of H. L. A. Hart, the Oxford scholar already quoted, as an 'open texture'. This is a term coined by Hart to describe a fixed written structure of norms, open to interpretation, that also allows a rethinking of the non-legal norm itself. This would seem to be acceptable to Muslims since it combines exegesis/*tafsir* with *ijtihad*/free reasoning beyond the holy scripture. Hart points out that all legal systems, whether traditionally handed down or legislative in character, represent a compromise between two legal requirements, 'the need for certain rules' and 'the need to leave open', adding: 'In every legal system a large and important field is left open for the exercise of discretion by courts.'[43] Hart reminds us that a recourse to the same handed-down law can have a different content in different times and different systems. Islamic legal history offers a classic example in support of this assertion. There exists no one single legal view accepted by the entirety of the culturally diverse and religiously sectarian *umma* of Islam. This *umma* is based on a transnational religion. As a civilization it would not be able to join the world community without opening itself to substantive legal reform, both for its self and for its interaction with others. This endeavour does not appear feasible under ideological conditions characterized by the rejection of any cultural borrowing from others, an attitude that at present characterizes the exponents of the *shari'a*. Under this consideration, Muslims need to be convinced of the authenticity of reform. If we yield to this, we need at the same time to vigorously oppose two extremes: the classical Islamic legal means of the *hiyal* (legal dodges; frankly: self-deceipt), and the literal understanding of Islamic law (for example, amputation of the hand as a punitive measure). The target is new outlooks; hence the question related to the potential for 'flexibilization' of the Islamic notion of law in Islamic terms. 'Flexibilization' is a technical term employed in the German juridical debate and refers to the non-rigid handling of legal norms in order to manage tensions between reality and dogma. This is not tantamount to a bending of law at the interpreter's discretion; rather, flexibilization conveys the notion of a certain pliancy in the process of lawmaking and jurisdiction. In the present crisis situation and in this juncture, I view flexibilization of Islamic law as the better alternative to the politicization of Islam that results in a totalizing *shari'a* based on the Salafist and dogmatic Islamic belief in immutability.

The truth is that – although it was always dismissed by the *shari'a* doctrine (according to which *bid'a*/innovation was seen as tantamount to disbelief) – change, even in legal reasoning, has always taken place in Islamic history. Islamists and Salafists alike argue *shari'a* is a revealed law never to be changed. Historical reality, however, belies Islamic and Islamist essentialism. This essentialism dismisses any legal reasoning that is committed to reform and is guided by a legal philosophy that would underpin the proposal to open the Islamic cultural system to 'change'. Again and again it is repeated that *shari'a* is God's revelation, and therefore is not subject to change. In reality, though, legal practice deviated from dogma and was actually adjusted to changed circumstances even as, in parallel, belief in the immutability of the legal norms was maintained. Hence the behavioural lag. It follows that a simultaneity of cultural persistence and real change is alleviated by behavioural conformism. Because a legal philosophy, as noted earlier, has been not only absent, but is rejected in Islam, the conformist adjustment was merely pragmatic in nature, avoiding any rethinking of values and norms. The flexibilization aimed for here would, unlike the former Islamic *hiyal* legal tradition, have to incorporate a full cultural awareness of social and cultural change. In my earlier work on *shari'a* I not only discuss the theory of law as an 'open texture' in Hart's sense, but also draw on juristic hermeneutics that could provide very helpful tools for efforts to modernize Islamic law. The aim is to establish an Islamic discourse of legal reasoning that runs – in the norm and in legal practice alike – from actual social givens to textual understanding, not vice versa, as the *ulama* and the *faqihs* in their *shari'a* reasoning mostly do. For these scribes, reasoning is restricted to interpreting the scripture, no more, no less. The result is pure or selective scripturalism, but a scripturalism that is strongly imbued with the orthodox way of reading the scripture. I do not want here to rehash that earlier work, in which I engage in a critical evaluation and draw on topical forms of thinking as an indispensable element in legal reasoning. It makes no sense to address the dogmatic system as such, but one can argue against the preconception that any system can be perfect and definitive.[44] The historicity of Islam speaks volumes against such a view, which blocks all reform.

The Islamists of the Arab Spring keep talking about *shari'a* and seem to overlook the need for religious reform based on an acceptance of the historicity of Islam. This would be the first step towards the de-essentialization of any system of *shari'a*. Then we come to distinctions. In Islamic law there is a distinction between *taqlid*, that is submission to the authority of the *faqhis*, and *ijtihad*, creative lawmaking through individual, independent legal reasoning. *Ijtihad* was the driver of Islamic modernism, which came into existence during the second half of the nineteenth century in Egypt.[45] The result has been the trend to gearing up for a reform of Islamic law in the twentieth century. In this context, attempts were made to revive the *ijtihad* tradition in Islam. However, the return of the sacred in the shape of political Islam is in no way a step in the direction of such a reform.

To sum up, Islamism pays lip service to the revival of scriptural *shari'a*, but the envisioned *shari'a*tization of the state is neither a reform based on an innovation and rethinking Islam, nor is it the traditional *shari'a*. A close look at the Islamist literature in which a call is put forward for a revival of *shari'a* reveals how much this is based on an invention of tradition, not on the revival of what is inherited – not even on the scripture.[46] For this reason, the term 'revivalism' is inaccurate as a description of Islamism. It does not reflect reality, which is that the Islamist recourse to *shari'a* is an 'invention of tradition'.

Conclusions: *shari'a*tized Islam is not a democratic constitutionalism

The analytical overview provided in this chapter acknowledges a strict distinction between Islamic orthodoxy (Salafism) and Islamism, without, however, overlooking the resemblance between the two: they both not only essentialize Islam, but also act intolerantly towards all Muslim reformers who introduce the historicity of Islam to Muslim thought. In the past, the medieval weapon of invoking *takfir* (the accusation of heresy to legitimate excommunication of a Muslim out of the *umma*, declaring a Muslim to be an unbeliever with the consequence he or she can be executed) was used against culturally innovative Muslims. As demonstrated above in reference to Nasr Hamid Abu-Zaid, this weapon of *takfir* continues to be used against bright and reformist Muslims. The religious orthodoxy of the past and radical Islamists of today share this weapon. *Tafkir* (topical thinking in Islamic law) is equated by Islamists with *takfir*.[47] Enlightened Muslim thought (see Chapter 3) includes philosophers like al-Jabri and others. Their reasoning is not only reassuring, it also revives the outlawed tradition of rationalism in Islam that provides better future perspectives for Islamdom.

I have decided to incorporate in the conclusions to this chapter comparisons between enlightened and Salafist Muslims, as well as different ways of looking at *shari'a*. I begin with the contrast between the Moroccan al-Jabri and the Pakistani Muhammad Muslehuddin. The latter has in fact a Western education and is a graduate of the University of London, but he is obsessed with a criticism of Western Orientalism in a binary mindset that derails his thinking to reach wrong conclusions. For instance, he is antagonistic against the late Malcolm Kerr, who throughout his life was a friend of Islamdom. Kerr was a highly respected political scientist from the University of California, Los Angeles, who served until his assassination by an Islamist in Beirut as President of the American University of Beirut. Kerr's accomplishments include basic research into efforts toward reform, in particular in legal thought in modern Islam.[48] In January 1984, Shi'ite Muslim fanatics murdered Professor Kerr in Beirut, even though he was highly sympathetic to Islam and Islamdom.

In his time as President of the American University of Beirut, Kerr was a consensus builder engaged in the bridging of civilizational divides. In contrast, Muslehuddin not only discredits all attempts at reform, but also engages in simplistic binaries. His apodictic statement is: 'Those who think of reforming or modernizing Islam are misguided, and their efforts are bound to fail. . . . Why should it be modernized, when it is already perfect and pure, universal, and for all time?'[49] In his view, therefore, the task of jurists is solely that of interpreting the *shari'a* in order 'to comprehend and discover the law and not to establish or create it'. For Muslims of this kind, only textual reasoning on exclusively scriptural grounds is permissible. Reform is dismissed with contempt as heresy. How could this Salafist essentialism contribute to democratization?

Salafism is a legal orthodoxy in Islam that prohibits free reasoning. It has this in common with the Islamist invention of *shari'a* tradition: both close the Muslim mind. Both Salafism and Islamism undermine any Muslim effort to think in terms of topically oriented interpretations that allow the introduction of religious pluralism and freedom of belief into Islamic thought. In Islamist legal thought, one often sees deductions by analogy, which generally indicate the absence of a perfect logical system. An example is Muslehuddin's critique of Kerr: it lacks any logic. He focuses on Kerr's rational, scientific method, which attempts to comprehend Islamic law in rational terms. Muslehuddin establishes a binary divide between any spirit of critique and the divine law that is constructed by humans but attributes to itself the character of divine revelation. Let us see how Muslehuddin thinks, in his own words:

Divine law is to be preserved in its ideal form as commanded by God, or else it will be devoid of its capability to control society which is its chief purpose. The mistaken view of the Orientalists is due mainly to the fact that the real good may be rationally known and that the law should be determined by social needs, while all such needs are provided for in divine law and God alone knows what is really good for mankind.

This statement reflects a mindset that contradicts any democratic understanding of law that underpins (not 'controls') the order of state and society. The prevailing contemporary highly uncompromising legal view of Islamism expresses the return of the sacred as a return of religion to public space with reference to *shari'a* law with a totalitarian mindset. This is an undemocratic order billed as the establishment of a God-given order. The reader is reminded that Islamist *shari'a* is not classical, traditional Islamic law, but a new religionized politics based on the *shari'a*tization of Islam in an invention of tradition. In view of the prevailing orthodox-Salafist and Islamist essentialization of Islam, politically empowered in the context of the Arab Spring, these facts cannot be repeated often enough. The result are conflicts and tensions.[50] These prospects alienate Islamdom from international society and from non-Muslims.

What is conceived by the would-be politically correct, as they deal with the envisioned Islamist rule of a *shari'a* state, as a purely 'cultural misunderstanding', is factually a source of conflict. People who upgrade Islamism in the name of respect for non-Western cultures act on a wrong footing. Non-Muslims can be respectful of Islam and critical of the *shari'a* state at the same time. There are also those critical-minded Muslims who dismiss a *shari'a* order for state and society on the grounds of enlightened Muslim thought. They deserve respect, too.

That stated, the first conclusion of this chapter is that the current return of *shari'a* to politics in the Islamist *shari'a*tization project precludes the rethinking of Islamic law as part of a commitment to opening the Muslim mind to cultural innovation. The implication of this conclusion is that Islamism is not a project of reform and cultural change. The obstacles standing in the way of the kind of critical reasoning that could lead to legal reform are great. In the age of the return of the sacred to public space as expressed by political Islam, the first victim of *shari'a*tization is the concept of rights, including the right to freedom of belief. Muslims of enlightened Muslim thought are among the victims. Unlike Islamists, they admit reform and cultural change as one of the prerequisites of a transformation of state and society towards democratization.[51]

The second conclusion is validation of the assumption that the new *shari'a* of political Islam, in contrast to the potential of a civil Islam, contradicts democratic constitutionalism. Furthermore, Islamist legal thinking is not receptive to the appeal for the integration of topical discourse into Islamic legal philosophy. In this reluctance, the mindsets of orthodoxy and of political Islam resemble one another. Nevertheless, the orthodoxy of Salafism and the invention of tradition by Islamism are different trends in Islamic civilization and should not be lumped together. The return of the sacred that has been discussed using the example of the constitutional claims of political Islam is based, not on traditionalism, but on an invention of tradition, and hence is in no way a revivalism.

Do these two conclusions matter for the future prospects of the Arab Spring? Contemporary Islamist movements which are the core opposition make instrumental use of democratization in their pursuit of *tatbiq al-shari'a* in the *shari'a*tization of politics (see Chapter 5). Their project is not a promising prospect for the establishment of a genuine democracy? Why is this?

Even if a political place is conceded for *shari'a* in Islamic civilization, some legal reform is needed that enables Muslims themselves to engage in a cultural vision that would facilitate a better future. Do not misunderstand me: the statement that change is blocked is not imbued with any essentialist Orientalism. My views on Islamdom are based on the idea of 'developing cultures' (see note 51). Change in economy and politics is legitimate; what inspires the present analysis is the need for a change of socio-cultural systems. Muslims of today are challenged to emulate their ancestors in learning from others to change their cultural world view. The call for the Islamization of law and for de-Westernization is nothing but a defensive cultural response to existing challenges: it leads to nowhere.

Ultimately, Islamism is the expression of a lacking of willingness to cope culturally with structural change. The so-called Islamization of law is an agenda of *shari'a*tization that not only shows no sign of cultural accommodation of change, but also precludes learning from others. It follows that the call for *tatbiq al-shari'a* (the implementation of Islamic law) into the overall contemporary phenomenon of the return of the sacred is not a blessing. This call is given by a religionized politics billed as religious revival, where in reality it is based on an invention of tradition. If it succeeds in driving the Arab Spring to end with 'Islamic states' based on Islamist *shari'a* – as is in fact happening – then no sign of democratization coupled with a commitment to the rule of law will be on the horizon.

So the third and final conclusion of this chapter is that the Islamist project of a *shari'a* state emerges from the contemporary crisis of Islamic civilization; it is challenged by a radically changing modern world. Under these conditions there is a need for a historically responsible response. The Islamist *shari'a* promises salvation, but not the response that is needed. The *shari'a*tization is the strategy pursued by Islamists who believe it to be the right resolution for this crisis. But the Islamist agenda is no solution, and in addition, it stands in serious contradiction to the democratic universal constitutionalism that would constitute grounds for the hoped for world peace. Rather, the Islamist *shari'a* is an obstacle in the way of Islamdom, hindering it from joining an international society that is based on universal law and committed to democratic peace, and from becoming an integrated part of its world order. One may add that the rule of the *shari'a* state is not what motivated the young, 'no-hope' generation to take to the streets to protest against authoritarianism in their hope for freedom and for a better life. The Arab Spring began from the bottom up as a series of grassroots, leaderless uprisings, but it seems to be ending up either in a *shari'a* state or in anarchy. Short of a miracle happening that redirects the ongoing development into a process of a genuine democratization, the existing prospect – of an emerging *shari'a* state – is not at all promising. Who believes in miracles?

This is my answer and it is a personal one. As a young Sunni-Muslim native of Damascus, I came to study in Germany in 1962 and had the great luck to meet the great German-Jewish philosopher Ernst Bloch in an unforgettable encounter in November 1995. Bloch not only gave me as a present his small book *Avicenna und die Aristotelische Linke*,[52] which inspired me to study the great traditions of Islamic rationalism (see Chapter 3); he also motivated me to read his magnificent three-volume magnum opus *Das Prinzip Hoffnung/The Principle of Hope*. From Bloch I learned that life without hope is worthless. So my answer is that the Arab Spring gave us a great hope that we should keep regardless of the outcome. If the authoritarian police states that caused the exasperation of the Muslim-Arab peoples can be toppled, then the *shari'a* state can be toppled too when people realize that this order does not meet their needs and expectations. As indicated at the end of the Introduction, in Libya this has already happened.

3 The challenge of the Islamist *shari'a* state to international order

Torn between the Westphalian synthesis, *Pax Americana* and *Pax Islamica*

At this stage of the analysis, the next task is to clarify the issue of the political order of the state and of the world at large – that is, basically, the world order. The rise of Islamist movements to power in the context of their empowerment through the Arab Spring moved this issue to centre stage. Among the 'tumultuous effects of the Arab Spring' is the quest of Islamist movements to seek, as a highly pertinent *New York Times* news analysis states, 'a leading political role for Islam in government'.[1] What is that?

The core argument of Islamists is that Islam is based on a concept for a political order that involves the unity of *din-wa-dawla*/religion and state. I shall discuss this view below and devote a full section to this theme. This view of Islam serves as a legitimation for the Islamist political agenda, the aim of which is to establish a *shari'a* state. The Islamist political argument is supplied by a religious undercurrent, and thus is presented as a religious faith. In this way, Islamists give their political ideology the ranking of a religious belief that has a claim to respect and acceptance. In doing this, they not only inoculate their ideology against criticism, but also ignore the basic facts about the religion of Islam and its history.

In this chapter I operate on the grounds of the facts established in the preceding two chapters to argue that the traditional Islamic *shari'a* is basically about a religious faith, the form of practice or worship of that faith, and a cultural world view based on ethics. I acknowledge that Islam was used in the past to legitimate a political rule, namely that of the caliphate. This acknowledgement does not, however, amount to viewing Islam as a political religion. Such a view would be wrong and therefore I reject it. Instead, I consistently look at Islam as a religious faith and an ethics.

The aim of juxtaposing Islamist ideology to facts is to de-legitimate the political order envisioned by Islamism. I pursue this aim in the Islamic terms of the development referred to as 'enlightened Muslim thought'. The core concern of Ali Abdelraziq, who – as Abdou Filali-Ansary rightly states – 'opened the way to the new direction', was to challenge and dismiss 'the claim that a particular form of state is prescribed by Islam'.[2] As established in the Introduction on the grounds of an Ethikon Institute debate run by the Muslim scholar Sohail Hashmi (see Introduction), Islam provides a political ethics, but never a system of government. Therefore, the aim of enlightened Muslim thought is to dissociate Islam from ideologies of political order, but not from politics in terms of the ethics of government. Abdelraziq's conclusion was that the classical political order of the imperial caliphate of the past did not form part of the Islamic faith. I add to this insight that the contemporary religionized politics of the *shari'a* state is not a matter of religious belief either; it is an order that is a novelty, unknown in Islamic history.

These preliminary introductory remarks make clear that the concern of this chapter is the incorporation of Islam into issues related to world politics and the world order under the conditions of modernity. At issue is a novelty introduced to Islamdom by Islamist thought. Islamic heritage knows of no concept of world order. This concept is a modern issue introduced to Islamdom by Islamism in an invention of tradition. In contrast, enlightened Muslim thought can authentically draw on a real, existing tradition in the Islamic heritage. This precious tradition is the *falsafa* rationalism in medieval Islam, of which the Averroism of Ibn Rushd is the civilizational peak of the positive heritage of Islam. The present chapter commences with this contemporary project of enlightened Muslim thought, which rests on this precious tradition, lays claim to it, and seeks to revive it in a creative accommodation with cultural modernity. In Arab debates this true revivalism is rightly dubbed '*mashru' al-Jabri*'/'the al-Jabri project'. The al-Jabri mindset is the inspiration behind the discussion of intra-Islamic concepts of political order as well as those of world order to be presented in this chapter, and therefore I will begin by outlining this Muslim approach.

Enlightened Muslim thought in an 'enlightened turn' on religion and political order

The commitment of the present inquiry to the 'enlightened Muslim thought' project has already been made clear in the Introduction as well as in the first two chapters. Enlightened Muslim thought is multifaceted and covers a broad range of issues stretching from epistemology to law. These concerns are addressed at various stages of the present inquiry, although without consolidating the relevant texts in a dedicated section. Devoting the first section of the present chapter to this matter in full is intended, not just to highlight the issue, but also to continue the reasoning of the great Muslim who 'opened the way' to this thinking in modern Islam, namely Ali Abdelraziq. His reasoning focuses on the abuse of Islam as a legitimation for a political order and claims to bring enlightenment.

The work of Abdou Filali-Ansary is the origin of the proposal to consolidate those contributions to Muslim thought that are inspired by *an* (i.e. not *the* European) enlightenment. The notion he coined for this project of consolidation is 'enlightened Muslim thought'. I also follow Filali-Ansary's proposal of abandoning the slogan of 'liberal Islam' to replace it with the notion of 'enlightened Muslim thought' (see note 2). This is not just because of the negative attributions to this slogan made by Islamists, but because of its association with a highly questionable Western reader bearing the title *Liberal Islam*. As discussed earlier, this approach by the reader's editor, Charles Kurzman, is deftly dismantled by Filali-Ansary as highly flawed.

In this section I do not exclusively focus on the present, as Filali-Ansary does. I see two sets of sources that serve Muslims as sources of inspiration to this enlightened thought: one in the past and the other in the present. I shall now briefly discuss both in historical order.

In medieval Islam, there existed highly significant seeds for an enlightenment that can be identified as an Islamic humanism. In my lifelong study of the history of ideas in Islam – which I will come to in a moment – I contend that this history includes an epistemology for a rationalist philosophy. In this tradition I see seeds of an Islamic enlightenment that predates the European one. I shall come back in a minute to this point.

Next come the sources of the present. Filali-Ansary refers to the work of three major twentieth-century modern Muslim thinkers (I suggest adding a fourth: Mohammed Abed al-Jabri) to exemplify 'key aspects' of this enlightened turn. At the top of the list he places Ali Abdelraziq, because this Muslim thinker was equally the founder and the precursor of the Muslim thought focused upon in this section. Filali-Ansary appreciates the work of this great and courageous thinker in this apt assessment:

> Abdelraziq examined the Qur'anic verses most often used to back-up the claim that a particular form of state is prescribed by Islam and found that . . . the first umma (community) of believers who Mohammed led from Mecca to Medina in 622 CE had none of the features of a polity. Abdelraziq's break with traditional notions stirred huge waves of protest, accusation, and attempted refutation.

I am in agreement with Filali-Ansary that the breakthrough started with Ali Abdelraziq's book *al-Islam wa Usul al-Hukm*. This is the first step in the project of an 'enlightened turn' in modern Islamic thought in which Islam is determined as a religious faith and dissociated from its abuse as an ideological concept for legitimating a political order.

Abdelraziq's reasoning was directed against the Salafist nostalgia concerning the restoration of the caliphate, which was abolished in 1924. In the year his book was published, 1925, the concept of a *shari'a* state did not yet exist, and neither did Islamism. Today, we can refer to Abdelraziq to build on his approach in arguing against the semi-modernist Islamist construction of a *shari'a* state, because his argumentation continues to be valid. Enlightened Muslim thought seeks a cultural accommodation of Islamdom to the present in the context of cultural modernity and the related order both of the state and of the world. Filali-Ansary describes Abdelraziq's work as a 'founding moment in contemporary Muslim thought and politics' because he 'dispels the misunderstanding and confusions surrounding religion and politics in Islam'. This is a major step in the accommodation that is needed, and it continues to be relevant to Muslim needs in the aftermath of the Arab Spring. For this reason, the critical thought of Abdelraziq is best understood when it is placed in the broader context of Islamic history of ideas.

Let me come back to the first set of sources for enlightened Muslim thought, which I briefly mentioned above. They are to be found in the medieval Islamic *falsafa* rationalism. In the twentieth century Mohammed Abed al-Jabri, honoured as 'the most significant Muslim thinker of the age' (Ali Allawi; see Chapter 6), devoted his life to reviving this tradition. I want to elaborate on the pertinence of this tradition to enlightened Muslim thought, and ask the reader to bear with me when I reference my own research in the final two decades of the past century, as it revolves around this subject. During that period I studied Islamic thought in depth in a close collaboration with the unforgettable Arab-Muslim Harvard professor of Islamic philosophy, the late Muhsin Mahdi. I learned so much from him; the debt I owe him is immense, and I acknowledge it in the study I completed at Harvard as a comprehensive history of political ideas in Islam.[3] The published book grew from the Harward project and includes extensive chapters each on Farabi, Mawardi, Ibn Taimiyya and Ibn Khaldun. The authority I draw on in my reading of these Muslim thinkers is Professor Mahdi, whose knowledge was unsurpassable. Muhsin Mahdi was for me – despite the fact that I had myself by then been a full professor for a decade – a great source of inspiration and a great mentor in the course of writing that book. Based on that solid research I maintain that the work of all four of the above-mentioned Muslim philosophers contains no foundation for the idea of a *shari'a* state. The idea of a *shari'a* state is recent and constitutes the core of contemporary Islamist thought. Furthermore, I argue with Abdelraziq that Islam is a faith that, despite its use in politics, does not entail a concept of any political order. In the Introduction to the present book I concede the existence of political ethics in Islam, but this does not equate to a concept of an Islamic government, still less of a *shari'a* state. The conclusion is that the Islamist *shari'a* state has no Islamic roots: neither in the Islamic faith nor in traditional Islamic thought. These are basic insights that I hold in common with enlightened Muslim thought.

In presenting a major aspect of enlightened Muslim thought, I combine the reasoning of great twentieth-century Muslims such as Abdelraziq with medieval Islamic humanism. Among the highlights of my academic life was not only the close and unforgettable collaboration with Muhsin Mahdi at Harvard, but also an encounter in Cairo with the late Mohammed Abed al-Jabri that made a deep impression on me. This great Muslim is the one who contributed to a revival of Islamic rational humanism. This encounter with al-Jabri took place at a symposium for a dialogue between Arab secular and Islamist thinkers organized by the Beirut-based Centre for Arab Unity Studies (the same centre that organized the venture for a reasoning on the 'Crisis of Democracy in the Arab World'; see Chapter 4). In that symposium the rift between those Muslims who were inspired by al-Jabri (who attended) and the Islamists of the *shari'a* state became most obvious. Two projects of Islamic revivalism were opposed to one another. One is a real revival and one is invented.

The magnificent work of al-Jabri, which Islamists dislike, is in my view one of the cornerstones of contemporary enlightened Muslim thought; hence my suggestion of adding him to Abdou Filali-Ansary's list of sources. The thinking developed by the truly Muslim revival of the classical Muslim enlightenment by al-Jabri is – in sharp contrast to the Islamist one pursued by al-Banna – the approach that Islamdom needs for a revival.

Taking the study of traditional Islamic thought and contemporary enlightened Muslim thought as the twin sources of my thinking, I look in this chapter at core issues of political order. I do this with two intentions: to rectify existing confusions (the ensuing section), and to screen the Islamist vision of a *shari'a* state from two angles, the first of which is the concern of democratization (the Arab Spring), and the second, its compatibility with the order based on the Westphalian synthesis that underpins the existing world order. I shall argue in this chapter for a dissociation of this order from its European origins in order to render it a 'neutral model' (Habermas, see note 35). It follows that the defence of the neutralized Westphalian synthesis for a world order is free from pro-Western apologetics, as will be shown.

In a commitment to the universality of knowledge and in adherence to the associated insights, I not only refer to Muslim sources, but also draw on the unsurpassable magnum opus of Marshall Hodgson on the history of Islam.[4] As already explained in Chapter 1, I have adopted from Hodgson's work the concepts of Islamdom and Islamicate. These terms relate to realities, and do not reflect the normative beliefs of a religious faith. The historical meaning of these terms also applies to the Islamist quest for a *shari'a* order. The Islamist drive drags contemporary Islamic civilization into a competition with other views and realities of order. In the first place these other orders are in our present time the Westphalian synthesis and the *Pax Americana*, to be distinguished from one another as will be elaborated on later in this chapter.

Basically, the present step in the argument moves the inquiry into the Arab Spring further on to relate the Islamist drive to establish a *shari'a* state to world politics. Thus, the new step leads into the core issue of international relations, which is the modern world order discussed with reference to Islamism in the tradition of Hedley Bull (see notes 10 and 33). Prior to the emergence of this order there were other historical Islamic concepts of order. On the top of these is the traditional imperial caliphate. One needs also to mention the pan-Islamic state of Afghani (see next section), not to be confused or conflated either with the caliphate or with the contemporary concept of a *shari'a* Islamist order. I hope that this section has established the pertinence of enlightened Muslim thought to the required understanding of these matters pursued in Islamic terms. The regional context of Islamism and the Arab Spring is fully embedded in this overall global context.

Great confusions of Islamic orders: the caliphate, pan-Islamism, and Islamist internationalism in the context of a new world order

Ahead of screening the three Islamic concepts of order listed in the heading (old, new, and in between) some groundwork needs to be done. This work has to be related to world order with regard both to US policies and US scholarship with a view to the assessment of the core concern of Islamism. Political Islam is about political order (not about violent *jihad*). Therefore, the argument already advanced that Islamism is not about religious faith has to be enhanced. The Islamist concept goes beyond the order of the state and foresees an overall order for the future of the world. However, the envisioned order is not the classical one of the imperial caliphate of the past, nor is it pan-Islamism. This Islamist order cannot be properly understood by relating it to an alleged 'trial of a thousand years', as in the Hoover approach with which I take issue (see note 34).

In the hope that the opening deliberations of this section will contribute to defining the point at issue, I begin by stating two sets of distinctions on different levels. First, on the global level, are those orders listed in the chapter title. Second, on the Islamic-civilizational level, there are concepts of order that are often confused with one another. These are listed in the heading to this section and they are here the matter in point.

On the grounds of the concepts and terms outlined in the opening chapter one can establish a historicity of Islam with the aim of overcoming all kinds of essentialism. In this understanding the first political order in Islam was the caliphate. This is past history. It is not to be equated with the Islamic *shari'a* state of contemporary history. The reader is reminded that neither of these reflects a religious faith, but rather that both are a product of Islamic history, past and contemporary. The caliphate was the political order established after the death of the Prophet in 632. Later, in 661, it was transformed under Umayyad rule into a kingdom under hereditary rule – as Ibn Khaldun described it. The caliphate is a post-Qur'anic construction that determined the real history of Islam from the seventh through to the twentieth century. There were three caliphates, the first in Damascus (the Umayyads), the second in Baghdad (the Abbasids) and the third and last in Istanbul (the Ottoman Empire). The rule of the caliph was abolished for good in 1924. The following year saw the publication of the ground-breaking *al-Islam wa Usul al-Hukm* by the Azhar professor Ali Abdelraziq, which, as already mentioned in the introductory section of this chapter, provided great momentum for the 'enlightened turn'. Abdelraziq paid dearly for his book, in which he de-legitimates the caliphate on Islamic grounds – he was dismissed and his livelihood was ruined. At that time, one thought that the new nation-states of the Islamicate had taken the place of the order of the caliphate for good.

After the order of the caliphate, I move on to the nineteenth-century pan-Islamist order, which needs to be distinguished from contemporary Islamist internationalism. The pan-Islamist vision was founded by the Islamic revivalist al-Afghani (1838–1897) with the support of the Ottoman Sultan-Caliph Abdulhamid in an effort to save the empire after the end of the Ottoman expansion. Pan-Islamism was not an internationalism at all, because it exclusively referred to 'Islamic unity' within the Islamicate, understood as territoriality. This was an application of the European pan-ideology of extended nationalism to Islamdom, not to the world at large. More than four decades ago I elaborated on this argument in my book *Arab Nationalism* (see note 2). By contrast, the *shari'a* state is a political order based on religionized politics driven by an internationalism that envisions a new order for the entire world based on the Islamist *shari'a*. This vision is not restricted to a call for Islamic unity as was Afghani's pan-Islamism. And neither of these envisioned orders – the one of pan-Islamism and the one of a *shari'a* state – reflects the order of the classical caliphate.

The caliphate was the traditional order of an asserted unity of Islamdom and the Islamicate. At the beginning this assertion corresponded with reality, but as early as the tenth century there existed three Muslim rulers, each of whom claimed to be caliph of all Muslims. Unlike the *shari'a* state, in the caliphate there existed a realm for politics in the sense of state administration (*siyasa*), practically separated from *shari'a* which was the realm of Kadis (judges) and Muftis. In Islam the *ulama-faqih*s act as Muftis who have the competency to issue an authoritative religious judgement, named *fatwa*. In the past they were never (and still are not) in any way political decision-makers. The foremost scholarly authority on Islamic *shari'a* law, Joseph Schacht, draws attention to the distinction between and separation of the realms of secular *siyasa* and religious *shari'a* in medieval Islamic history.[5] After Schacht, and in the same context, I draw on the research of Sir Hamilton Gibb, who established Islamic studies at Harvard. He clearly shows that *shari'a* merely served as *post-eventum* legitimation of decisions that were taken by the political rulers on the grounds of convenience, not on religious tenets (see Chapter 1, note 9). This is a basic feature of the history of the caliphate. In addition to the scholarly evidence of Schacht and Gibb, I have drawn on authoritative Muslim scholars in Chapters 1 and 2 to question the religious foundation of the caliphate.

These historical facts are ignored by some scholars (I have been exposed to some of them in their function as peer reviewers). They not only disregard these facts, but also accept the Islamist claim that the *shari'a* state is nothing but a revival of an Islamic state order of the past. I will cite anonymously one review that led to the dismissal of my work. This review was based on the allegation that the *shari'a* state is not a novelty as it is already grounded in the work of Mawardi, Ibn Taimiyya and even Ibn Khaldun. This is utterly wrong. I have studied very closely the work of all of these medieval thinkers and published a big research-based monograph on this subject, discussed above (see note 3). This is how I know how unfounded this allegation is, and that it reveals a lack of the required knowledge, coupled with a deplorable drive to curb academic freedom. Familiarity with the work of Mawardi, Ibn Tamiyya and Ibn Khaldun shows that these classical Muslim thinkers deal in different ways with the traditional caliphate, but this should not be confused with the *shari'a* state, which is a modern pattern that did not exist in those times. If one fails to distinguish between past and present, naturally one can only reach wrong conclusions. I have reason to repeat: neither order – that is, neither the caliphate nor the *shari'a* state – is grounded in the Islamic faith.

The fact of the abuse of *shari'a* in politics does not elevate this abuse to make it a part of religious faith. The prudent Muslim scholars of enlightened Muslim thought, standing in the tradition of Abdelraziq, reject the use of religious faith for political ends. In response, Islamists call them names. The most prominent example of this is the Islamist sheykh Qaradawi, whom I cited in the Introduction calling Muslim dissidents ' . . . disbelievers . . . wrong-doers and truly wicked'. This seems to be exemplary of the way Islamists view Muslim dissidents. The name calling reveals their attitudes towards pluralism and diversity. For Western scholarship Qaradawi is a model of 'moderation', and is even presented as a source of 'liberal Islam', as Charles Kurzman wants us to believe in his reader of that title.

Based on the distinctions I have introduced between orders within Islam, my inquiry takes issue with existing confusions and establishes its own position within enlightened Muslim thought. First is Islamism with its claim to reverse the process referred to as the 'end of history' in their project of a nostalgic 'return to the history' of civilizations in the pursuit of *Pax Islamica*. For Islamists this would be a return to the political order in the glorious past of Islam. This nostalgia happens in opposition to the hegemonic order of *Pax Americana*. Make no mistake: the opposed order envisioned by Islamists is not, as it is misconceived to be in Western scholarship and politics, a restored caliphate.

After the envisioned *Pax Islamica*, there is the real politics of *Pax Americana*. The ideology of the latter is represented in the approach pursued by the Ajami–Hill Working Group on Islamism and International Order based at the Hoover Institution. This approach will be discussed in more detail in a later section, and some readers might quest the anticipation of that debate here. I think, however, that it is right to take issue at this juncture with Hill's arbitrary centuries-long history *A Trial of a Thousand Years* (see note 34). The *Pax Americana* approach also engages in replacing communism by Islamism in a new Cold War. This Hoover position is wrongly held as a defence of the Westphalian synthesis. This is utterly wrong and therefore I strongly disagree with it. It is appropriate to state here that I do not criticize the Islamist vision of *Pax Islamica* for the sake of defending *Pax Americana*, as Hill and Ajami do. In contrast, I stand for a real democratization (and pluralism) in a global civil society – not for a choice between *Pax Islamica* and *Pax Americana*. Although I reject both these, I am neither Islamophobic nor anti-American.

I reject the imagined *Pax Islamica* along with the existing hegemonic *Pax Americana* in favor of the Westphalian international system, which I dissociate from its European origins to turn it into a neutral model. For this reason I dissociate the Westphalian synthesis not only from any approval of a US hegemony over the world, but also from its modern European origin, with the aim to 'stylize it into a spatio-temporally model' (Habermas). This can be justified on universal humanist grounds. Based on this thinking, I strongly reject the approach of the Hoover Institution's working group on Islamism and world order and its equation of *Pax Americana* with the Westphalian order, just as as much as I discard the *shari'a* state from a standpoint of universal-humanist democratization, which is not to be equated with an apologetics for US policies.

In a nutshell, the insight at the end of this section is that the Westphalian synthesis should not be confused with the *Pax Americana*, as much as the caliphate should not be confounded with the *shari'a* state.

Is the order of a *din-wa-dawla* Islamocracy an Islamic democracy compatible with democratic world peace?

The next step, after delineating the classical order of the caliphate and the pan-Islamic order of the nineteenth century (and taking issue with those who confuse them), is to place the discussion of the envisioned Islamist order within a general debate on political order. Adhering to universal principles in this context does not mean that people of different cultures follow the same pattern and live in accordance with it. For instance, there are culturally different practices of democracy (see, for example, the observations of the French philosopher Tocqueville on democracy in America). Nevertheless, democratic rule honours values that are similar in substance, which are referred to in terms of unity and diversity. Does the reference to an order of an 'Islamic democracy' fit into this reasoning?

We Muslims have our particularisms, but we are members of the same humanity. So why a specific Islamic democracy (Islamocracy), and why a specific Islamic law (*shari'a*)? In compliance with the idea of one humanity in a need for commonalities – despite all respectful cultural particularisms that underpin diversity – I argue with Muslims of enlightened thought for universality of knowledge and for cosmopolitan law. On these grounds I accept the legitimacy of the Kantian vision of a democratic world peace. It was hoped that this peace would prevail at the end of bipolarity, and in the course of the Arab Spring this vision received first a great boost, then a blow. Arab states make up the South and East of the Mediterranean, which was historically the centre of the history of civilizations. Democratization in that part of the world would therefore be a great contribution to democratic world peace. But how real is this perspective? To answer this question we need to know what Islamists want and deal with the order they envision. They are the chief beneficiaries of the Arab Spring and thus have gained the power to determine the aftermath.

Since Hasan al-Banna, Islamists have argued that Islam is about politics and have pronounced their core principle of *din-wa-dawla*/unity of religion and state order. This notion reflects the salient feature of Islamism. Studying the Islamist ideology that politicizes Islam to an Islamism provides ample evidence that it is not favourable to democracy. Unlike the religious faith of Islam, and even to its use on the surface as a legitimation for political rule in historical Islam, contemporary Islamism is not only basically, but almost exclusively about governance. Someone coined the term Islamocracy to argue that democracy is Western, not universal, with the incredible conclusion that this Islamocratic *shari'a* rule – as an 'Islamic democracy' – is more suited to Muslim people. This reflects a kind of Western patriarchy. For example, a US professor (Amitai Etzioni, in: *The National Interest*, 2011) whose research is not basically on Islamdom, thinks, in endorsing Islamocracy, that he knows what is best for Muslims. For enlightened Muslim thought (see note 2), the only correct thing about the coinage 'Islamocracy' is that the new term reveals what Islamism is all about, namely about governance, not religious faith. The rest is better forgotten, although with this note: Professor Amitai Etzioni is a respected scholar, but can to my knowledge in no way claim to be an expert on Islam and Islamism. For this reason he seems not to realize that the design with *din-wa-dawla* Islamocracy is not to restrict it to the Islamicate, but to raise it to an order of the world that would replace the present order of the international state system based on the Westphalian synthesis. I wonder whether Etzioni would accept an Islamocracy as a world order; I doubt whether he would.

In the recent past, particularly since the Arab Spring, institutional Islamist movements have found out by experience that elections are much more promising than *jihad* for the seizure of state power. In contrast, jihadist violence leads to nowhere. The Muslim Brothers have been successful; al-Qaeda failed. The shift in Islamism from jihadism to institutional participation in electoral politics is neither a moderation, nor a democratization. The change is in the means employed, not in the political agenda. Make no mistake: the Islamist *shari'a* state, the goal, is an Islamocracy, not a democracy. Neither is it the traditional caliphate. It is a new order, called in modern Arabic: *nizam islami*. Close scrutiny of this order reveals that it would never fit into a world peace based on pluralism and democracy.

One more rectification: the shift from jihadist violence to Islamist institutionalism is not an indication of post-Islamism. The shift has taken place within Islamism in favour of institutional politics at the expense of jihadist Islamism. This shift is not combined with a change in either the mindset or in the political agenda. It is safe to say that the political record of the Arab Spring of 2011 – which in 2012 has seemingly become an unpleasant winter – supports the validity of this assumption of a shift. It is utterly wrong to suggest that Islamist movements in this shift are embracing democracy, because the *shari'a* state is, as has been already plainly argued, not about democratic rule.

The origin and major source of the idea of an Islamist *shari'a* state is the work of Hasan al-Banna and Sayyid Qutb. However, the most powerful and systematic formulation of this idea is to be found in the book trilogy of the global TV Mufti Yusuf al-Qaradawi on *Hatmiyyat al-Hall al-Islami/The Islamic Solution*. In line with Qutb who claims to see 'the end of democracy and its bankruptcy', Qaradawi rejects democracy in a wholesale manner among the 'imported solutions' that have allegedly plagued the world of Islam in the context he calls the 'invasion' of 'the Crusader West'/'*al-gharb al-salibi*'. For Qaradawi, 'the only cure is a return to Islam' and hence he coined the term 'the Islamic solution', which has become one of the strongest Islamist slogans, translated into a mobilizational ideology.[6] Its most powerful expression is the role of Islamism in the aftermath of the Arab Spring. This solution is the 'Islamic *shari'a* state', outlined in the second volume of Qaradawi's trilogy. The evidence that this state is not a democracy is there in Qaradawi's work. After repeating the accusation against the 'Western colonial crusaders' who have Westernized (that is, secularized) legal structures in reducing *shari'a* to a personal law, he pleads for the imposition of *shari'a* as 'the only source of law applied to all aspects of life . . . every law that contradicts *shari'a* is utterly subject to invalidity'. It is not the elected parliament, but an unelected supreme council of *faqih*s (sacral jurists) knowledgeable about *shari'a* 'that is in charge of compatibility of any law with *shari'a*'. Among the rules of the implementation of *shari'a* are the *hudud* (penal code of physical punishments, such as lashing, stoning and cutting parts of the body), approved by Qaradawi. Then he asks: How could this all be achieved? The answer is given in his chapter on 'The Islamic State'. It is this: the *shari'a* state ensures the implementation of *shari'a* in all realms of life, whether public or private, and this is the solution. This *shari'a* order 'establishes the Islamic society aspired for . . . purified – intellectually, psychologically and behaviourally –

from all alien bodies and hidden viruses that infected Muslims, such as nationalism and secularism.' The legal purity that Islamists such as Qaradawi attribute to the *shari'a* state order does not indicate a democratic rule, but rather is one of the six core features of Islamism that are incompatible with democracy. The new understanding of purity in the Islamized *shari'a* law is something also shared by all Islamist movements regardless of whether they are jihadist or institutional. It is based on the distinction between what is accepted as Islamic and what is rejected as 'un-Islamic' and to be punished by applying the *hudud* to ensure purity.

I acknowledge that the analytical, facts-based distinction between jihadist and institutional Islamism does not overlook the reality of boundaries that can at times be blurred. There are Islamist movements (e.g. Hezbollah in Lebanon, some Islamist parties in Iraq and Hamas in Palestine, among others) that participate in balloting to send their members to elected parliaments, but at the same time maintain their militias and related jihadist practices. Nevertheless, I keep the distinction, although modifying it by acknowledging the existence of hybrid patterns within Islamism.

What matters most to the present venture is the pertinence and validity of generalizations that do not overlook nuances and particularisms, as well as mixed forms of the general type in a Weberian sense. What matters most is the validity of the statement of six general features of Islamism that are shared by all related movements whether peaceful or violent. It follows that post-jihadism is neither moderation nor post-Islamism.

There are also new hybrid regimes with a mixed type of rule (e.g. the tribal-Islamist rule in post-Qadhafi Libya). However, these must not be confused with either democracy or the traditional caliphate. The classical order dealt with by Mawardi and others is the caliphate, not Islamocracy – something different as it grows from a contemporary *shari'a*tization of Islam. In short, the Islamist order of *din-wa-dawla* Islamocracy is a hybrid order that never existed before in any period of Islamic history. Thus, it is not a revivalism, but is based on an invention of tradition.

In this context the reader is reminded yet again of the strict distinction made between Islamism and Islam. This distinction is so fundamental to understanding the contemporary phenomenon of religionized politics – so important – that it cannot be repeated often enough. If this distinction is ignored, it is impossible to acquire a proper grasp of the contemporary ideology on which the actions of Islamist movements rest. It is wholly unfortunate that this distinction is not shared knowledge, and is often rebuked. If this were not so, so many of the numerous, often fruitless debates could be saved. These debates are often ideologically biased; they mostly take place in a partisanship caught in an oscillation between the extremes of Islamophobia and Islamophilia, as shown in Chapter 1, and they burden Western scholarship.

An outline of the major issues: religious faith and religionized politics

Based on the foregoing analysis, I put forward the contention that Islamism is not Islam although it is an ideology that has emanated from a politicization of

Islam. As I have made clear, this is a process culminating in the call for an Islamic state based on *shari'a*. In the text of the Qur'an, the Arabic terms *dawla*/state and *nizam*/order do not appear. These are newer Arabic terms introduced or adopted by Islamists. Since the Arab Spring in 2011 there has been a convenient, but most disturbing upgrading of Islamism in the West in a drive to undo the 'Islam bashing' seen in the aftermath of the 9/11 attacks. To this recent political correctness may be added the charge of a proclivity to political expedience, as practised earlier in Western Afghanistan policies. In May 12, 2010, an op-ed commentary by Maureen Down in the *New York Times* stated simply: 'everybody here (in Washington) lies'; she referred to 'serious flaws' and to how these were 'put to rest' while delaying the 'inconvenient truth'. It is unfortunate to see this Washingtonian kind of politics – a combination of 'delaying inconvenient truth' (*New York Times*) and an appeasement of Islamism – has also entered scholarship, as demonstrated in Chapter 1. The truth is that there is no such thing as radical Islamism and moderate Islamism. The truth is also that all Islamists share the goal of an Islamic *shari'a* state as well as everything else, except the resort to violence. They mostly disagree about the means to be employed for grabbing power. In my work I propose viewing non-violent Islamists who approve of electoral politics – wrongly regarded as 'moderate' – as 'institutional Islamists' (because they participate in institutions) in contrast to the violent jihadists.

In the course of my earlier research, conducted over the past 30 years in twenty different countries of the Islamicate, I established in a trilogy of books the interpretation of Islamism as a political religion that affects post-bipolar politics as a religious fundamentalism embedded in a global context (see Chapter 1, note 14). Islamist movements act in global networks, at home, in the Islamicate, as well as in the Islam diaspora in the West. Islamism is, however, not an outcome of post-bipolarity, and neither does it derive from local and regional conflicts, such as the Arab–Israeli conflict, as often wrongly stated by some Western scholars.

I share with other established scholars the view of an overall context for contemporary Islamic history. This context is Islam's internal crisis, which has been generated by the encounter with modernity.[7] Islamism grew from this context and has benefited from the popular discontent caused by the legitimacy crisis of the existing authoritarian regimes, coupled with the disruptive effects of failed development. All of these factors have contributed to the politicization of religion in the search for an alternative that provides more promising options for a better future. The secularization launched earlier, having failed, has been replaced by a process of de-secularization carried out by Islamism.

Under conditions of a combination of crisis and uncertainty Islamists seem to establish an appealing solution, '*the* solution'/*al-hall*. This slogan is embodied in the envisioned political order of the *shari'a* state. The religious slogan in Arabic, therefore, is '*al-hall huwa al-Islam*'/'the solution is Islam'. Islamists believe that the solution of all pending problems is their Islamist rule. For a proper understanding of these complexities in the context of the interplay between religion as a cultural system and politics, society and socio-economic development, I propose an analysis based on the following assumptions, to be tested as hypotheses in the present chapter. I put them in the following order:

First, Islam is a faith and a cultural system that determines a way of life for ordinary Muslims. Islam is not a framework for a *political* state order. Islamists believe in contrast that the order of the state based on a totalizing *shari'a* lies at the core of Islam. This is an invention of tradition which functions as an Islamist response to the exposure of Islamic civilization to a globalizing modernity. The backstory is a crisis of modern Islam. At the outset Islamist ideology reflects a defensive cultural response to modernity. It then moves into the offensive with a claim to remake the world. Islamists are challenged, but they turn the tables and emerge as the challengers. The call for a *shari'a* state is their challenge to the order of the world and to the international system of secular sovereign states.

Second, Islamism is a binary ideology (self-victimization based on a perception of The West vs. Islam) that with its binary world view creates obstacles for Muslims in the way of joining an international community based on democratic peace. In a nutshell: Islamism revives the claim for Islamic supremacy/*siyadat al-Islam*. By including this slogan in their logo, the Muslim Brothers acknowledge the claim to superiority. Islamism thus impedes peace between Muslims and non-Muslims on a basis of equality. Non-Muslims are perceived as minorities and are supposed to live as inferiors under Islamic *shari'a* rule. In this way minorities are denied basic individual human rights by the implementation of the *shari'a* on them as subdued unequals.[8] This Islamist agenda stands in contrast to democratic world peace for the twenty-first century based on pluralism. A civil Islam is a better alternative to Islamism for both Muslims and non-Muslims.

Third, a democratization of the states of Islamic civilization is a viable option, but an Islamization of democracy in a *shari'a* state is not. This is because an order which is in conflict with all values of the political culture of pluralism cannot be embedded in a global democratic peace. Islamists reject pluralism and power sharing. In contrast to Islamism, a liberal–civil Islam admits 'rethinking Islam' as grounds for religious reform that makes Islam compatible with the concept of democratic pluralism, having abandoned the claim to superiority. There exists no essential Islam that is beyond change. Islamists essentialize Islam.

Against any binary thinking I argue for an inclusive 'open Islam' (along the lines of Sir Karl Popper's 'open society') based on enlightened Muslim thought as discussed above. At issue are intra-Islamic tensions that relate to different understandings of Islam. There is no one essential Islam. In my earlier work I looked at Islamism in a scholarly manner through the lenses of Hannah Arendt, not, however, as an outsider, but with the spirit of a civil Islam. I was surprised to find that this phenomenon fulfils most of the criteria of Hannah Arendt's work on totalitarian movements.[9] I know it is politically incorrect to attribute a totalitarian character to Islamism, but take the liberty to state what I see as a Muslim scholar. Based on this knowledge, I cannot share the belief that Islamism can be accommodated in a democratic game, and will not buy into the thinking that looks at Islamism in terms of moderation. In the past we have seen Islamists – for instance, Hamas and Hezbollah – go to the ballot box, but refuse to comply with the values and rules of the political culture of democracy. Despite all these reservations I continue to argue for inclusion and engagement with Islamist movements, but this must be conditional on averting any switch from engagement to empowerment, as has happened in Egypt under the presidency of the Muslim Brotherhood by the Islamist Mohammed Morsi.

The pivotal question is: How can a totalitarian ideology on which Islamist movements rest be accommodated if the ideology itself is not revised by the Islamists themselves? If the pluralist culture of democracy is not negotiable, then what is one to do? Despite all odds I am against exclusion and therefore continue to argue for inclusion even of Islamists; but we must beware naivety, and act without illusions. I admit to not having a clear concept that combines inclusion and engagement with avoiding the empowerment of Islamism in the name of democratic participation. Unrestricted engagement would ultimately end up in a *shari'a* state that practises exclusion in the form of outlawing opposition as *kufr*/heresy. Islamists reject diversity in favour of a single united *umma* devoid of pluralism. A strong example is the contemporary Islamist sheykh Qaradawi, who speaks with contempt of all Muslims who fail to follow him. He calls them names such as those already cited in the Introduction: 'disbelievers, wrongdoers and truly wicked'. What kind of mindset of tolerance towards dissent is that?

Is institutional Islamism a moderation? Or is it a variant of religious fundamentalism?

In the Introduction to this book I rejected the term 'radical Islam' employed by some to identify the politicization of Islam, along with the biased association in many minds of Islam with violence. Instead I introduce a distinction between institutional and jihadist branches of Islamism. I keep to my intention to combat prejudice and am not astray when I argue against the view that institutional Islamists are 'moderate Islamists', just because they do not fight physical *jihad*. Nonetheless, I consistently keep my commitment for engagement with Islamist movements and against their exclusion. Is this manageable? How? The distinction between institutional and jihadist Islamism makes it easier to understand that the venture of engagement only applies to the institutional Islamists, without overlooking the fact that their reference to democracy is merely instrumental.

One cannot be silent about the fact that the Islamist pursuit of an Islamist *shari'a*-based state contradicts the basic values of democracy on a variety of counts. For Islamists, every means appears justified. Based on the study of political Islam cited above, I see barely a difference between Qutb's '*hakimiyyat Allah*'/'God's rule' and the order of the *shari'a* state envisioned by contemporary Islamists.

The separation between the public and the private in the polity is essential to any democracy. The objection to this separation by Islamism is of itself a statement that belies the contention of some pundits that the *shari'a* state may be seen as an expression of democratic constitutionalism. One must be accorded the right to counter these writers who are favourable to Islamism. In claiming this right I reject the self-deception practised in a 'flight of the intellectuals' – to use Paul

Berman's formula. The liberal Western third-worldist perception of Islamism, misconceived as a cry of the 'wretched of the earth' against the injustices of globalization, is utterly wrong. Islamism is rather an agenda for a reordering of the world along politico-religious lines. We are back to the issue of 'order in world politics', leaning on Hedley Bull and adopting the phrase from his work.[10]

If one adds to the notion of order the attribute 'democratic', then a question arises regarding the compatibility of the Islamist *shari'a* state with global democratization.[11] In the Kantian model of a democratic peace, only democratic states could be engaged in such a venture. Could Islamists as fundamentalists do so? According to the research carried out in the context of the 'Fundamentalism Project' at the American Academy of Arts and Sciences (research unfortunately mostly either rejected or simply ignored), religious fundamentalisms – such as Islamism as a variety of a global phenomenon – could result in political religions. A leading Egyptian Islamist, Hasan Hanafi, established the term *usuliyya*[12] in Arabic for such a political religion.

The term '*usuliyya*'/'fundamentalism' is a recent addition to Arabic and other languages of Islamdom, but the phenomenon itself predates the introduction of the word now used to designate it. Historically, the Movement of the Muslim Brothers[13] is the first fundamentalist movement in Islam. It was established in the year 1928 by Hasan al-Banna. The phenomenon called religious fundamentalism is the same as Islamism/*al-Islamiyya*, or as political Islam. In French the phenomenon is referred to with the term '*intégrisme*'. Although some Islamists accept the term '*usuliyya*', most of them prefer to speak of '*al-sahwa al-Islamiyya*'/'the Islamic awakening'.[14] This is also shared in the official ideology of the state propaganda of the Islamic Republic of Iran. We are dealing with a political concept based on religion. Therefore, I am in favour of viewing Islamism as the Islamic variety of religious fundamentalism. Religionized politics is not a true religious revivalism, as the term 'awakening' wrongly suggests. On this basis one can qualify scholarly contributions that take such a suggestion at face value as not useful, to say the least.

The conclusion is that those who view Islamism as a revivalism, with the implication that it indicates a *sahwa Islamiyya*/Islamic awakening, are misled. This view is baseless given the basic feature of Islamism as an Islamist invention of tradition. Great differences exist between true revivalism and modern Islamism.

Many authors not only fall into the trap of confusing the invention of tradition with revivalism, but also engage in a further confusion. The resulting contributions fail to understand Islam's predicament with modernity at all. This predicament is embedded in the process of globalization. Is it difficult to understand the contradiction that a tradition is being referred to, but in an invention that is itself imbued with modernity? Authors who think like this not only naively view the Islamists as revivalists, but also attribute to them the function of modernizers who 'engage with modernity'.[15] This is deplorable scholarship.

Religion, embedded in a cultural system, can never be explained in a reductionist manner. Despite the reference to globalization, I refrain from interpreting political Islam as a mere reflection of constraining structures. Independent of globalization, the framework of the Islamic tradition is fully considered and included in the politicization of Islam; it leads to the emergence of a defensive culture that then moves to become a mobilizing force in the shape of an activist revolutionary internationalism. The Islamist, even the jihadist, is a political man, but this male conceives of his self as a 'true believer' because the 'meaning of religion' matters to him. The reference to religion is neither a pretext nor instrumental.

If one considers the meaning of religion, one can avoid looking at Islamism as just a reflection of social reality. To say otherwise would be mere reductionism. For this reason it is not only silly, but entirely inappropriate to dismiss jihadism and its deeds as 'un-Islamic', as is often done. At issue is a combination of reality and meaning; it can be described in many ways. The established terms are: political Islam, Islamism, religious fundamentalism, *intégrisme* (the French term) or – as already stated – the preferable Islamist label *al-sahwa al-Islamiyya*/Islamic awakening, a formula coined by the Islamists themselves, even though the equation of fundamentalism and revivalism is utterly wrong.

In fact, there are many perceptions and interpretations of Islam, indicating the diversity within Islam. However, the 1.8 to 2 billion people of a global humanity of more than 7 billion share the same view of themselves, namely as belonging to the imagined community of *umma*. It is safe to state this common reality without falling into the trap of essentialism. Even Muslims in the diaspora in the West share this world view. Even though the *umma* is characterized by tremendous, ever-changing religious and cultural intra-Islamic diversity, there exists a Salafi belief in an essential Islam that is shared by those involved in the politicization of Islam. It is important to realize that Islamists are among the beneficiaries of globalization. They not only act at home, but enjoy the use of global networks that facilitate their activities in Europe and worldwide. In the diasporic ethnic culture they abuse the lack of integration of young Muslims to recruit and mobilize some of the latter for their goals, again in global networks.[16]

Islamism is a cultural essentialism that, in essentialist language, reads the ideology of an Islamic state based on *shari'a* and *jihad* into the Islamic past. The core issue of a remaking of world order was expressed by Sayyid Qutb. The mobilizatory ideology of Islamist movements was designed by Sayyid Qutb, the *rector spiritus* of Islamism.[17] The difference within Islamism refers to the means – participation in institutions or *jihad* – not to the goal, which is Islamic order and governance. As John Kelsay puts it:

> In its broad outlines, the militant vision . . . is also the vision of critics . . . they do not dissent from the judgment . . . that the cure . . . involves the establishment of Islamic governance . . . the problem of militancy is not simply a matter of objectionable tactics. The problem is the very notion of Islamic governance.[18]

The *shari'a* state is viewed as the manifestation of true and authentic Islamic governance. Here one can see the 'family resemblance' of all religious fundamentalisms despite their variations. This insight makes it possible to engage in analytical generalizations. In other words, one can apply a general concept in the study of religion to fundamentalism to view it as a general phenomenon. Yet, among the differences in religious fundamentalism, one finds some religious fundamentalists with universal claims and others who lack such universalism in their religious outlook. Hindu fundamentalists, for example, are concerned only with an imagined Hindustan as the territoriality of Hindu civilization, while the Islamist universalist imagination of '*dar al-Islam*'/'the abode of Islam' as a global entity is reflected in a world view that extends its agenda to all humanity. Qutb thus argued for an 'Islamic World Revolution' waged through a cosmic *jihad* that would bring about an Islamic world order. The 'Islamic state' with its 'Islamic order' is only one step in this direction and is not restricted to an imagined territoriality of *dar al-Islam*, but considered to be valid for the world at large.

In a nutshell, the universal Islamist claim resembles communist internationalism, albeit articulated on religious grounds. The visions of both are in conflict with the opposed idea of global pluralism and democratic peace. The Islamist vision for the world in the twenty-first century is based on the following major characteristics of political Islam (Islamism, or religious fundamentalism), which are:

- *Politically*: The concept of *din-wa-dawla*, i.e. interpreting Islam as a political religion prescribing a divine order for the state, which is to be a *shari'a* state run by an Islamist government.
- *Legally*: The extent to which the Islamist *shari'a* goes equally beyond the Qur'anic meaning of morality and beyond the traditional concept of Islamic law. Traditional *shari'a* is, in its origin, civil law for *mu'amalat*/interaction as it covers marriage, divorce, inheritance, etc., but is not for determining the order of the state. By contrast, the new *shari'a* is the totalizing state law of a political order. The new concept results from a politicization of religion within the framework of an invention of tradition.
- *Culturally*: The Islamist perception of all 1.8 billion Muslims as the Islamdom of one monolithic *umma*, reflecting their view of an imagined community that is supposed to share the exact same culture. Although this perception is not in line with reality, it serves to underpin Islamic internationalism. Uniformity of Islamic clothing (veils for women) and symbols (beards for men) in addition to other features serve to support the claim for one Islamic culture that rejects the cultural diversity, not only of the world at large, but also among Muslims themselves, denying them religious pluralism. Understood in this way, the *umma* tends to become a perception of a unified gated community. However, this gated community ('Islam under siege') is not the end objective of Islamism. Islamists want to transform the *umma* into a leader of humanity. Through proselytism this *umma* community is envisioned to expand to encompass the entire globe. This objective, in reality, is an expression not just of religious imperialism, but of a totalitarian mindset.
- *Militarily*: The Islamist reinterpretation of the traditional Islamic concept of *jihad*, which goes beyond the original Qur'anic and traditional meaning of *jihad* to become '*jihadiyya*'/'jihadism'. Unlike traditional *jihad*, the new

jihadism legitimates a war without rules – hence the proposed term 'irregular war' – in the sense of holy terrorism, but for unholy ends.[19]

Nuances exist within Islamist movements, so not all of these general features are shared by all of them in all varieties (although most of them are). The basic intra-Islamist differentiation relates to participation in elections versus the use of violence, and therefore I base the distinction between institutional Islamism and jihadist Islamism on this differentiation. The most prominent example of institutional Islamism is the Islamist AKP that had ruled Turkey since 2002. The most prominent case of jihadist Islamism is al-Qaeda. There exists a hybrid Islamism, for which Hezbollah stands in Lebanon. This movement has ministers in the government and members in parliament. At the same time its militias – composed of irregular warriors – continue to be in action. Hybrid Islamists go for both: maintaining a violent militia and sending some as members to parliament. They claim to be moderate, though at the same time they act as warriors. One may say: they want to have their cake and eat it.

AKP Islamists have proved that it is more promising to pursue Islamist goals through political participation in existing democratic institutions. These 'institutional Islamists' of the AKP continue the efforts of Turkish political Islam established by the *Selamet Partisi* in the early 1970s, but more successfully. Since the Arab Spring of 2011, AKP Islamists have been cooperating closely with the Movement of the Muslim Brothers and also claim leadership for the entire Middle East.[20]

In contrast to institutional Islamism, the opposite extreme, is jihadism. Jihadism is best represented by al-Qaeda and its networks. Despite this acknowledgement of a basic distinction between violence and moderation within Islamism, however, I dissociate the study of Islamism in general from its association with terror. I prefer to shift the focus from violence to the study of political order. Both brands of Islamism, institutional and jihadist, are a challenge to international security.[21] A clearer look at the perception of political order that emerges from the Islamist world view reveals this challenge.

The world view and ideology of Islamism: origins

It is common sense to state that all Islamists, regardless of the distinctions that exist among them, are Muslims. Moreover, they believe they are the true believers. In a benign spirit some Westerners not only dismiss the radical part of Islamism as deviant extremism, but also dissociate it entirely from Islam. Like the former British Home Secretary Jacqui Smith, they view it as 'un-Islamic'.[22] There need to be other ways to dissociate Islam and its followers from prejudice, apart from the extremes of exonerating and maligning, that do not involve tampering with facts. Some make the wrong assessment and engage in virtually excommunicating Islamists from the *umma* just to keep Islam clean. This is a reversal of the intolerant religious weapon of '*takfir*'/'excommunication' applied to fellow Muslims by Islamists themselves; to excommunicate the Islamists and place them outside Islam would be to act oneself like an Islamist. Like other Muslims, Islamists share a view of the world based on inherited religious tenets, but this world view can mutate in different directions even when articulated with the same religious symbols.

To understand the point at issue, it is helpful to refer to that fact of an inherited Islamic world view. This view of the world has been adopted by Islamism, but one encounters it there in a new shape.[23] The Islamist phenomenon is a political one, but it is also intrinsically imbued with a religious meaning. This is the hallmark of religionized politics and it must not be ignored. Failure to truly grasp this hallmark makes one liable to fall into the trap of reductionism and thus to derive fundamentalism from its social context. In other words, an analysis of political Islam that is based exclusively on sociological variables, with no reference to religion, would lead to wrong conclusions. In so arguing, I am not ignoring the social environment of fundamentalism, which is extremely important. I am only emphasizing that ideology and world view matter equally, and it is by no means an essentializing culturalism to take this into account. The religious fundamentalist has a political-social agenda, but he is not a secular man. In his self-perception this male sees himself exclusively as the 'true believer', and this is why the religio-ideological background, and the world view associated with that background, are as important for the analysis as is the social context. For Islamists, the commitment to political *shari'a* is the defining issue that determined who is a true believer and who is not.

Pursuant to the stated methodological requirement of looking at 'development' from the perspective of a multifaceted 'interplay' between various underlying constraints, I move back to the case of Islamism to pinpoint the different historical stages of its rise. In 1928, the first fundamentalist movement in the world of Islam, the Society of the Muslim Brothers, was established. The movement was equally involved in the politicization of general Islamic beliefs to advance the concept of a *shari'a*-based *'nizam islami'*/'Islamic order/government' and in practicing jihadism as terrorism. In this process the religious doctrine of *jihad* and the concept of *shari'a*/law were coupled and given a new meaning. In the course of this return of the sacred in a political garb, the traditional Islamic world view changed as well. This process is documented in the writings of the founder of the Muslim Brotherhood, Hasan al-Banna. Of course, the work of Sayyid Qutb has also spread around the world of Islam, far beyond the country of its origin, Egypt. Unlike the practitioner al-Banna, Qutb provided the Society of the Muslim Brothers with a firm ideological foundation. His ideas, combined with those of al-Banna, continue to be the cornerstone of Islamist ideology.[24] The recent transmitter of this continuity is the work of the TV Mufti Yusuf al-Qaradawi.

As earlier argued, there is no revivalism in the Islamism of al-Banna, of Qutb and of Qaradawi. Once again, their thinking is best understood as an invention of tradition. It follows that the ideologues and the practitioners of the Muslim Brotherhood are not clerics but modern Islamists. The Muslim Brotherhood Islamist president of Egypt has a PhD in engineering from a US university. In its formative years between 1928 and the execution of Sayyid Qutb in 1966, the

Movement of the Muslim Brotherhood established the seeds of this new direction within Islam, referred to here as an Islamic fundamentalism that is imbued with modernity but is against it. The Brotherhood was successful in spreading its ideology of a *shari'a*tized Islam far beyond the boundaries of Egypt, its country of origin. Until the Arab Spring, the Muslim Brotherhood remained at the fringe and failed to transform Islamism into a mobilizatory ideology. In the years from 1928 to 1967, therefore, political Islam was not the mainstream as it has been since the 1970s, in particular since the Arab Spring of 2011. The backstory is as follows.

The breakthrough for Islamism happened along the contemporary historical watershed of the Arab defeat in the Six-Day War of 1967. This generated a legitimacy crisis in the Arab world, with the result that the secular ideologies of Nasserism and Ba'thism that had prevailed until 1967 were de-legitimated. The de-legitimation gave a boost to Islamism in the Arab world.[25] From this cultural core of Islamic civilization, great spillover effects were generated which resonated throughout the Islamicate as the civilizational world of Islam and its Islamdom. At this point political Islam moved from the fringe to centre-stage, in this way becoming a mobilizing power.[26] This happened far beyond the Middle East, presenting the ultimate alternative of the 'Islamic solution' to the '*anzimat al-hazima*'/ 'regimes of defeat'. The solution presented is the order of a *shari'a* state for the whole world. Egypt continues to be the intellectual–religious core. The idea of the 'Islamic state' has been advanced as the basic challenge to the nation-state order throughout the world of Islam. The Arab Spring of 2011 gave the Islamist movements the greatest boost ever in this drive.

The family resemblance mentioned earlier between the ideological currents of the global phenomenon of religious fundamentalisms can be observed in the three major goals shared by all varieties of religionized politics: (i) de-secularization, (ii) the remaking of politics and political order, and (iii) the de-Westernization of society in an act of purification. In non-Western civilizations, these goals determine the overall framework of the new 'Revolt Against the West'[27] best grasped by Hedley Bull. The revolt is directed against Western values of cultural modernity. It is not just about Western hegemony. As will be argued later in this chapter, the criticism of US hegemony is legitimate, but the conclusion – to replace a *Pax Americana* with a *Pax Islamica* in the Islamist quest for a new world order – is not acceptable. The ideology (and world view) of Islamism gives top priority to challenging the existing secular world order, and thus to challenging the West itself. Islamist pronouncements reveal a cosmic binary world view. The reader is reminded of the religious sources of Islamism mentioned above. In the past these were the thoughts of Hasan al-Banna and Sayyid Qutb. In the present, Yusuf al-Qaradawi maintains their tradition and acts as the top sheykh-mentor of Islamism.

The overall contemporary context is a competition over the shape of the order of the world that takes place in a 'war of ideas'.[28] The effects of this are more important and more powerful than the terror of al-Qaeda itself. In Qutb's book *Ma'alim al-Tariq*/*Signposts Along the Road*[29] it is made clear that a two-step strategy is at work. The first is to establish *hakimiyyat Allah* for *dar al-Islam* in a replacement of the secular nation-state. In a second step, a reordering of the world at large is the target. This is considered to be a goal of the Islamic world revolution, to accomplish world peace under conditions of *siyadat al-Islam*/supremacy of Islam over the entire globe. The design for this is the idea of an Islamist internationalism. For Qutb it is a *farida*/obligation on every Muslim to adhere to a *jihad* in the modern understanding of a 'World Revolution of Islam' that pursues this agenda of remaking politics on a global scale. In this project, the formation of a *shari'a* state is the cornerstone. Asked to define Islamism in one phrase, one might say: Islamism is the political ideology of a *shari'a* state.

References to the political thought of Qutb and his vision of a 'World Revolution of Islam' to save the world from *jahiliyya*/pre-Islamic ignorance (i.e. '*kufr*'/ 'unbelief') are dismissed by some Western pundits and scholars by the remark that Qutb was a marginal figure. Western readers, therefore, need supporting evidence for the great significance rightly attributed to Qutb and to his thinking. After all, we are not talking about the radical Islam of an insignificant minority, but about a call for a new order for the state and for the world. This is what Qutb's thinking is all about. Let me refer to Roxanne Euben, an established expert on fundamentalism, who says: 'Qutb's prominence seems an accepted fact . . . Qutb's influence is undisputed.'[30] The impact of Qutb is not restricted to the jihadist al-Qaeda, but also extends to peaceful institutional Islamism as in the case of Turkey. Educated Muslims know this well and need no supporting reference to serve as evidence for Qutb's impact. At issue is not a sect within a radical sect, but a major direction in contemporary Islam of great pertinence to global politics. In David Cook's words, Qutb acted

> from Egypt, the very center of Arab Muslim political, intellectual and religious debate, and his life and achievements parallel and exemplify the rise of political Islam . . . he joined the Muslim Brotherhood . . . and quickly became its dominant intellectual figure.[31]

Today, Egypt continues to be the centre from which the very same – once clandestine – political–religious organization of the Muslim Brotherhood continues to act, particularly in the aftermath of the Arab Spring of 2011. This action is driven by the same Qutb demand: a remaking of politics in the pursuit of the *shari'a* order for the state and for the world at large. Most bizarrely, this Islamist agenda is billed as the democratization of the Middle East. Pundits seem to ignore, not just the jihadist backstory of the Muslim Brothers, but also the fact that al-Banna is the founder of jihadism. I was amazed to read in some of the post-Arab-Spring apologetic publications that al-Banna is the precursor of Islamist participation in democratic elections. To ignore and to be ignorant/*jahil* are the words – cognates – for this mindset. In Islam, *jahl*/ignorance ranks among the top sins with regard to knowledge. Qutb continued with vigour what al-Banna started to establish. Today's Islamists stand in this tradition – better, invention of tradition – and do their job in a variety of ways.

Finally, a note regarding Qutb. His world view and ideology are not an indication of Salafism because he was an Islamist, that is, not a traditionalist. His concept of an Islamic world order based on the *shari'a* state is a great challenge to the sovereign secular nation-state. This Islamist agenda generates competition, not only between the religious and secular order of the world, but also between *Pax Americana* and *Pax Islamica*. Due to this significance the next section is devoted to embedding Qutb's ideas in a general discussion on the order of the world.

The Islamicate: torn between incorporation into the Westphalian synthesis and the vision of a *Pax Islamica*

Islamists are very smart people who do their homework well. Only then do they turn to face their external enemies. Accordingly, Qutb's attention is directed first to the Islamic community itself; his aim was to dismantle Islamic conformism of the nineteenth century.[32] In the nineteenth century, faced with the expansion of international society based on the territorial sovereign state, Islamic traditional conformists had sought to establish a basis for the incorporation of Muslim territoriality to the modern order of the world. The most prominent of these *ulama* was the Moroccan thinker Ahmed Bin Khalid al-Nasiri (1835–1887), who developed a Muslim conformism that made it easier to deal with the changed circumstances of a global world order in Islamic terms. In contrast to him, Qutb, the *rector spiritus* of Islamism, rejected any accommodation; instead he developed an alternative, namely an Islamic world order based on the *shari'a* state to be accomplished in a project to remake the world. Qutb's thinking on this issue is documented in his two globally disseminated booklets *Signposts Along the Road* and *World Peace and Islam*. This is the most powerful Islamist formulation of the quest for an Islamic world order.

Qutb puts forward his belief in the following words: 'There is only one road to Allah, and no other beside it.' This road 'alone is the *nizam islami*/Islamic system and anything else is to be dismissed as *jahiliyya*/pre-Islamic ignorance.' The specific meaning of this contention in terms of world order is expressed by Qutb himself in other words:

> There is an Islamic territoriality which is *dar al-Islam* (the abode of Islam) that rests on the Islamic *shari'a* state . . . The borders of this *dar*/territoriality are determined by the prevalence of the *shari'a*; this is the criterion for determining what lies beyond it as *dar al-harb*/the house of war. The relations between Muslims and this non-Muslim territoriality are determined either by *qital*/war or *hudna*/temporal peace.

Then Qutb returns to addressing individual Muslims to emphasize his belief that 'the only home for a Muslim is the territoriality in which [*tuqam fihi al-shari'a*] *shari'a* is implemented'. For Qutb there exists 'only one *shari'a*'; he admits no diversity. The history of *shari'a* in Islam is, however, characterized precisely by diversity, not by a single monolithic *shari'a*. But the *shari'a* state is based on an Islamist *shari'a*. I discuss this as a challenge to the existing world order, although with some clear caveats about the red line not to be crossed if one accepts the prudent principle that the West should avoid offending Islam and Muslims. I certainly follow the Qur'anic ethics of *shari'a*, which is very dear to Muslims. What I oppose is merely the *shari'a*tization of Islam in an ideologically blinkered project. At issue is a challenge to the secular order of the state and the world which is not the *shari'a* prescribed in the Qur'an.

The overall context of the challenge to the existing order of the state and of the world is much broader than the Islamist agenda of a *shari'a* state. Two facts must be kept in mind: the first is the imposition of the modern world order based on the Westphalian synthesis on the non-Western rest of the world in the course of the past few centuries; the second, the decline of Europe in favour of *Pax Americana* since the Second World War. Since the late twentieth century and the turn to the new twenty-first century, non-Western peoples have been engaging in a process dubbed by Hedley Bull, the late Oxford scholar of international relations (who was the first to see it), a 'revolt against the West' (see note 27). This is a new kind of revolt that emerges in the context of a discrepancy between cultural particularisms and economic structural globalization. I place the Islamist revolt against the order of the nation-state and the order of the Westphalian synthesis in this overall context. One need not be an Islamist to lament against 'Westphalian Eurocentrism'. Today, such sentiments emerge from identity politics. Due to the heat of the debate, whatever terms you use, you enter a minefield.

For a scholar like myself who is poised to combine the study of conflict with cross-civilizational bridging in a spirit of conflict resolution, the complexities that exist can only be managed if distinctions and subtle nuances are established and consistently kept in mind. Thus, the order of the Westphalian synthesis needs not only to be freed from Eurocentrism, but also to be strongly dissociated from a pattern of Western hegemony, above all from *Pax Americana*. Otherwise the level of acceptance will be zero. No rational person can expect Muslims to accept being subject to American hegemony in the name of consent to an international order. If Westphalia and *Pax Americana* were the same, no criticism of Islamism would make any sense.

In recent years, contributions to the theme of this section have been published in abundance. I read most of them not only with great disappointment, but with intense dismay. However, there are some positive exceptions. Among the few laudable analyses that continue to be unique and valuable is the article by Daniel Philpott in *World Politics* cited above. This contribution stands in the highly respected international relations tradition of the late Hedley Bull, who studied world politics in terms of order. Philpott not only chooses the apt title 'The Challenge of September 11 to Secularism in International Relations', but also delivers what the title promises.[33] This is a rare quality! Myself a Muslim, I join Daniel Philpott and Hedley Bull in defending the Westphalian world order, but only after dissociating it from its European origins to make it a neutral model. In this venture I risk being defamed and even ridiculed by some reviewers as already mentioned in the Introduction (see note 5). In view of this minefield in a highly contaminated environment one has to couple the statement of an awareness of an Islamist 'threat' to this order with an effort at dissociating the analysis from others who address the same phenomenon, but with clearly different – I may add: not respectable – intentions. I have in mind analysts who engage not only in binaries and polarization, but also in partisanship favouring US hegemony in world politics. I mentioned a case at the beginning of the chapter, which will be elaborated upon in the next section. My thinking reflects adherence to enlightened Muslim thought as outlined as the beginning of this chapter.

Bottom line: the Westphalian synthesis is not *Pax Americana*

For a world order to be a house order that can be shared by the whole of humanity, one condition has to be fulfilled: the rejection of any claims to hegemony or supremacy. Following this mindset, I choose to prefer the Westphalian synthesis dissociated from its European origins to become a neutral model based on the Westphalian principles of an international system of sovereign states. I therefore reject the claims made for *Pax Americana* in a book by Charles Hill, *Trial of a Thousand Years: World Order and Islamism*, sponsored by the Hoover Institution and strongly endorsed in a highly questionable foreword by Fouad Ajami.[34] Both Ajami and Hill attack Islamism from this perspective. My take on Islamism is very different from the Cold-War-oriented one of the Hoover Institution. In contrast to Ajami and Hill, I argue for inclusion of Islamist movements, with the provision that one must beware of naively confusing or conflating engagement with empowerment.

I find it quite embarrassing to be taking issue with these two authors whom I once respected, as I know both in person and earlier had extraordinarily high regard for them both and for their work. Sadly, this attitude had to change after I read their new work on international order. Scholarly integrity stands above all considerations and compels me to dissociate my analysis from the recent work of these authors. I do this in clear terms without ambiguity, for the sake of the mindset identified toward the end of the preceding section.

Hill's book is published in the series 'Islamism and International Order' of the Hoover Institution at Stanford University. I met Hill at Yale in 2009 and shared with him in respect the critique of the Islamist threat to the secular world order. We were in agreement to defend this secular Westphalian order against Islamism. Years later I read this book of his with dismay, because the consensus reached seems to rest on foundations I do not share. I find it distasteful and even a misinterpretation to view *Pax Americana* as a continuation of the 'Westphalian order'. In their untenable venture, Hill and Ajami cross the red line I mentioned at the end of the previous section. Most dismaying is the binary thinking that places the issue in 'a trial of a thousand years'. Hill engages in the Christendom/caliphate binary – viewed as a duality with no further distinctions – to then add to it the new binary Islamism/world order. The modern world order has nothing to do with the revived classical binaries. I find myself not only in strong disagreement with this thinking, but also compelled to dissociate my work vehemently from these binaries that have been established as the Hoover approach to the study of what is called 'Islamism and international order'. What I am trying to do is to make the defence of the Westphalian order of the world compatible with a civil Islam that allows Muslims to accommodate to modernity. No Muslim can reasonably defend *Pax Americana*. If this US hegemony is equated with the Westphalian order, then

Muslims have the right to oppose it and I would be the last scholar to deny them this right. As a staunch critic of Eurocentrism I do not overlook the European origins of the international system. However, as a supporter of universally shared cultural modernity – of course in the sense of the al-Jabri project – I dissociate the Westphalian system (it has become global) from its modern European origins to 'stylize it into spatio-temporally neutral model'[35] with universal validity. This thinking separates me from Hill, Ajami and their Hoover-based Working Group on Islamism and International Order.

One should beware, not only of falling into the trap of the earlier Cold War mentality, but also of prejudice against Islam. There is no doubt that Islamism is a threat to the Westphalian world order, but this is neither a continuation of the old Cold War once fought by the US, with Islamism perceived as a replacement for communism, nor does this conflict relate to the binary Christendom vs. caliphate. This Hill–Ajami thinking amounts to an apologia for US wars in the Islamic world, which are deplorably presented under cosmetic make-up as 'the foreigner's gift' (the title of a book by Ajami on the Iraq War, discussed below). The present analysis takes a strong stand against Ajami's apologetics, seeking to be as balanced and impartial as possible. In recent years the debate on world order has revolved around US wars in the Islamic world, and it is therefore worth dwelling on this theme to rebuke the core aspect of the Hill–Ajami–Hoover approach.

In an effort to be sound in the judgement on the Iraq war I draw on Richard Haas, who is a knowledgeable and reasonable author. He seems more balanced than Ajami; he also served as a policy advisor in the White House and US State Department. Despite this, he succeeded in avoiding any apologism for US wars – not to speak of their distasteful description as a 'gift'. Haas rejected the Iraq war and wrote this in an important book that he concludes with this assessment: 'the second Iraq war was a war of choice that was ill-advised . . . wars of choice are thus largely to be avoided.'[36] In contrast, Fouad Ajami, whom I previously defended against critics as an enlightened Arab intellectual, now turns to defend *Pax Americana* in the least reasonable way. The alleged US 'gift' to the Iraqi people proved to be more of a curse as it was a poisoned 'gift'.

I am against Islamist anti-Americanism, but am not contradicting myself when I criticize and reject US hegemony in a *Pax Americana* for the world. It is deplorable that Charles Hill and Fouad Ajami defend at Hoover this *Pax Americana*, a project I could never approve. We do not need this hegemony. What the world needs instead is cross-civilizational bridging in a political culture for the world that is based on pluralism. This goal could never be accomplished with a *Pax Americana* – or, conversely, with a *Pax Islamica*. Islamists have the right to reject a world order that is reduced to *Pax Americana*, but not the right to demand in its place a *Pax Islamica* to replace US hegemony by an imagined Islamist one. In my view, the model based on the Westphalian synthesis of a world order of sovereign states could be considered a neutral order in the sense outlined above (see above *note 35 cit.*). In this sense it is an order that entail no hegemony, neither of the one nor of the other. This is why the Westphalian synthesis rightly underpins the UN Charter, which is based on universal tenets supposed to be acceptable to all.

I refuse to demonize Islamists and I reject a wholesale dismissal of their political thinking. The problem with Islamists is not their criticizing of US wars in the Islamic world, but the wrong conclusions they draw from their criticism. True, these US wars are evil and they do harm to Muslims. For this reason I do not share the binary thinking that one can detect in the work of Ajami and Hill. In my first reading of Fouad Ajami's book on the Iraq war, entitled *The Foreigner's Gift*, I disliked the apologetic overall tone, but I acquiesced to the unseating of the dictator Saddam Hussein. Nonetheless, the Iraq war was – as Haas put it – a war of choice, not of necessity. For ordinary Iraqis this US war was a curse. It was also a violation of the rules of the Westphalian synthesis, which respect the sovereignty of states. These rules can be overridden for humanitarian reasons, but not violated by wars waged for the *Pax Americana*. In a second reading of Ajami's book I became aware of some highly partisan and imbalanced implications of his presentation of a war of aggression as a 'foreigner's gift'. This is untenable. When this second reading was combined with reading Ajami's foreword to Hill's distasteful book, which justifies not only a *Pax Americana* but also a new Cold War (see below), I woke up and it became clear to me what is on the mind of Hill and Ajami. This is something of which I utterly disapprove. Now I am in a position to recognize that we – Hill and Ajami on the one hand, and the present author on the other – live in different worlds. I shall come back to these differences in the concluding section of this chapter to resume the debate on *Pax Americana* and the Westphalian order to support my criticism with quotes and more details.

Dissociating my work from any apologetics for *Pax Americana* and taking issue with those who defend US hegemony upgrades my critique of Islamism by giving it integrity. It is therefore very important to make quite clear that this is not about a reckoning with the apologetic work of Hill and Ajami. It is the issue itself, which is far more significant than any personal views. Unlike these two pundits I do not demonize Islamism. On the contrary, I do agree – although without any anti-Americanism – to the Islamist criticism of the US military incursions in the Islamic world. The difference is, however, that I do this in a defence of the principles of the prevailing Westphalian secular order of sovereign states, not to speak in favour of *Pax Islamica*. Since my thinking is free from any anti-American bias whatever, there is no contradiction when I criticize US wars and at the same time reject the political claims of political Islam to remake the world.

It is impossible to overemphasize the concern for credibility and the need for integrity. For this reason, I admit the following question: Is it hypocritical to support a universal order that emerges from Western civilization, while countering the efforts of the competing universalism of Islamic civilization to establish its own Islamist order? As a Muslim scholar committed to 'preventing the clash of civilizations'[37] and equally to the present secular world order, I think this question has to be faced squarely. In a spirit of civil Islam based on enlightened Muslim thought, I also admit this question: Is it hypocrisy to criticize the Islamist challenge of a *Pax Islamica* based on a *nizam islami*/Islamic order and at the same time to defend *Pax Americana* and its wars for US hegemony? In the search for proper answers we need a sound debate.

This quest has to acknowledge the need for an order of the world on which global politics rests. In this context I draw on the work of Daniel Philpott and Hedley Bull,[38] to both of whom I give credit for being among the very few international relations scholars who address and discuss the real issue, namely: world order and the challenge to remake the existing order of the world. In the article already cited, Philpott rightly says that Islamism 'challenges the authority structure of the international system. This . . . is the tradition behind al-Qaeda's attacks'. This authority structure rests, as Philpott continues, on 'the peace of Westphalia (that) marked a victory of the sovereign state'. With regard to the matter in point, the late Hedley Bull is the foremost authority in international relations theory. His work on world order is pivotal to the study of international politics. This concern is very different from the Hoover working group's approach to Islamism and international order. In my view Bull does a better job of elaborating on the issue, saying that '[i]nternational order is order among states . . . (the present) world political system, has been the expansion of the European states system all over the globe, and its transformation into a state system of global dimension' (see note 33). The Westphalian synthesis, which is at present under fire from Islamism, is indeed the origin of this world order, but it is by no means identical with the hegemonic order of *Pax Americana* nor with the colonial European past. Waging wars in the Islamic world is a disservice and should not be allowed as a justification for any world order whatever. I add to these insights the reference made above to Habermas's view on cultural modernity as cited above (note 35). My preference for the Westphalian synthesis is combined with the precondition that it becomes a neutral model dissociated from its European origins.

Prudent Muslim philosophers, such as the late Mohammed Abed al-Jabri, reject a thinking based on cultural particularisms and on authenticity. They argue instead for universally valid knowledge. Consequently, they accept an order of the world based on universal law and on principles of universal law that are shared by all.

To support this mindset, a reference to medieval Islamic rationalism that provides the paradigm is helpful. In order to take issue with the claimed authenticity of the *shari'a* state I draw on this Islamic universalism, combining its thinking with references to basic facts. Such a position can only be tenable and maintained if it is credible. The conclusion is that any defence of the Westphalian order would become incredible if it, first, follows the Hill–Ajami–Hoover approval of *Pax Americana* and second, if it fails to dissociate this order from its European origins as discussed above.

For a moment I return to the overall world-historical context addressed at the outset to touch on the undisputed historical fact of the Islamicate as an Islamic civilization that not only predated the Western one, but also had its own pattern of expansion. The Islamicate dominated major parts of the world from the seventh to the seventeenth century. The rise of the West changed the world and also the balance that had existed until then. In parallel with a military revolution that brought to a halt the global Islamic *jihad* project, the West was created as an expanding civilization. The greatest world-historical pain caused by this novelty for Muslims was the fact that their expansion was replaced by the European expansion. This is the real history of two models for globalization; one was partly successful, but fell short of its goal (Islamic expansion), while the other (the West – not Christianity) succeeded in mapping the entire globe.[39]

On the grounds of these facts it is utterly wrong to mobilize Christianity against the caliphate to address the present conflict in a 'trial of a thousand years' as Hill does. This pundit confuses modern Western globalization with the old Christendom–caliphate dichotomy.

The chief problem today is the Western hegemony that also maps the Islamic world. I cannot emphasize enough how important it is to make clear that 'cultural modernity', on which the universality of the modern world rests, is something that must be distinguished from Western hegemony (see note 35). The universality of 'cultural modernity' (Habermas) admits – in principle – democratic pluralism and global civil society for all civilizations on equal footing. As yet, however, this is only the model, not the reality. Westerners and Muslims who confuse the secular and rational principles of 'cultural modernity' with the hegemony of the West are not only wrong, but also end up in an awkward line of reasoning. An amusing example of this kind of thinking is the conclusion of a Muslim thinker, Sardar, that Enlightenment Cartesianism is an 'epistemological imperialism'. This thinking is laughable, but it is extended by some others to the Westphalian order itself. If you approve this order then you are 'the accused'. This is why there is a need for criticism in the pursuit of epistemological clarity. This criticism has to be politically extended to those who confuse the Westphalian synthesis with the hegemony of *Pax Americana*. I strongly reject this confusion, as much as I reject the other one that equates rationalism with 'epistemological imperialism'.

To shed light on the sources of the thinking developed in this context, I draw again on the work of the late Mohammed al-Jabri and his Islamically founded rationalism. He not only was among the great rationalists of modern Islam, but also engaged in the 'enlightened Muslim turn'.[40] In this line of reasoning it is possible to criticize Western hegemony and – at the same time – to maintain the universality of modernity that includes the principles of the secular world order based on modern rationality. This order can be dissociated from its European origins to make it 'spatio-temporally a neutral model', as established earlier in this chapter. As has already been stated, reality is yet not in line with this model, but this is no reason to dismiss the world order. In a similar vein one can argue that the violations of human rights in US policies[41] can never serve as a reason for dismissing these rights as such. US foreign policy is one thing and universal human rights are another! It is no contradiction to reject the one and approve the other. Likewise, in this line of reasoning Muslims critical of US hegemony can approve the Westphalian synthesis without being caught in contradictions.

Further, in the same line of reasoning it is possible to dismiss the Islamist *shari'a* state in favour of the secular nation-state that is challenged by Islamism. Contemporary developments paved the way for advancing the demand for that divine order to a popular public choice against the nation-state. Despite my dispute over 'clash' rhetorics and the related disagreement, I fully agree with Huntington that 'modern democracy . . . is democracy of the nation-state and its emergence is associated with the development of the nation-state'.[42] To argue for the universality of this state pattern is to endorse the universality of secular democracy. Now, it is this very modern world order that Islamists reject. The emergence of this order goes back to the Peace of Westphalia of 1648. The pre-eminent sociologist and social historian Charles Tilly comments on this issue in an early study that remains of seminal importance: 'over the next three hundred years the Europeans and their descendents managed to impose that state system on the entire world. The recent wave of de-colonisation has almost completed the mapping of the globe into that system.'[43] Continuing his research, Tilly writes 15 years later: 'Something has changed in the extension of the European state system to the rest of the earth', adding: 'Europe created a state system that dominated the entire world. We live within that system today. Yet the world outside Europe resembles Europe no more than superficially.'[44]

Any siding with the secular nation-state against the *shari'a* state has to acknowledge that this modern state pattern is not yet well established in most countries of non-Western civilizations. It is a fact that most nation-states in the Islamic world are nominal, sometimes even failed states. The conclusion is that nation-states in non-Western civilizations lack substance. They are only in a nominal sense nation-states, really quasi-states.[45] In international relations research, the expansion of the West is presented as an expansion of international society. Most parts of Asia and Africa were first colonized and then emerged during their post-colonial development as sovereign states. Through de-colonization, former colonies obtained sovereignty, nominally evolving into nation-states in international politics. Thus they became legally mapped into the modern international system of sovereign states. In this development the Islamic world, though an Islamicate civilization viewed as the territory of *dar al-Islam*, was no exception. Muslim people constitute an Islamdom characterized by cultural diversity, but the Islamicate has no more than an imagined territorialized community. In reality the Islamicate is subdivided into a great number of nation-states.

Earlier, in the course of de-colonization, Muslim leaders made an effort to accommodate the new international environment by joining the international system of nation-states. Regrettably, the new states were mere nominal states. Islamists of today want to reverse this historical process through a return to glory: *Pax Islamica* as an imperial power.[46] This mindset that undergirds a Muslim public choice makes it necessary to address the envisioned Islamist reversal of the prediction of 'the end of history' into a demand for 'the return of history'. For this reason I shall take issue with Francis Fukuyama's belief in a triumph of Western values. The rise of political Islam since 1928 compels us to question this triumphalism.

At the outset, when the Movement of the Muslim Brotherhood was established in 1928, Islamism was marginal. Only in the aftermath of the 1967 war did the consequences of that war generate a development that was favourable to the growth of Islamism.[47] This development reached a height after 1989 (the end of bipolarity) and culminated in 2011 (the Arab Spring), with the result, at the time of writing in late 2012, that Egypt, Libya and Tunisia are ruled by Islamists. This development contradicts Fukuyama's forecast. The consequences of the fall of the Berlin Wall (1989) cannot be imposed on Islamdom. This became crystal clear in 2011. This global perspective of Islamic civilizational self-assertion seems not to be well taken in the West, where public views are determined by powerful pundits. They indiscriminately talk about 'democracy' and 'transition' while ignoring the reality on the ground.

Islamism and the Western triumphalism of 'the end of history'

The Islamist vision for the future rests on Islamic nostalgia based on Islamist collective memories. The past of an imperial glory of Islamic civilization provides an orientation for an imagined *shari'a* order that expresses the Islamist demand for a return of history. This demand defies the already contested Western triumphalism of 'the end of history'[48] based on the perception of a victory for Western values. One needs to reconstruct the overall historical context to understand this well. I will therefore provide a brief summary of the backstory, to support the argument with historical evidence.

The process of decline of imperial Islamic civilization in favour of nation-building resulted in the creation of new entities that are only nominally nation-states. In reality these are 'tribes with national flags'.[49] The new nation-states in the Middle East are not underpinned by the necessary institutional structures, nor do they have the political culture associated with nation-states. In addition, they have very poor legitimacy. This is not, however, *prima facie* evidence for the allegation that the model of nation-state building itself is wrong.

Islamism rejects the modern order of a nation-state. It views it as an imposition on the Islamicate and envisions its replacement by the *shari'a* state. In the footsteps of the late Qutb, the leading Egyptian Islamist of today, the Muslim Brother Yusuf Qaradawi, regarded as Qutb's heir, addresses the issue by rejecting nation-building altogether. In his three-volume *Hatmiyyat al-Hall al-Islami/The Islamic Solution* (see note 6) Qaradawi dismisses wholesale any adaptation or adoption based on cultural borrowing from Western civilization. At the top of the list of these rejections are democracy and the nation-state. This dismissal is pronounced in the name of purification and authenticity.[50] In total ignorance about political economy, Qaradawi focuses on religion and culture, blaming the '*hulul mustawradah*'/'imported solution' for all ills resulting from the failed development in the Islamic world.

As a scholar who in recent decades has focused his academic life on cultural analysis, I am the last to question the significance of religion and culture in the development of state and society. Nonetheless, I follow Alan Richards' and John Waterbury's seminal work *A Political Economy of the Middle East* and (as I stated in the Introduction) share with them their answer to the question 'Is Islam the solution?', namely, 'the answer is no'. Today, the core problems pertain to economic development, not to culture. To support their 'no' answer, Richards and Waterbury add: 'Islamists do not offer any intellectual theory of economics founded on reasonable assumptions.' Instead, they, the Islamists, believe 'that the imposition of Islamic Law . . . offers clear, coherent and straightforward solutions to the problems facing Muslim societies.'[51] Richards and Waterbury do not share this belief; neither do I.

The misleading argument of viewing adoptions from others as *hulul mustawra-dah*/imported solutions serves not only as a tool for purification, but also as a formula that underpins the attitude of self-victimization. Islamists engage in putting all blame on the West to make it responsible for all ills in the Islamic world. On these grounds Qaradawi argues for a wholesale 'healing' de-Westernization to purify Islam of the Western virus. For him, this purification is a precondition for the Islamization of the entire world, the 'solution' that Qaradawi presents. However, the envisioned return to *shari'a* viewed as a return to Islam is not as authentic as Qaradawi and other Islamists contend.

The real world of Islam is not the monolith Qaradawi has in mind. He himself is a Sunni Islamist and there exists another competing call for an Islamic solution, namely a Shi'ite one, coming from the Iranian Revolution that took place in 1979. Having generated spillover effects all over the Islamic world, Iran has been able to stretch its Shi'ite networks to reach out to Iraq, Syria and Lebanon. Of course, there have been sectarian forces constraining the Iranian impact. The competition between the Sunni and the Shi'ite elements of Islamic fundamentalism is based on deep sectarian trenches within the Islamicate.[52] The Islamic Revolution in Iran could not overcome existing diversity, nor will Qaradawi be able to do so. Nonetheless, Islamism in Iran not only successfully demonstrated that Islamists are able to seize power and establish an 'Islamic state', it also showed the ability to advance a state involved in proliferation to become a nuclear power capable of threatening the West.[53] On these grounds, the claims that are also being put forward for a remaking of politics on a global scale become more powerful. However, the Arab Spring dealt Iran – the ally of the Alawi–Shi'ite Assad regime in Syria – a great blow, as will be discussed in more detail in Chapter 4. To this may be added the fact demonstrated in the Iranian case that Islamists promise but fail to deliver what they promise: development, freedom and prosperity. Nonetheless, the example of North Africa supports the statement made by François Burgat: 'The revolution of Khomeini breathed life into Islamist movements everywhere.'[54] One has to beware, however, of rhetoric – breathing life means reinforcing an ongoing process, not putting a new life into it. The Islamic Revolution in Iran was and continues to be a Shi'ite event, and this sets limits to its impact. It strengthened the development of Islamism, but did not give birth to political Islam. Islamism existed earlier in a powerful Sunni variety that developed a half century before. Today – with the sole exception of Bahrain – the Arab Spring of 2011 is an exclusively Sunni phenomenon. The Sunni Islamist Turks of the AKP, not the Shi'ite Iranian Islamists, are the beneficiaries of the Arab Spring.

What matters here is the claim of a return of history. What does it mean with regard to the political order of the state and the world? A proper answer again requires engagement in further distinctions and nuances. Note that traditional Islamic universalism is not the nineteenth-century pan-Islam, nor the contemporary Islamist political internationalism directed against the present international system. The Islamist ideology and its world view, whether Sunni or Shi'ite in character, politicizes the traditional Islamic claim to universality. Religious neo-absolutism is elevated to an internationalism paired with a world-historical nostalgia. The subject matter of this nostalgia is collective memories about the glory of the Islamicate in the past, to be restored in a 'return of history'.

Given this backstory, the prediction of the 'end of history' by the famous political scientist Francis Fukuyama, who has my great respect, seems to have been premature, to say the least. When Fukuyama wrote his book *The End of History* he was thinking of a victory of Western values to prevail following the breakdown of communism. It did not happen. It is unfortunate that he does not discern the process in which old Islamic doctrines and precepts are presented by Islamism in an invention of tradition. This process not only rekindles the classical historical tensions between Islam and the West as civilizations, but also claims to remake the world in parallel to the thriving Islamist nostalgia. This is a call for the return of glorious Islamic history on the grounds of *Pax Islamica*. Despite all the references to the past, however, this is modern history and not Charles Hill's 'trial of a thousand years'. The modern Islamist revolt against the West is breathing new life into the historical collective memories related to a competition between rival models of expansion and globalization, as grounds for a remaking of world order.

Islamism invents itself and constructs a lot of myths, but the civilizational competition it generates over the order of the world is not 'constructed', as wrongly suggested by some politically correct scholars. At issue is a real political conflict. The reality is that Islamism presents a quest for a new world order based on religion. This agenda employs a reference to history that involves Islam and Christian Europe, but it is not the history Charles Hill seems to have in mind. The accurate, knowledgeable and telling identification of these issues by John Kelsay provides a much better analysis, summed up in words that deserve to be quoted in full:

> Much of the contemporary return to Islam is driven by the perception of Muslims as a community . . . having a mission to fulfill. That this perception sometimes leads to conflict is not surprising. In encounters between the West and Islam, the struggle is over who will provide the primary definition of world order. Will it be the West, with its notions of territorial boundaries, market economies, private religiosity, and the priority of individual rights? Or will it be Islam, with its emphasis on the universal mission of a transtribal community called to build the social order founded on the pure monotheism natural to humanity? The question for those who envision world order, then, is, 'Who determines the shape of order, in the new international context?' The very question suggests a competition between cultural traditions with distinctive notions of peace, order, and justice. It thus implies pessimism concerning the call for a new world order based on notions of common humanity.[55]

This is a different and highly nuanced narrative of history with an effort at social scientific conceptualization that is by far more helpful than the 'trial of a thousand years' thinking of Charles Hill. At issue is globalization and the use of collective memories in response to its effects. In the past, Islamic expansion was the first world-historical model of globalization, though it was not fully successful in mapping the entire world into its territoriality, as did European expansion. Still, the effort at a globalization of the 'Islamicate' in medieval history continues to be a historical fact. However, the reference by Kelsay to the Islamic caliphate that failed to become the dominant order of the world does not confuse the old order with the new one, as Hill seems to do.

Today, the West continues to prevail in the world at large, politically, economically and also militarily, but its values are not only culturally questioned, they are rejected. Fukuyama's assumption about 'the end of history' as a victory of European values has proved wrong. The return of the history of civilizations after the collapse of the East–West bipolarity is a backlash against the ideologically driven repression of history and of culture of the Other. Non-Western people, Muslims among them, once considered by arrogant Westerners as 'people without history', are now rising in a new 'revolt against the West'.[56] Unfortunately, this return of history has the pitfalls of anti-Westernism, anti-Americanism, and in some cases even an evil antisemitism.[57] Therefore this trend is *not* a sign of a promising future, as it ignites tensions and hatred that lead to conflict and even to violence. To relate this development to the theme of this book, one needs to point at the Islamist claim that the *shari'a* state indicates a return of history in the sense outlined above of a return to Islamic glory. If the argument of this chapter holds, that the *shari'a* state is not the classical caliphate, then it becomes clear that the claim of a return of history is based on a bogus idea; it is not a return to the classical order of the caliphate, it is a novelty. This is why I totally reject Charles Hill's historical construction of a 'trial of a thousand years', not just because it is not in line with the real history, but because of its strong bias. Hill not only in general confuses different periods and stages in history, but also specifically confuses the real history of Islam and the tradition invented by Islamists. Thus, he fails conspicuously, even though he addresses the right question: 'Which world order?' His answer (endorsed by Ajami in the foreword), which is '*Pax Americana*', is extremely distasteful as well as ridiculous, especially when given at a time in which prudence outlaws any advocacy of a hegemonic order. *Pax Americana* is nothing other than a hegemony.

Conclusions: which world order? The Westphalian synthesis, *Pax Americana* and political Islam in competition. The need for a democratic world peace

This chapter has broken fresh ground for discussing Islamism's international pertinence in a global context. Given the Islamist vision of an Islamic world order based on religious tenets, one can state the existence of an Islamist internationalism that entails a design for remaking the world. This is not the traditional Islamic concept of order, namely the classical caliphate. Nor is it the nineteenth century's pan-Islamism. This chapter has brought Western and Islamist misconceptions into the debate and has corrected erroneous views. These earlier concepts are often conflated in Western scholarship with the new vision of a *shari'a*-based world order advanced by Islamism. I have selected Charles Hill's book *Trial of a Thousand Years*, sponsored by the Hoover Institution, as a strong example to demonstrate basic misconceptions in order to correct them, also in an exemplary manner.

The biggest mistake is the confusion of the past with the present. Current Islamist responses have nothing to do with the 'rise of Islam' in the seventh century, as Hill contends. In these conclusions I look at the Hill–Ajami–Hoover approach,[58] not just to correct common mistakes, but also to make clear that the establishment of a *Pax Americana* in international relations as 'a revitalization of the procedurally based Westphalian state system' is a damaging effort. A rational debate on world order that is also accepted by Muslims cannot be run this way. Hill's drawing of centuries-long historical lines to outline 'three world historical events . . . most consequential . . . affecting the problem of world order' is a highly arbitrary undertaking. In a prejudiced manner, Hill refers to 'the rise of Islam' in a derogatory way as one of these three 'events' identifying a threat. By 'event', Hill means this: 'Islam with its great Arab conquests . . . These were followed by an establishment of an international caliphate.' Then he jumps – again with no supporting evidence (no footnoting at all to supply the allegations) – over centuries up to the present to state the problem in these words: 'Today's problems of Islamism and world order is that Islam . . . has been . . . unsuccessful and, in part, adversial.' One is compelled to liken the Islamist's confusion of *Pax Americana* and the Westphalian order of states with Hill's approach, which does the same. Hill speaks as Islamists do of 'world order and its chief protector – the United States'. He defends *Pax Americana* for the sake of a stable world order; Islamists oppose it.

Of course, there is a backstory of Islamism – which is not to be equated with Islam. Islamism is a current issue that has not fallen from the void, but its backstory is certainly not the one Hill tells us in a highly deficient narrative that evinces an obvious lack of the required knowledge. It is true that Islamism divides, rather than unifies, humanity, but it is also a fact that ordinary Muslims are not Islamists. A spirit of civil Islam allows – indeed encourages – bridging efforts to jointly build up foundations for a democratic peace on a global scale for all humanity. The threat to world peace is posed by Islamism; it is also a threat to intra-Islamic peace. In the pursuit of *Pax Americana* the US waged a war in Iraq that ended a Sunni dictatorship to replace it by a Shi'ite one. This is not a contribution to democratic world peace. The US promise of liberation resulted in a situation in Iraq in which Muslims kill one another. Is this the 'foreigner's gift' to Iraqi Muslims? What they need is not subordination to a US 'center of gravity', as Hill puts the issue in strategic terms, but to learn in their own way how to dissociate their religion from Islamist *shari'a* politics, in order to address the real issues underlying the crisis of their civilization alluded to earlier.

It is true that Islamists have engaged in stigmatizing their critics as purveyors of xenophobia and Islamophobia. This will be the theme of Chapter 6, with which the present book concludes. To avert this instrumental use of Islamophobia by Islamists, Western scholars are advised to beware of a mentality that contributes to a continuing of the old Cold War as a war against Islam and Islamism. The sincere misgiving that lies behind this warning is underpinned by my reading of the deplorable Ajami–Hill volume from the Hoover 'Working Group on Islamism and World Order' (cited above). In his foreword to that volume, Ajami acknowledges a view that leads to this suspicion, as he says precisely: 'The cold war . . . guided a good deal of Hoover's work . . . no sooner had communism left . . . than a huge challenge arose . . . the Islamic world.' He then adds, outrageously and with no hesitation, 'Islamists are strangers and determined enemies. They war against world order and against Pax Americana that guards peace.' Such a critique of Islamism guided by a binary mindset engages in demonization and loses all legitimacy. Even worse follows with the confusion between US hegemony and world peace alongside the equation of *Pax Americana* with the Westphalian synthesis.

This demonization combined with the erroneous equation of a world peace based on the Westphalian synthesis with the hegemonic order of *Pax Americana* does great disservice. Hill himself states unambiguously that 'world order and its chief protector – the United States' are the issue. Not only do I strongly contradict; I argue to the contrary with vigor. In my view, democratic world peace should never be equated with US hegemony. A staunch critic of Islamism, I distance my work from the mindset of the Hoover 'Working Group on Islamism and International Order' as documented in Hill's book and Ajami's foreword. I and the Hoover group may share the purpose of taking issue with the order that Islamists envision, but we do it with two completely different mindsets. I would never, ever defend *Pax Americana* against Islamism; and if I did, then my criticism of the Islamist *shari'a* state would be de-legitimated and become trash. The Kantian world peace based on cosmopolitan law I defend is something entirely different from the hegemonic peace criticized here, be it *Pax Americana* or *Pax Islamica*. My approval of a world order based on the Westphalian synthesis presupposes looking at it – as discussed above and referenced in note 35 – as a neutral universal model. This approval rests on Islamic humanism,[59] not on a submission to the West and to its hegemony.

A basic conclusion of this chapter is that a world order acceptable to all humanity under conditions of cultural diversity and plurality of religions has to be neutral: that is, not only religion- and culture-blind, but also free of hegemony. For this reason, *Pax Americana* and *Pax Islamica* are not suitable orders, as they are both concepts of a world order based on hegemony, whether real or envisioned. Unlike both Hill and Ajami, I count myself as a person who – in the tradition of Ernst Gellner – was among the few scholars able to understand fundamentalism, and to criticize it with integrity. In my case this is done in a mindset committed to enlightened Muslim thought in particular and to enlightenment in general.[60] To use Islamism as a cover for replacing communism with a new enemy in a new Cold War would be to do a disservice to preventing 'the clash of civilizations' in favour of democratic peace in the Kantian sense.[61] To avoid the self-fulfilling prophecy that the West needs a new enemy, one has to beware of conflating Islamism and Islam. I find this spirit lacking in the questionable Hoover approach to studying Islamism and the international order, despite its use of the notion 'Islamism'. And the Hoover volume is only one example of many.

To really end the 'clash of civilizations' one needs to engage in a de-legitimation of Islamism by a civil Islam, but one should never wage a new Cold War, Hoover style – not even against Islamism. It is better and more promising to address the sources of tensions in a spirit of bridging guided by the principles of conflict resolution. I do not deny that an inter-civilizational conflict exists, but I do not see any solution in a *Pax Americana* that legitimates US hegemony, or at least, none acceptable to Islamdom. *Pax Americana* is the problem, not the solution. A dialogue for bridging requires a new policy that can only be successful if achieved in the form of conflict resolution. This task cannot be accomplished if the West fails to see the distinction between the tolerant religion of Islam (faith and ethics) and the totalitarian ideology of Islamism.[62] For the West to continue to maintain its hegemony over Islamdom would add further fuel to the fire. Under these conditions, Islamism, with its quest for *shari'a* order for the world, would continue to thrive and increase its constituency, with no democratic peace in sight.[63]

At the present crossroads of world history the West has two options: either to take its own liberal values at face value and establish credibility in a dialogue with Islamdom, or to fall into an opportune policy that replaces the earlier close collaboration with the toppled authoritarian rulers by a new one with the empowered Islamists. The latter is already happening in Egypt, as will be shown in Chapter 4. The alternative partner to Islamism, and a better and more appropriate one, would be those Muslims of the valuable tradition of Islamic humanism and rationalism that today is continued in the form of enlightened Muslim thought. In the course of the Arab Spring, Western policy-makers unfortunately seem to prefer to do business with institutional Islamism, labelled as 'moderate', just for convenience.

No cross-civilizational bridging can be achieved if the real conflict between the democratic order of pluralism vs. the divine order of *shari'a* state is overlooked or simply ignored. Western policies are doomed to failure if they continue the self-defeating self-deception of an 'Islamist democracy'. The conclusion drawn from these first three chapters of the present book is that the *shari'a* state is no democracy. There can be an ethics of government based on a reform Islam compatible with democracy, pluralism and civil society – of course – in the context of religious reform and cultural change,[64] but no 'democratic Islamism', the latter being truly a contradiction in terms. An authentically moderate Islam can only be a civil Islam, which is not to be confused with Islamism.[65] Civil Islam does not preach an ideology in the pursuit of an Islamic *shari'a* state, the political order envisioned by the Islamist movements. A world order based on the idea of democratic world peace is compatible with civil Islam. The ascendance of the *shari'a* state gives the lie to the frequent wishful thinking of some Westerners that the post-Islamic era has arrived. It is a misconception that the decline of jihadist Islamism heralds an end of Islamism. Far from it, in reality Islamism is thriving, thus there is no post-Islamism.

In drawing these conclusions I find myself anticipating the theme of wishful thinking and self-deception, which will be addressed in the next chapter. I would not be surprised to see a policy of *Pax Americana* that for convenience accommodates the rule of Islamism in a *shari'a* state to its own needs and interests.

The signs of this scenario have become clear by the end of 2012. In the past, all of us were exposed to the many opportunistic references in US foreign policy to democracy and human rights. Parallel to these rhetorical proclamations, which in the past were belied by US practice, the US was doing business with dictators and authoritarian rulers in Islamdom. Therefore, it is most important to underline some clear distinctions. In addition to the one between Islam and Islamism, there is also the other one between the Westphalian synthesis (updated by the revival of the Kantian utopia of democratic peace) and the binary policies of *Pax Americana*. Based on these distinctions I conclude that the hegemonic order of *Pax Americana* is neither the Westphalian synthesis nor a democratic peace. One loses credibility if one rejects *Pax Islamica* merely to replace it by *Pax Americana*. Neither is desirable. Islamism is a vision of a hegemony in reverse. Islamists are right when they criticize *Pax Americana*, but wrong when they present their alternative, *Pax Islamica*. The argument of this chapter has been that these competing concepts of order are detrimental to the democratization of the Middle East and North Africa. The people of that region did not take to the streets to support hegemonic rule; they were fighting for freedom and the fulfilment of their urgent social and economic needs to improve their daily lives.

Finally, I return to the core theme of his chapter, political order, to dissociate the analysis not only from *Pax Americana*, but also from the work of those less knowledgeable and less benign pundits who identify Islamism with terror. They overlook the fact that Islamism is about the order of the state and the world, not about violence, the latter being marginal and merely a means employed in a political pursuit. All Islamists, regardless of whether they are jihadists or non-violent, are in agreement among themselves that what they are fighting for is the *shari'a* state. In this understanding, Islamism is one variety of the global phenomenon of religious fundamentalism. Drawing again on the work of the American Academy of Arts and Sciences, I remind the reader of the research-based fact that an envisioned 'remaking of politics' is the driver of all variants of religious fundamentalisms.[66] Islamism is only one variety of this global phenomenon, though a powerful one. The major distinction within Islamism relates to how to accomplish the political goal of a *shari'a* state, not the choices between moderation and radicalism. Thus, the intra-Islamist dispute is about jihadism in contrast to the approval of political participation in institutions in order to seize political power peacefully.

Of course, there are hybrid forms of Islamism. But when it comes to the political goal at issue, namely to demand a 'leading role for Islam in government' (see p. 75 *note 1 cit.*) in terms of the *shari'a* state, then there are no radicals in contrast to moderate Islamists. This is a mere fact in a reality that I neither invent nor can be silent about. Of course, I acknowledge the existence of grey areas between the two, but nevertheless I stress that the core distinction between jihadist and institutional Islamists relates to the means, not to the agenda itself. Grey areas are relevant for a policy dealing with Islamism, but they are not important for a careful study of the political order Islamists envision. Those who not only ignore this commonality, but polemically reject it as 'lumping Islamists together', are fooling themselves. Fooling should never replace proper knowledge.

4 *Shari'a* and Islamism in the 'Arab Spring'

From the promise of a blossoming spring to a frosty and lethal winter

The Arab Spring conveniently opened a delicate window of opportunity for the well-connected Islamist movements in the Arab Sunni-Muslim world. In the past, when these movements were still in opposition, their basic slogan of oppositional politics in a crisis-ridden environment was 'Islam is the solution'. The slogan was translated into a politics on which their demand for '*tatbiq al-shari'a*'/ 'implementation of the *shari'a*' rests. This is their solution to the crisis. The Arab Spring helped these movements to move centre-stage and finally to seize power in the context of a 'democratization', the meaning of which has been reduced to 'balloting'. Does *shari'a* promise a spring?

The notion of a spring brings to mind the most beautiful season of the year. Its use in politics – supposedly as a feature of a political phenomenon – seems to promise beautiful prospects. Does this feature apply to the phenomenon named the 'Arab Spring' and to its aftermath, an empowerment of Islamist movements? Does the political process that took place in 2011–2012 in the countries of the Middle East and North Africa (MENA) justify the use of this label?

To understand the phenomenon of the Arab Spring properly, and perform the analysis needed to arrive at solid answers to these questions, it must first be placed in its broader context. That is the assignment I have set myself in the present chapter.

Was the uprising really a spring?

The political process referred to as the 'Arab Spring' began in January 2011 in a series of events that took on world-historical significance. Starting on a regional level in the MENA, it soon became a world-political phenomenon. No one (not even the top experts) expected what happened in Tunisia, even less its spillover to other countries. The pace of events was feverish and breathtaking. Not only was the uprising unexpected, its development was unpredictable for the simple reason that it took place in countries ruled by ruthless police states. These states are all equipped with great surveillance capabilities – both modern and pre-modern – to keep the entire population in check. For instance, Syria and Libya were in a way territorialized jailhouses for the entire population. People there used to say fearfully that 'not even a fly can escape the surveillance of the *mukhabarat*/secret police'; they even feared their relatives. At some point the oppression went overboard and the fears were dispelled, facilitating the uprising. All of us were taken by surprise when this miracle materialized; it was a most admirable one. But is its outcome admirable too? Does the rule of the Islamists remove the exasperations that were the driver of the Arab Spring?

A basic fact is that most of the rebelling people are in the young 'no-hope generation' that has 'nothing to lose, except their life'. By Middle Easterners' cultural values, it is better to die in dignity than to live a miserable life as a prisoner of a ruthless dictatorship. I repeat the notion of 'unpredictability', but add to it some knowledge about the 'leaderless young generation' of the rebels who were acting in the vacuum that emerged after the breakdown of the oppressive security apparatus. These conditions led to a specific prediction, or rather to a misgiving, about one power that managed, on the basis of secretiveness, clandestine organization and global networks, to escape existing surveillance and get a head start in the Arab Spring. This power was the effective Islamist movements. The vacuum created by the powerful effects of the Arab Spring allowed these movements to come out of hiding, first to exert great impact, and then to succeed to power, ostensibly filling the vacuum by replacing a secular authoritarianism with a religious one.

As one of the scholars who has studied Islamism, I have worked for the past 30 years on these Islamist movements – long enough to know how effective they are. Thus I was aware and fearful of the potential for an Islamist hijacking of the Arab Spring in the name of democracy. I aired this misgiving in a section on the Arab Spring added to my book *Islamism and Islam* in the final stages of its preparation for publication. At the time of the present writing, the Arab Spring is almost two years old. What has been become of it?

A *New York Times* correspondent, David Kirkpatrick, reports about the hopes of post-Qadhafi Libya, but knows 'that hope for democracy, however, is now imperilled by lawlessness in Libya and . . . sectarian war in Syria . . . (and) the victory of Mohammed Morsi an Islamist . . . (becoming) President' of Egypt.[1] Kirkpatrick is an honest Westerner and forthrightly acknowledges in his report that for the West 'the greatest promise of the Arab Spring (is) that political participation could neutralize the militant strand of Islam'. Clearly, this concern is about security and the politics of countering terrorism, not about what the Arab world needs, namely freedom for all and development of a kind that fulfils the basic economic and social needs of the suffering population. What happens when these jihadist Islamists become rulers and turn peaceful? Will these needs be fulfilled? Do we get then democracy? Kirkpatrick is a practical observer who focuses on specific cases. Those who 'took up arms . . . to bring Islamic (*shari'a*) law' have now 'refashioned' themselves as 'politicians running for local office, looking to the ballot box to promote Islamic values'. Is this democracy?

Islamists say 'the Qur'an is the only constitution', as Kirkpatrick rightly quotes. But for true Muslim believers the Qur'an is '*kitab hidaya*'/'a book of guidance', not a constitution. The late sheykh of al-Azhar Jadulhaq Ali Jadulhaq said the same in an interview lasting many hours that I ran with him back in September 1989 in his office in Cairo. The Qur'an is not a political constitution. It is a book or source of *iman*/belief. Islamists bill the law of their movement as a divine *shari'a* law and claim respect for their ideology as a religious belief. This is not the original promise of the Arab Spring, and the *shari'a* state was never the aspiration of the people who took to the streets demanding freedom and a better life. Rather, it is an order imposed on them.

Given the state of flux of post-Arab Spring developments, there would not be much value in engaging in a narrative of day-to-day events, and this is not the trajectory of this chapter. The Arab Spring broke out when my fourth book on political Islam, *Islamism and Islam*, was almost complete. I wanted to conclude my career with that book, and it was on its way to the printer. Fortunately, my editor at Yale University Press, William Frucht, restrained my repeated efforts at updating. In the coda on the Arab Spring added to the final chapter of that book, I quote Bill Frucht's advice that even if the book 'is completely up to the minute when the proofs are finished and sent to the printer something will happen the next day and the day after that. The world overtakes it before the ink is dry on the paper'. This most valuable advice also applies to the present chapter of a book I did not expect to write, as I shall acknowledge later on. I continue to follow it here, where it helps to avoid topicalities in order to focus on 'big structures, large processes, huge comparisons'[2] in the mindset of the methodology of historical sociology. This is the framework for dealing with the Arab Spring; a few topical references only will be made on the side.

The Arab Spring started in Tunisia, followed by Egypt. The events happened at the grassroots level and seemed very promising, to an extent that justifies the hopeful and sunny term 'spring'. However, the spillover of the peaceful rebellion into Libya and Syria ceased to justify the use of the term. No well-informed observer would qualify the bloody tribal and sectarian strife in Libya or the ruthless sectarian bloodshed in Syria as 'a process of democratization'. What was going on in 2011–2012 indicates, not a spring, but something like a day of reckoning among tribal and sectarian foes. Nonetheless, for ease of reference, I shall continue to employ the term 'Arab Spring' in the common sense throughout the present book.

What compelled me to write this book was an inescapable and bewildering combination of hope and sadness. As I have stated before, I am a Sunni Arab-Muslim native of Damascus and thus among the victims of the oppressive sectarian regime in Syria. I sensed it as a duty to unravel what has been named the Arab Spring – in a hope for democratization. The cherished hope of a spring was shattered by the lethal winter that has followed. Some of my readers may remonstrate that I had already announced my departure from the stage in 2012 in *Islamism and Islam*. I can only plead guilty, but explain why in a section below, and ask for forgiveness.

Pertinent questions about the Arab Spring

Some readers may be asking why this chapter on the Arab Spring is Chapter 4 rather than Chapter 1 of this book? The reason is simple: the dominance of Islamists in the aftermath of the uprising makes it necessary to deal with the *shari'a* state, the order that is likely to be the outcome of the Arab Spring. I contend that no one can properly understand the Arab Spring without detailed reference to its contemporary historical context. The crisis was the background that allowed the existing vision of a new political order – called the *shari'a* state – to move centre-stage. To grasp these ramifications properly, beyond any chronicling of the Arab Spring, I had to establish the overall context needed to understand it as a current phenomenon. Providing this context is the aim of Chapters 1 to 3. Only on such solid grounds will the phenomenon itself be seen clearly.

Next, the phenomenon itself in this chapter. A first question is about the place of Islamism in the rebellion (it is not yet a revolution). The rebellion was not of an Islamist making, so how come Islamists prevail? Let us first state the positive features of this promising 'spring'. For the first time in modern history, political change happens when people rebel: not army officers in a coup d'état, but ordinary people. The people want political freedom – call it what you want – coupled with the fulfilment of social and economic needs. All the political regimes ruling the MENA states are not only authoritarian, but have also presided over a failure of development. These are the issues that generate the need for change. Are these concerns of the people now being considered? Or has there simply been a change of rulers? Let us look at some cases.

As a Syrian-born student of the Middle East I know that my country of origin is the worst case. In Syria a minority of Shi'ite Alawis has been suppressing the majority Sunni population since 1970. For more than four decades the Alawi sect, which constitutes 10 per cent of the population, has been able to dominate the entire country in a police-state style, turning it into a prison. They were able to do this by entering the army and the similarly established sectarian security forces until they outnumbered all others. In Syria the revolt is against sectarian rule. In January 2011 I was live in Vienna on Austrian ORF-TV and in Zurich on Swiss DRS television to speak as an expert. I confess that by then I did not believe that the miracle of Tunisia and Egypt could be repeated in Syria and Libya. I was wrong, and I am happy that I was wrong; but I am not happy about the bloody outcome. In Syria, strife erupted and escalated the process of violence to a grave extent, resulting in mass murder. In 2011–2012 and continuing into 2013, the killing of more than 100,000 of the civilian population by the tanks of the predominantly Alawi army and its infantry became almost a daily media headline. Two million innocent Sunni-Syrians became displaced, fleeing the killing to the neighbouring Sunni countries of Turkey and Jordan, but not to Shi'ite Iraq. This fact is a statement in itself.

People knowledgeable about Syria predict that if the Alawi regime collapses, there will certainly be a payback: revenge, not democratization, not even a trial for crimes against humanity as in Serbia and Kosovo. Because the executioners know that, they fight to the last man. What is 'spring-like' about these atrocities and the potential for revenge? This is one of the core pertinent questions.

The next case I glance at is Libya. In that country tribal militias have established their violent fiefdoms, replacing the murderous secret police of the toppled and brutally executed dictator Muammar al-Qadhafi. Disorder has followed the tight rule of a dictatorship. Of course, an ordered *shari'a* state is better than the disorder of criminal tribal militias, but would such a state be a democracy? At the time of writing, Libya has managed against all odds to run elections and to build a new government based on an Islamist–tribal coalition. The rest remains to be seen. I shall come back to this case later in a section on Libya.

Then we can move to the most important country of the MENA region, Egypt. The modern history of Egypt, since the modernization of Mohammed Ali (1805–1849), teaches us that what happens there matters and affects the entire region.[3] In Egypt the Islamists won the parliamentary elections of 2011–2012, but the Supreme Constitutional Court dissolved the elected parliament on the grounds of Islamist faking and tampering with election law. It was doubtful whether Islamists would generate democratization, since Salafists and Muslim Brotherhood-Islamists were poised to establish not democratic rule but a *shari'a* state. Is it a democracy when tyranny emerges asserting its intent to impose a majority rule over minorities including non-Islamist Muslims? Does the use of democracy as legitimation justify the suppression of all others? The Islamists view non-Islamist Egyptians as a minority – what then about Christian Copts? Where is democratization then? What 'spring' is that? These questions were shelved in mid-June 2012 when the Supreme Constitutional Court ruled that the Islamist-dominated parliament must be immediately dissolved. However, the questions surged again when the Islamist president Morsi 'forced key military leaders to step down', and – without 'constitutional authority' – dared to nullify the parts that had been added to the constitution.[4] In a later section on Egypt I shall address these questions in more detail and take pains to provide a well-founded assessment.

At this stage, however, pursuant to the case-related questions asked above, I shall focus on more general issues. The first question relates to the already mentioned positive character of a 'spring': can one generally continue unabated to refer to the uprising as a 'spring' even though it became a lethal season at the turn from 2011 to 2012?

The study of rising Islamist movements indicates a hegemonic ideology. These hegemonic groups have succeeded in taking over the 'spring'. As already stated, the rebellion was not at the outset carried out by these groups. It was the young, leaderless 'no hope'generation that acted in the hope of a better future. In contrast to them, the Islamist groups were better organized, and were simply fighting for political power. Earlier they had been mostly jihadist in nature, but they underwent a process of learning and abandoned the ideology of violent action. The change away from jihadism towards institutional participation persuaded some Western pundits prematurely to view this shift as moderation.[5] As will be demonstrated below, this assessment has been translated into a policy of US–Islamist cooperation in Egypt.

The learning process of Islamists happened because they became aware that terror *jihad* leads to nowhere. The sum total of al-Qaeda's achievements provides the evidence for this. This is why Islamists have recognized that there is more future in getting on the democratization train. Is it right to view this shift as a moderation? These hegemonic groups have abandoned violent action (although in fact not consistently), but they have not abandoned their Islamist ideology that calls for hegemony, a premise on which the political thought of Islamist movements rests. These groups impose hegemonically, in the name of majority rule, their agenda of the *shari'a*tization of state, society and polity. The victims of such a hegemony are not only non-Muslim religious minorities (Christians, Jews, sects), but also all non-Islamist Muslims who disapprove of the *shari'a* state and refuse to submit to its rule.

It is a fact that the 'Arab Spring' has not always been a pleasant, sunny season. It also had an ugly face: for instance the increasing antisemitism, disguised as anti-Zionism. This antisemitism is a basic feature of Islamism.[6] Next to this unpleasant feature is the outlawing of discord as treason in the *shari'a* state. In the Introduction I quoted the foremost sheykh of Islamism, Yusuf al-Qaradawi, defaming Muslims who disagree with his agenda as 'disbelievers, wrong-doers and truly wicked' (see Introduction, note 7). This is not a reassuring mindset!

Islamist regional state actors and the US in the Arab Spring

At present, there are in the MENA region two non-Arab states that are ruled by Islamists. These are the predominantly Sunni Turkey under the Islamist AKP, and Iran under the Shi'ite mullahcracy. Egypt under the rule of the Muslim Brothers seems to be adding to this. These states have been using the Arab Spring to establish their dominance over the region of the Middle East. Turkey coordinates its politics with the US and supports the Movement of the Muslim Brothers, which has emerged from the Arab Spring in a powerful position. In Egypt the Muslim Brothers were able to seize the presidency. It follows that Turkey seems to have better cards than Iran. Iran also supports the Arab Spring, but the Iranian mullahcracy and its ally in Lebanon, Hezbollah, are caught in a dilemma: both support the Alawi-Shi'ite Assad dictatorship in Syria. Because of this great contradiction Iran not only lacks credibility, it is hypocritical. In the competition between Turkey and Iran, therefore, Iran is possibly the loser. This competition is neither about democracy nor moderation, it is about regional power and hegemony. Let me illustrate this with a reference to two efforts supportive of the Arab Spring. These took place in two big conferences, one held in Turkey, the other in Iran.

In the first week of February 2012 Iran organized a big event in Tehran to support the Arab Spring as a sign of 'Islamic Awakening'. As the *New York Times* reported: 'It was meant to be a crowning moment in which Iran puts its own Islamic stamp on the Arab Spring.'[7] However, this propaganda effort was 'marred' by its exclusion of the uprising in Syria against the Alawi-Shi'ite regime of the Assad clan. Not only did the cynical accusation of the West of 'ferment[ing] sectarian conflict in our society' fail to convince, but it was also laughable to brand the Syrian protesters as 'foreign agents' of the 'Jews and Israel'. In actual political reality the uprising in Syria, close ally of the Shi'ite-Islamist state of Iran, dealt a large blow to Iran's claim to (regional) leadership. Another blow followed by the end of August 2012 when Iran hosted the assembly of the heads of the non-aligned states (the Third World) in Tehran. Among the guests was Mohammed Morsi, the new Islamist president of Egypt. In his speech in front of the Iranian leadership, the Sunni-Islamist Morsi used strong words to blast the bloody crackdown of the Syrian regime against the Sunni population.

Ahead of that non-aligned assembly, in mid-July 2012, the Iranian and Syrian ministers of foreign affairs met in a demonstration of solidarity between the two states, and in a public communiqué again blamed 'Israel and the Jews' for inciting and supporting 'terrorism' against the Syrian regime that 'stands up to Israel with Iranian help'. As July turned into August in 2012 – parallel to the bloody fight between the Assad regime and the rebels in Aleppo – Iran became more active. While Syria's airforce was bombing the residential areas of Aleppo, killing thousands of innocent civilians, the supreme leader of the Islamist Republic of Iran, Ali Khamenei, dispatched his top aide Saeed Jalali to Damascus to assure Assad of his support and commitment to the 'axis of resistance' (Iran, Syria and Hezbollah). The *New York Times*, which covered this meeting in its *International Herald Tribune* global edition,[8] published in the same issue an editorial with this comment: 'al-Assad's security forces are continuing to kill Syrians in large numbers . . . the conflict has already intensified splits among the Sunni and Alawi . . . communities.' The Alawite community disposes of formidable armed forces on the ground and in the air, and with Iran's assistance it could prevail militarily. The question in this protracted conflict is: How long will it take?

A week ahead of the Iranian 'Arab Spring Rally' in February 2012, Turkey organized a conference on Sunday, January 29, to support the Arab Spring in Syria in which 'Iran's assistance in the Syrian government's crackdown on protesters' was denounced. The *New York Times* report cited earlier (see note 7) rightly states 'Iran's Shi'ite faith is also a serious obstacle in a region where Sunni Muslims are the majority and sectarian tensions are on the rise'. This gives rise to further questions: What is an Islamic Awakening, and what is spring-like about these sectarian tensions and the related competition between Turkey and Iran to dominate the MENA region? Where is the 'democratization' in Iran's courting of Hezbollah in Lebanon as a replacement in case Assad should fall? In another *New York Times* report one reads this assessment:

> Bashar al-Assad could fall. Iran relies on Syria as its bridge to the Arab world, and as a crucial strategic partner in confronting Israel. But the Arab revolts have shaken Tehran's calculations with Mr. Assad unable to vanquish an uprising. . . . Tehran is scrambling to find a replacement of its closest Arab ally.[9]

However, Iran kept its loyalty to the Assad regime and provided all means including the training of the murderous militias.

Despite all doubts, either those I have squarely expressed or those just inherent in this portrayal of the Arab Spring in the shadow of Turkish–Iranian rivalry, I would never say that a great and admirable change has not been taking place. The agenda of a real democratization that brings freedom can no longer be shelved. However, a regime change in Syria resembling the one that took place in Iraq is not desirable. In Iraq the US waged a costly war, and the winners were Iran and the Iraqi Shi'ite Islamists.

Specifically, Syria and the earlier Iraq under the rule of the fascist Ba'th party are (and were) the most severe examples of mighty dictatorships established in the name of secular pan-Arabism.[10] The human rights violations of these regimes presiding over 'republics of fear' resemble Nazi barbarism. The rule of the Ba'th party in Iraq under Sunni Saddam Hussein and in Syria under the Alawite Assad clan was based on the legitimacy provided by the populist pan-Arabism ideology. The Syrian Assad dictatorship and the earlier Iraqi one under Saddam (until 2003) were regimes that resembled each other in merciless tyranny. In other words, the rule of the Ba'th party in Syria and Iraq was in every respect the same. So why did the West restrict its outlawing to only one of them?

Syrians, like Iraqis, do not trust US pro-democracy pronouncements. For convenience, the US cooperated with Assad's Syria during the Gulf War of 1991. The US worked closely with Ba'thist Syria against Ba'thist Iraq, and from mere opportunism supported the dictator Assad against the other dictator Saddam. The price the US paid was not only toleration of the Syrian military occupation of Lebanon, but also the suppression of the human rights of the Sunni majority of the population. The US did this to get Syrian Ba'thist approval for its Gulf War of 1991. The EU was not very different, as it also approached Assad's Syria in the naive hope of striking a deal for a Middle Eastern peace to be mediated with the state of Israel. Middle Easterners have long collective memories regarding the good and the evil.

One focus of these memories is the war the US waged in Iraq. And what was the outcome of the US liberation of Iraq? The post-Saddam Iraq of today is no democracy. The suppression of the Shi'ite majority in Iraq by the Sunni-Takrit clan of Saddam Hussein has been reversed. Today, it is replaced by Shi'ite dictatorship supported by Iran to suppress the 20 per cent Sunni minority. These new victims, the Iraqi Sunnis, do not believe in the US liberation. I shall come back to Iraq later on to reject the model presented by Fouad Ajami as 'the foreigner's gift' (discussed in Chapter 3).

The US support of Islamism in the post-Arab Spring era in the name of promoting democracy and the 'transition to civilian rule' follows similar lines, and that is why it fails to generate any more trust in a Western policy of democratization of the MENA region. It is amazing to read, in a policy article in *Foreign Affairs*, a recommendation to US policy-makers to work closely with emerging Islamist regimes in the MENA region. The article, by Daniel Byman, demonstrates the West's unabating obsession with counter-terrorism in response to al-Qaeda. It is a fact that the basic issues related to the Arab Spring do not relate to al-Qaeda as Byman keeps contending (see the section on Syria). The concern of the US pundits seems not to be democratization, but rather the fight against an imaginary al-Qaeda: 'From a counterterrorism point of view, a greater role for Islamists could be good news.'[11] Byman knows well that the Muslim Brothers' 'commitment to true democracy is uncertain', but, amazingly, this does not bother his thinking at all in view of the fact that 'there is bad blood between the two organizations', that is al-Qaeda and the Muslim Brothers. In this sense 'the United States needs to catch up'. One may ask: Catch up how? The answer one gets is this policy recommendation: 'the United States should develop efforts to train the intelligence and security forces of the new regimes that emerge. The first step is simply to gain their trust . . . Developing such co-operation will take time and patience, but the United States should make this a priority.' One year after the publication of this article, its recommendations became reality. Following a deadly clash with jihadists in Sinai in August 2012, a US–Islamist collaboration emerged under the presidency of the Muslim Brother Mohammed Morsi. The *International Herald Tribune* reported on August 13, 2012: 'The shared threat of extremism . . . could also overcome reservations . . . in Washington about Mr Morsi's affiliation with the Muslim Brotherhood,' an organization which was in the past – as the report continues – 'reviled by US officials for its anti-Western views and Islamist politics.' This is a specific policy example of the shift that the 'moderation' thesis announces.

The reader is reminded of the fact that the peoples of the MENA region rebelled in the first weeks of the Arab Spring precisely against the oppressive 'intelligence and security forces'. The rebels had their own needs and security concerns were not among them. Now security recurs in the name of democratization. The US security community is not bothered about the rule of *shari'a*. One more naive question: Do US policy advisers confuse their obsession with 'counter-terrorism' with democratization?

As a European Arab democrat and cofounder of the Arab Organization for Human Rights, I cannot consider people who recommend such policies as allies (see Chapter 3). The point of departure for dealings with Islamists must therefore be free from any obsession with counter-terrorism. At issue is rather how to overcome the ruthless dictatorial rule combined with the social and economic misery. In short: the issues are democratization and development. Counter-terrorism is of minor concern if any in the context of the Arab Spring. Nor is the regional security a great concern. The already cited *International Herald Tribune* of August 13 includes the report 'Turkey and US Team Up on Syria'. This could be a preparation for a takeover of the Syrian Muslim Brothers after the fall of Assad with US–Turkish assistance. In addition to the regional actors (Turkey and Iran) and the global ones (the US, Russia and China), there are other actors such as the tiny Qatar and the Wahhabi monarchy of Saudi Arabia who push forward their own interests in the name of support for the Arab Spring. I do not think that any comment is needed on the notion of Saudi Arabia as a champion of a democratization process in the MENA region.

Back to the exemplary case: Egypt

In general, Egypt is the MENA country that matters most. It is also the best exemplary case of authoritarian rule coupled with failed development, as the study of the political economy of Egypt under Nasser and Sadat (and later Mubarak) clearly demonstrates. The two most authoritative books on this subject by the foremost scholarly authority on Egypt, John Waterbury, contain the best analysis based on solid evidence that supports what is stated here.[12] We will start with the first of these books, on the failed development under Nasser. Waterbury identifies this development as the source of a crisis that overtook Egypt in 1965–66. It was first felt in 1964 and was exacerbated, but not caused, by Egypt's military defeat in 1967. . . . It was caused by the gross inefficiencies of a public sector called upon to do too many things. . . . It was also caused by the neglect of the traditional agricultural sector . . . [which] was not reformed, so as to become an engine of growth in its own right.

This crisis continued under the Sadat regime, reached its height under Mubarak, and finally led to the breakdown of Mubarak's regime in February 2011. The first book by Waterbury that provides this analysis was published in 1983. It was followed ten years later by a second one – written jointly with Alan Richards – as a general analysis of the political economy of the Middle East. This book not only demonstrates cross-regional facts about failed development throughout the MENA region, but also offers a critical assessment of what Islamists propose as a solution. The Egyptian Muslim Brother Islamists coined the slogan: '*al-Islam huwa al-hall*'/'Islam is the solution' to overcome failed development. Waterbury and Richards look at Islamist strategies underlying this slogan through the lenses of political economy to reach the conclusion that 'no, it is not the solution'.

At the time of this writing, Egypt has a strongly empowered president based in the party of the Muslim Brothers, the Freedom and Justice Party. This is the strongest and best organized Sunni-Islamist party, not only in the country, but in the MENA region in general. This party has issued a 'party platform' or election manifesto in which it outlines its vision for Egypt under Islamist rule. Whatever else, one has to credit the Muslim Brothers' Freedom and Justice Party with some honesty regarding their reference to *shari'a*. Its election programme (currently available on the internet at http://fjponline.com/articles.php?pid=80) professes to be 'founded on fundamental principles, which represent the great purposes of *shari'a*'. The Freedom and Justice Party further acknowledges that its ideology 'requires a new constitution with enlightened principles of *shari'a* as its frame of reference and the source to its articles'. Do not, by the way, conflate the use of 'enlightened' in the Freedom and Justice's Party's election programme with the 'enlightened' Muslim thought (introduced in the first section of Chapter 3) that inspires the present book. The constitution that the Islamists imposed in Egypt by the end of 2012 is neither 'enlightened' nor democratic; it is an Islamist constitution, a design for a *shari'a* state. The violent crackdown on non-Islamist opposition to this constitution that followed is not an indication of a will to engage in a democratization that allows dissent and power sharing.

Let us continue the reading of the election manifesto of the Islamist Freedom and Justice Party of Egypt. It lists the 'characteristics of the state', namely an 'Islamic democracy based on *shari'a*'. This Islamist party manifesto consistently speaks of 'the *shari'a*' not of 'a *shari'a*', suggesting that there is a single specific *shari'a*. In so doing, it completely ignores the fact that, as the late Muslim Oxford scholar Hamid Enayat stated on the basis of his research findings, 'there is no such a thing as a unified Islamic legal system' called *shari'a*. He continues: 'But one must not forget that despite the *shari'a*'s grasp . . . a unified Islamic legal system enshrined in integrated codes, and accepted and acknowledged unquestionably by all Muslims' never existed throughout Islamic history (see Chapter 1, note 10). Based on this conclusion of an authoritative scholar, I ask: What are the Egyptian Muslim Brothers talking about when they speak of 'the *shari'a*'?

The outcome of the Arab Spring in Egypt, often wrongly called a 'revolution', has been a change of rulers, not yet one of social structures. Egypt is not yet a *shari'a* state although it is ruled by the Muslim Brother Islamists with an Islamist *shari'a* constitution (characterized above). It guarantees the incremental Islamization of polity and society. The Islamists engage in tactical coalitions simply for convenience, abandoning them as soon as they no longer need them. Barak Barfi wrote from Cairo in the *International Herald Tribune* of August 8, 'the generals . . . forged an alliance with the Islamist Muslim Brotherhood . . . As the military and the Brotherhood jockey for power, they are ignoring the reforms Egyptians demand.' The US that gives its political blessing to the Muslim Brother–military coalition is also 'neglecting Egypt's larger problems . . . Lost in Washington's myopic focus on democratic transition is an understanding of the socio-economic problems that brought Egyptians into the streets . . . What united the disparate groups was exasperation.'[13] Only a week after the publication of this insightful commentary on the deals the Muslim Brothers struck with the military, the same newspaper reported a few days later (August 13) on its front page: 'Morsi forces key military leaders to step down.' This is only one example for the short-lived tactical coalitions the Muslim Brothers engage in, wrongly presented by people with myopic vision as 'power sharing'.

Clearly, the grievances of the Egyptian people are ignored by the major local players, the Muslim Brother Islamists and the military, as well as by the global players, the US and the EU. The latter two focus on what is regarded as a transition to full civilian (formally elected) rule, billed as a democratization. I am in full agreement with Barak Barfi's assessment that 'a handover of power to the country's new civilian rulers will not resolve the country's dilemmas. In fact, it may only exacerbate them'. The Brotherhood's concerns are to restructure the judiciary and the military in a power struggle, just as the Islamist AKP did in Turkey, to eliminate its foes in these two institutions. Otherwise the Muslim Brothers have no policy that will placate the exasperation of the Egyptian people with their social and economic malaise. This transformation of rule was never the driving motivation of the rebellion dubbed the Arab Spring. The rebels wanted real change in society.

Whatever the variations between Arab countries – and there are many – one thing is true of all of them. It is this: that everyone who has travelled in the MENA region (not, of course, as a tourist or a journalist who does not speak the local languages and lives in Westernized hotels) knows very well how fed up the people of that region are with the way of life imposed on them by their rulers – all their rulers. The name chosen for the pre-Arab Spring movement of protest in Egypt was '*kifaya*' which translates: 'it is enough'. The change they aspire to is not a change of rulers, but of the conditions of their lives. The explosion has been just a matter of time. For many decades the ruthless security apparatus of the *ancien régime* was able to prevent or, rather, delay the explosion, but in the end, in January 2011, it happened, beginning in Tunisia and spilling over from there to Egypt and later to other parts of the Arab world. The outcome has been a state guided by an Islamist *shari'a*. Will this order bring freedom and prosperity? And how about Egypt under the rule of the Muslim Brotherhood? Most of us can only wait and see. Those who can wait may consider the assessment this chapter provides. Due to the great significance of Egypt, I shall come back later to this case.

Western wishful thinking about an 'Arab Spring' confronted with non-Islamist Arab critical reasoning

In Chapter 1 of the present book I took issue with Western scholarship and its wishful thinking on Islamism. Here I continue this criticism. This section aims to confront Western thinking about the MENA region with the reasoning of non-Islamist Arab opinion leaders about what they themselves term the 'crisis of democracy' in their homeland. The point of departure is the just rebellion named the Arab Spring. This revolt reflected the outcry of politically oppressed and economically impoverished leaderless people rebelling at the grassroots level. For real change, a process of democratization requires the fulfilment of some basic preconditions. Among these are a process of consolidation at various levels, ranging from institution building and political organization to behavioural change (from submission to representation), and, above all, a pluralist political culture of democracy. *No hegemonic group can fulfil these preconditions*. Because, in the MENA region, all of these requirements are missing on the ground, the leaderless rebelling masses were always liable to lose in favour of groups with strong leadership. The Islamists have at their disposal well-organized movements that have been able to survive the suffocation efforts of the security apparatus at two levels: first, the highly efficient clandestine organization they have at home, and, second, their ability to abuse the Muslim diaspora in Europe to establish Islamist networks. As early as the first weeks of 2011, the suspicion of such a shift came to the fore and then materialized. Islamists were able to hijack the rebellion. They did this very successfully. The question still remains: Will there be a successful democratization in the MENA region after the Arab Spring?

The deplored contemporary Western naivety in matters Middle East and democracy is a present case that resembles an earlier pattern documented in a highly influential book, *The Passing of Traditional Society: Modernizing The Middle East* by Daniel Lerner.[14] The book was first published in 1958 and later went through many editions, with great impact and tremendous dissemination. Just as, earlier, Daniel Lerner believed in a swift transformation from 'traditional to modern society', the naive Western alliance of today believes in a swift transformation from ruthless dictatorship (palliatively named 'authoritarianism') to democracy. Luckily, this naivety is not shared by non-Islamist Arab thinkers, as will be discussed in this section. Naivety seems to have become a feature of Western thinking, not only in this matter, but seemingly in general when it comes to the non-Western cultural Other.

Today, an incidental political-correctness-minded alliance consisting of many well-meaning but not well-informed scholars, journalists (opinion leaders) and politicians dominates the view of the Arab Spring. A valuable book on 'the controversy over Islamism and the press', Paul Berman's *Flight of the Intellectuals*, takes issue with their faulty assessment of Islamism.[15] The present book contributes to the clearing up of a misconception of the role of Islamist movements in the Arab Spring. Opinion leaders were in agreement among themselves to view the just uprising or rebellion as 'the Arab Spring', but later in their prevailing narrative they overlooked the shift to an unpleasant season. In fact, the people of the Middle East and North Africa deserve a real spring of dignity after the long dark decades, but what they got was a development that was no choice of theirs. For sure, it would have been great if such a spring had come about to make the prevailing narrative true, but it did not happen. The core assumption behind the positive labelling of the rebellion is the belief that there was a swift transformation from authoritarianism to democracy. Only a few cautious observers failed to share this naive optimism.

Throughout this book I keep my commitment to 'enlightened Muslim thought', on which I base my sharing of the views of the Moroccan democrat and essayist Abdou Filali-Ansary. As discussed in Chapter 3, he is among those Muslims who represent an 'enlightened turn' in contemporary history, as he distinguishes between enlightened Muslims and Islamists. The first group consists of those Muslims who accept 'universalist moralities, beyond political and cultural boundaries . . . (and have) respect for civic spheres. . . . To enlightened Muslims, both this acceptance and this respect are matters of principle.'[16] In contrast, the moderate Islamists are not genuinely democratic, as their approval of democracy is based on 'merely grudging tactical concessions'. For them 'democracy and freedom . . . are instruments Muslims should use to achieve their community's goals and defend its interests.' As will be shown later in this chapter, a well-informed expert, Eric Trager (see note 38), tells us that this Islamist mindset identified by Filali-Ansary can be demonstrated in the case of the Freedom and Justice Party of the Egyptian Muslim Brotherhood, which makes instrumental use of democracy.

The reader is reminded of consolidation needed at various levels as the ground for democracy. Democratization can never be restricted to balloting. Economic, institutional, cultural, political and social preconditions must be fulfilled to serve as the needed foundations. All of these were absent, and continue to be so. Against the prevailing views among Western pundits, non-Islamist Arab thinkers proved as long ago as the early 1980s that their reasoning about democracy in the Middle East is not only more mature than that of dozens of Western pundits, it is also characterized by more realism when it comes to democracy in the Arab homeland.

Let me introduce this enlightened Arab-Muslim reasoning on freedom, taking the example of three Arab debates that were published between 1980 and 1997. At all three meetings Arab democrats presented papers that continue to be highly topical for understanding the democratization needed in the aftermath of the Arab Spring. In Tunis, leading Arabs were allowed to meet in October 1980 (ahead of the Ben Ali dictatorship) to debate about '*Les Arabes face à leur destin*'.[17] The then acting director of Centre d'Etudes et de Recherches Economiques et Sociales (CERES), the host institution in Tunis, Abdelwahab Bouhdiba, acknowledged at the outset the 'state of hopelessness', asking: 'Who are we? And where do we go from here?' He frankly deplored 'the dominance of tyranny in politics as a rule and the oppression under the pretext of the urgency of pending problems, the violation of dignity and the lack of freedom on all levels.' Alluding to the title of the conference, '*Al-Arab amam masirahum*'/'The Arabs Face Their Destiny', he challenged participants to engage in a form of reasoning that would be able to deliver a future perspective, so that hope would not be lost.

Despite the dominance of the culturalist-francophone approach in the Tunis debate, the convening Arab scholars acknowledged the problems on the ground. Among these is the great discrepancy between the enormous demographic growth and the slow economic growth. Lack of the policies needed to tackle the burning issues led to a failure of development. The spread of education does not conceal the high rate of illiteracy. The lack of democracy was an issue in the Tunis debate, but the reluctance to address this lack – because of fear – was obvious. In looking for alternatives, Habib Janhani made it clear that Salafism is not the future prospect that the Arabs need.

Three years later, some 70 Arab thinkers assembled in Limassol, Cyprus, in November 1983 to discuss '*Azmat al-Dimuqratiyya fi al-Watan al-Arabi*'/'The Crisis of Democracy in the Arab World'. At this conference they also established the Arab Organization for Human Rights. There were some noteworthy circumstances surrounding the choice of Limassol as the venue for the conference. It was supposed to take place in Cairo. The reason why this was not possible gives a good illustration of the atmosphere in the MENA region of that time. Cairo had to be replaced by Limassol as a venue for discussing the crisis of democracy in the Arab world because the Egyptian government, which at first had given its approval, had to bow to Saudi pressure; it revoked the permission. *Arab democrats had to go to a non-Arab place to think*. The proceedings of that meeting, documenting mature and realistic Arab thinking about democracy in the Middle East, were published in Beirut in a big volume.[18] Although the book was placed on the blacklist of oppressive regimes, this could not prevent its dissemination in Arabic throughout the Arab world as a document of a great historical significance. The participants were well aware that the transition to democracy was never going to be a walk in the park.

With the hindsight of three decades of reviewing Arab contributions to the theme of democracy in the Middle East, I qualify the Limassol debate of November 1983 as the most important discussion conducted among Arab democrats in recent history. In his introduction to the published proceedings, Saad Eddin Ibrahim deplored the lack of pluralism and participation in political life in Arab societies. He pointed to the fact that the authoritarian regimes kept justifying the failed freedom under the 'pretext of the need to focus on the preparation of the great battle for the liberation of Palestine'. This shows just how damaging the Arab–Israeli conflict was: it served as a pretext for shelving any process of democratization. The convening Arab opinion leaders, recruited from three generations, who convened in Limassol did not accept this logic, as they were discussing democracy, not the Arab–Israeli conflict. In fifteen papers and forty-two written comments they debated for five days, in a mindset of freedom of thought and pluralism, the notion of democracy itself as it relates to the Arab world. The Arab contributions to an accommodation of democratic thought and to political participation were discussed both at a general level and also in case studies, at the end of which future prospects were outlined. Whatever their disagreements, these Arab democrats were in agreement over the need for a '*mashru' hadari'*/'civilizational project' for the MENA region based on democracy, justice, independence and proper development. Saad Eddin Ibrahim ends his long introduction to the 928-page book of the proceedings by mentioning a fact combined with an inference. The fact is that on the final day a group of the participants established the Arab Organization for Human Rights. The inference is that 'this is the first practical result of the debate on democracy, and it indicates an Arab sense of responsibility of Arab thinkers that they need to act, not just talk.' None of the convening Arab democrats predicted any uprising like the one of the Arab Spring. The authoritarian regimes, by contrast, were aware of the perils and kept the debate under surveillance. During the convention a Syrian journalist asked me for an interview and I consented. During the interview a participant pulled me politely to whisper in my ear 'be careful, this journalist is a Syrian agent of the *mukhabarat*/secret police'. That was a telling moment!

The third example relates to a debate that took place in the Middle East, but outside the Arab world. Three Arab democrats and social scientists were invited to Istanbul to join an internationally supported debate among Middle Easterners on Islam, civil society and democracy.[19] The three Arabs were Saad Eddin Ibrahim, Sadik J. al-Azm and myself. We all argued for secularization, the creation of a cultural underpinning for civil society and democracy in Islamic terms, and for an 'accommodative politics of inclusion', as Ibrahim put it.

The three debates on democracy in the Arab world summed up in this section are evidence that there were 'pre-Spring' Arab efforts to discuss democracy. Although they took place as much as 30 years before the Arab Spring, they deserve to be considered in the present debate because their reasoning continues to be pertinent.

The three Arab debates in the 1980s and 1990s in Tunis, Limassol and Istanbul reflect not just insider knowledge, but also maturity combined with a high degree of political prudence. In contrast, many US and European pundits naively think today, as like-minded others did in the past, that if autocrats are removed, democracy will automatically follow. Torn between these two standards one is challenged how to view the Arab Spring properly. Because of their continuing pertinence, I recommend undertaking this task in the light of these earlier Arab debates. The reasoning on democracy and democratization published in the years before the Arab Spring is very important. Among the enlightened Muslims who contributed to this are the already quoted Abdou Filali-Ansary (see note 16) and also Ali Oumlil. The latter was among the Limassol combatants for democracy back in 1983. A decade after that conference, Oumlil published a small but remarkable book to defend the *haq fi al-ikhtilaf*, that is the 'right to dissent'. In that book he rejects the ideology of national unity that the authoritarian regimes promoted to outlaw, not just any opposition, but diversity and pluralism altogether.[20] By the same token, Oumlil rejects the religious unity of the *umma* as it is also directed against pluralism and discord. Oumlil argues for *'shar'iyyat al-ikhtilaf'*/'the legitimacy of discord' against all ideologies of unity, be these nationalism or *shari'a* Islamism. He states that what Arabs need is not the unity of the nation or of the *umma*, but rather the 'three basics, democracy, pluralism and individual human rights'. Does the *shari'a* state admit these needs? No, the study of the Islamist ideology reveals that it does not.

The most admirable feature of these non-Islamist Arab-Muslim debates of the 'enlightened turn' is that they are free from wishful thinking and thus from the high and unrealistic expectations made by Westerners in an assessment that does not accord with what has been happening on the ground in the Arab world. In view of these valuable contributions from Arab thinkers of the enlightened turn, it is not just wrong, it is distasteful when Fouad Ajami accuses Arab thinkers indiscriminately of living in a 'dream palace'.[21] The portrait he paints of them in his book ignores wholesale the positive Arab-Muslim contributions cited above, and simply advances prejudice.

Grounded in reasoning committed to the three debates covered above, I move to the realities of the Arab Spring. First I shall deal with some particular cases, to be followed by a more general assessment. Due to the high complexity of the case of Syria as the most unpleasant one in the Arab Spring, and also for personal reasons (to be spelled out and explained in a separate section), I start first with Syria and then move on to Egypt and Libya. I proceed on the basis of solid information combined with the spirit of an uncensored enlightenment that does not seek Western favour. I have spent more than 40 arduous years in Western scholarship, but these were combined – in a double life – with participation in the Arab fight for democracy in the MENA region. I shall be at pains to establish a balance between these two segments of my earlier scholarly work, on which the present analysis rests.

The sectarian case of Syria and its coverage in the Western media

The argument that the Syrian case of the Arab Spring is the most complex one rests on two grounds: one factual and functional, which I will address in this section, and the other personal, which will be addressed in the following section. With regard to the former, it can safely be said that the possible toppling of the dictatorship in Syria does not simply relate to an unseating of a ruler, or to his clan, as was the case with toppling the dictators of Tunisia, Egypt, Yemen and Libya. Parallel to the unseating of Ben Ali, Mubarak, Saleh and Qadhafi, a regime change took place. Why can this easy scenario not be repeated in Syria?

In Syria the dictatorship is not restricted to the Assad clan; the regime rests on an entire sectarian community. The regime recruited Alawis for its military forces and security apparatus, and trained them as army officers. The Alawi minority (approximately 10 to 11 per cent of the total population) has been ruling since 1970. The core of the officers of the armed forces (30,000 out of 34,000) consists of Alawis. The oppressive *mukhabarat*/security apparatus are also recruited from this Alawi minority. With this armed power it has ruled the country since 1970, when Hafez al-Assad seized power in a coup d'état. The fall of the regime is inevitable, but how will it happen? If Hafez's son Bashar, who inherited the bloodthirsty dictatorship, gets desperate and thinks of fleeing, the Alawi generals and security officers will not let him go. The leaders of the Alawi community may offer Bashar al-Assad as a scapegoat in a negotiated settlement that keeps the regime and its Alawi-dominated armed and security forces. The Sunni rebels will not buy into such a settlement. They want to end the sectarian Alawi hegemony, and nothing less.

I have no high regard for the intelligence community, but I appreciate the realism of a CIA analyst who said on CNN: 'The Alawis will fight to the last man.' All prospects for the future of the ongoing violent fight (since 2011) speak for a protracted and bloody civil war, not for a spring concluded with regime change directed by the hope for democratization.

In passing I mention the other reason for the difficulty of the analysis. Not only do I happen to be a Sunni native of Damascus; I was born into the centuries-old Damascene Sunni Ashraf (aristocratic) family of Banu al-Tibi. More on this in the ensuing section. At this point I am focusing on sectarianism as a source of complexity in the Syrian case, but in doing so I feel the need to repeat in all honesty my commitment to a non-sectarian civil Islam based on enlightened Muslim thought (see Chapter 3). Enlightened Muslim thought respects not just cultural diversity, but also denominational differences within Islam. According to this mindset one should combat sectarian prejudice on all sides and fronts, and I do so. To decry the barbarism of the Alawi-dominated army and security apparatus of the Syrian state is not to deviate from a sincere commitment to non-sectarian civil Islam. It is unfortunate how fashionable it has become to look at conflicts in merely political, social and economic terms, thus overlooking the role of religion and ethnicity. People who do this deny the negative effects of religion and ethnicity in a mindset of political correctness. To deny the fact that Alawis are killing Sunnis in Syria collectively is to side with the butcher Assad, who denies the sectarianism of his dictatorship.

Assad legitimates massacres against the Sunni population as a fight of a sovereign state against lawless terrorists. Let me illustrate this ideology with the case of the massacre of Houla in Syria, where Alawi soldiers jointly with the Alawi al-Shabiha militia gangs literally butchered about 1,000 mothers along with their children. The men of these families were mostly out of reach because they were on the run, fleeing ahead of the arrival of these Alawi killers. Probably they trusted the non-sectarian belief that the Arab-Muslim code of honour outlaws the killing of women and children. But the Assad regime did not hold back from this evil. It not only denied the crime, is also faked facts, alleging that among the soldiers were Sunnis and that the Houla victims were Alawis. Some Western media went along with this fake story which inverted the facts. Blindly ignoring sectarianism in the fashionable way, the biggest German daily, the *Frankfurter Allgemeine Zeitung* (*FAZ*), seriously denied the sectarian character of the Houla massacre in many reports. The author of these reports, Rainer Hermann, is a German reporter based in Abu Dhabi, far from the scene of slaughter, and thus lacks insider knowledge. Through these denials, shamefully, the *FAZ* reports virtually adopted the Syrian state propaganda, and even spread it.

It restores the honour of the German press that the German weekly *Der Spiegel* published witness accounts of the Houla massacre that belie the denial of sectarianism and clearly evidence the origins of the perpetrators: they were Alawi soldiers acting jointly with the Alawi militia. In its edition of June 18, 2012, *Der Spiegel* said: 'F.A.Z. reports that the (Syrian) opposition is responsible for the massacre,' and asked, 'Why should the (Sunni) rebels massacre their own people, and then participate in the funeral of the massacred Sunni victims?'[22] This, however, did not deter the major German television channel ARD from running a long propaganda interview with Assad on Sunday, July 8, in which the dictator repeated the lies and denials. I watched the long interview, aired on TV in prime time, with a combination of outrage and disgust. A few days later, the *International Herald Tribune* covered this interview with the wondering remark that 'the Syrian leader rarely grants interviews'.[23] So why did he?

The interview was run by a former German politician, Jörg Todenhöfer, who is obviously favourable towards Assad, as he allowed him – without any contradiction – to air his state propaganda. Among the many lies was the one that the rebels were 'anti-government gangs' and 'terrorists', who kill 'my supporters'. The *International Herald Tribune*'s account of this interview reported: 'The victims of the Houla massacre in May [were] among [my] his supporters.' Assad not only claimed in this shameful interview that he had 'broad public support', but also lied in stating that the deaths of his supporters killed by the 'terrorists' 'outnumber those among civilians killed in the Syria conflict'. The German interviewer did not question this contention. How could one believe that civilians could kill more soldiers than soldiers could civilians, despite the military superiority of the Alawi armed forces equipped with tanks, attack helicopter gunships and artillery? And this interview was broadcast, not on Syrian state television, but by Germany's main public television channel. Assad assured his German viewers that he would remain in power thanks to the 'public support for his rule [which] meant he would remain in office'. This lie – 'I still have public support' – was repeated in the *International Herald Tribune* report of the interview.

The exemplary case of the Houla massacre committed by the Alawi-dominated Syrian army and its allied Alawi Shabiha militia reveals many eye-opening facts about the sectarian character of the conflict. The case compels the following lessons to be learnt:

1   The Arab Spring has become a sectarian bloody conflict in Syria, and elsewhere (in tribal Libya). Is not spring the pleasant season of the year? This uprising is no spring; it is a bloody and hazardous winter.

2   The Syrian dictatorship denies the sectarian feature of its killers and contends that it is fighting US-style against the 'terrorists' of al-Qaeda ('counter-
terrorism'). There is no al-Qaeda presence in Syria.

3   Those Westerners who – in a 'benign' mindset directed against prejudice – believe they are seeing (in the language of the established discourse) a 'fight
for democracy' against 'authoritarian regimes' tend to deny the existence of
bloody sectarianism and thus end up, whether they wish to or not, adopting
the propaganda of the Syrian Assad regime.

4   The ideologically blinkered anti-Western 'Third Worldism' that also prevails
among some Western liberals, and unfortunately determines the views of the
left, has to be put into question. It is the US (even if not wholeheartedly) and
the European Union, the two pillars of the West, that condemn the crimes of
the Assad regime (if, however, without acting). In contrast, the states of China
and Russia not only impede condemnation of the crimes, but also any related
action to stop the killing. Russia also provides instruments (e.g. attack helicopters) to facilitate the crimes against civilians. As a European Muslim with
a leftist past, I profess to be pro-Western and could not care less if the present
left accuses me of conservatism and blames me for – allegedly – arguing on
the right! The bottom line is this: When it comes to fighting crimes, there can
by only a humanism that goes 'beyond left and right' (Anthony Giddens). A
commitment to a humanist mindset is based on a philosophy that has roots in
medieval Islam. This humanism is more promising than the ideology of Third
Worldism.[24] The values of humanism matter more to world peace than an
incomplete democracy reduced purely to the ballot box that disregards who
wins.

5   The Alawi dictatorship recruited some token Sunnis (e.g. General Mustafa
Tlas and, earlier, Abdul Halim Khaddam) as a cover to hide the sectarian
nature of the regime. Some Western pundits on CNN viewed this recruitment,
unbelievably, as a Sunni–Alawi alliance. This is pure nonsense. Are pundits
who operate on such misconceptions qualified to give proper briefings about
the Arab Spring?

What lessons can we learn about conflict coverage when it is produced in a culture
of politically correct restrictions that fails to distinguish between what is right and
what is wrong? Living as a Syrian exile in Germany, I cannot be silent about some
German journalists and politicians who adopt Syrian state propaganda, not only
(*FAZ*) denying the sectarianism that exists, but also (ARD) handing the Syrian
dictator Assad an opportunity to present his atrocities against the Sunni population
as a politics for 'countering terrorism'. I watched speechless as the former German politician Jörg Todenhöfer expressed his worries about the fate of the Assad
family, but not about the Syrian people. This propaganda interview, on prime-time
public German television, ended in whitewashing Assad and wishing him and his
family well. The world turned upside down!

Although I acknowledge the much higher quality of the *New York Times/
International Herald Tribune*, I often shake my head over some of its reports.

In the issue of Wednesday August 22, 2012, the *International Herald Tribune* published a top story on its front page, covered from 'Inside Syria'. The report is continued on a full page 4 under the heading 'Lives Reshaped by Syria's Civil War'. This huge report does not mention once that the rebels are Sunnis and the executioners of the regime are Alawis. These two parties are fighting one another in a protracted sectarian conflict. This is not an example of good journalism that cares about informing readers properly about what it is reporting.

As noted above, the German interview on the ARD channel on July 8, 2012, was covered by the *New York Times* on July 10, 2012. The day after the interview was broadcast, Monday, July 9, Todenhöfer appeared again on ARD, not only to reiterate the lie that Assad is fighting against al-Qaeda terrorists, but also to request President Obama to engage in a 'peace dialogue with Assad', to justify – as Todenhöfer put it – 'that he deserves the Nobel Prize for Peace awarded to him'. Comment is superfluous, except to remind the reader of the editorial column of the *Wall Street Journal* of June 15, 2012, which recognized Assad's game playing with the UN in the search for peace: the only peace Assad was looking for, it said, was 'the peace of the grave for his opponents'.[25] A few months later the *International Herald Tribune* did a better job than before. Confirming a reality that corresponded with what the *Wall Street Journal* editorial had assumed, on August 27 it reported on the front page: 'Mass Graves Evidence Slaughter by Assad Forces.' The report continues: 'Syrian soldiers searched house to house, killing as they went.' What spring is this?! Is this the peace that German and other Western pacifists are asking the Syrian rebels to submit to after laying down arms to dialogue peacefully with Assad? Those who designed the Nobel Prize for Peace and awarded it to Obama had a different concept of peace and how to qualify for it than the one employed by Todenhöfer. His recommendation to President Obama is simply scandalous.

The Arab Spring began for my home country Syria, and in my beloved Damascus, as a promise of freedom. Unfortunately, it also ignited a sectarian conflict of enormous consequence. The devastating flames of this conflict have made the place look like the wrath of God.

Sectarianism is an evil reality that resembles an 'irritating fly' (J. P. Sartre): it flies around you most disturbingly, and you can ignore it, but ignoring it does not mean that it ceases to exist. The conflict in Syria has not been, as some inadequately put it, 'threatening to become' a sectarian civil war in 2012; it is that already in full. The facts on the ground are that since the 1970 coup d'état in 1970 by the current president's father Hafez al-Assad, the Alawi Shi'ite minority of 11 per cent of the population has dominated all ranks of the army and security forces, and in so doing has enabled the Alawis to establish their grip over the entire country in a bloodthirsty (in the literal sense) dictatorship that knows no forbearance. The Arab Spring encouraged the suffering Sunni majority to rise up against this sectarian tyranny.

The protesting began in peaceful demonstrations in many Syrian cities. The Alawi-dominated army responded with artillery fire – heavy shelling assisted by attack helicopters – killing tens of thousands of innocent Sunni people. Can there be, under such conditions, any compromise in a peaceful solution? Some in the West naively believed there could: the UN envoy Kofi Annan – in his most unsuccessful mission – was one, and so were many Western pacifists. Aware that he had failed, Annan gave up. He failed to recognize what the *Wall Street Journal* had seen: that 'the killings have multiplied to include at least four massacres in two weeks . . . Mr. Assad and his protectors aren't going to accept any cease-fire or peace plan until it is the peace of the grave of his opponents.' The Alawis act hereby along the well-known 'Hama rules' (see note 27 below) of mass killing followed by bulldozing all traces, first to destroy the evidence and then deny it. The Assad regime practises these rules in the belief that it can only prevail by silencing (in the sense of the silence of the grave) the rebelling Sunni majority, rightly fearing the revenge of this community for the suffering it underwent throughout the past four decades of dire oppression enforced literally by slaughter.

In fairness, and without any acquitting of my Syrian Sunni community of the evil of sectarianism and of some evil intentions against Alawis that I believe I am free of, I contend that the incitement to sectarian resentment started on the hegemonic Alawi side. It was later – in reaction – also adopted by Sunnis. In Syria, as in other parts of the neighbouring countries, the difference between city culture and rural areas is a deeply civilizational one. It is described in the classic *Muqaddima* by Ibn Khaldun in the fourteenth century. The Alawi sect is based in a group of villages in the countryside of North Syria. With their ascendency as rulers of Syria under Hafez al-Assad after the coup of 1970, which was carried out by Alawi officers, the peasant villagers of the north started to move to the capital, Damascus. This migration was continued in the following decades, with the result that the Alawis incrementally dominated the city. Gradually the well-to-do residential parts of Damascus (e.g. the aristocratic Abu-Rummana, or Mazra'a) became Alawi residential areas. These resemble the exclusive white parts of South African cities under the apartheid regime, which were built at the expense of the native people. No wonder that they incite Sunni resentment.

Despite the Ibn Khaldunian tremendous civilizational gap between city and village dwellers, the rural Alawi conquerors of Damascus displayed a despicable superiority toward the original Sunni population of the city. The Alawi prejudice has been expressed in this Alawi saying describing the people of Damascus: '*Kul shami lahu alama wa hiya al-la'ama*'/'Every Damascene is marked by a sign and it is the vileness'. This sectarian prejudice heavily determines the response of the military ruling Alawi class against the oppressed Sunni city dwellers. I deeply deplore that the rebelling Sunni population also responds to the oppression with sectarian resentment. One has, though, to concede that the rebellion started peacefully (e.g. non-violent demonstrations in the streets), but it had to turn violent in reaction to the shelling by the regime's armed forces. Peaceful demonstrations were replaced by armed rebels because non-violence had no chance against shooting tanks and artillery. Non-violence became suicidal. It is extremely difficult for a scholar who happens to be a Sunni native of Damascus to keep cool and detached in response to this unfolding story of ruthless violence on both sides. Nonetheless, I continue to be fair and accuse both sides in the conflict of violent sectarianism.

Why write this book after leaving the stage? Confessions of a Sunni native of Damascus

The reference to Syria in the context of my identity is one of the two reasons mentioned at the start of the foregoing sections for the complexity of the sectarian reality involved. I cannot be silent about the place of my Sunni family of Damascus. It would be dishonest not to acknowledge its place in my thinking.

The leading Sunni Kadis and Muftis of the city from the thirteenth to the nineteenth century emerged from my family. In the late nineteenth century my grandfather Sadiq Pasha was the first to deviate from that tradition, serving as a general in the Ottoman army. Sadiq Pasha of Banu al-Tibi fell in 1907 in Yemen in defence of the Sunni Ottoman empire. Given these family roots in Damascus, no one can reasonably deny me outrage in response to the heavy shelling of the residential parts of the city of my birth by a military power that claims to be the national army of Syria. The tragedy is combined with the fact that I was part of all three of the Arab-Muslim ventures on democracy in the MENA region discussed above. All of these reasons create the context for my return to the stage after retirement to write this book. I decided to place the necessary justification for my return to the stage in this chapter on the Arab Spring, not in the Preface or Acknowledgements because this Spring is the core reason for writing this book. My story is as follows.

Following the completion of *Islamism and Islam* at Yale University I not only retired, but also left the stage in 2009. Exceptionally, though, in 2010 I accepted an affiliation as a senior fellow at the Center for Advanced Holocaust Studies in Washington, DC, for the simple reason that this fellowship provided a window of opportunity for revising the manuscript of my Yale book following a heavy reviewing process. Then came, unexpectedly, the Arab Spring in 2011. It was breathtaking and took every one of us by surprise. At first I started to update my Yale book, before it went to print, but thankfully the highly experienced and prudent senior editor, Bill Frucht, at Yale University Press, whom I quote with admiration in the opening remarks to this chapter, restrained me. In the end we agreed – despite all odds – to include in a last minute effort a sub-chapter to the one on democracy. This addition was facilitated by a delay in publication to 2012. Nonetheless, the acknowledgement to that book includes this firm decision: 'This book – apart from a collection of my unpublished papers (Routledge 2012) – would be my last one.... I end my public and academic life.'[26] Why did I then revoke this decision after the publication of these two books in 2012? I shall try to respond with honesty, hoping to be persuasive to avert possible remonstrations. I also need to justify the personal way of addressing the issues in point. I do this at length because the explanation is part of the assessment of the Arab Spring. In my view this political phenomenon named the 'Arab Spring' is just an indication of a simple hope for change. If it had not touched my heart and soul, as it does, I would have stuck to what was announced in my Yale book, but that was simply impossible.

By Western standards scholars are supposed to keep their emotions out of their books and articles to avoid the accusation of 'unscholarly sentiments'. In their rhetoric Western scholars allow a 'diversity' of cultures. If the lip service paid to this wisdom were honest, then there would be no problem and one would allow me to be personal at this juncture. It must be permitted to combine scholarly thinking and detached writing with human emotional involvement, as we Middle Easterners in our culture often do. I am a Middle Easterner. Even by Western epistemological standards, knowledge is based on the 'subject–object' interrelation and on the interaction between the two. No objectivity can keep the subjectivity (not to be confused with subjectivism) of the researcher out of the process of the search for knowledge. In the Introduction to this book I addressed the matter of culturally different styles of presentation and argumentation. I will not repeat them here.

How happy would I be if the Arab Spring were really a political season bearing the features of a spring. I would accept even an Indian summer, but not a terrible humid and blazing summer to be followed by a dark and lethal autumn to end up in a dreadful, not only frosty but murderous winter. I am a Sunni native of Damascus who found refuge in democratic Europe and I proudly hold European-German citizenship. This citizen identity does not, however, annihilate my culture of origin. For a Middle Easterner it is imperative to attend the funeral of one's parents. The Ba'th–Assad dictatorship prevented me from complying with this ethical duty. Had I gone to Damascus to fulfil not only an emotional need but also an Arab-Muslim ethical duty, I would have been escorted afterwards by the Alawi *mukhabarat* to suffer the barbarism of torture in the regime's prison. So how can I be silent about the ongoing change despite the announcement in my Yale book? I am an ethical person, not a coward!

In terms of bloodshed, Syria is today the worst place in the MENA region. The same applies to the lack of freedom and human dignity on all levels. How can this be changed? All the enlightened Arab intellectuals who met in Tunis, Limassol and Istanbul (see above) were not only in agreement about the high value of freedom needed by all Arab peoples in their suffering under dictatorship, but also that this freedom does not come from nowhere. Muslim-Arabs of the enlightened turn were full aware of the thorny path to a democracy that cannot be reduced to balloting after the unseating of a dictator. It follows that the democratization of the MENA region requires much more than just regime change. Saddam's regime in Iraq was as murderous as is Assad's in Syria. From the Iraq war we have learned that a simple regime change does not result in democracy. The Iraq of today under the rule of the Shi'ite Da'wa party is clearly not a democracy. True, the new ruler Maliki is not as bloody as Saddam was, but this does not make him a democratic ruler. This is a lesson for my home country Syria. Military intervention by the West – as happened in Iraq and Libya – could be damaging and is no help. What can we do to curb the crimes of the Syrian army? There is no clear recipe.

How could an army act in this barbarian manner against the people of the country that it is supposed to represent? As a schoolboy in Damascus I was exposed to state propaganda which focused on legitimizing the denial of individual freedoms and justifying high military expenditure at the expense of all basic needs. The central reference in that propaganda was to preparation of 'the core battle' in the fight against Zionism and Israel. Today, the officers of the Syrian army originate basically from the Alawi-Shi'ite sect. With the assistance of co-religionist snipers imported from Lebanon (Hezbollah) and Iran (Republican Guards) they murder thousands of civilians including children, women and elderly unarmed people. These brutally committed crimes are undertaken by tanks and infantry financed by the Syrian victims. The Sunni civilian population financed the killer army with their taxes.

Unlike the Turkish and Egyptian armies which are symbols of national unity and pride (even for Sunni Islamists), the Syrian army of today is a symbol of sectarian suppression. It kills Syrian people en masse (witness the atrocities in Damascus and Aleppo in July and August 2012, in Islam's holy month of Ramadan). Whenever the Alawi dictatorship ends, the present army will have to end with it. I am, however, fearful that there will be no democratization after Assad's fall. The potential for a payback against the Alawi officer corps by the Sunni majority of the Syrian population is large. In the Middle East, collective memories last a long time. In 1982 Hafez al-Assad, the father of the acting dictator Bashar al-Assad, established and put into practice the 'Hama rules', aptly described by Thomas Friedman as: 'no rules at all. . . . You do whatever it takes to stay in power . . . just defeat your foes. You bomb them in their homes and you steamroll them.'[27] These things happened in spring 1982. They were only practised in the form of a deterrent in the city of Hama to set an example for all Syrians. At that time, Assad the father ordered the overnight killing of about 30,000 innocent people by his sectarian Alawi army. The victims' crime was merely to dare to rebel against the sectarian Alawi dictatorship. The new uprising in Syria, which has been going on since 2011, has given the sectarian Alawi regime a pretext to commit a series of massacres that are turning the country into a mass grave. This process means in Syria that Assad the son is extending the Hama rules to the entire population, including the Sunnis of my home city Damascus. What kind of a spring is that? How could I stay put and be silent? My answer to this tragedy is this book. I hope that this sad story persuades the reader to forbearance.

Sunnis and Alawis killing one another in Syria: the lethal season of 2012 is no spring

In the first section on Syria I expressed my dismay at the Western coverage of the crimes in Syria against my people. Although I believe that the *New York Times/ International Herald Tribune* is no exception, I want exceptionally to praise a few of its reports. In one of the best reports published in this newspaper on the Syrian massacres, one reads the well-known fact that Assad's 'community are the Alawites . . . They closed ranks . . . As Syria's conflict escalates to new levels of sectarian strife . . . the Alawite core of the elite security forces is still with him (Assad).'[28] Other media are silent about these facts. It is acknowledged that a tiny fraction of the Alawi sect reasonably fears future repercussions (i.e. Sunni vengeance) and thinks 'that Mr. Assad is risking the future of the Alawites by pushing them to the brink of a civil war with Sunni Muslims'. However, the Alawi majority continues the commitment to the Hama rules as the only way to survive. Some Alawi fanatics blame the son Bashar 'as being torn soft, saying that his father and

predecessor as president, Hafez al-Assad, would have quashed the threat by now.'
True, the killer-father was a real butcher who ordered the killing of around 30,000
people in Hama. This 'job' was done in just a few days. Thereafter, these Alawi
executioners bulldozed the evidence. In contrast, son Assad needed more than a
year to kill as many innocent civilians as his father did in a few days.

The Alawi dictatorship that has lasted in Syria since 1970 cannot continue for
ever, not even with the shameful support of the superpowers China and Russia,
which not only obstruct international condemnation of the crimes, but also any
action to stop them. Hillary Clinton asked at a session of the UN Security Council:
'How can this be done without the risk of paying a price for this?' When the time
comes that this dictatorship falls, there will be a price. I also fear a sectarian day
of reckoning, with bloodshed of dire vengeance and a great hatred for Russia and
China. As a non-sectarian Sunni Damascene I am fearful of the future. I would
condemn any revenge as much as I condemn the Alawi crimes against my community – but this kind of balanced sentiment counts for little in this heat!

To be sure, the reference to the potential of a bloody future prospect of sectarian payback does not reflect my thinking, but merely a realist assessment of what
may happen. As a Sunni Syrian I feel on the one hand great outrage at the action
of the Alawi killers, but – on the other – as a follower of civil Islam I would never
approve revenge. I cannot repeat often enough the expression of this attitude and
the statement that the prospect of sectarian strife is merely a description of facts,
not the tainting of an uprising against a ruthless dictatorship. Of course, I acknowledge the true character of the revolt as a call for freedom against dictatorial rule.
However, one would have to be blind not to note three important facts:

- The oppressors are Alawis (approximately 10 to 11 per cent of the population),
  while the oppressed are Sunnis (the majority of about 80 per cent of the population). This self-awareness and identity politics determines both groups.
- Sectarian divide means a lot in the culture of the Middle East. This is not my
  contention but a fact of everyday life in that region.
- Middle Easterners – of whom I am one – have long collective memories
  with regard to both the positive (gratitude) and the negative (reasons for
  vengeance).

I mention these facts as a scholar, not in my capacity as a Sunni-Muslim native
of Damascus. In my young years in Damascus I was a pan-Arab nationalist (Nas-
serist) and thus against any sectarian division of the Arab nation. When I became
a Marxist in German exile in Frankfurt I adhered to a universalist humanism that
outlaws any sectarianism. Today, I belong to those Muslims who subscribe to civil
Islam of the 'enlightened turn'. Thus, religious fanaticism is alien to me. In all
three stages of my life I rejected sectarian identity and all that relates to it. But I am
a scholarly analyst who avoids wishful thinking. In this capacity I see no spring,
but a sectarian strife that threatens to be followed by vengeance.

Under the present conditions the feared payback seems inevitable, and therefore
I ask this question: would a counter-action by the Sunni Muslim Brothers against

the Alawi sect in Syria be the launch of democratization? In the example of post-Nazi Germany one sees how Hitler's henchmen were punished under the rule of democracy. It is certain that in Syria there will be no legal Nuremberg-style trial for the Assad clan and its Alawi executioners. After the fall of Hitler there was no bloody revenge. Syria resembles Libya rather than Germany. The illegal shooting of Qadhafi is a clear case. I may say as a believing Muslim – Allah/God forbids the shedding of blood in revenge, but as an analyst I fear that this prospect may become a reality. Assad's destiny resembles Qadhafi's. In this case, however, his entire community is also at stake.

What are the future prospects for Syria? At the time of writing – the second half of 2012 in the holy month of Ramadan – it seems to be certain that the Assad regime will fall, but no certain predictions can be made concerning the timing. Knowing the dire future prospects for their sectarian community, the Alawi army officers will presumably fight endlessly, regardless of how many thousands of Sunni people they kill. So the realistic forecast is: there will be a protracted bloody conflict. No one can foresee when it will end. It could take several years of continued crimes by the regime against the civilian population.

How long will the 'international community' be silent about the crimes of the Alawi-Assad regime? There is an International Criminal Court in The Hague – will it act? Lydia Palgreen thinks, in a *New York Times* article, that 'Mr. Assad is likely to evade prosecution'.[29] Why? Because the court cannot act without the approval of the United Nations Security Council. As much as the US would veto the prosecution of its friends (e.g. the king of Bahrain), Russia and China, being the powerful allies of Syria, would never allow the court to indict the crimes of Assad. Palgreen quotes the reproach directed against 'an inherent selectivity of the court's prosecution'. The court applies its so-called justice only to insignificant 'outcast leaders', primarily low-key politicians in sub-Saharan Africa, while letting all top murderers continue their crimes – as Assad does – and in this to 'proceed with impunity'. Commenting, she rightly asks 'whether the failure to prosecute autocrats of the Arab Spring will erode faith in the movement toward a truly universal system of international justice.'

I have to keep repeating that this chapter, like the book in general, has no intention to catch up with events related to the Arab Spring in an effort to update, not even on Syria. The intention is rather to analyse the overall phenomenon in order to understand it. In the case of Syria one is caught in the difficult job, on the one hand, of showing the place of the Islamists in the rebellion, and on the other, of contradicting Arab dictators, like Assad, who legitimate their crackdown on the opposition with the fake claim of 'countering the terrorism of al-Qaeda', hoping for US support. While security-obsessed US experts (e.g. D. Byman, quoted in Palgreen's article; see also p. 119 *note 11 cit.*) project their obsession with al-Qaeda into the Syrian rebellion, Syrian rebels complain to the *New York Times* that 'every now and then we hear about al-Qaeda in Syria, but there is so far no material evidence'. It is quite reassuring to read in a *New York Times* report the acknowledgement that 'mainstream Syrian rebels are nearly uniformly opposed to a role of al-Qaeda in their popular uprising'.[30] The truth is that the development of the sectarian Sunni–Alawi conflict will burden Syrian society for decades to come, in particular in the aftermath of the Assad dictatorship. The *New York Times* report just quoted acknowledges the truth in this statement of facts: 'the battle evolved into a sectarian war between a Sunni dominated opposition and . . . security forces dominated by the Alawi minority.'

The same *New York Times* edition of July 26, 2012 includes an editorial comment by Thomas Friedman, whom I repeatedly quote in this chapter. Under the heading 'Syria is Iraq', Friedman refers to the sectarian feature addressed here. First he reminds readers of the 'Hamas rules' notion he coined earlier (see p. 135 *note 27 cit.*) to describe the crimes of the Assad regime, and then he frankly acknowledges the sectarian character of the Ba'th rule that uses pan-Arab nationalism as a legitimation, when in fact it is sectarian, not pan-Arab at all. All Sunni Arab states are against Assad-Syria; the only regional ally of this dictatorship is Shi'ite Iran. Friedman writes: 'The Assad regime deliberately killed demonstrators to turn this conflict into a sectarian struggle between the ruling minority Alawi sect, led by the Assad clan, and the country's majority of Sunni Muslims.'

So what is going to happen when the massacres of the 'Arab Spring' in Syria end? It is in no way an expression of Orientalism when Friedman states this traditional piece of wisdom: 'In the Middle East the alternative to bad is not always good. It can be worse.' However, he is wrong if he means that a vengeful Sunni *shari'a* state in Syria would be even worse than the bloodshed that has been going on since 2011. No *shari'a* state could ever be as bloodthirsty as the Alawi–Shi'ite regime of the Assad clan. I do not share Friedman's view despite my fears of a payback. For a better understanding of what may happen after the fall of the Alawi Assad regime, it is important to reveal what this regime's army did to Sunni Muslims, especially in the holy month of Ramadan 2012. I do not believe that even the Muslim Brothers would do anything like this.

In Islamic belief Ramadan is not only a holy month of fasting, to fulfil the fifth pillar of the Muslim faith; it is also a month of peace, respect and devoted observance. Conspicuously, this does not apply to Syria under the sectarian Alawi-dominated Ba'th regime of the Assad clan. At the beginning of Ramadan the ground forces of the regime, assisted by attack helicopter gunships provided by Putin's Russia, invaded the Sunni city of Aleppo after the technically successful bloody crackdown on rebels in Damascus. For Muslims, Ramadan ends with *'id al-fitr*, a religious feast of breaking the fast which in its significance resembles Christmas for Christians. At the time of writing, the time of the ending of the fast and the expected joy of *'id al-fitr*, Syrian Sunnis of Damascus and Aleppo were under bombardment from the Alawi air force of the Assad clan. On August 21 the powerful Arabic newspaper *al-Hayat* (printed in London) on its front page reported hundreds of victims in Damascus. After killing, their corpses were beheaded. What an *'id al-fitr* in Syria.

With the help of the international media, I followed all these crimes with great distress and pain from my home in German asylum. I am most grateful for this safe refuge in Europe, but I repeatedly deplore the inability of the German media to learn from their shameful Nazi past. With the exception of the

July 1941 Stauffenberg attempt to topple Hitler, the Germans submitted and were not as courageous as the Syrian rebels in their uprising against the Assad Alawi dictatorship. During the last weekend of July 2012, the impression that German viewers were given by the powerful public broadcasting, with its two major television channels ARD and ZDF, is that the Syrian army was successful in taming 'the terrorist criminals and people on drugs' in Damascus, thereafter to turn on them in Aleppo. On Sunday July 28 (at 7 p.m.), ZDF reported – just like the Syrian state propaganda – on the persecution and alleged crimes of Sunnis against the Shi'ites in Damascus. This is a complete reversal of the reality on the ground. The German media failed miserably to provide a balanced and well-informed coverage of the massacres committed by the Alawi regime on the Sunni majority population. The German public television channel ARD stood in great contrast to others – for instance, the balanced BBC television – when on July 26, 2012 it covered the Ramadan offensive of the Alawi troops against Aleppo, the largest Sunni city of Syria, with pictures and information adopted from the Syrian government's television propaganda. The story told was that the Assad regime is 'fighting terrorists'. The investigation run by the ARD reporter in Damascus consisted merely of interviewing fled Alawis in his luxury hotel. They told him the government is after 'terrorists' and 'people on drugs'. Based on my knowledge of my home country Syria under Assad, I am quite sure that the interviews were arranged by the Syrian secret police. In Syria under Assad, no foreign journalist can do anything that escapes regime surveillance. What shameful journalism, and what wrong coverage of what is called 'the Arab Spring in Syria'. This kind of journalism happens in a country, Germany, that is supposed to honour people who stand up to fight tyranny. The rebels of Damascus and Aleppo display a courage that was lacking in Germany under Hitler. At least the German journalists could have explained to their viewers – had they had some knowledge and sensitivity (but they did not) – what it means for Muslims for two great cities of Muslim history, Damascus and Aleppo, in the holy month of Ramadan, to be shelled by the artillery of the ground forces and from the air by attack helicopters. Neither the medieval crusaders who came to Damascus, nor the modern French colonial troops that colonized Syria, ever committed any crime of this magnitude. The executioners are the officers of the military force composed of Muslims too, who are not only Syrians, but also members of the Alawi sect. How can a crime like this be allowed to pass unpunished? How can one call this lethal season a 'spring'?

To sum up: what happened on the ground, in particular in the sectarian case of Syria, gives the lie to Western views. The contrast between the wishful thinking about an 'Arab Spring' and the reality on the ground is tremendous. The unchecked assumption of a swift process of democratization is invalidated. Such views, as they operate on a weak basis, are wrong. In contrast, the reasoning of Arab opinion leaders (see notes 17–19 and Abdou Ansari-Filaly, who speaks for those Muslims engaged in an 'enlightened turn') provide better alternatives for thinking about democracy in the Arab world. The West would be well advised to listen to their voices, introduced above and in Chapter 3 of this book.

The precarious balance of the Arab Spring: the cases of Tunisia, Egypt and Libya

The other cases of the Arab Spring are less dramatic, but they too are not promising as they are not delivering the promised democratization. In Tunisia and in Egypt 'the Arab Spring' went smoother than in Syria. However, the unseating of the dictators did not yield what the rebelling people have expected.

The rule of the toppled dictatorships was highly varying in degree of oppression: Ben Ali and Mubarak were not as bloody and brutal against political opposition as Qadhafi was and Assad still is. Ali Saleh of Yemen was a caricature of himself. However – with the exception of Tunisia, where it is coupled with great doubts – the hoped-for foundation of democracy has not taken place, nor is it in sight. The Arab rebellion (not yet a revolution) of 2011 was not of an Islamist making. In 2012 it became clear, however, that Islamist movements have been able to successfully hijack the rebellion and put their imprint on it. For them, 'democracy' serves as a tool to climb up the ladder to power.

Tunisia is a unique Arab country with a civil society and a strong secular tradition that dates back to de-colonization under Habib Bourguiba, the secular founder of modern Tunisia. After the unseating of Ben Ali, Tunisian An-Nahda Islamists were able to adjust and compromise in order to establish a coalition government with non-Islamists. For how long? In the second half of 2012, Western media focused on Syria and mostly ignored what was happening in Tunisia. In August 2012 a draft for a new Tunisian constitution was discussed. In article 26 this draft abolishes the gender equality that existed earlier under Bourguiba, who introduced constitutionally based gender equality among other items of modernity. In this regard Tunisia was the first and the pioneer among all Muslim states to introduce women's rights. In August 2012 there were huge demonstrations by women in Tunis protesting against the abolition of these rights under the new Tunisian Islamocracy, but there was no coverage of this outrage by the *New York Times*, for instance, or by most Western media. Nonetheless, the slaying of the leader of secular Tunisian opposition Chokri Belaid on February 7, 2013 by Islamists was covered in the West.

In an article that I published two decades ago in *Human Rights Quarterly* on 'Islamic Law *shari'a*' (see note 67) I demonstrated the incompatibility of this law with most of the individual human rights including the right to gender equality. The Tunisian Islamists knew what they were doing when they drafted the new constitution in 2012. On August 20, 2012 *al-Hayat* published on its front page a report on the Egyptian case under the heading '*Mutalabat al-Ikhwan bi Tatbiq al-Shari'a*'/'Brotherhood Demand Implementation of *Shari'a*'. This demand did not set 'any limits for this implementation'. How could *shari'a* law, which outlaws individual human rights, be part of a democratization agenda? This section is directed by the question of why – apart from balloting – the Arab Spring did not result in laying some cornerstones for genuine democracy in the Arab world. I operate on the understanding that the democratic rule hoped for in Arab countries is much more than the ballot box. I do not see one single promising sign of a process of a genuine democratization, unless one believes that democracy consists merely of a ballot box regardless of the outcome and of the nature of the new rulers.

Egypt is the most important country of the MENA region. There, the Islamists promised a mere non-hegemonic participation and to abandon a claim for presidency. At the end of the game these promises proved to be fake. Instead of keeping their promise, the Islamists imposed their own candidate Mohammed Morsi. The Muslim Brothers managed to get the presidency of the country. In a game of various tactics the Egyptian Islamists have been able not only to sideline but also to silence all secular parties and to subdue the Coptic Christian minority. The Supreme Constitutional Court stood up to the Islamists and took the decision in a constitutional ruling to dissolve the fake and therefore illegal election of the parliament.[31] The Islamists tampered with the rules of the election and the court rejected this as illegal. But in overriding the court's decision the new Islamist president Morsi seems not to comply with constitutional law.

This is the story: in terms of proportional representation Egyptian election law reserves one third of the 508-member assembly for individual candidates competing in winner-takes-all races. Only two thirds of the seats are designated for party lists. The Freedom and Justice party, the institutional extension of the Muslim Brotherhood, tampered with the legal rule and sent its members also to campaign, illegally, as individual candidates. This Freedom and Justice Party won 135 seats according to its party list; however, it won an additional 100 seats through organized Islamists who were elected as individual candidates. This is illegal and unconstitutional. This is why the Supreme Constitutional Court invalidated the election and dissolved parliament. That was a decision of the court, not of the military, as some biased Western media wrongly reported, thus doing a favour to the Islamists.

After the tampering I have described, the election ended in an Islamist-led parliament and all non-Islamist parties had a poor showing. The results reflected the deficient parliamentary election that was prematurely pushed for jointly by the US and by the Muslim Brothers. From Cairo, David Kirkpatrick wrote in the *International Herald Tribune* after the dissolution of the parliament: 'Some lawmakers said they welcomed the dissolution of Parliament though it cost them their seats. They were afraid of the power of the Islamists, said Emad Gad, a leader of the secular Social Democratic Party's parliamentary bloc.'[32] The Muslim Brotherhood was ready for the election, but non-Islamist parties were not. The Muslim Brothers ignored the legal rules. Kirkpatrick also reported from Cairo that 'the Muslim Brotherhood . . . Egypt's best organized political force . . . almost immediately began preparing for elections.' This included the tampering with the rules I have mentioned in a 'misapplication of rules for independent candidates'. The Supreme Constitutional Court did not wait long and invalidated the elected legislature in response. What happened then? How did Islamists react?

The new Islamist president of Egypt had little respect for the Constitutional Court's ruling and insisted on being sworn in in front of the dissolved parliament. This did not work to the extent that he compromised and finally accepted being sworn in in front of the Supreme Constitutional Court. He did this to avoid an escalation that might have cost him the office of the presidency itself. However, once an empowered, constitutionally sworn-in president he paid back afterwards by overruling the court in an illegal action: he refused to recognize the court's dissolution of the parliament. The front page headline of the *International Herald Tribune* of July 10 was: 'Egypt Court Rises to Morsi Challenge.' The illegal action of the new Islamist president in ordering the return of the dissolved Islamist-led parliament was intended to cast into question the authority of the Supreme Constitutional Court: it was a challenge to the court's ruling that the composition of the parliament was unconstitutional. The *New York Times/International Herald Tribune* (*NYT/IHT*) reported that, in full respect of the court's ruling and its authority, non-Islamist members of parliament refused to attend the ordered session. The human rights lawyer Ahmed Ragheb told the *NYT/IHT* that 'Morsi used his power as president just like the military used it'. And the Egyptian Nobel Laureate and one-time non-Islamist candidate for presidency Mohammed ElBaradei qualified Morsi's decision to overrule the Constitutional Court as 'turning Egypt from a government of law into a government of men'.[33] Although elected, these men are positively not democrats but Islamist activists. The *NYT/IHT* rightly commented that the Islamist president has set 'a dangerous precedent by overruling Egypt's Supreme Constitutional Court'. This politicized conduct does not indicate respect for the rule of law in a democracy. Morsi not only challenged Egypt's Supreme Constitutional Court, he did the same to US justice. As the *NYT/IHT* informed readers in a news analysis, the Islamist president Mohammed Morsi requested from US president Barak Obama the release of the jihadist sheykh Abdul Rahman. This 'notorious terrorist' (*NYT/IHT*) is serving a life sentence in a US prison after being convicted of seditious conspiracy in connection with the terrorist assaults on New York in 1993, among other crimes. This sentence was handed down by a US court. Islamists challenge the US and ask it to ignore the law of its own justice system in the name of respect for other cultures.

The new Islamist president Mohammed Morsi has not only challenged the Supreme Constitutional Court but also the Muslim Brothers' most powerful enemy, the army. The future prospect is therefore of a fight between the Islamist Muslim Brotherhood and the secular army. The precedent for this fight in the MENA region is the struggle in Turkey between the AKP and the Kemalist army. Islamists have the resolve to establish a rule of a believed majority against all kinds of minorities and they bill this new tyranny as a democracy! What a democracy charged with *shari'a* rule!

The next case to look at in taking stock of the Arab Spring is post-Qadhafi Libya. An Oxford University survey conducted in Libya revealed that most Libyans do not yearn for democracy, but rather for a strongman to restore the order that has been lost in the anarchy caused by the dominance of armed militias. In this account I shall quote two *NYT/IHT* reports on Libya. Both support the doubts about the ballot box as the stairway to democracy. It is a mere illusion. In September 2011 the two *New York Times* correspondents of the first report from Libya, Rod Nordland and David Kirkpatrick, tell us: 'For an uprising that was overwhelmingly secular and populist, the growing influence and power of Islamist people with hard-line or fundamentalist views, who want a society governed by Islamic principles, is striking.'[34] The most important political leader among these Islamists is Sheykh Ali Salabi, while the most important commander is Abdul Hakim Belhaj, a former jihadist with an Afghan background. This sheykh 'made it clear' to the *New York Times* 'that what he and his followers want is for a political party based on Islamic principles to come to power through democratic elections.' In the second report the reader is enlightened about the way elections take place in Libya. They look like this: 'Militias could bully voters, suppress voters or otherwise dominate the process, leaving Libya mired in internecine violence.' What could the solution be? Kirkpatrick's report continues: 'Libya may now expect . . . the rise of a new strong man.' The reference to the poll among Libyans mentioned above (conducted by an Oxford University research centre) includes these findings: 'Libyans appear to distrust democracy . . . only 15 percent of more than 2000 respondents said they wanted some form of democracy . . . while 42 percent said they hoped Libya would be governed by a new strongman.' This strongman could be a modernized Islamist imam who acts as a political leader, that is, with a reference to the traditional meaning of a legitimate imam who acts as a ruler of the *umma*.[35]

Under the outlined conditions of lawlessness, elections took place on Saturday July 7 in Libya with surprising results, but – nonetheless – as expected with tribal effects and results. Libya is a country composed of tribes, not a real nation. The winner of the elections was Dr. Mahmoud Jibril of the Warfalla tribe. The turnout for him was over 60 per cent. The Warfalla is the most populous of the Libyan tribes; it accounts for one million out of an overall population of six million people. Next behind it is the Misrata tribe, characterized by a deep enmity towards the Warfalla that has existed since the Italian occupation of the country in the last century, when a leader of the Misrata was killed by some Warfalla warriors. This kind of enmity is a central component of tribal culture. The Misrata tribe controls forceful militias. In Libya there are approximately 200,000 armed tribesmen organized in hundreds of militias. Next to these there is the Muslim Brotherhood with its branch in Libya. This movement formed a bloc that went to the elections, but failed to attain a majority because of the prevailing tribal loyalties. To harm the reputation of Jibril, who holds a doctorate in political science from a US university, Islamists hurled accusations at him, referring to his years in the US coupled with the words 'liberalism' and 'secularism'. These can be harmful in the world of Islam. Jibril is a wise and educated man who knew how to respond properly, asking: 'Do you think they (the Islamists) are more Muslim then we are?' In a *NYT/IHT* news analysis in July 2012, Scott Shane cited this statement by Jibril, noting that 'Jibril went out of his way to reject the secular label of his National Forces Alliance and reached out to the Islamists'.[36] This is an indication of an alliance between tribes and Islamists that reflects a kind of an agenda for Libya that sees a coalition, half tribal and half religious, to rule the country in a modest *shari'a* state. After the parliamentary elections, a new government was built in 2012 that reflects this religious–tribal coalition.

A preliminary assessment

As I have stated, I do not wish to chronicle or provide a survey of the events related to the Arab Spring; I take pains to keep up with the big picture. This happens with an orientation to historical sociology (see note 2). At this point the empirical part provided in the previous sections on the cases of Syria, Tunisia, Egypt and Libya stops, and I return to the overall assessment of the Arab Spring.

In all the country cases discussed above, the hoped-for democratization has been used by Islamists to promote their project of the 'implementation of *shari'a*'. As earlier argued, this is neither the understanding of *shari'a* as it stands in the Qur'an (see Chapters 1 and 2), nor the traditional *shari'a* in Islamic history (see Chapter 5). Islamism focuses on a new vision for a state order and for the world at large. In the aftermath of the Arab Spring everything seems to revolve around the issue of *shari'a*. The question that arises is this: Why was it not possible to foresee these developments, to restrain the high expectations regarding democracy that arose shortly after the Arab Spring? To answer this question properly one needs to review the background.

Prior to the Arab Spring, the Arab world, caught in the resistance of its rulers towards the global third wave of democratization, stood outside this world-historical process. It is fortunate that not all Western observers shared the naive enthusiasm prevailing at that time, propelled by wishful thinking, about global democratization. One contemporary realist, Robert Kaplan, asked: 'Was democracy just a moment?'; he pretended that his 'pessimism (is) just a foundation for prudence'.[37] On these grounds he painted a 'murky record' of the 'Third World's venue for democracy'. Underlying this pessimist realism is the fact that 'civil institutions are required for successful democracy'. The truth is that in most non-Western states there is a great lack of such an institutional underpinning for democracy. Added to this is the lack of a political culture of pluralism and power sharing. A democracy reduced to the ballot box can only be a poor democracy, if one at all. In this context Kaplan reminds us that 'Hitler and Mussolini each came to power through democracy. Democracies do not always make society civil.' The bottom line is this: that 'states have never been formed by elections'. States are based either on civil institutions, or authoritarian rule. If you topple an authoritarian regime and fail to build civil institutions – as is happening for instance in Libya after the Arab Spring and even after the elections of July 7, 2012 – then you either smooth the way for a new authoritarianism (e.g. the *shari'a* state) or you open the door to 'the coming anarchy'. These two trends existed at the same time in 2012 in post-Qadhafi Libya.

I profess that I am mostly in agreement with Kaplan's assessment, which was published back in 2000. Eleven years ahead of the Arab Spring he outlined the potential for a possible outcome. At that time and in that book, Kaplan displayed a rare honesty that is missing, not only in most scholarly books on global democratization, but also in most policy pronouncements of Western politicians, whether they originate from the US or the European Union. Kaplan acknowledges this about Western policy: 'Of course, our post-Cold War mission to spread democracy is partly a pose . . . We praise democracy, and meanwhile are grateful for an autocrat.' This autocrat could be Hosni Mubarak in pre-Arab-Spring Egypt or the Muslim Brother Mohammed Morsi, the new president of the country, accepted and applauded by the West. In this context one is reminded that democracy means also the rule of law. The first action of the new Islamist president of Egypt was to override a ruling of his country's Supreme Constitutional Court. He simply ignored the court's ruling that parliament should be dissolved based on the evidence that its composition was unconstitutional.

Kaplan was not quite alone, however; a few others had similar foresight. Among the dozens of articles by battalions of pundits, I have found only a very small set of really knowledgeable and therefore helpful contributions that are an aid to understanding the Arab Spring in its overall context. Among the noteworthy contributions are two pieces by Eric Trager and an article by Raymond Stock. The first piece by Trager, which I have already discussed in the Introduction to this book, bears the title 'The Unbreakable Muslim Brotherhood: Grim Prospects for a Liberal Egypt', a telling title which is a statement in itself that needs no comment; the second article I will come to in a moment.[38] I shall start here with two questions posed by Raymond Stock: first, how could one trust an authoritarian movement based on secrecy and clandestine action, and characterized by doublespeak intended to deceive? And, second, how could a movement that is structured hierarchically on the basis of a totalitarian ideology be a champion of true democratization? Bravely, Raymond Stock states clearly that the Muslim Brotherhood is a movement

> with an implacably anti-Western, anti-secular, anti-Christian, antisemitic, anti-female, Moslem-supremacist ideology . . . Yet, most of the world still sees its leaders not as they are but as they wish them to be: moderate, liberal, interested more in economic well-being than holy war . . . but we have no evidence at all that they have changed so far.[39]

As demonstrated in Chapter 1, this wishful thinking prevails in the dominating Western narrative on Islamism, on moderation and on the Arab Spring.

Stock lived for 20 years in Egypt and knows the Egyptian bittersweet sense of humour. Using the figure of the donkey as it is used in Egyptian jokes as a vehicle to ridicule stupidity, Stock fears that the West will 'be the donkey on which the Muslim Brotherhood and its fellow travellers ride to ultimate power in Egypt and in the Middle East'. Unlike those theorists who are obsessed with abstract models of 'moderation', both Trager and Stock know the country and its culture well and speak the local language. They also know many of the actors involved in person. They are more credible than those who lack these attributes. At issue is also the credibility of the Islamists, whose pronouncements approve democracy and power sharing, but are belied by their action. How serious and trustworthy is this? Let us examine the political conduct of the Brotherhood.

One of the most knowledgeable scholars of political Islam (whom despite some disagreement I highly respect), Emad Shahin, notes in an article on the Arab

Spring in Egypt that the Muslim Brothers joined the uprising of Tahrir Square in a coalition with non-Islamists on this basis: the Brotherhood 'agreed not to raise any of its religious slogans and gave assurances that after Mubarak's ouster, it would not field a candidate [for the presidency] nor would it run for more than 35% of the seats of the parliament.'[40] Shahin also tells us that among the basic features of the uprising 'was the leaderless nature . . . [it] had no leading figure, group, vanguard, or movement'. It is unfortunate that Shahin fails to add that the Muslim Brotherhood abused this leaderless revolt. They made promises that they do not keep and continue to do exactly the opposite to their pronouncements. They abused the Arab Spring and conned the world. So how could one trust them?

To continue the process of this clearing, I turn to the second of the articles I mentioned by Eric Trager, which enlightens best, giving in a few pages authentic knowledge about the Muslim Brothers in Egypt that cannot be found in many volumes of Western Islamic studies on this matter (see note 38). His concern is to understand how to make sense of the politics of a movement that has 'risen swiftly from the cave to the castle', that is, from the underground of clandestine action to ruling with one of its leaders as the president of the largest Arab country. The Muslim Brothers' head start is due not just to its popularity, but also to its ability to mobilize on the basis of temporary tactical coalitions with non-Islamists. They make promises to the latter that they do not keep, and form coalitions for simple convenience. Therefore, these coalitions 'are typically short-lived', as Trager notes. These coalitions have pursued 'unity projects' for a few months and helped 'enable the brotherhood to build up its profile as a leading political party', but once the Brothers' goal was reached, they abandoned the coalitions. The inclusion of non-Islamists in Islamist politics is thus 'more about symbolism than genuine power sharing'. After all, the 'Brotherhood Guidance Office' operates professedly on '*shari'a* principles', although with great caution and flexibility. For instance, the Muslim Brotherhood engages with the Supreme Council of the Armed Forces (SCAF) 'apparently in hashing out a deal . . . while tabling other areas of disagreement', and does this most successfully. One result of this politics has been the deal for SCAF to approve the presidency of the Islamist Mohammed Morsi. Trager rightly notes: 'The Brotherhood's arrangement with the SCAF is not surprising.' Such a deal is acceptable to the Islamists so long as it contributes to their 'achieving power incrementally'. Morsi told Trager in an interview that 'our program is a long term one, not a short term one', and therefore he is against 'rushing things . . . this leads to a real stable position'. However, when the Muslim Brotherhood is empowered, it acts differently. Trager comments: 'The brotherhood's attempt to appear inclusive while also accommodating . . . will not last.' Only a few weeks after the publication of Trager's enlightening remarks about the Brotherhood's short-lived coalitions and about the deal it struck with SCAF, real life validated his assessment. On Monday August 13, 2012 the front page of the *NYT/IHT* announced: 'Morsi Forces Key Military Leaders to Step Down', thus ending the coalition. At the end of the 'long game' the Muslim Brotherhood will be empowered to the extent of being able to accomplish the goal of a *shari'a* state billed as an 'Islamic democracy'. This is what matters most.

Some Western pundits accept Islamist pretensions, in which democracy and the *'shari'a* state' are confused. For instance, Noah Feldman argues for 'the necessity of Islamic democracy' in the 'process of democratization in the Muslim world'.[41] He wrote this in 2003. One has to give credit to Feldman for some realism as he stated in 2003 that the idea of an Islamic state 'may never manage to bring about the . . . downfall of the Egyptian dictatorship. No realist could claim . . . such a development'. Well, Mubarak fell and one of the best Egyptian political scientists, Shahin, tells us (see note 40) it was the people of Egypt, not the idea of *shari'a*, that toppled the dictator.

In that early book Noah Feldman states his trust in Islamists, which is based on his belief that 'Islamists everywhere enjoy a reputation for sincerity . . . Islamists speak a language of truth'. 'Everywhere' includes Egypt and the Muslim Brotherhood. The belief in the 'sincerity' of the Islamists not only overlooks their tradition of double-speak (see note 41) but also betrays an astounding naivety. This judgement was published ahead of the Arab Spring. US decision-makers, for whatever reason, listen to and accept this kind of thinking. Five years after that book Feldman published a new and more serious one, but he continues to maintain his illusions about Islamism. These are demonstrated in the new book as follows: *'shari'a* can provide the necessary resources . . . *shari'a* aspires to be law . . . no one is above it.'[42] The reader is advised to rectify this misconception through the evidence presented in Chapter 2 because I do not want to repeat it, but ask: What is wrong with Feldman's argument? The answer is: Most of it.

After the election of the Islamist Mohammed Morsi, the US Secretary of State Hillary Clinton rushed to Cairo in mid-July to endorse him. There she was received by protesting members of the Christian minority that is suffering under the Muslim Brothers. The demonstrators were carrying signs with slogans such as 'Clinton, you are not welcome in Egypt'. In both the books I have cited, Feldman confuses Islam and Islamism, using the terms interchangeably in an inconsistent manner. He seems to know the literature as he also quotes the first of my book trilogy on political Islam. Had he read Chapter 8 on 'The *Shari'a* State' and Chapter 9 on 'Democracy and Democratization: An Alternative' in *The Challenge of Fundamentalism* he quotes, he would have reconsidered. To avoid misunderstanding I repeat what I wrote in the Introduction, namely that democracy in the Islamicate needs some Islamic legitimacy; it could and should rest on Islamic ethics,[43] but this is not tantamount to an approval of the *shari'a* state disguised – as the Muslim Brotherhood disguises it – as 'Islamic democracy'.

Everything is subject to change and Islamism is no exception. However, the work of the major political ideologue of Islamism, Sayyid Qutb, continues to provide the guidelines and the main source of inspiration. Even though he spent part of his life in the prison of one of the authoritarian regimes, Egypt, and in 1966 was hanged in public by the executioners of Nasser's regime, Qutb was not favourably disposed towards democracy. Many Western scholars ignore this mindset and continue to believe in swift democratization with Islamist assistance and leadership. Qutb never shared the hopes of those Muslims who yearn for democratization. In his major pamphlet *Ma'alim fi al-Tariq*/Signposts Along the Road, he sets off on the first page with this derogatory statement: 'Democracy is finished in a way that resembles bankruptcy'.[44] Later in the same booklet he presents the alternative, namely 'the Islamic state dominated [*tuhaymin alayha*] by the *shari'a*'. Given that the idea of a *shari'a* state stands at the core of Islamist political thought, one is compelled to ask: Will this order be the outcome of the Arab Spring after its hijacking by Islamism? Will the empowered Islamist movements really contribute to democratization and be part of this effort? And, last but not least: Have the Islamists changed the views on democracy that they adopted from Qutb and Qaradawi? I fail to see the change imputed to Islamists by the theorists of moderation.

'People ignore predictions they dislike'

Aware that my analysis of Islamism may not be welcomed by the establishment of Islamic studies, and also by political advisors, I draw a comparison between my warnings about Islamist movements and the ignored warnings of a looming financial crisis. The warnings about the financial crisis were referred to in a commentary published in the *Financial Times* of December 30, 2008 under the heading: 'People Ignore Predictions They Dislike'. The columnist argues that the crisis was predicted, but the prediction was disliked and therefore largely ignored. My point is that the West deals similarly with predictions about the Islamist *shari'a* state. The prevailing Western narrative prefers to ignore all realist predictions related to the *shari'a* state, insisting instead on wishful thinking.

Here is my personal experience. I spent about two decades in various affiliations at Harvard with a research focus on Islamism in the context of the study of religion and politics in international relations. This most fruitful affiliation ended in 1998–2000 with a tenure as the Harvard Bosch Fellow at Harvard University's Weatherhead Center for International Affairs. The research produced in that period was documented in my book *Islam between Culture and Politics* (2001), the publication of which was sponsored by Harvard. In 2004 I returned to Harvard on sabbatical as a visiting scholar, this time however with an affiliation at the Center for Middle Eastern studies. In the context of the new affiliation I was invited to join in the 50th anniversary of Islamic studies at Harvard (1954–2004). The anniversary took place in the shadow of the Islamist assaults of 9/11, but most attending scholars were highly reluctant to deal with this unpleasant challenge seriously. At that anniversary I failed to generate a debate on Islamism. Therefore I acknowledge my continued happiness that the Harvard book mentioned above was for obvious reasons published in association with another Harvard Center, namely the Weatherhead Center for International Affairs, definitely not with Harvard's Center for Middle Eastern Studies. The basis of my Harvard affiliation in the most inspiring years, 1982–2000, was several appointments in international studies, not in Middle Eastern studies. It was the right choice.

My research agenda for the academic year at Harvard's Center for Middle Eastern Studies in 2004–2005 was the completion of a new edition of *Islam between Culture and Politics*. In view of what happened after the assaults of 9/11 executed by al-Qaeda, representing the jihadists (that is, the violent branch of the more general phenomenon of Islamism), I had to look at Islamism. I hasten to add (in an attempt to pre-empt unjustified attack): I know that there are non-violent peaceful Islamists, and I know of the related distinctions. Moreover, in my work (including the present book) I argue that the non-violent branch of Islamism is growing at the expense of jihadism. For sure, Islamism is not about terrorism. However, I do not buy into the unchecked assumption about its moderation. In contrast to my rich years at Harvard's international studies, I found the environment of Harvard's Middle East and Islamic studies neither encouraging nor supportive of my research. The lack of interest in the research I was doing at that centre induced me to leave Harvard in 2004, accepting an offer to spend the second half of my sabbatical academic year as a senior research fellow at the Asia Research Institute (ARI) of the National State University of Singapore (NUS). There I found a much better, inspiring environment for my research on Islam and modernity. My point is not the difference between Islamic studies at Harvard and at the NUS, but rather between two different set-ups for dealing with Islam and with politics. Despite all odds, I finished the new edition of *Islam between Culture and Politics* at Harvard before leaving for Singapore.

In Singapore there were more challenging tasks, namely a research project on Islam, modernity and pluralism in Asia. Unlike Islamic studies at Harvard, where I had to be a lone scholar with no one to communicate with, I was fortunate at ARI in Singapore to be in a research team in the cluster 'Religion and Globalization'. There I made research presentations discussed in workshops held at ARI to my benefit, and the papers from these workshops were later published.[45] Some in Singapore may have disliked my predictions about Islamism, but – fortunately – they did not just ignore them, they engaged in discussion with me.

In the Preface to the new edition of *Islam between Culture and Politics* I complained about the lack of freedom in the world of Islamic civilization (Islamdom) from which I originate. Then I expressed (in 2004) the hope that it would become 'an open society promoting the rights of free speech and freedom of faith'.[46] This hope meant that the ruling dictatorships (authoritarian regimes) would be overcome on the way to democracy and prosperity. I then added this statement:

> Not only the ruling autocrats are the enemies of open society, but also the opposing Islamists who aim at toppling them. The theocracy of the Islamic (*shari'a-*) state is not the proper alternative to the existing rule. The lack of freedom in the world of Islam seen in the context of open society and its enemies is home made and not the outcome of a conspiracy by the West against Islam.

This prediction alienated me from my colleagues at Harvard Middle Eastern studies, who were not ready to listen to my critique of the *shari'a* state and to my refutation of the mindset of Orientalism in reverse. Being ignored did not discourage me from continuing to stand by this assessment and from completing a new part for the new edition, which was published 2005. I repeat the *Financial Times* phrase: 'People Ignore Predictions They Dislike' and use it in general, not only with reference to the establishment of US Islamic studies. That is why this book started in Chapter 1 by taking issue with these studies, in an inquiry into the politicization of Islam as a process that seeks a name.

The present book has a different focus to *Islam between Culture and Politics*. After the unseating of the Ben Alis, the Mubaraks, the Qadhafis and (potentially) the Alawi Assad clan, one is confronted with the propspect that the Muslim Brothers may replace the dictators not only in Egypt, but also in my home country of Syria. If Islamists prevail, there will presumably be no democracy, but rather an undemocratic *shari'a*-Islamocracy. I know that this perspective on the Arab uprising against long-standing authoritarian regimes is not a popular one. Apart from being ignored, my work also faces rejection by the establishment. Nevertheethe-less, I dare state the truth about Islamism, also in this book, in a true belief in academic freedom.

The Arab Spring has been clouded in the aftermath by the fogs of Islamism. I keep repeating the fact that the young leaderless grassroots protesters who took to the streets fought for the prospect of democratization, not for a *shari'a* state, yet in no country can one say that democracy has been firmly established – or is at least on the way to it – not even in civil Tunisia after Ben Ali, nor in Egypt after Mubarak, nor in Libya after Qadhafi. This applies also to the other embattled territories. The earlier hope that the Arab Spring might help the MENA countries join the post-bipolar process of global democratization has failed to become reality. It is shrouded in great uncertainties. In 2000 Kaplan rightly predicted that, despite the burst of idealism, democracy was 'just a moment'. The Arab Spring ushered in such a moment in the struggle for freedom.

After the comparison with predictions of the financial crisis published in the *Financial Times*, let me engage in another comparison: war and democratization. The case in point is Iraq in the aftermath of the toppling of Saddam's regime. The US sent its troops into Iraq in 2003 with the vision that regime change leads to democracy. When the US troops left Iraq in 2011, the Shi'ite Islamist Da'wa Party took over. That meant the end of the US-imposed democratization project based on power sharing among Iraqis (Shi'ites, Sunnis and Kurds). In other words: for Iraq this meant the end of the promise of real democracy. A valuable *NYT/IHT* editorial commentary headlined 'Iraq's Latest Battle' made this hard-headed assessment:

> After the last American troops departed. . . . Prime Minister Nuri Kemal al-Maliki, a member of the Shi'ite majority, . . . is showing a greater interest in reprisals against the Sunni minority, than in encouraging inclusion. . . . Shi'ite-led post-Saddam government . . . [of] Mr Maliki recklessly threatened to abandon an American-backed power-sharing government.[47]

The *NYT/IHT* assessment is shared by Ayad Allawi, Osama Nujaifi and Rafe Essawi, the leaders of al-Iraqiyya, the most important opposition party. This is a Sunni party, but with a clear secular, non-sectarian orientation. These leaders take stock of the democratization of post-Saddam Iraq with a reference to the election the US imposed before leaving Iraq in these words:

Since Iraq's 2010 election, we have witnessed the subordination of the state to Prime Minister Nuri Kamal al-Maliki's Dawa party, the erosion of judicial independence, the intimidation of opponents and the dismantling of independent institutions intended to promote clean elections and combat corruption. All of this happened during the Arab Spring. . . .[48]

What has happened in Iraq can be repeated elsewhere in the MENA region. Given the failure to establish democracy in the aftermath of the Arab Spring, it is crucial to examine not only the potential of Islamist participation in a process of democratization, but also the peril of its hijacking by an empowered Islamism. This misgiving seems to have materialized. The story seems to repeat itself in post-Arab-Spring Tunisia, Egypt and Libya, and perhaps soon – though after a bloody civil war – in post-Ba'th Syria.

Islamism and the abuse of democratization in a claim to moderation

Unfortunately, in great parts of the Western discussion the role of Islamists is often misperceived. This discussion continues to ignore all predictions about their rule. Islamists have not been the leaders of the uprising; on the contrary, like cautious Leninists, they have been hoping to take over with the help of the exceptionally sophisticated organizations of their movements. As demonstrated in the case of Egypt, games of short-lived coalitions combined with the use of the ballot box have proved helpful to them to climb the ladder of power. The fact that ruling dictators in the Middle East (e.g. Qadhafi and Assad) have typically presented themselves to the West as the alternative to the Islamist movement indirectly gives undeserved credit to Islamists. In this understanding Islamist movements were misconceived as opponents of dictatorship. This dynamic makes it harder to touch on the core issues frankly. A sound assessment of Islamism and the winds of change in the Arab world requires an adequate understanding of the forces that are in operation, free from the limits imposed on this debate by the Islamist movement. The deplored naivety of Western politicians, illustrated in the Introduction to this book with the example of the EU foreign affairs representative, boosts the pro-Islamist public opinion prevailing in the West.

Among the few exceptions that I applaud is Thomas Friedman. In a column in the *International Herald Tribune* of March 23, 2011 he describes the Middle East as a 'region that has been living outside the biggest global trends of free politics and free markets for half a century', and then states that the current Arab uprising helps Arab Muslims to 'join history'.[49] Yet Friedman is among the not so many US commentators who are aware of the 'hard choices'. Friedman knows well and states in his March 2011 column the misgiving about the uprising that 'Sunni fundamentalists . . . if they seize power could suppress all those . . . they don't like' – anyone, that is, who is not an Islamist. Would this be a contribution to democratization or a step towards *shari'a*-Islamocracy? Can the Middle East democratize under Islamist rule?[50]

Thomas Friedman is absolutely right: Islamists have no liking for non-Islamist Muslims, even when they – in double-speak (see note 41) – pay lip service to democracy and to pluralism in the Western media. Muslims of the enlightened turn know well that they will not have an easy time in an Islamist *shari'a* state. Thomas Friedman visited Egypt a few months after the publication of the column cited above and wrote another, again published in the *International Herald Tribune*, entitled 'Pay Attention', in which he asked Obama to understand 'how to complete the transition to democracy in a situation where liberal Muslims made the revolution and the Muslim Brotherhood can now take it'.[51] Friedman rightly asked readers to pay attention to 'who gets to write the rules for the new Egypt'. If the Islamist Muslim Brothers do it, then there will be a totalitarian *shari'a* state, not a democracy. These are 'grim prospects', as Eric Trager calls them in an article (see note 38) that provides exceptionally more realism than most Western contributions do with their wishful thinking about the democratization of MENA countries!

As early as the end of March 2011 the major trend was clear, and by the end of that year it had fully materialized. On March 25 the very competent *NYT* Cairo reporter Michael Slackman reported from there:

> In post-revolutionary Egypt . . . religion has emerged as a powerful political force, following an uprising based on secular ideals. The Muslim Brotherhood . . . is at the forefront . . . . It is also clear that the young, educated secular activists who initially inspired and propelled the nonideological revolution are no longer the driving force. . . . As the best organized and most extensive opposition movement in Egypt, the Muslim Brotherhood was expected to have an edge in the contest for political influence.[52]

In November 2011 one of the *NYT/IHT* reports had the heading 'The Brotherhood Flexes Its Muscles'.[53] By the beginning of 2012 it had become unmistakeably clear that the Islamist movement of Muslim Brothers had abandoned the tactical talk about sharing power in short-lived coalitions. In the final months of 2012 the empowered Muslim Brotherhood seems to be ruling the most important state in the MENA region: Egypt under a *shari'a* constitution.

Enlightened Islamic and secular parties lost in the democratic competition because they did not have enough time for the necessary institution building that would enable them to compete with the well-organized and externally funded party of the Muslim Brothers, and with the Salafist Nour Party funded by millions of petro-dollars transferred by wealthy Gulf sheykhs and Saudi Wahhabis.

By and large the idealism of the Arab Spring died in the same year it was born, in the course of the process of empowerment of Islamist movements. This shift was referred to by Anthony Shadid, a very competent *NYT* observer, as a shift from 'spring' to a 'blazing summer'. The following season was even worse. Shadid provided this assessment:

> The idealism of the revolts . . . revived an Arab world anticipating change. But . . . [it also] illustrates how perilous that change has become. . . . The

intentions and influence of Islamists in their ranks are uncertain. . . . The pro-
longed transition of Arab countries to a new order may prove as tumultuous
to the region . . . uncertainty is far more pronounced. . . . [The only certainty is
that] Islamists have emerged as a force in Egypt, Syria and elsewhere.[54]

The order these Islamists envision is clearly the *shari'a* state and they imposed it
when empowered. By all standards this order is not a democracy.

The caveat that the non-Islamist rebellion has been hijacked by Islamist movements does not negate the fact that the Arab Spring was an indication of change in
the Arab world. At issue is a process of a world-historical significance. The rebellion has radically changed the Arab part of the Middle East at all levels. Rulers
had to go. Earlier, there were only four ways to unseat a Middle Eastern despot as
a political imam: removal by Allah (natural death), murder, a military coup d'état,
or foreign intervention, as happened to Saddam Hussein in the Iraq war. The great
novelty now is that it is the Arab people who unseated their rulers. Ben Ali fell in
Tunisia, followed by Husni Mubarak in Egypt, as well as Qadhafi in Libya. On the
side I mention Ben Saleh in Yemen. It appears that this unseating may continue
to happen to other rulers (e.g. Assad), since the uprising against the dictators has
been spilling over at a great pace throughout the region. Even as a student of the
Middle East for 40 years, I was, I confess, among those taken by surprise. I know
of no one who was not. I admired the Egyptian and Tunisian people, but I had no
expectation that the Arab Spring could ever be stretched to Libya and Syria. A
miracle happened. Nonetheless, I do not think this breakthrough is leading to an
overnight democratization. I repeat: The underlying underpinning needed for such
a process is lacking, and no consolidation seems to be in sight.

In spite of being taken by surprise, I believe to be right in my assessment that
the Arab Spring will not lead to a swift transition to democracy. In his *NYT/IHT*
column 'Democracy is Messy' Nicholas D. Kristof wrote from Cairo in April
2011: 'The Muslim Brotherhood has been brought into the power structure
. . . it seems increasingly likely that Egypt won't change as much as many had
expected . . . Islamists will play a greater role in society and government.'[55] This
prediction already came true in the second half of 2011, and since June 2012 the
Islamists have been in power in Egypt. In other words, the rise to power of the
Islamists – certainly a change with important political consequences – will mean
that any transition toward genuine democracy will be significantly constrained.
Islamists want a *shari'a* state. It cannot be repeated enough that their approval of
democracy is 'merely a grudging tactical concession'[56] restricted to permitting the
ballot box, and a concession that is anyway time-limited (e.g. short-lived coalitions). As repeatedly argued, democracy is not merely about the ballot box: it is a
culture of pluralism and power sharing. For Islamists, by contrast, democracy is
an easy way to climb to power, not a culture for political life in the public square.

The critical assessment of Islamism does not overlook the insight that no honest democrat can afford to bypass Islamist movements. Any democratization has
to engage Islamism, but it must do it without illusions. The Islamist ideology is
represented by various movements supported by on average approximately 20 to

30 per cent of the population, and unfortunately it also appeals to the non-Islamist majority. Therefore, one cannot deny Islamist movements political participation. The issue, however, is not whether Islamists should be allowed to engage in politics (of course they should be), but whether political hegemony should be handed over to them. In the latter case the empowerment would inevitably lead to a *shari'a* state. Can this be democratically averted?

I am against exclusion and, as stated, argue for engaging with Islamists, but with an awareness of the democratic choice between engagement and empowerment. As the cases of Egypt and Tunisia demonstrate, a hasty process of democratization reduced to a formal voting procedure will help Islamists seize power. This is no democratization as happened ahead of the Arab Spring in Gaza, Lebanon and Iraq. This mistake has been repeated with US support in Egypt as well.

Professor Amr Hamzawy of Cairo University acted in the Arab Spring as a non-Islamist politician. He founded a secular social-liberal party in post-Mubarak Egypt opposed to the *shari'a* state. He argued against the premature referendum in March 2011 on the prematurely redrafted constitution with these arguments: for decades, the Mubarak regime oppressed any democratic opposition, and the breakdown of authoritarianism generated a vacuum. Under these conditions it was clear that democratic forces need enough time in a democratization process for institution building. Islamist movements had the experience and privilege of a clandestine political organization (again, the comparison to the Leninists is apt) that was able swiftly to fill the vacuum. This is a great head start for the Islamists who were in a position to take over, and this is exactly what they did, or are trying to do. In contrast to these misgivings expressed by Hamzawy, the leader of the Muslim Brothers vehemently supported early elections, and the Brothers were the winners.

Do not be mistaken: engaging the Muslim Brothers as participants in the public sphere is not the same as empowering their movement and should not be confused with it. This confusion also applies to the power Islamists have gained to design the constitution. The warning of Mohammed ElBaradei at an early stage, that Egypt would get an 'unrepresentative parliament writing an unrepresentative constitution', is highly pertinent. Mohammed ElBaradei is the Egyptian Noble Prize Laureate for Peace who retreated from his candidacy for the presidency following the empowerment of the Islamists. ElBaradei is quoted above accusing the Islamist President Morsi of confusing a 'government of law' with a 'government of men', that is, democratic rule with a kind of new authoritarianism.

The liberal Egyptian Khairi Abaza, fearful of an Islamist *shari'a* constitution, wrote in a *NYT/IHT* op-ed column in December 2011:

> The drafting of the new constitution will afford the army another opportunity to make good, ensuring that minorities are heard and the majority does not become tyrannical. If the military elites are wise, they will referee Egypt's political process, rather than dominating the whole game.[57]

In December 2012 the army did not intervene when Islamists drafted a *shari'a* constitution and enacted it. The army is still in place as a political actor. The foreseeable future prospect for Egypt is a fight between the army and the Islamist movement. This is in no way a democratic competition.

Well, this is not the place for a resumption of the old debate on the military and politics. Older readers may recall the early debate in US Social Science on the military elites that projects onto them the role of an agent of modernization parallel to the post-colonial development in the 1960s. The expectations of successful modernization did not materialize.[58] Nonetheless, it is wrong to judge without country-related distinctions. The role of the army in Kemalist Turkey and in Nasserite Egypt is not to be confused with the reactionary military of Latin America or the tribal gangs occurring as national armies in sub-Saharan Africa. The officers of the Egyptian army are closely observing the Islamist AKP in Turkey, which succeeded in stripping the secular Kemalist army of all of its power in the name of democratization. Even though the Egyptian Islamist president succeeded in imposing retirement on top officers in August 2012, one may assume that the Egyptian army would not allow the Muslim Brothers to do in Egypt what the AKP did to Kemalist officers in Turkey. I will content myself with these basic remarks on the future prospects and continue my analysis on the place of Islamist movements in the post-Arab Spring from the point of view of a shift in the debate from modernization to the democratization of state and society.

The policy choices: between engagement and empowerment

I am committed to democracy and acknowledge accordingly that Islamism is a popular political choice. Thus, it is necessary to engage with Islamist movements. No democrat would ever allow the repression, sidelining or outlawing of any opposition. But engaging with illiberal parties in terms of political participation is not to be confused with empowering them when it is clear that in power they may abolish civil liberties. The core issue, then, is how to design the right strategy for dealing with Islamism in the process of democratization. The democratic options are indicated in the heading to this section. The consideration of engagement requires the ability to recognize the moderate pro-democracy Islamists and to see what distinguishes them from the jihadists. The latter are the radical Islamists who are committed to violence. Unlike the jihadist hardcore Islamists, who say clearly what is on their mind, the so-called moderate Islamists engage in double-speak (see note 41). They disavow violence, but disguise their agenda of pursuing a *shari'a* state and eliminate this concept from the discussion, speaking only about democracy. In contrast to both brands – the violent jihadists and the pro-democracy moderate Islamists – civic non-Islamist Muslims offer the best hope for a better future. This is the hard choice facing the West. Will the West work with the civic Muslims of the enlightened turn who oppose Islamism? Or will it choose the pragmatic, opportunist policy of working with moderate institutional Islamists?

In the journal *Foreign Affairs*, a highly influential policy forum, the US pundit Marc Lynch and others of a like mind upgrade the Islamist movements to the status of a worthy partner for the West. According to press reports the US State

Department has invited Lynch to speak and advise on this matter. However, any defence of moderate Islamism is deeply misplaced. In the West there is a need to understand that a civic Islam based on 'enlightened Muslim thought' (see Chapter 3) is the appropriate cultural underpinning for a democratic society. Those who promote Islamism ignore or even sideline the community of enlightened civic non-Islamist Muslims.

The uprising dubbed 'the Arab Spring' is not yet a revolution. By definition a revolution engages in a structural transformation of state and society. True, the unfolding of the events named the Arab Spring indicates a development of world-historical magnitude, but no structural change has happened or is in sight. The Arab Spring gave rise to the vision that a strong civil society and democratic free-dom are feasible in the world of Islam, but it seems unlikely that these goals are attainable under the present conditions of Islamist rule.

It is a fact, which the Islamists themselves admit, that the current Arab upheaval against authoritarian regimes is not of their making. On the contrary, it was made by a grieving young generation suffering from a combination of poverty and polit-ical oppression. At the outset the prevailing slogans of the Arab Spring were, not the Islamist slogans, but 'bread, justice and freedom'. The revolt was clouded by another fact: the rebelling people were leaderless; they were neither well organ-ized (because their action lacks an institutional framework), nor did they have a clear agenda for democratization. At the outset the rebels were an amalgam of individuals from all walks of life, and they simply aspired to change in the hope of a better outlook. They believed that toppling an authoritarian regime opens the way to a better future. In contrast, the Islamists joined in as a well-organized power. Their experienced leaders know what they want and pursue an agenda of an Islamic *shari'a* state, which is the driver for a clear political agenda. The Islam-ists' inner strength – namely, their strong and clandestine organization (similar to their organizations in the diaspora in Europe) – helped them to hijack the rebellion made by others and to prevail. They have now become the engine for a future mobilizing force. There is thus a parallel between Islamism and Leninism: both were established not at home, but in the diaspora of Western Europe – Lenin was based in Bern in Switzerland, and today's Islamists have headquarters throughout Western Europe.

Earlier in this chapter I argued that abuse of the Muslim diaspora in Europe by the Islamists helped the Muslim Brothers to escape persecution. This assess-ment is supported in recent research by Lorenzo Vidino. He provides solid empiri-cal evidence for the existence of a powerful Islamist establishment in Western Europe.[59] The inadequacy of current debates in the West results from the claims of the previously ruling dictators, who represented themselves as the secular alternative to Islamism, even though some of them (e.g. Qadhafi) drew instrumen-tally on Islam for the purposes of legitimation. The fact that two distinct repres-sive forces – the dictators and the Islamists – opposed each other does not turn either one into a force of liberation. The fact that Islamism stands in opposition to these authoritarian regimes only contributes to a moral and political upgrading of Islamist movements. By the same token, the Islamists' opposition to the dictators becomes a tool with which to discredit the critics of Islamism. One cannot repeat frequently enough the distinction between Islam as a faith and Islamism as a political ideology. Confusing them leads to wrong conclusions. The real alternative to the toppled authoritarian dictators is not closed-minded Islamism, but a civic, non-Islamist, open Islam that would be compatible with democracy. Indonesia is a paragon of civil Islam. It is unfortunate that not one single Arab country fulfils this characterization of an open and enlightened Islam. The Islamist *shari'a* state the Islamists strive for is not compatible with the pluralism of a civil society. Democracy requires this pluralism and acceptance of diversity as a minimum standard for freedom. In contrast to the *shari'a* state, civil Islam can deliver.

In the general pondering about the choices of engagement versus empowerment, one has to be flexible in view of the fact that the Arab world is not a singular, homogeneous space, but is characterized by great diversity; each of its societies, as Friedman put it, 'has different ethnic, tribal, sectarian and political orientations'. Islamist movements know their way around this variety in a way the West does not. Nonetheless, nobody is perfect, and neither are Islamists. Sometimes they manage, sometimes they do not. In Egypt they were able to prevail and to take over. They imposed an Islamist presidency and a *shari'a* constitution. But in Libya Islamists had to cope with the existing tribal structure of the country and created a tribal-Islamist government. Tunisia has a coalition with a large Islamist proportion in it, as the Islamists are not able to rule alone. But the region continues to be in turmoil, and Islamists act in troubled waters.

Is the West able to deal with this complexity? It does seem most unlikely. When I lived in Washington, DC, my experience was that the US State Department is not always well advised. People there prefer to listen to the misguided and misleading so-called Islam experts who recommend that the US embrace Islamists as their new partners. A former US congressman, Curt Weldon, acknowledged with honesty after a visit to Tripoli that the West has no plan for a post-Qadhafi Libya: 'no one has a plan, a foundation for civil society has not been constructed and we are not even sure whom we should trust.' This lack of orientation reminds one of exactly what happened earlier on the eve of the Iraq war. Then, the US had no advance planning for a post-Saddam, post-war Iraq. What happened in Iraq is now being repeated in Libya and elsewhere. Let us look at the earlier case.

Following the departure of US troops from Iraq in late 2011, the Shi'ite Islamist Da'wa Party of Maliki established its grip on power in parallel to the loss of leverage of the US. In August 20, 2012 the *International Herald Tribune* reported on the undermining of US sanctions against Iran by the Iraqi government that came to power with US assistance. Within Iraq, the Maliki government ended the system of power sharing once imposed by the US. Is this what the US fought a costly war for? The dismal experience in Iraq can be repeated in other places. To be sure, Islamists should be engaged in political processes and the US policy in this regard is not wrong. The problem is that Islamists should not be trusted. Engaging them has to be kept distinct from empowering them. In the MENA region, any signal of approval sent toward Islamist groupings contributes to delaying democratization. Ultimately, empowering Islamism in a defeat of the Arab Spring that turns into a gloomy Arab winter does not indicate the democratization of the MENA region. At the time of writing, this outcome seems to be the real prospect.

Whither the Arab Spring? Trends and some future prospects

Throughout this chapter the question: 'Will the Arab Spring bring democracy to the Arab core of Islamic civilization?' has been the driver of the analysis. We have seen that the notion of a 'transition to democracy' combined with the false comparison with post-communist, post-1989 Eastern Europe is not helpful. This thinking reflect Western wishful thinking more than it reflects knowledge of what is going on on the ground. The reader is reminded of an earlier reference to the classical work with the similar wrong forecast put forward in 1962 by Daniel Lerner (see p. 123 *note 14 cit.*). With the hindsight of half a century, one can today argue as follows: just as the disruption of traditional society did not result in a modern state – but rather in a failure of development – the fall of authoritarian regimes seems not to result in democratic rule. The assumption that an Islamist *shari'a* state will contribute to the rule of democracy is based on incorrect knowledge. The Islamist *shari'a* state does not provide a system based on rights, on the political culture of pluralism and on power sharing. In contrast to Islamism, a civil Islam based on religious reform and cultural change could provide the cultural underpinning and deliver the legitimation needed for such a democracy.[60]

It is an indisputable fact that in the world of Islam most states are underachievers in democracy. The core of Islamic civilization, the Arab Middle East, is the worst in this regard. It is dominated by authoritarian regimes that suppress all kinds of dissent. This is why, until the Arab Spring, no opposition could emerge and thrive. All opponents were suffocated by the security apparatus of the *mukhabarat*/secret police. The only exceptions are the Islamist movements, because they were able to escape surveillance to thrive as an organized opposition for two reasons: first, the very efficient, clandestine structure based on extreme secrecy, obedience and strict patriarchical (hierarchical) authority, and, second, their ability to establish a foothold in the European Muslim diaspora, while enjoying the right of political asylum and related democratic civil rights with which European civil society provides them. For instance, Rashid Ghannouchi and his An-Nahda movement acted from London just as Lenin did from Bern before the October Revolution in 1917. However, until the Arab Spring – despite their power in the underground at home and in the parallel societies in Europe – the Islamists failed to manage a seizure of power. Then came the Arab Spring and it opened a great window of opportunity for them. In the competition between violent jihadism and institutional peaceful Islamism, the latter won, but the outcome is not a moderation, but only a shift within Islamism.

There are pundits who not only believe that they can see a moderation, but go a step further and even speak of 'post-Islamism' (see p. 110). This is self-deception. Islamist movements have emerged as the winner who have benefited from the fall of authoritarian regimes in the course of the Arab Spring, but without going beyond Islamism as the term 'post-Islam' suggests. The basic explanation for their success is their high organizational efficiency. The young, leaderless, rebelling, non-Islamist no-hope generation, by contrast, lacks any of the organizational capability that is needed. The Islamist movements have hijacked the Arab Spring.

With regard to the question posed at the outset of this section, it can be stated that the MENA region started well in 2011, but in the second half went into a dark and very long tunnel with seemingly no light at the end of it. The current prospect is that if Islamist movements rule alone – that is, with no power sharing with non-Islamist partners – there will be a *shari'a* state; there will not be democratic rule based on law in an order of a pluralist civil society. As I have repeatedly and clearly shown, this assessment runs against the view prevailing in the West, which is favourable to Islamism. Therefore, one needs to question the unchecked assumptions that underlie the favourable assessment of Islamism. Some pundits give Islamists credit for the fake moderation they wrongly attribute to them, and assume that Islamists support democracy. They also view Islamist movements as potential political parties willing to join the democratic game of competition under conditions of sharing political power. This assumption has so far remained unchecked. As I have repeatedly stated, the Muslim Brotherhood is an organization based on clandestine action, hierarchical membership and indoctrination and follows an ideology that is not compatible with democracy. The Muslim Brothers have formally established a political party in Egypt named the Freedom and Justice Party, but to date they have not changed their ideology or their organization in a way that might be reassuring.

In the Egypt of today, after Mubarak, Islamists continue their inherited structures of clandestine politics and oligarchy. The president of Egypt, Mohammed Morsi – although he has formally resigned his membership in the Muslim Brotherhood – continues to be one of the top bosses of this movement that restricts its democratic action to the ballot box and its approval of power sharing to short-lived coalitions with non-Islamists.

There is a discrepancy between the promise given by the Arab Spring at its outset in January 2011 and its outcome at the end of the year 2012. To state a few preliminary prospects, it is safe to argue that the thread of the unfolding development is visible and compels a rejection of any comparison between the Arab Spring and the developments in formerly communist Eastern Europe around 1989. In Poland, for instance, there was already in existence a democratic movement that rallied around the trade union Solidarność. The democratic state of Poland took the decision to include a comparison between the Arab and the Polish Springs at the thirtieth anniversary of Solidarność, held at Gdansk, the birth city of this movement, in September 2011. I had the honour of being invited to that event to join the panel discussing the question 'Are Cairo and Tunis Repetitions of Gdansk?' Sadly, my Polish hosts proved to be wrong in their comparison. At present one can state the following prospects based on clear, observable trends. These prospects and trends are as follows.

First, at the local level there is a tremendous empowerment of the Islamist movements. Again, these were not the engine of Arab Spring at the beginning, though they participated in it. The answer to the question why these movements have been easily able to climb up the political ladder was given to the *New York Times* by a Libyan democrat in these words: 'The Islamists . . . seem more influential than their real weight. . . . Most Libyans are not strongly Islamic, but the Islamists are strongly organized and that's the problem.'[61] In the earlier section on Egypt and Libya I repeated that Islamist militants have become political leaders in a process of empowerment. Of course, the country-related differences are acknowledged, but the statement that these Islamist movements share the same agenda – the Islamist *shari'a* state – is not an indication for lumping them together. This is a political order they have in common, as they themselves state. This order is not democracy, nor is it an Islamic variety of democratic rule.

Second, at the regional level, Turkey under the rule of the Islamist AKP is moving to the fore as leader. The first statesman to visit all three successful countries of resurgent Islamism – Egypt, Libya and Tunisia – was R. T. Erdogan in mid-September 2011, in what was dubbed 'Erdogan's Arab Spring Tour'. Ahead of the visit, Erdogan fired off rhetorical broadsides against Israel in an al-Jazeera television interview and expelled the Israeli ambassador. The pay-off for this muscle flexing was a welcome by the Movement of the Muslim Brotherhood in Cairo as the 'hero of Muslims' and rising popularity. An Associated Press news analysis provided this assessment: 'Erdogan has sought to leverage the Arab uprisings into greater influence for Turkey in a region where, as the seat of the Ottoman Empire, it once ruled for centuries.'[62] Nabil Abdel Fattah, an analyst of al-Ahram Center in Cairo, thinks that Turkey 'meant to promote itself as a political power in the Arab region and spread its influence'.[63] This is the neo-Ottoman variety of Islamism designed and pursued by the Turkish Minister for Foreign Affairs Davotoglu as Turkish foreign policy, claiming regional hegemony in the Middle East.

In wrapping up the future prospects, the question whether there will be democracy at the end of the tunnel under the rule of Islamist movements is central. The lip service paid to democracy by these movements does not match their political conduct when they are empowered. They claim that their vision of a *shari'a* state is compatible with democracy, but then they reject democratic principles and limit their approval to tactical concessions. How is this to work?

Conclusions

Ahead of drawing conclusions I want to quote what an Islamist told Anthony Shadid of the *New York Times* in Cairo. This Islamist Mohammed Nadi, a 26-year-old student at a recent Salafist protest in Cairo, asked, 'Is democracy the voice of the majority?' then continued: 'We as Islamists are the majority. Why do they want to impose on us the views of the minorities – the liberals and the secularists? That's all I want to know.'[64] At the beginning of Chapter 5 I shall quote authoritative Muslim Brotherhood politicians who express this mindset in an understanding of democracy reduced merely to balloting. But, in contrast to this mindset, democracy is above all a practised value system of a political culture of pluralism that averts despotic rule, even of a majority. Given this contrast, it may be concluded that if the Islamist presentation of democracy prevails – in the form of the rule of the assumed majority over all minorities – then the Arab Spring will end in a new authoritarianism. One is reminded of John Stuart Mill's warning, in his classic *On Liberty*, of the 'tyranny of the majority'.[65]

Based on my long years of study of Islamism, I conclude that the Islamist *shari'a* state provides no promising prospect for genuine democratization in the MENA countries. One is intrigued by the thinking of a distinguished US political theorist, Amitai Etzioni, who coined the term 'Islamocracy'. He did this in the aftermath of the electoral victory of the Islamist An-Nahda of Sheykh Rashid Ghannouchi in Tunisia in October 2011. The conclusion that there is a contrast between Islamocracy and democracy runs against the views of Etzioni, as it recognizes the incompatibility between the two that Professor Etzioni ignores. He identifies Islamists as 'illiberal moderates', but argues in favour of Islamism in an article in *The National Interest*. For him, 'Tunisia . . . (is) on its way to becoming the first Muslim nation to combine the rule of *shari'a* with elements of democracy.'[66] In contrast to this baseless allegation, which is not supported by knowledge on the issue in point, I argue: the *shari'a* state named 'Islamocracy' by Etzioni is the very opposite of democracy. At the outset of 2013 the leader of the Tunisian secular opposition was assassinated by An-Nahda Islamists. Professor Etzioni is a highly respected scholar, but his expertise does not include the study of Islam, *shari'a* and Islamism. Well, he knows that an Islamocracy 'is likely to introduce one form of censorship or another'. This seems not to disturb him at all, as he is not worried about freedom in Tunisia, but rather is concerned with a legitimation for averting a rerunning 'of the Danish cartoons of the Prophet, or a Tunisian edition of *The Satanic Verses*'. Again, the problem is that some distinguished scholars like Etzioni who are neither experts on Islam nor on the MENA region take the liberty to make strong, but in effect valueless recommendations. Real experts know very well that none of the Tunisian opinion leaders of enlightened Muslim thought ever has *anything* in mind that resembles what Etzioni uses as a legitimation for censorship. To date, apart from secular Kemalist Turkey and the Indonesia of civil Islam, Tunisia is the only one out of 57 Islamic countries to have a secular law that allows women – against *shari'a* rules – to ask for divorce, and generally prescribes a gender equality that is denied by *shari'a* rules. Etzioni believes, as he writes, that the Islamists will change existing law in a 'new constitution' that follows *shari'a* to reflect 'views of marriage, divorce and inheritance that strongly favour men over women'. Despite this, he pleads that Americans should 'accept Islamocracy' and recommends: 'We should accept that Muslim republics will incorporate some moderate elements of *shari'a* into their governments . . . We should hold that these countries . . . qualify as regimes with which we can work.' Etzioni is silent about the complete incompatibility of *shari'a* and individual human rights. Etzioni published this article in 2011. In 2012 the Islamists drafted a new constitution for Tunisia that abolished the hitherto constitutionally enshrined gender equality. Could one cogently conclude that the 'Islamocracy' of the 'illiberal moderates' is to be accepted as an 'Islamic particularism' that is the outcome of the Arab Spring?

The views I have cited of Etzioni and others of like mind who approve Islamocracy mostly reflect a thinking that emanates from a cultural relativism that recognizes cultural particularisms at the expense of the universal validity of the values of cultural modernity. This recognition of cultural particularisms ends up approving Muslim particularisms despite their rejection of individual human rights.[67] There are democratic Muslims such as Reza Afashari who argue against this kind of cultural relativism in favour of the universality of the discourse of human rights and democracy.[68] This is the point to bring in a reminder of the heritage of Islamic humanism, which in its universalist scope facilitates cross-civilizational bridging. This Islamic tradition provides arguments against Islamocracy and for the universality of precious goods which are shared by all humans and are therefore universal. Top of the list of these are rational knowledge, democratic freedom and individual (not just collective) human rights. Among the enlightened Muslims who argue for this universality of law against the *shari'a* particularisms is Abdou Filali-Ansary. He states: 'Some form of universal rule of law . . . would help to define a framework . . . that is compatible with democratic ideals on the scale of humanity.'[69] The conclusion is that *shari'a* – construed by Islamists as a law – cannot accomplish this function, not only because it is not compatible with universal democratic ideals, but also because humanity is not defined by the particularism of belonging to Islamdom. No religion and no cultural particularism can ever serve as a defining criterion for what humanity is and for its needs.

At the top of the needs of humanity is a universal rule of a cosmopolitan law that has to stand above cultural particularisms. This need is contradicted by the Islamist *shari'a* state. I repeat the conclusion that *an Islamocracy is the negation of democracy, not a cultural variant* of it. At the beginning of this chapter I applauded the Arab Spring, though without sharing any of the Western naivety. The aftermath of the Arab Spring has given the lie to the assumption of an easy transition from ugly Arab authoritarianism to the hoped-for democratic rule.

Earlier in this chapter, the debates of Arab intellectuals on democracy in the Arab world and on the future of Arab Muslims were discussed to remind the reader that these Arab democrats had the insight that democracy presupposes some basics that are to be achieved in a process of consolidation. The analysis provided here leads to the conclusion that the rule of Islamist *shari'a*, which has been named 'Islamocracy', is not the agenda needed for such democratization, nor is it the basis for the democratic rule aspired to to allow Islamdom to join in democratic peace. This global peace needs to be based on the universal rule of law so as to prevent the eruptions of conflicts to which some, wrongly, apply the formula 'clash of civilizations'. To 'prevent the clash of civilizations',[70] in an effort at inter-civilizational bridging, one needs to engage in real dialogue to reach an inter-civilizational consensus over shared values and a concept of cosmopolitan law. The rhetoric of the 'convergence of civilizations' is not only worthless playing to the gallery, but also a reversal from the extreme of clash to the other extreme of convergence, a move from maligning to exonerating. Instead of this unpromising approach – also promoted by Wahhabi Saudia Arabia – what is needed is conflict resolution based on addressing the existing conflicts of values. One of these is the conflict between the democratic state and the *shari'a* state. This approach to dealing with Islamism in the context of the Arab Spring seems to be more promising than the Western wishful thinking deplored in this chapter and in Chapter 1. The Western thinking that assumes a moderation of Islamism, without inquiring into whether this so-called moderation is underpinned by a change in values, leads nowhere.

The alternative to the *shari'a* state, presented in this book, is 'enlightened Muslim thought' (see note 5). The first source of this thought – the work of Abdelraziq – argues that Islam is a religious faith, not a political order. Enlightened Muslim thought offers a better solution than the *shari'a*tization project of Islamism and its political order of a *shari'a* state. In the Introduction I quoted Ali Abdelraziq rejecting the use of the Islamic faith to legitimate a political order, and I end this chapter by applauding Abdou Filali-Ansary for his upgrading of the work of Abdelraziq to the position of first source of 'Muslim enlightened thought'; as he states, Abdelraziq 'dispels . . . confusions surrounding religion and politics in Islam'.[71] This thinking is therefore 'a founding moment in contemporary Muslim thought on politics', to which this book adheres, a thinking that is highly topical for making conclusions about the post-Arab Spring era.

5 From traditional *shari'a* reasoning to Islamist *shari'a*tization of politics in the post-Arab Spring

At the outset of the preceding chapter on the Arab Spring, I quoted the two major Islamist slogans, *'al-Islam huwa al-hall'*/'Islam is the solution' and *'tatbiq al-shari'a'*/'implementation of the *shari'a*'. However, in the formative weeks of the Arab Spring, Islamist movements preferred to play games and therefore refrained from using these slogans in favour of prevarications. One of the best-informed Egyptian political scientists, Emad E. Shahin, tells us that the most powerful Islamist movement, the Muslim Brotherhood, 'agreed to not raise any of its religious slogans'[1] in a tactical submission to the plurality of the Arab Spring in Egypt. However, only a year later, following their empowerment, the Islamists abandoned everything they had previously promised to do, including their commitment to consensus over power sharing, freedom of expression and liberty of opposition, together with a lot of other related things. The focus of the present chapter is on the religious slogan about *shari'a*. On the basis of Islamist empowerment this slogan seems to have become translated into state policy in Egypt, a country ruled by the Muslim Brotherhood since 2012. Egypt has an Islamist president and a government dominated by the Muslim Brotherhood. Still, the extremely cool institutional Islamists are putting their agenda into practice with tactical prudence, implementing it incrementally in a such a careful manner that one is compelled to admire their efficiency.

The 'implementation of *shari'a*' slogan in politics

On August 21, 2012, the Arabic daily *al-Hayat* published on its front page a story (continued on page 4) on the unveiling of the true face of the Muslim Brothers done authentically by their own leaders. The newspaper also covered the responses of non-Islamist elected Egyptian politicians of three oppositional parties to a statement made by Isam al-Erian, chairperson of the ruling Freedom and Justice Party of the Muslim Brotherhood. This Muslim Brother stated in public that the election of his party gave it the political mandate 'to implement *shari'a*'. His logic, as he himself argued, was this: that the majority of Egyptians are Muslims, and democracy means the rule of the majority – that is, the rule of *shari'a*. The three leaders of the three non-Islamist parties quoted in *al-Hayat* rejected this 'implementation' and complained – as reported in *al-Hayat* – that 'the slogan of the implementation

of the *shari'a* is advanced without any further explanation of any point of substance related to the matter and without setting any limit to the scope of the agenda
of an implementation of *shari'a*'. They also state their agreement to *shari'a* as
ethical-legal orientation, but not to it as law. Earlier in this book, in Chapter 1,
I quoted authoritative Muslim scholars including Hamid Enayat who presented
evidence that there is no such thing as 'the *shari'a*' in Islamic history as 'there is
no such thing as a unified Islamic legal system . . . accepted and acknowledged
unquestionably by all Muslims'.[2] The Muslim Brotherhood ignores this history
and speaks of 'the *shari'a*' to be softly imposed on all in the name of 'democracy'
as a 'majority rule'. This *shari'a* is, however, not the classical *shari'a*, but rather
an Islamist one. It is not law in general, but the law of Islamist movements.

Among the findings of Chapters 1 to 3 of the present book is the fact that 'the
shari'a' that Isam al-Erian has been announcing is not based on the traditional
shari'a of Islamic history. In the Qur'an, *shari'a* is ethics. When *shari'a* was translated into law from the eighth century onwards, it was characterized by various
ways of law-making, so there was no '*the shari'a*'. Today, one may refer to these
different interpretations of *shari'a* in a modern phrase as a plurality. Traditional
multi-faceted *shari'a* honours the reality stated by Hamid Enayat that there is no
common understanding, nor an enshrinement in integrated codes for what *shari'a*
as law could ever be. Thus, the addition of the definite article 'the' to '*shari'a*'
contradicts all the historical facts and heralds a political agenda enacting an imposition. In the present chapter I shall look at *shari'a* reasoning throughout Islamic
history, and also show that there were other traditions that do not fit into this
shari'a reasoning. Before doing so, I feel a strong inclination in this opening section to quote an editorial of the *New York Times/International Herald Tribune*.
It is unsigned and may thus be taken to express the view of the newspaper itself,
and it characterizes the pursuit of 'implementation of the *shari'a*' by the current
Islamist presidency of Egypt (which rests on the empowerment of the Brotherhood) very aptly, as follows:

> Many Egyptians worry that Mr. Morsi and the Brotherhood are seeking to
> monopolize power, including imposing serious restraints on freedom of the
> press. . . . but criticism of political leaders should not be a crime, especially
> in a country aspiring to be a democracy. . . . Critics worry that the crackdown
> on journalists shows that the Islamists intend to exert tight control over every
> aspect of life.[3]

The 'implementation of *shari'a*' mindset, as reflected in the described conduct of
policy by the Muslim Brothers in their capacity as political leaders of the state,
gives just a taste of what is yet to come. Although Egypt is not yet a *shari'a* state,
this editorial seems apt, pointing just to the direction of this process that began
with the empowerment of the Islamists. These preliminary remarks serve merely
as an introduction to the theme of this chapter, which attempts to place the Islamist
shari'a state within the history of *shari'a* reasoning in Islam. The intention is to
place the Islamist post-Arab-Spring policy of the 'implementation of *shari'a*' in

a historical perspective, then to question the authenticity of this Islamist venture. In a way one can state this: the Islamist *shari'a* advanced in the post-Arab Spring reflects the most recent stage in the history of *shari'a* reasoning in Islamdom.

Islam and the tradition of *shari'a* reasoning

With reference to what has been said, the point of departure is the research-based argument that the political agenda of a *shari'a* state is a novelty hitherto unknown in Islamic history. This identifies the new order as an Islamist invention of Islamic tradition. The new Egyptian constitution pushed through in December 2012 is a case in point.

The overall context in modern history is the abolition of the Islamic order of the caliphate in the year 1924 by the founder of modern Turkey, Kemal Atatürk, parallel to the introduction of the secular nation-state and its application to the territoriality of the Islamicate. A few years later Atatürk also abolished the *shari'a*.[4] In 1925, a year after the abolition of the caliphate an Azhar professor, Ali Abdelraziq, published his famous and ground-breaking book on Islam and patterns of government. At the outset of Chapter 1 and later in Chapter 3 I endorsed Filali-Ansary's praise for Abdelraziq, ranking his work as the first Muslim contribution to the modern 'enlightened turn'[5] in Islamdom and one of its cornerstones. That book by Abdelraziq includes the following argument that I adopt:

> The addition of the caliphate to Islamic beliefs has been a crime (*jinaya*) of kings and oppressors of Muslims to mislead them and to deny them light in the name of religion . . . The truth is that the religion of Islam is innocent of the caliphate imposed on Muslims and also innocent from all the related ills . . . No, the caliphate is not part of the religion of Islam.[6]

In so arguing, Abdelraziq dissociated *shari'a* from politics and thus from the political rule of the caliphate. He restricted *shari'a* to the religious beliefs of Islam as a faith and to the performance of religious worship. The abolition of the caliphate coupled with the cultural enlightened change induced by Abdelraziq removed tensions between Islamdom and the rest of the world.

The topicality of Abdelraziq's thinking and of his work to our present lies in the fact that his criticism of the caliphate also applies to the Islamist *shari'a*. The current context for this topicality is the fact that the once-abolished *shari'a* is back in politics in a new shape. It has become one of the most burning hot-button issues, but it is often debated on poor grounds, not only without proper knowledge, but also with a low intellectual quality of debate, often expressed in an aggressive, polemical manner. This has become a feature of this war of ideas which I know only too well from my own observation combined with personal experience of exposure.

As I mentioned in Chapter 4, I had planned to conclude my career with my 2012 book *Islamism and Islam*. In the course of four rounds of reviewing, one of eleven readers maintained that there is no distinction between 'Islamic' and 'Islamist' *shari'a* and accused me of imposing a construction. I was therefore compelled to engage in a further elaboration of the argument that there *is* such a distinction with regard to *shari'a*. I did not raise any complaint, but instead was rather grateful for that challenge, which had a positive result, namely the adding of a chapter on *shari'a* to that book, improving it. In the added chapter I presented more succinct delineations with an awareness based on bad experience that I needed to inoculate my argument against unfavourable attack – clearly distinguished from constructive criticism. Of course, I shall not rehash here what I wrote there, and therefore ask the reader to consult that chapter (see note 6) as I prefer to move on and present new research, though always in continuity with my earlier reasoning – in the present case with reference to the Arab Spring.

The start has to be a reminder for the reader of the textual fact, referenced in Chapter 1, that the Qur'an lists *shari'a* only once in terms of moral conduct, commanding the good (*al-amr bi al-ma'ruf*) and forbidding the evil (*an-nahi an al-munkar*). It is understood as morality, as stated by Fazlur Rahman among others, not as law (for references see Chapter 1). Nonetheless, there is a post-Qur'anic Islamic tradition of *shari'a* reasoning in which *shari'a* has been elevated to law, but clearly not to state law. I add to this the contemporary insight that this traditional classical *shari'a* is not the same *shari'a* as the one that Islamism claims to represent in its drive to establish an Islamic state based on *lex divina* as legitimation.

In the venture undertaken in this chapter, one of the most remarkable contributions to illuminating the classical tradition of *shari'a*, John Kelsay's book *Arguing the Just War in Islam*, has proved most helpful.[7] Unlike the focus of Kelsay's book, which is the use of *shari'a* to legitimate *jihad* as a just war, my focus in terms of Islamist *shari'a* reasoning is the order of the state and of the world. Nonetheless, Kelsay's research and his authority are most pertinent to my theme, and so Kelsay's thinking is central to arguments in the present chapter in dialogue with Kelsay.

The term '*shari'a* reasoning' was coined by John Kelsay in the aforementioned book on political–religious thinking throughout the history of the civilization of Islam. His differentiations matter greatly to this chapter as they provide light at the end of the tunnel in the contemporary confusions that prevail in Islamic studies. Kelsay's work deserves (and enjoys) high esteem, in contrast to the dip in quality I see reflected in other recent studies compared to the standards reached earlier in the work of Joseph Schacht and N. J. Coulson. Kelsay's work helps to rectify the flaws in the scholarship of the intervening period.

Although I acknowledge the centrality of *shari'a* reasoning in Islam, some nuances and modifications need to be added to allow more differentiations. In particular, I think that the introduction of a distinction between the *fiqh* orthodoxy and the *falsafa* rationalism in the past, and also of distinctions between secularists of all types, reform Muslims, and Islamists in the present, would be helpful. As to the past, I argue that the *falsafa* rationalists of medieval Islam (e.g. Farabi and Ibn Rushd [Averroes]) were not guided by *shari'a* reasoning. As to modern history, one can argue that Arab secularists of all kinds (liberals, nationalists, socialists) of the late nineteenth and twentieth centuries were not affected by any pattern of *shari'a* reasoning. These Muslims did not invoke *shari'a* in their reasoning.

It follows that the generalization about Islamic history that it mostly reflects various efforts at *shari'a* reasoning is on the one hand correct, but on the other it is wrong if it serves to maintain that Islamic intellectual history can be summed up as a history of *shari'a* reasoning. In light of these differentiations, I maintain that the intellectual history of Islam goes beyond *shari'a* as it includes more schools of thought, as will be argued later. Nonetheless, the centrality of *shari'a* reasoning in the Islamic tradition in the shape of *fiqh* is an undisputed fact – only, this reasoning was traditionally not about a *shari'a* state.

In the history of ideas of the past, the medieval text by Ibn Taimiyya on *al-siyasa al-shari'yya* is the most important one with regard to the genre under discussion. At present, Islamists emulate Ibn Taimiyya, citing him as a 'precedent'. Current citations of medieval texts by most Islamists, however, blur the line between past and present. Medieval theology is referred to in order to legitimate contemporary political decisions. In general, a major feature of *shari'a* reasoning is that it revolves around the search for a historical precedent. This is not only a major argument, but also the underlying concern in the reference to the text. As Kelsay puts it: 'the citation of texts . . . involves a search for a fit between history and the present.' This interpretation by Kelsay explains precisely the preoccupation of contemporary Muslims with 'the authority of the text'. Texts by Ibn Taimiyya rank today at the top in this process. This ranking is translated into educational politics in the indoctrination of the members of Islamist movements.

The use of Hobsbawm's notion of an invention of tradition to conceptualize the Islamist legitimation of a venture that draws on medieval texts is most helpful (see note 27 below and cit.). The Islamist commitment to the procedure of a search for *sabiqa*/precedents to acquire authenticity affects the historical context of the contemporary *shari'a*tization of Islam.

The Islamist acknowledgement of the authority of the text underpins a susceptibility to dogmatic thinking. This dogmatism does not, however, conceal the fact that Islamist *shari'a* reasoning in our present era is embedded in a specific modern context. For scholars, historical reality is supposed to stand above the text. Although the Qur'an acknowledges diversity in *Sura al-Hujarat*, in Islamic history the ideal of one Islamic *umma* had always established a binary of *dar al-Islam*, the authentic house of belief, contrasted with the alien abode of the non-Muslim rest of the world. Non-Muslims, despised in their characterization as *kuffar*/infidels, were always the unequal non-Muslim other. I wonder why Western scholars ignore or even whitewash this kind of 'othering'. The accusation made towards unbelievers of *jahiliyya* (ignorance) underpins this binary. This is a burden that is rooted in traditional *shari'a*. For today's Muslims this burden charges their world view with an evil they need to abandon. One relevant problem of this thinking in Islamic doctrine is that this world view of one *umma* continues to reject pluralism. The implication of *shari'a* is that the religion of Islam proclaims to be the natural religion of humanity and thus claims superiority to all others. This religion also makes provisions to engage in *jihad* against any deviation, to correct any regarded as being an error. There is an Islamic tolerance that engages with those who do not accept the Islamic mission, but only on the grounds that they 'enter into a tributary relationship . . . (and) acknowledge the supremacy of Islam . . . as the true religion'. This is the source of a dilemma for those Muslims who prefer to maintain the claim to *siyada*/supremacy. There is no doubt that this thinking prevents them from accepting a pluralism of cultures and religions, such as is needed for cross-civilizational bridging in a global civil society.

Any serious reconstructing of the Muslim view of the world (*Weltbild*) as one based on a *shari'a* reasoning must lead to the conclusion that the Islamists envision remaking the world along their understanding of the provisions of Islam as the natural and final religion of humanity. It is true that traditional historical *shari'a* also views the Islamicate – the civilization of Islam (*dar al-Islam*) – as the centre of the world that is expected to map the entire globe into one entity. However, the Islamists of today reshape this ideal to determine a new thinking that is to be imposed, not just on the people of the civilization of Islam, but on the whole of humanity. Islamists have a problem with the non-Muslim other who may not be willing to accept the impositions of *shari'a*. They also have great problems with pluralism and diversity.

The contemporary Islamist invention of the tradition of *shari'a* has been the ground for a fruitful debate with Kelsay that has lasted for years. I have no doubt that his analysis covers properly the Islamic world view based on a universal *shari'a* reasoning. This analysis of Kelsay is accurate and – although a few corrections need to be made – fully valid. I also admit that the appeal of the Islamist *shari'a* lies in the fact that it employs the slogans of Islamic tradition. Now, everything is changeable and Islam is no exception. Although the world view described survived change throughout past centuries, modern times are challenging it vehemently. The bottom line is that Islamism is not a traditionalism. Some propose viewing the mix between tradition and modern items adopted by Islamism in terms of hybridity. I prefer to see it as a 'semi-modernism', a concept elaborated upon in my earlier work. The notion of semi-modernism conceptualizes a reality in which the adoption of modern technical and scientific instruments (items of modernity) is coupled with a wholesale rejection of modern values (cultural modernity), which is defamed as 'Western'.

The tradition of classical *shari'a* doctrine in the light of contemporary realities

The mix-up between what is revelation and what is human reasoning ended, in Islamic legal history, in an essentialized classical doctrine that tends not only to ignore historical changes but also to reject the historicity of Islam. Nonetheless, the doctrine engages in conformism, which facilitates adjustment but lacks any cultural ability to accommodate change by rethinking the religious doctrine. The confusion between *shari'a* (revealed by God) and *fiqh* (human reasoning on *shari'a*) is to be placed in this context. The equation of *shari'a* and *fiqh* leads to a belief that attributes immutability to the historical *shari'a* on the grounds that it is a revelation and thus supposed to stand above history.

In modern history, the new power of industrialized Europe gave the lie to the Muslim belief in Muslim supremacy – a belief which ignores the necessity of dealing with changes that have been taking place. Thus, contemporary *shari'a* reasoning continues to assume the shape of *fiqh*, the major source of thinking for those Muslims who have become Islamists. In their aspiration for guidance, they seek *sabiqa*/precedents in the classical doctrine. The context of this Islamist venture is the uncertainty that has been generated by the exposure to the challenge of modern times. This is the phenomenon I refer to in the title of my book *Islam's Predicament with Modernity*. The core argument of that book is that failure to culturally accommodate modernity creates tensions, and that these lead to conflict.

The topicality of *shari'a* in contemporary Islam is related to the rise of Islamism. Ibn Taimiyya serves Islamists as a major source in their search for a precedent to which they can refer. Prior to the rise of Islamism, Muslim *ulama*/scribes were poised, under the conditions of globalization in the nineteenth century, to engage in a type of *shari'a* reasoning referred to as 'conformism', i.e. they were engaged in an effort to reinterpret *shari'a* anew – but not to rethink it – to establish a fit between its claims and the new, changed conditions. These scribes were, however, not willing to reform the religious doctrine by going beyond scripturalism. In their venture, these *ulama* invoked *shari'a* in a new setting to respond to the challenge of modernity within the frame of reference determined by *shari'a* reasoning.

Again, I draw on Kelsay's help for a proper understanding of three Islamic patterns of response to the challenges involved. The first is the radical response that legitimates armed struggle; Kelsay focuses on the example of al-Qaeda. Kelsay consistently speaks of *jihad*, but I prefer the term 'jihadism', because what is at issue is an invention of tradition, best covered by a new term. Jihadism is not classical *jihad*.

The second response pattern is that of the religious establishment and moderate institutional Islamists who criticize the overriding of the rules of traditional *jihad* by contemporary jihadists. This establishment stops short of distancing Islam completely from the resort to violence; the jihadists' practices are questioned, but not the goals they pursue.

The third pattern is that of Islamic democrats who respond by addressing the issue, more or less, in its broad scope. These are not only a minority, but also highly inconsistent in their thought (e.g. Abdullahi An-Na'im), and tend have little impact on their communities. These Islamic democrats are not identical with Muslims of the 'enlightened thought' and should not be mistaken for them.

In Chapter 2 I reminded the reader of the distinctions within Islamism, in particular those between peaceful and violent/jihadist Islamists. When it comes to governance in terms of a *shari'a* state, however, intra-Islamist tensions disappear. Kelsay tells us: 'In its broad confines, the militant vision articulated by al-Zawahiri is also the vision of his critics.' This contention is made clear in the statement that those critics of jihadism reject the resort to violence and qualify the means of terror as 'wrong or counterproductive, or both. But they do not dissent from the judgment that . . . the cure for the ills . . . involves the establishment of Islamic governance'. Kelsay adds: 'The problem of militancy is not simply a matter of objectionable tactics. The problem is the very notion of Islamic governance.' This notion translates into the *shari'a* state being the hallmark of Islamism, irrespective of whether moderate or violent. To reject this insight is to prefer the self-deception of equating 'moderation' with 'approval of democracy' – a way of thinking that simply steps around all the pertinent questions. Merely overlooking or denying the budding conflict does not, unfortunately, mean that it will subside.

While it is easy to be critical of the first (jihadist) group, it is more difficult to take issue with institutional Islamists who have successfully invaded the religious establishment. And as regards the third group, it is deplorable to see the great lack of consistency in Islamic democratic thought. This is clearly seen in the writings of some Muslim democrats, in particular those of Abdulaziz Sachedina.[8] Another Muslim democrat, Abdullahi An-Na'im (with whom I earlier shared a concern in joint projects of introducing individual human rights to our civilization), began as a voice of 'Islamic reformation', but then took a big step backwards, shifting course in a U-turn from rejecting the notion of *shari'a* as constitutional law to approving it in these words: '*shari'a* should be . . . a source of liberation and self-realization.'[9] In his early work, An-Na'im requested in a highly promising book on Islamic reformation, published in 1990, that Muslims must either do away with or revise the historical *shari'a*. These references demonstrate a lack of consistency, and therefore a loss of credibility. To pay lip service to democracy and pluralism without embracing the civic culture that goes with them, and without detailing a programme of religious reforms, is not enough to make this Muslim democratic position tenable. Enlightened Muslim thought is more consistent and thus is free from such ambiguities.

Unlike the inconsistent Muslim contributions referred to, the religious establishment consistently maintains a version of traditional *shari'a*, but does so in an attempt to establish a conformism aimed only at adjustment, devoid of any cultural accommodation of the changed reality. In the past this sentiment was best represented in the multi-volume work of the nineteenth-century Moroccan Ahmed al-Nasiri. Al-Nasiri's work seeks a balance between inherited *shari'a* and reasoning – mostly in regard to the changed realities of the nineteenth century.[10] The significance of al-Nasiri (1835–1897) lies also in his role during his time as an advisor to the then Sultan of Morocco. He recommended to him the suspension of *jihad*, given that the Islamicate was deprived of its power to establish hegemony. This nineteenth-century tradition was continued in the twentieth century by al-Azhar's textbook *Bayan lil-Nas*.[11] In contrast to the conformism of the religious establishment represented by the sheykh of al-Azhar, Jadulhaq Ali Jadulhaq, the sheykh of the Islamists, Yusuf al-Qaradawi, is a rejectionist. He acts as the heir of Sayyid Qutb and calls for a *shari'a* state to replace the nation-state. This replacement is viewed as the *hall al-Islami*/Islamic solution to the crisis. This position of a *shari'a*tized Islam, not al-Qaeda terrorism, is the real challenge of Islamism to the international order based on the Westphalian synthesis.[12]

Alternatives to *shari'a* reasoning in Islamic civilization

In scholarly terms, the repudiation of the Islamist contention that Islam rests on a concept of a *shari'a* state has to be placed in a context of 'big structures, large processes and huge comparisons' in order to make it possible to understand properly what is happening on the ground in the aftermath of the Arab Spring. In Islamic terms, this kind of reasoning, which confronts Islamism in the mindset of the tradition of the humanism of Islamic *falsafa* rationalism, has to be pursued with Islamic legitimacy. It is a confrontation embedded in the history of ideas and is characterized by a deep-seated conflict between *fiqh* and *falsafa*.[13] This Islamic past is continued today in the new conflict between Islamism and enlightened Muslim thought. The Islamic *falsafa* rationalism, which can be identified as the seed of an Islamic version of a secular enlightenment, was a culturally innovative, forward-looking direction in Islam. Unlike the philosophers of the European Enlightenment (e.g. Voltaire), the Muslim philosophers (e.g. Ibn Sina and Ibn Rushd) never polarized *fiqh* orthodoxy. They were willing to establish bridges, even though they were not willing to participate in '*shari'a* reasoning'. Some of them paid lip service to *shari'a* (e.g. Ibn Khaldun), but this was simply to inoculate their rationalism from attacks by the orthodoxy of the *fiqh* establishment.

The al-Jabri Islam project of the twentieth century, which carries the name of the great late Moroccan philosopher Mohammed Abed al-Jabri, was and continues to be a project to revive *falsafa* rationalism in Islam.[14] This civil Islam is the alternative, not only to the tradition of *shari'a* reasoning in classical Islam, but also to the one of *shari'a*tizing Islamism in our present. Ibn Rushd was a rationalist and served al-Jabri as a paragon for emulation in the pursuit of an accommodation of cultural modernity. The fight between rationalism and *fiqh* orthodoxy is embedded in big structures of Islamic history.[15]

In contrast to these Muslim philosophers, the *fiqh* scribes draw a clear red line between faith and rationalism.[16] As Mawardi put it in medieval Islam, every Muslim is exposed in his thinking to the alternatives '*bi al-aql aw bi al-wahi*' ('either by reason or by revelation') when it comes to sources of knowledge. For the *fiqh* orthodoxy there is no middle in this binary. In the past as well as the present, it may be seen that those Muslims who are inclined to accept the primacy of reason run the risk, not just of being demonized, but of being excluded from the *umma* as heretics and executed. A crude scripturalism contributes to this separation of *al-aql* (reason) from *al-wahi* (revelation). Muslim rationalists were fearful of this exposure. The last great philosopher in Islam, Ibn Khaldun (died 1406), was a rationalist, but distanced himself verbally from philosophy in an act of self-protection. The lip service I mentioned earlier that he paid to *shari'a* can only be understood properly when one considers the deeply rational work of a reason-based philosophy of history articulated in his *Muqaddima*. In this great work one will not find any *shari'a* reasoning at all. Ibn Khaldun states that religion is not a primary source of '*asabi-yya*/esprit de corps which is – according to his philosophy – the driver of history.

The tensions between *fiqh* and *falsafa* ended in the past in favour of the *shari'a* reasoning of the *fiqh* orthodoxy. I remind readers of the philosophy of *al-Madina al-Fadila* of al-Farabi and the epistemology of Ibn Rushd, asserting that these great Muslims did not follow the Islamic tradition of *shari'a* reasoning. In contrast to them, Ibn Taimiyya in his *al-Siyasa al-Shar'iyya*, and Mawardi in his *al-Ahkam al-Sultaniyya*, asserted the authority of *fiqh* against philosophy. In that medieval competition within Islamdom, Ibn Taimiyya and Mawardi were more successful than the *falsafa* rationalists and thus ended as the winners.

Apart from the al-Jabri project in contemporary reform Islam to revive Averroism, there are Muslims discussed earlier, such as al-Ashmawi, who repudiated the Islamist concept of the *shari'a* state on scriptural grounds. Given the authority of the text in Islamic civilization, al-Ashmawi views *shari'a* in the Qur'an and considers the traditional *shari'a* reasoning, to conclude first that there is no *shari'a* state in this scripture and second that this order is the contemporary invention of political Islam.

The work of Mohammed al-Jabri goes a step further: 'The survival of our philosophical tradition, i.e. what is likely to contribute to our time, can only be Averroist.'[17] Averroist philosophy does not rest on the method or principles of *shari'a* reasoning. Rather, it rests on the Hellenization of Islam and the related combination of rationalism and humanism.[18] It is sad to see that *shari'a*tized Islam is more appealing to contemporary Muslims than the Islamic heritage of Averroist rationalism which is poised to accommodate cultural modernity. There is a most important survey on these failed attempts at true revival in the brilliant study carried out by Anke von Kügelgen.[19] In the aftermath of the Arab defeat in the 1967 war, enlightened intellectuals made a further effort in this direction, but they also failed. This post-1967-war development lasted for only three years. Prior to this development there was another alternative, but it also failed.[20] This was the short period of liberalism and secular nationalism.

The backstory is the encounter with the West in the nineteenth century. Muslim thinkers wanted to engage in cultural borrowing from Europe. Muslim liberals at that time made the bottom line clear: only adoptions were to be admitted that did not contradict or violate the rules of *shari'a*.[21] Islamic modernism aimed to establish a synthesis between *shari'a* reasoning and cultural modernity, but it did not work. Then followed the age of secular liberalism, which was not committed to *shari'a*. The failure of this liberalism paved the way for the illiberal populism of secular pan-Arab nationalism, which had nothing at all to do with *shari'a* reasoning.[22] In the course of the de-legitimation of secular ideologies in the aftermath of the Arab defeat in 1967, this secular nationalism waned in favour of the rise of political Islam with its agenda of *shari'a*tization.[23] This development has been the indicator for the resumption of *shari'a* reasoning in a new shape, in an invention of tradition. The climax of this development is the empowerment of Islamist movements in the course of the Arab Spring.

Historically, the Arab defeat in the Six-Day War of 1967 was a watershed. It allowed a short interval of post-1967 Arab enlightenment (see note 20), but at the end of the day the defeat resulted in the return of *shari'a* in the Islamist shape of a counter-enlightenment based on the authority of the scripture, not on reason. The result was the victory of political Islam.[24] This process started first in the

Sunni-Arab part of Islamic civilization. A decade later, the Shi'ite Islamic Revolution in Iran (1978–1979) followed as a latecomer, with a Shi'ite variety of *shari'a* Islamism.[25] Since the Sunni vision of a *shari'a* state is what has moved centrestage in the broader context of the Arab Spring, the focus here is on Sunni Islam.

The return of *shari'a* reasoning in an invention of tradition

In modern times, liberal and nationalist secularism failed to strike roots in the world of Islam, just as earlier Islamic *falsafa* rationalism did in the medieval period. Nevertheless, both periods can be pointed to as evidence that there existed periods in both classical and modern history that were not determined by *shari'a* reasoning. The recurrent *shari'a* is so powerful that it can be observed even in the foremost secular republic of the world of Islam, in Turkey. Secularists in Turkey are in retreat. Although the Republic of Turkey continues to enshrine secularism in its constitution, the ruling AKP Islamists have been successful in launching a process of de-secularization. The victory of the AKP is a victory for *shari'a* reasoning in Turkey and serves as a model for Islamists in the Arab Spring. The Movement of the Muslim Brothers enjoys excellent relations with Turkey and has its support.[26]

The Islamist project of *shari'a*tization of state and society invites the adoption of Hobsbawm's notion of the 'invention of tradition'. Hobsbawm tells us that 'inventing traditions is . . . characterized by reference to the past . . . where a tradition is deliberately invented and constructed. . . . The difficulty is not only one of the sources, but also of the techniques . . . in symbolism and ritual.'[27] The new *shari'a* of political Islam can be interpreted along these lines. The invented tradition is then combined with the political agenda of imposing an authoritarian state order that claims to be based on divine law. This is not the constitutionalism that the Harvard law professor Noah Feldman believes he sees.[28] The *shari'a* state is a totalitarian order, distinct from more traditional forms of despotic rule. In my book *Islamism and Islam* I draw on the work of Hannah Arendt to examine the hypothesis that Islamism can be conceptualized as totalitarianism. The result of this examination is positive: the *shari'a*tization of Islamic polity fulfils all the criteria of a totalitarian order.[29]

At this juncture, there is a need to repeat the reference to the distinction between Islam (tradition) and Islamism (the invention of tradition) in order to understand properly what al-Banna and also Qutb did to the *shari'a* to make it useable as a frame for establishing *hakimiyyat Allah*/God's rule. The *shari'a* state – by some wrongly called Islamic constitutionalism – is a concept that never existed in quite this form in any earlier Islamic tradition. This is why, in terms of the legacy of al-Banna and Qutb, I speak of a combined jihadization and *shari'a*tization of Islam. This combination results from the process of an invention of tradition. If one accepts the argument of an 'interval' in Islamic history that occurred twice (*falsafa* rationalism in the past, and secularism in contemporary history), there can be agreement over the place of a return of *shari'a* reasoning as an Islamist venture taking a new shape. In short, I not only propose to consider the 'interval' mentioned, but also suggest that the return of *shari'a* reasoning takes place as an invention of tradition. This is why it is wrong to view al-Banna's thought as a 'revival' of tradition, as his grandson Tariq Ramadan contends in a highly questionable book.[30]

While I would not wish to endorse Huntington's rhetoric of a 'clash of civilizations', I submit in fairness that the late Harvard scholar contributed, albeit in a distorted manner, to the revival of the study of civilizations in politics. In this context, a conflict is stated in civilizational terms. A conflict is not necessarily a clash. A conflict can be peacefully resolved; a clash cannot. With this understanding in mind, I propose to see in the course of the revival of divine law in Islamic civilization a conflict and a competition between 'secular' and 'political–religious' concepts of order; however, I reject the 'clash of civilizations' formula for conceptualizing this conflict because it is based on an essentialism. It is more proper to speak of a 'new Cold War' taking place in a competition between secularism and the return of the sacred.

To be sure, one can employ a new understanding of *shari'a* for ethical guidance in politics, but no more than that. *Shari'a* is not itself constitutional law, as the Islamists claim, and get support from some Western scholars. This claim abuses the text of the Qur'an to legitimate a new variety of Oriental despotism wearing the religious garb of either Wahhabi or Islamist Islam in the name of constitutionalism. The difference between Hanbali-inspired Wahhabi orthodox Salafism and Islamism is the difference between despotism and totalitarianism. These two ideologies engage, each in its own way, in *shari'a*-based reasoning to legitimate pre- or undemocratic political rule.

At present, the argument for secular law and legal universality is challenged by the Islamist project of the *shari'a*tization of Islam. Truly, the *shari'a* in Islam is a pendulum swinging between ethics and politics. Ethically, the Qur'an prescribes piety and general rules of conduct. This guidance (*hidaya*) is not a legal system (the reader is reminded of facts listed in Chapter 1). The 'legal system' of *shari'a* is therefore a post-Qur'anic structure erected by humans. As a tradition it is, however, confined to *mu'amalat* (civil law), cult (*ibadat*) and a penal code (*hudud*). Islamic clerics are learned men of religion (*ulama* or scribes), and some of them act as religious jurists or *faqih*s (Arabic plural: *fuqaha*), not as theologians (*mutakallimun*). In medieval Islam a religious tradition of *kalam* (theology) developed. These scribes deliberately confused their *fiqh* with divine *shari'a*. In contrast to them were the Mutazilite theologians, who were 'defenders of reason', but they – unlike the *fuqaha* – never succeeded in becoming mainstream in Islamic civilization.

The *fiqh* (Islamic sacral jurisprudence) possessed and continues to possess a monopoly over the interpretation of religious affairs in Islam, and it is presented as *shari'a*. Most of the jurists did not deal with politics and they were never independent in their *shari'a* reasoning, because they were subservient to the caliph. There was a separation between law (*shari'a*) and the politics (*siyasa*) of the state. I prefer to follow Joseph Schacht rather than Hallaq, and to adopt his way of describing this separation: that the sovereign pretended 'to apply and to complete the sacred law. . . . [but] in practice to regulate by virtually independent legisla-tion matters of police, taxation, justice, all of which had escaped the control of the Kadi'.[31] This field, as Schacht continues, was 'later called *siyasa* . . . As a result of all this, a double administration . . . one religious . . . on the basis of *shari'a*, the other is secular exercised by political authorities on the basis of . . . – sometimes – arbitrariness of governmental regulations.'

The Schacht quotations reveals that a virtual separation between *siyasa* and *shari'a* existed in Islamic medieval history, but this is ignored in the Islamist *shari'a*tization of law. This project claims to be in the tradition of *shari'a* rea-soning, but in reality it is engaging in an invented tradition. In the past, *shari'a* reasoning took a new political direction in the work of Ibn Taimiyya. This implies on the one hand a 'conservative practice in the sense that it . . . follows the line of precedent';[32] on the other hand, however, it seems 'to suggest the necessity of fighting' in a kind of 'just revolution'. This is a novelty expressed in a tension between two contradictory provisions, and may explain the life of Ibn Taimiyya: he preached obedience to authority, but at the same time, as Kelsay reminds us, he spent most of his life in prison as a punishment for disobedience. In the age of the return of the sacred with an invented *shari'a* law, the writings of Ibn Taimi-yya are highly instructive for understanding Islamism. Islamists themselves refer to Ibn Taimiyya and claim universality for *shari'a*. In so doing, they not only generate inter-civilizational conflict, but also call for disobedience to the existing rule, which they qualify as un-Islamic. In so doing, they engage in the same con-tradiction that characterized the life and work of Ibn Taimiyya.

Both continuity and discontinuity exist in the development from the historical background I have outlined to the present of Islam. This development generates a conflict-ridden situation. There is the reality of a diversity of legal systems that exist in parallel to the diversity of cultures and civilizations. Salafi Muslims and Islamists reject secular law as a Western notion and also challenge its claim to universality. Instead, they prefer to refer to the Qur'an, imposing on it their under-standing that it is the only valid source of law as well as of an Islamic constitution. While they reject the universality of secular law, they give to their own views on *shari'a* the feature of universalism. To understand how the particular can be made universal, a reference to the Oxford jurist H. L. A. Hart is worthwhile. Hart shows how European-structured law becomes international law, binding for new states:

> It has never been doubted that when a new, independent state emerges into existence . . . it is bound by the general obligations of international law. . . . Here the attempt to rest the new state's international obligations on a 'tacit' or 'inferred' consent seems wholly threadbare.[33]

This statement is correct, but it is also correct that humanity needs a universal law on which the international system rests. As argued in Chapter 3, the 'Westphalian synthesis' is a system which is secular and therefore is more promising than the return of the sacred embodied by Islamism. International law has to be secular, since it is for the whole of humanity. There is no single religion for the whole of humanity on which any law could rest and be cosmopolitan. I will confine myself here to this remark, given the detailed analysis of this issue provided in Chapter 3.

The reference to the existing Westphalian system is nonetheless justified by the Islamist drawing on law traditions constructed along the lines of the traditional concept of sacred law but applied to the present. This *shari'a* law establishes a reasoning based on the belief that it is revealed by God, even though it is derived by humans interpretatively from holy scripture. These religious tenets are intended to replace the secular 'Westphalian synthesis'. In modern democracies, the law-makers are elected parliamentarians acting in legislative institutions, whereas in Islam, non-elected *faqihs*, in their capacity as interpreters of scripture, are not only legal scholars but also those who determine what the law is and what is legitimate authority in the name of Allah. The Islamists apply this *fiqh* not only to Muslims and their Islamicate, but also to the whole of humanity, globally. It is a global imposition that generates conflict, not peace.

Thus, one may contrast two competing legal traditions with one another: legislative secular democratic law versus interpretative authoritarian divine law (*lex divina*). The contemporary Islamist *shari'a* reasoning reaches a peak in the process of *shari'a*tization of law which legitimizes a project of de-secularization. It is viewed as a project of de-Westernization, to be accomplished through Islamization of the law as an expression of a politics of cultural purification. This process is clearly imbued with anti-democratic implications. Currently, in most Islamic countries, positive law is flatly rejected in favour of the agenda of a *tatbiq al-shari'a*/implementation of *shari'a*, as mentioned at the beginning of the present chapter. The landslide electoral victory of the pro-*shari'a* Islamists in general in the context of the post-Arab-Spring era has led to their empowerment. This outcome casts great doubt on the future of the world of Islam as well as on the prospects for its incorporation into a world community based on secular law. If the new *shari'a* reasoning, based on a *shari'a*tization of the state, were to prevail, the situation will be worth despairing over, because it leads to tensions and to geopolitical conflict.

An important excursus: *shari'a* reasoning in the Islamic diaspora in Europe

Right at the outset of this book, I listed Islamism's safe footing in European exile as one of the two reasons for the ability of Islamist movements to survive political persecution by authoritarian regimes. Despite its significance, this theme does not form part of the trajectory of the analysis pursued in the present book. Nonetheless, the digression undertaken in this section (before moving on to the conclusions) is pertinent. *Shari'a* reasoning has relevance for the Islamic diaspora in Europe, a diaspora that has emerged in the contemporary context of global migration.[34] Westerners who are not knowledgeable about Islamic beliefs confuse migration in Islam with migration in general, thus failing to grasp the issue properly, and as a result they draw utterly wrong conclusions about integrating of Islam into Europe on the grounds of allowing space for an 'Islamic culture within Europe'. This issue is best grasped by John Kelsay in an earlier work, where he says: 'Given the increased presence of Muslims in Europe and North America . . . it is important to see . . . an account of an exchange,' and then adds towards the end:

> the traditions we call Western and Islamic can no longer strictly be identified with particular geographic regions . . . The rapidity of Muslim immigration . . . suggests that we may soon be forced to speak not simply of Islam, but of Islam in the West. What difference will this make? . . . Islamic communities form a sort of sectarian enclave in the context of a larger, Western culture . . . , but not of it.[35]

In his more recent *Arguing the Just War in Islam*, Kelsay makes the following insightful comment regarding migration in Islam:

> The migration to Medina, *al-hijra*, constitutes a defining moment in the story. For the time being, the community would carry out its mission not only by means of preaching and worship, but by means of fighting and other political activity.[36]

Given the Muslim view that a *sabiqa*/precedent serves as an orientation for the future, the tough question as to whether this *shari'a* provision is also valid for the Muslims of the diaspora in Europe should not be evaded. It is a question that relates to the rapidly increasing diaspora that has been emerging from the new wave of migration. There are Europeans who naively believe that in the context of multiculturalism Europe could accommodate the 'implementation of *shari'a*'. Paul Berman does not share this naivety, and dismantles the idea of a 'Muslim counter-culture', speaking of a 'counter-culture in the West to assume a shape of its own under the name of a Western Islam'. For Berman this 'means a Salafi reformism, and not a Westernized Islam'.[37] At issue are two different understandings of Islam for Muslims living in Europe: either a European Islam (Euro-Islam) – as Islam in Senegal is Afro-Islam, or Islam in Southeast Asia is Indonesian Islam – that allows Muslim migrants to become European citizens, or a *shari'a*tized Islam of a 'sectarian enclave' (Kelsay). The latter allows Islamist movements to recruit in the European exile and to establish a safe haven for their global networks in an ethnicized diaspora existing in parallel societies.

The study of Islam in Europe and in its Islamic environment is a minefield. I have myself squarely faced how people evade and bypass all the questions involved. I will restrict myself here to a reference to a EU project on 'democratization in the European neighbourhood' that demonstrates the linkage.[38] This process matters to the integration of the Islamic diaspora. I add this insight: No doubt, Muslim immigrants can only be integrated as citizens of the heart in a secular polity. They can only do this if they can be induced to abandon the combination of *hijra* with proselytization for the spread of Islam by all means. If, however, *shari'a* reasoning is more binding on them than loyalty to secular, non-Islamic laws and to the con-stitutions of the states where they live, there can be no integration, only illusion that overlooks the reality of an Islamization that leads to conflict. Can democracy be transferred to the Mediterranean part of the Islamicate via the Islamic diaspora in Europe? The question betrays wishful thinking!

As one of these migrants myself, I think one can counter Islamization that leads to a misgiving of an 'ethnicity of fear', that occurs if the integration fails, if the extension of the *shari'a* is replaced by an abandoning of *shari'a* in a Europeanized Islam. This is my concept of a Euro-Islam free of the trinity *da'wa*/proselytizing, *shari'a* and *jihad*. This trinity does not do Muslims any good, either in the Islamicate itself or in Islamdom in Europe. There are better alternatives.[39] A general alternative is enlightened Muslim thought; an example of a specific case is civil Islam in Indonesia.

Conclusions: Islamist *shari'a* vs. the Arab Spring

Having studied Islam in global politics in the past three decades, I share the view of John Brenkman that the world of Islam is in turmoil, an overall situation that reflects an intra-Islamic 'civil war'.[40] Since 9/11, the violence within Islamic civilization has expanded to become a geopolitical war. A part of this war is a war of ideas in which Islamist *shari'a* reasoning claims geopolitical space for the establishing of a new order. In the name of 'respect', Islamists and multiculturalists demand recognition of this *shari'a*tized Islam, including in the European diaspora. The only response is to point to the facts that no single essentialized Islam exists, and no single *shari'a*. To this one can then add that there is an Islamic alternative to *shari'a*tized Islam, namely in the context of a 'peace of ideas' – the tradition of Islamic humanism.[41]

At issue are not only concerns about the two billion Muslims living all over the world, out of the seven billion people that make up the world population, but also the non-Muslim rest of humanity, defined by Islamists in *shari'a–jihad* terms. Thus, the secular-universal outlook that underpins the unity of one humanity is threatened by the Islamist binary world view, which is determined by the *shari'a* reasoning analysed in this chapter. Religious reform and cultural change are needed in Islam to facilitate an accommodation to secular cultural modernity. The pertinence of this need is not restricted to the people of Islamic civilization – it affects everyone. In my study of Islam's predicament with modernity I placed the inquiry into how Muslims could embrace the values of pluralism and a philosophy of a secular law at the top – next to the universality of knowledge and of human rights.[42] These are the core issue areas of the predicament. One cannot pay lip service to pluralism and continue at the same time to approve a *shari'a* reasoning that denies diversity in favour of a false unity. The classical Islamic concept of peace is based on subduing non-Muslims as unequal *dhimmi*. This concept has been revived by Islamism in a new binary, although it had been phased out. A *shari'a* state based on this ideology is an obstacle to Muslims who want to see Islamdom as a part of an international community, because it alienates them from the non-Muslim other.

Peace can only be established on the grounds of *mutual* recognition and respect between Muslims and non-Muslims. This would be a true pluralism. In a study completed at the National University of Singapore, Asia Research Institute, a research team proposed a concept for the pursuit of this end which they called a 'democratic pluralism of cultural modernity'.[43] This concept runs against the Islamic concept of 'dhimmitude' revived in Egypt by empowered Islamists. The traditional Muslim understanding of toleration under conditions of subjection is no longer acceptable in the twenty-first century. At issue is not only to open a space for Islam, but also a space for the non-Muslim other (e.g. as in Malaysia) to live with Muslims as equals. To create such space for non-Muslims, the Islamist hegemonic project of a *shari'a* state has to be abandoned, because it precludes the placing of the non-Muslim other on an equal footing and thus contradicts the spirit of pluralism at all levels. Without the acceptance of cross-civilizational bridging based on pluralism and equality, there can be no end to 'Islam's geopolitical war'.

The Arab Spring is relevant, not only to the needs of the rebelling people, but also to the need for cross-civilizational bridging in global politics.[44] Make no mistake: this is not the dishonest European–Saudi rhetoric of an 'alliance of civilizations'. An honest will to conflict resolution requires *abandoning* the Islamist concept of a supremacist *shari'a* order for the state and for the world at large. If the Arab Spring ends with establishing this *shari'a* state, neither the promise of democracy nor a peace based on bridging will be within reach. The order of a *shari'a* state contradicts the early Arab Spring that was driven by a pluralist and liberal–secular democratic mindset. To contribute to democratization, we need a civil Islam based on enlightened Muslim thought. A *shari'a* state would fail to accomplish anything in this direction and thus could never fulfil the hopes pinned on the Arab Spring. The exasperation that caused the rebellion would continue, though in a different shape. Enlightened Muslim thought, which decouples the faith of Islam from ideologies of political order, proves the better alternative – in spite of its weak constituency in Islamdom and the West.

In view of the existing conflict between civil Islam and Islamism in Islamdom, it cannot be repeated often enough that the critique of the *shari'a*tization of Islam never doubts the compatibility of Islamic ethics with democracy. Enlightened Muslim thought is open to learning from others, including the Western concept of an open civil society as a requirement for a genuine democracy. The core idea of Karl Popper's open society is that it is a misconception to view democracy as the 'rule of the majority'. The basic concern of a democracy is to avert *any* despotic rule, not to establish the rule of the majority. In a working paper of the Madrid-based think tank FRIDE ('A European Institution for Global Action'), the Muslim writer Moataz El-Fegiery asks in the title: 'A Tyranny of the Majority? Islamists' Ambivalence about Human Rights.'[45] Underlying El-Fegiery's question is the fact that Islamists argue that an Islamic democracy reflects the rule of the majority. They infer from this argument that, given the Islamic majority of the population, advocacy of the *shari'a* state is a binding rule for everyone of Muslim faith. Is this genuine democracy? All Islamist 'programmes, statements and literature' give a positive answer to this question, but closer scrutiny provides the evidence that in a 'public order based on *Shari'ah*' – as El-Fegiery states – 'human rights will be endangered'. He continues:

Islamists assert in their model of an Islamic state . . . that there are fixed rulings in *Shari'ah* that cannot be open to change. . . . So, under the model of the Islamic state advocated by these Islamist groups, one specific understanding of Islam would be institutionalised and adopted by the state as authentic. In consequence, any religious belief that differs from the mainstream of . . . *Shari'ah* would be denounced as heresy.

These ideological views compel a questioning of the sincerity of Islamists, in particular when they 'vow to respect the right to freedom of expression' among other democratic rights, but act to the contrary. Based on solid evidence, El-Fegiery emphasizes that 'the Islamists' bleak record in practice in this area casts doubts on the official positions'. In short, in the name of an 'Islamic democracy' in a '*Shari'ah* state' Islamists establish 'a tyranny of the majority'. One may add: and the Islamists may not even be a majority in Islamdom.

6 Torn between combating prejudice and the accusation of Islamophobia

The *shari'a* state and policing speech in the debate 'Whither Islamic civilization?'

The Arab Spring could have been a blessing as a promise of a democracy, but it is one that stands on an unsure footing. The empowerment of the Islamist movements has enforced the trend towards a *shari'a* state. In the political culture of an open society it must be allowed – with freedom of speech – to discuss the outcome and to ask: Is the *shari'a* state a democracy? Is it possible to ask this question without running a risk?

In a democratic polity, civil liberties are always defended against the power of the state. The protection of citizens' and minorities' rights, viewed as entitlements in civil society, is underpinned by strong institutions that are committed to safeguarding these entitlements in a culture based on the values of pluralism. These institutions guarantee to citizens the practice of human rights – again, as entitlements. A state is democratic only when its power to intervene in the life of its citizens is not only limited but also controlled by the efficient institutions of a civil society determined by law.

The *shari'a* state is not in line with the model I have outlined, which is supposed to be a universal one with regard to its nature. In a *shari'a* state, citizens have no right to contest what is presented to them as *shari'a* rules with which they have to comply. In spite of diversity, there should be no difference between what is Western and what is Islamic when it comes to rights as entitlements in a democracy. Cultural diversity admits differences, but not when these cross the red line of rights. Differences should be allowed only when they pertain to details of practices, not to the substance of democracy itself as a culture of rights. In this understanding, which determines the nature of the present chapter, I not only state – on the basis of the evidence presented in the preceding chapters – that the *shari'a* state is incompatible with democracy: I also ask whether scholars do not have the right to conduct an inquiry that states these findings without being exposed to accusations and defamation. This chapter conducts this debate, and ends – as does the book – with arguing for the legitimacy of a free inquiry on: 'Whither Islamic civilization?'

No to a culture of imposing limitations

An op-ed piece by a representative of the US independent watchdog organization Freedom House in the *International Herald Tribune* defends the freedom of belief next to that of free speech (see note 60 below). With regard to combating prejudice against Islam and Muslims, the article strongly recommends that 'governments should not be in the business of policing speech'. There are other ways to combat prejudice.

One financially powerful state does not heed the Freedom House recommendation. It is most intriguing that this state, namely Saudi Arabia, is one that denies its citizens all individual human rights including the freedom of belief and of speech. At the same time Saudi Arabia is the core actor in the imposition of a culture of limitations in the name of fighting 'Islamophobia'. Saudi Arabia is endlessly at pains to impose global limitations on speech in the name of respect for Islam. Saudia Arabia was the foremost power in building the Organization of the Islamic Conference (OIC) when it was founded in Morocco in 1969. The OIC acts in the Saudi–Wahhabi mindset and it is – along with Iran – the source of the birth of the questionable notion of 'Islamophobia'. At issue is an illiberal policy based on a culture of accusations and outlawing. As Stephen Schwartz of the Center for Islamic Pluralism has written, Saudia Arabia uses the OIC to define

> Islamophobia with considerable and questionable latitude, as any criticism of Muslim individual, institutional, ideological, legal, or cultural behaviour. Combating Islamophobia as it conceives it, OIC seeks to prevent free discussion about Islam or the lives of Muslims under, for example, the radical Islamists dominating Saudi-Arabia and ruling Iran.[1]

Another author, Pascal Bruckner, refers to the second source of the prevention of freedom of speech, namely Iran, saying:

> At the end of the 1970s, Iranian fundamentalists invented the term 'Islamophobia' formed in analogy to 'xenophobia'. The aim of this word was to declare Islam inviolate. Whoever crosses this border is deemed a racist. This term, which is worthy of totalitarian propaganda, is deliberately unspecific. . . .[2]

In the mindset identified in both quotations, Islamists claim that the *shari'a* state is an Islamic democracy, in parallel to their outlawing any critical inquiry with the accusation of Islamophobia. A closer look at the nature of an Islamist *shari'a* state reveals that it is not a democracy. The instrumental limitations imposed on freedom of speech are based on the grounds of the 'legitimation' I have cited. In Chapters 1 to 3 of this book I have demonstrated that enlightened Muslim thought argues that Islam is not bound to a state order. This enlightened thought can deal with prejudice against Islam and Muslims using the power of criticism and ethics, but it does not respond to it by calling for impositions aimed virtually at curbing freedom of speech. As I showed in Chapter 3, this enlightened Muslim thought started in 1925 with Ali Abdelraziq's critique of the caliphate, in which he rejected the caliphate as an abuse of the faith of Islam, which is a religious belief, not an ideology for a political order.

The line of reasoning established in Abdelraziq's work is continued today by

Muslims of the 'enlightened turn', who similarly accept *shari'a* as the source of ethical conduct but not as an order of the state and of the world. Therefore, the *shari'a* state in Islamic terms is rejected in the present book. In this concluding chapter I argue for freedom of critical speech and relate this thinking to those who attempt to taint criticism with the accusation of Islamophobia. Enlightened Muslim thought not only takes issue with Islamists, but also combats prejudice against Islam when it really exists – but criticism should be distinguished from prejudice.

So, for the final step in this journey this chapter defends the liberty to criticize the *shari'a* state and deals with the related risk of exposure to defamation. The preceding five chapters have provided ample evidence to validate two assumptions: first, that the Islamist *shari'a* state has no roots in the Islamic historical record, and, second, that the Islamist *shari'a* state is not a democracy. After all, Islamism is not Islam. Is it not permissible to criticize the *shari'a* state in a scholarly analysis on the grounds of research findings without running the risk of offending anyone?

Let us first look at an abstract case before moving to a concrete answer. What would be the response to an unnamed state model that not only is based on prohibitions and duties, but also denies its citizens rights as entitlements; even more, it prescribes inequality between believers of different religions as well as gender inequality, in addition to limitations imposed on free speech and personal behaviour. I imagine that the responses of people committed to democracy would unanimously be not only unfavourable, but would amount to rejection. They would also feel quite comfortable about expressing this kind of response. If, however, you add a name to this state model – in this case 'the *shari'a* state' – the respondents start to feel uncomfortable and most likely seek evasion, preferring to escape into silence. This kind of response occurs not just in order to comply with the illiberal stipulations of political correctness (often practised as an unrestricted form of postmodern censorship), but also out of concrete fear of being exposed to accusations. These name-callings may range from racism to Orientalism and Islamophobia. The official legitimation for this culture of restricting the freedom of speech is 'respect for Islam'. But is this respect real? Is there only one Islam? Does not enlightened Muslim thought, to which this book adheres, also deserve respect? I shall come back to this question in the concluding section of this chapter.

The accusation of Orientalism and Islamophobia in the war of ideas

The post-bipolar global environment is marked by an atmosphere in which Western civilization finds itself under fire. As an illustration, let us look at an exemplary case. When in December 2010 the French parliament debated a bill for punishing the denial of genocide, there was no problem with this venture as long as no specific case was addressed. However, when a particular case was mentioned, namely the mass murder committed against Armenians in 1915, the Islamist AKP government of Turkey reacted with strong words. The Islamist Turkish Prime

Minister Erdogan rebuffed the French bill as 'a clear example of how racism, discrimination and anti-Muslim sentiment have reached new heights'.[3] Why should identification of the killing of Armenians as genocide be an offence to Muslims? In a similar vein one may ask, why should an attempt to take issue with the *shari'a* state – which strips its subjects of all rights – be an expression of Islamophobia?

I found the response of the then French president Nicolas Sarkozy to Erdogan's accusations correct and well balanced. According to the *International Herald Tribune*, Sarkozy professed his 'respect (for) the conviction' of Turkish Muslims and for their 'grand civilization', but went on to say 'and they must respect ours'. He defended the right of Europeans to defend their own convictions – such as the one that qualifies a mass killing as genocide – and that a state without a culture of democracy is not democratic. The report quotes Sarkozy as saying that to yield on one's convictions is always 'cowardice, and one always ends up by paying for cowardice'.

The price the West pays for what is misconceived as 'respect for Islam' has been described by Paul Berman in a book on Islamism and the press in these words: 'The Islamist movement, in prospering, has succeeded in imposing its own categories of analysis over how everyone else tends to think. . . . Islamist judgments end up getting adopted by Western and non-Islamist journalists.'[4] I am a Muslim scholar who refuses to submit to this Western kind of censorship. I have taken the liberty to write this book in the critical mindset based on enlightened Muslim thought, and I request respect.

Continuing the theme of the dispute between Nicolas Sarkozy and Erdogan in 2010, I want to conclude the present book with a continuation of the debate that I started out with in Chapter 1. I want to ask this question: Is it allowed, in the contemporary post-Cold War debate, to discuss and criticize with scholarly rationality the Islamist quest of reordering the world? The issue is much more than just whether or not the *shari'a* state is a democratic rule. No expert familiar with Islamism would ever doubt the prominence and significance of Sayyid Qutb, the foremost Islamist thinker. Qutb made it unequivocally clear that it is the design of world order that is the core issue. 'The *dar al-Islam*/territory of Islam is the place for the Islamic state in which *shari'a* prevails. . . . The home of Muslims is the place where this *shari'a* is implemented.' For this implementation, Muslims need to fight for an 'Islamic world revolution' to establish *hakimiyyat Allah*/Allah's rule in a *shari'a* state, not only in the world of Islam, but also in the world at large. In pursuit of this, it is 'prescribed to Muslims to fight *jihad* to establish God's rule on the globe to save humanity.' This salvation occurs on the grounds of *shari'a*, viewed 'as universal law for the entire world'.[5]

At the end of Chapter 5 I quoted a prominent book on political theory after 9/11 by the New York University political theorist John Brenkman, in which he claims to discern an Islamic 'civil war', sprawling into 'Islam's geo-civil war' that affects the entire world. Brenkman might be right or wrong, but the Islamist claim to a *shari'a*-based world order, in which non-Muslims submit to Islamic rule, is a political reality that generates geo-civil conflict. In an Islamic order, non-Muslims have to accept paying *jizya* (a non-Muslim poll tax). Such an order is surely unacceptable not only to non-Muslims; it is also in general – applying international standards of democracy – incompatible with democratic order. In fact, the *shari'a* state generates global tensions that develop towards a conflict in global politics. Brenkman assumes a 'civil war' within Islam that turns into a global 'geo-civil war', causing international instability.[6] In contrast to Brenkman, there are self-defeating Western scholars and policy-makers who prefer to give in to the challenge of impositions, and keep silent about such a threat in order to avoid being accused of Islamophobia. As stated above, in Sarkozy's opinion, this attitude would be 'cowardice', and it is paid for by accepting the forbidding of any criticism of the Islamist venture of the politicization of Islam through the ideology of Islamism. Against this cowardice, a critique of the dominating narrative in Western Islamic studies needs to be admitted. To study the *shari'a* state, viewed as a component of an Islamist (not Islamic) agenda for a reordering of the world, includes, essentially, being able to deal with impositions on ways of thinking.

To be sure, religious faith is among the basic human rights. The religionization of politics does not, however, form part of these rights. Ideologies based on political religions are not a faith or belief as these are understood in human rights terms. Those who relate religion to politics and practise it in terms of a political ideology engage in a distortion of religion. One has the right to criticize them, and such criticism is not an offence to believers. Religion and politics are here separated not just with secular intent, but also motivated by the ethical concern of keeping religion away from abuse for political ends. The Islamic faith is spiritual and is a practice of worship, based on the *arkan*/five pillars recognized in common by all Muslims and discussed at the outset of Chapter 1, which are: *shahadah* (the profession of faith), *salat* (prayers), *siyam* (fasting in Ramadan), *zakat* (alms for the poor) and *hajj* (pilgrimage). None of these five relates to politics. In the religion of Islam, the call for a *shari'a* state is not found among the pillars of faith. So, to what right do Islamists refer when they politicize Islam to Islamism?

The reader is reminded of the fact that Islamism is based on an invention of tradition aimed at re-interpreting Islam as a concept of political order. This venture has been undertaken in the name of religious faith with the intention to religionize politics. Criticism of this venture does not infringe on the human right to religious practice. No doubt, one has the freedom of one's own opinion; one does not have the freedom of one's own facts. It is a fact that Islamism is not Islam. I devoted a university press published book to presenting the evidence for this contention.

The normal consensus is that the right to disagree is among the fundamental elements of academic freedom, and I should like to ask why this principle does not apply to criticism of the use of religion in politics in an ideologically blinkered new interpretation. The statement of fact, that the politicization of Islam in the form of Islamism is not a part of the Islamic faith, is neither an expression of Orientalism nor is it Islamophobic. Of course, one needs to beware of both the evils of Orientalism and Islamophobia. I do not deny the existence of these evils, and commit myself to countering them. This is, however, not the issue here. Islamists defame any scholarly critique of Islamism and relate it in a general way to these evils. In so doing so, they are pursuing their own agenda, which is to conceal, not to reveal, and above all – as already stated in the Introduction to this book and in its first chapter – to outlaw any criticism of Islam and Islamism.

In view of the above-mentioned limitations imposed on free research, this book concludes with an attempt in this chapter to provide a legitimation for the free study of politics, religion and ideology in contemporary Islamic civilization. The three areas of politics, religion and ideology are at first separate from one another, since politics deals with the *politeia*, religion is faith and ideology reflects a distortion of reality. However, there is a social reality in which these three intermingle, as religion can be politicized to become an ideology. The result then is religionized politics, of which Islamism is a case in point. In 1962 I came as a Muslim student to Europe and found it unacceptable to join Westerners in their ways of dealing with religion. Many Westerners, in particular European scholars, not only miss the meaning of religion in their reductionism, but also fail in every religion to distinguish between faith and social fact. Emile Durkheim's sociology of religion views religion as a *fait social*, a social fact. I believe that Durkheim's approach continues to be more helpful for determining the place of religion in society. However, we also need to acknowledge the meaning of religion. The three notions under discussion, politics, religion and ideology, matter to research on Islam and Islamism. Beyond cowardice, I dare to contradict those who are poised to outlaw such an approach altogether. Scholars committed to academic freedom need to unanimously resist impositions on academe in order to keep the integrity of scholarship.

Despite having a great disagreement with Edward Said, I honour his intention in his book *Orientalism* to outlaw prejudice against Islam as a humanist venture. Said had a point but he was too simplistic, to an extent that compelled a Yale-educated Muslim scholar of the Damascene aristocracy, Sadik J. al-Azm, to accuse him of reversing the prejudice (turning racist prejudice into anti-racist racism), ending up with an 'Orientalism in reverse'. Among the Western followers of Said, some have popularized and simplified his views, acting with even more simplicity than Said ever did. These 'Saidists' have distorted Said's noble humanist intention to fight prejudice, which guided his development of the notion of Orientalism. The Saidists pervert this humanism into an ideological weapon of censorship employed to police the work of scholars who are not willing to kowtow and are determined to continue the tradition of Western scholarship in the study of Islam.[7] I was a friend of Said and al-Azm, and we published an important book together.[8] However, Said disliked al-Azm's criticism of the notion of Orientalism as well as the accusation of 'Orientalism in reverse', and that created great tensions between the two. I tried to mediate between them, but failed.

In the ensuing 'war of ideas'[9] between Saidists and their foes I was compelled to take sides against Said. Worse is what happened in the recent past when a new notion was added to the highly ideologized debate, namely the construction of an even more rampant Islamophobia. Now some highly respected and well-established scholars such as Bernard Lewis were defamed with this invective of Islamophobia and insulted as 'rogue academics'.[10] This is a shame that drives one to John Stuart Mill's *On Liberty*, the classic text on democratic freedom of thinking and expression, to protect freedom of thought. Mill not only deplores the 'tyranny of prevailing opinion',[11] but also views its imposition as an infringement of democratic freedoms. Knowledge and, equally, liberal civil politics can only thrive if freedom is secured to guarantee their development. That said, Said's rampant notion of Orientalism derailed the originally justified humanist intention to combat prejudice. What the Saidists do is as wrong as the recent campaign based on the accusation of Islamophobia. In contrast to these people, Sarkozy is right when he warns of cowardice.

In this book, and throughout my work published in the course of the past 40 years, I look at Islamdom as an Islamic civilization.[12] In its past this civilization flourished when the great Muslim rationalists had the freedom to defend their *falsafa* rationalism against *fiqh* orthodoxy and decayed when this tradition was suppressed. Today, Islamism continues the fight against enlightened Muslim thought. Some Westerners suggest that 'Islamism is a term we should abandon'[13] and thus impose restrictions on free scholarship. But outlawing the study of Islamism would be an interference in the freedom to pursue knowledge. Chris Mooney thinks any interference of this kind 'constitutes a fundamental assault on the integrity of science'.[14] In the conclusions of the present chapter I shall come back to this issue at greater length. Here I confine the argument to stating that no one has the right to impose the abandoning of a concept useful in the study of the politicization of Islam to an Islamist ideology, unless the freedom of scholarship itself is to be abandoned.

At present, critiquing of the *shari'a* state runs counter to the dominating narrative in US Middle Eastern studies. The clear distinction between Islam and Islamism is not welcome. As a distinction between religion – to be respected as a faith – and a political ideology, however, it is of great significance. And indeed, there is a great difference between Islam as a tolerant religious faith, on which a magnificent civilization rests, and the religionized politics of the political ideology of Islamism. It is no repetition to state that no contradiction is involved in honouring the great accomplishments of Islamic civilization and arguing for respect for the Islamic faith, while at the same time being critical of Islamist religionized politics. In addition, it needs to be understood that Islamism is not about militancy, nor is it merely a propensity toward violence. The core argument of this book is that *Islamism is about governance and political order* in a drive at remaking the world. The *shari'a* state can be imposed through the ballot box, as has happened in Egypt and elsewhere.

There is an Islamist agenda that prescribes this remaking of the world as a religious obligation undergirded by new values based on an invention of tradition. At issue is the replacing of existing political orders by a system of governance believed to be Islamic. I discussed this at length in Chapter 3, where the Islamist concept of *nizam*/order was shown to be one opposed to the sovereign nation-state, as well as to the existing world order based on the Westphalian synthesis.[15] Make no mistake: Islamism is not about the restoration of the caliphate, since the envisioned Islamist *shari'a* state is a novelty; it is an invention of tradition. Islamists prefer the notion '*nizam islami*'/'Islamic order'. Double-speak is one of the most disturbing features of Islamism (see note 41 in Chapter 4). When you talk to Islamists, they successfully prevaricate and pretend a commitment to democracy.

They also deny any distinction between Islam and Islamism. The founder of Islamism, al-Banna, viewed the *shari'a* order as an indication of what he sees as proper Islam. The outcomes of dialogues with Islamists are mostly delusions that promote the Islamist course in the pursuit of '*al-hall al-islami*'/'the Islamic solution', which is based on a belief in 'Islamic governance' in a *shari'a* state, not democracy. These are the facts. So let me keep asking: Why is the critical study of the *shari'a* state not only improper, but also defamed as Islamophobic? Is it a vice to deal with these issues in Middle Eastern studies in order to inform and to enlighten? Why does the dominating narrative create obstacles in the way of the unravelling of prevarications about Islamism?

Of course, no decent person could afford to keep silent when real Islamophobia is at work. This occurs in particular when some Western self-appointed or self-proclaimed 'experts' are obsessed with associating Islam with terrorism. But is limiting freedom of speech the right response to malicious Western profiling of Islam? Two wrongs do not make a right. The reversing of 'Islamophobia' by Islamophile scholars is wrong; this is the same as the mindset in which Orientalism is replaced by Orientalism in reverse.

The overall context for this deplorable state of affairs is the process of politicization of Middle Eastern and Islamic studies that is currently taking place in the West, especially at US universities. The extremes of Islamophobic and Islamophilic narratives clash at the expense of sober scholarly analysis. In the process, great obstacles emerge in the way of any balanced study of Islamism as an ideology of the Islamist *shari'a* state.

The critique of the *shari'a* state seeks an unbiased assessment that dissociates the faith of Islam from the ideology of Islamism. To argue that Islamism has grown out of a conflict in a crisis-ridden situation is not to engage in polarization. The driver of my thinking is inter-civilizational bridging.[16] Although I staunchly criticize Islamist movements, I never engage in the vilification or demonization of Islamism (see Chapter 3). I argue for engagement of the Islamists, while warning against empowering them, which would mean surrendering to the *shari'a* state. Before one can make any attempt at conflict resolution, one must be able to name the conflict one seeks to resolve.

The failure to understand Islamism as a venture for a *shari'a* state

Let me repeat that Islamism is about neither extremism nor violence. Of course, there are violent Islamists who are identified as jihadists. However, violence is not the proper criterion by which to identify Islamists. Rather, the core feature of Islamism is 'Islamic governance', i.e. a *shari'a* state. This is the defining issue. With the decline of al-Qaeda in the course of the negative repercussions after the 9/11 attacks, major Islamists have reconsidered and come to the conclusion that violence not only damages their cause, but does not get them anywhere. A ride on the democracy train, however (with the option to get off in due time), promises a much easier power grab. Does this constitute moderation?

In the first chapter of this book I identified the confusion of Islamism with Islam, combined with the false assessment of Islamism in the prevailing narrative of Islamic studies. Instead of promoting enlightenment, some outlaw critical study of the Islamist ideology and the movements that rest on it. These features seem to determine the prevailing narrative, which is challenged in this book and its conclusions. The issue is not about 'good' versus 'bad' Muslims; these are images that are not useful for serious analysis. The distinction is rather between a political religion and a religious faith based on truly spiritual tenets. The differences between Islamism and Islam are also not a matter of language or rhetoric, since they refer to realities which are different, although not entirely separate from one another. Those Westerners who argue that Islamism does not in reality exist, and attribute it to the mere invention of Western language, appear to be ill-informed. The term 'Islamism' can be traced back to Hasan al-Banna himself, who not only coined the term, but also acted as the founder of the Movement of the Muslim Brotherhood, giving the term an authoritative meaning in a political reality that has existed ever since. The Arabic term *al-Islamiyya* is the name of the political reality that underpins the concept: namely, the Movement of the Muslim Brotherhood.

As stated in Chapter 4, the inspiration to write this book was generated by the Arab Spring and the way in which Islamists hijacked it. Earlier, in the course of my three decades of research on Islamism, I faced the twists and turns in the minefield of contemporary Islamic studies. The field is torn between Islamophobia and Islamophilia in the shift from Orientalism to Orientalism in reverse, and the resulting mindset seems to prevail both in scholarship and in public policy. Particularly in Washington, DC, where I lived for most of 2010, I felt the heat of the politicization of US Islamic and Middle Eastern studies and the repercussions this caused. Once again I cite John Stuart Mill's *On Liberty* to argue for a commitment to free as well as balanced and detached scholarship. In Washington, DC I read *Islamism: Contested Perspectives on Political Islam*, a Middle Eastern Studies Association proceedings volume that documents the US debate. I took issue with this – highly representative – publication in Chapter 1 and come back to it here because one of its contributors (quoted above, see p. 188 *note 13 cit.*) seems to prohibit the use of the concept of 'Islamism'. Richard Martin and Abbas Barzegar, the volume editors, abstain from taking a position, maintaining in their introduction that they cannot resolve the debate. They fail to present a decisive cogent assessment.[17]

Although Islamism was neither the launcher nor the engine of the Arab Spring of 2011 against authoritarian regimes, the ongoing politicization of Islam to Islamism has determined the outcome of this radical change. Islamism has reached a peak in the course of this world-historical development. Why is the US Islamic studies establishment so reluctant to provide the assessment of it that is needed?

The politicization I have referred to relates to a crisis which is also 'the crisis of modern Islam'.[18] In full awareness of the distinction between Islam and Islamism, I argue that the rise of contemporary Islamism results from this crisis. It is twofold: a crisis of legitimacy and a crisis of failed development. Islamist ideologues argue in relation to this crisis that '*al-Islam huwa al-Hall*'/'Islam is the solution'.

Does 'the *shari'a* state' provide a solution for this crisis? One of the few exceptions in the US community of Middle Eastern studies, John Waterbury, responds in his admirable 'Political Economy of the Middle East' with a 'no'.[19] It is an answer that cannot be repeated enough.

Anyone who agrees that it is legitimate to admit critique of the prevailing narrative, and who shares the view that giving in to the increasing limitations impinges on the spirit of free inquiry, would endorse the according of unlimited academic freedom. To be sure, the scholarly spirit of such freedom does not permit demonization, and for this reason I am against the exclusion of Islamist movements and argue for their engagement. I have reason to repeat the distinction between their engagement and their empowerment, i.e. including Islamists to allow their participation in the process of democratization, but not handing over power to them, thus allowing them to establish hegemony. The case of Egypt under the Islamist Muslim Brother Morsi serves as an example of empowerment. Non-Islamist Egyptians complain about the 'Muslim-Brotherizing' of the state apparatus by the ruling Islamists. In contrast to Egypt, the participation of the Islamists in politics in Morocco is an example of engagement.

There are clear Islamist attempts to ward off any criticism based on the diversity within Islam. When Islamists argue, wrongly, that there is only one Islam, that one is always the one they represent, i.e. political Islam. In fact, Islamists have been very successful in their endeavour to intimidate their critics and, finally, silence them. In contrast, there are also 'the other Muslims',[20] often exposed to all kinds of harassment and threats, not only by Islamists, but also by some Westerners. It is bizarre to see some Islamophile Westerners joining forces with Islamists against intra-Islamic enlightenment, and against a civic Islam based on the enlightened turn and on the resultant enlightened Muslim thought. When Islamists act in the name of combating Islamophobia, then one has reason to worry about freedom of thought. It is a profound cause for concern that some Western academics, in the name of respect for Islam, side with Islamism against enlightened Muslim thought, and thus with their power also sideline the champions of this enlightened turn. This is an academic world turned upside-down.

The strong rejection of the equation of Islam and Islamism is based on dissociating Islam both from political ideology and from terrorism. The distinction made is without any demonization of this new direction within Islam. I do not doubt that Islamists are Muslims, I only argue that most Muslims are not Islamists. A proper understanding of Islamism requires a better grasp of the *shari'a* state that is presented as the solution for the crisis that led to the Arab Spring. However, Islamists are a strong reality in the present world of Islam that no one should overlook. There are other options for Islam in the context of development and change. For Muslims of the enlightened turn who also follow the al-Jabri project, Averroist Islam, which stood in the past against the Salafism of *fiqh* orthodoxy, is the basis of a civil Islam to set against Islamism today.[21] Sincerely loyal to the buried tradition of Islamic humanism, I profess my normative commitment to pluralism and therefore admit rival interpretations of Islam. It follows that there are different Islams competing with one another. The

commitment to the tradition of Averroism and to its Islamic medieval rationalism is only one direction in Islam that is opposed to *shari'a*tized Islam and to the
contemporary ideologies that rest on it.

The reference to these basic intra-Islamic distinctions is blurred in the contemporary war of ideas in which the prevailing narrative of the US Middle Eastern
and Islamic studies establishment seems to take the side of Islamism in the context
of the Arab Spring. Many US scholars of Islamic studies sympathize with Islamist movements and recognize them as the alternative to the rotten authoritarian
regimes that fell, one after the other, in the course of the Arab Spring. These scholars overlook the reality expressed by the Egyptian-American political scientist
Saad Eddin Ibrahim, who sees the fate of contemporary Muslims as torn between
'autocracy and theocracy'. The conclusion is that the Islamist *shari'a* state does
not reflect the yearning of young hopeless Muslims in their fight for freedom
against dictatorship. In my view, the Islamist venture for a *shari'a* state seems not
to be well understood in the West and the original drive behind the Arab Spring
is overlooked.

The prevailing narrative that dominates the debate on Islamism in the West
does not admit the thinking articulated in the present book. Why? A tentative
answer was given at the outset of this chapter in the assumption of existing impositions and limitations. These were addressed in the context of Sarkozy's warning
of 'cowardice', for which one has to pay a price. Based on this thinking shared
with Sarkozy, the present book takes the freedom to freely address core issues and
identify three major sources of the ideology of Islamism: the ideas of, first, Hasan
al-Banna and, second, Sayyid Qutb in the past, and, third, the work of Yusuf al-
Qaradawi in the present, which continues to determine in a new shape the process
of the politicization of Islam to Islamism.[22] Referring to the research accomplished
within the framework of the Fundamentalism Project of the American Academy
of Arts and Sciences,[23] I develop the following three insights.

First, the return of religion to the public square. This process unfolds in a politicization of religious precepts in a crisis-ridden situation related to local as well as
to global constraints. This situation is exacerbated through a civilizational crisis,
which will be discussed toward the end of this chapter.

Second, the global character of this phenomenon, which is not restricted to the
world of Islam; it can be observed in all world religions.

Third, this process of the politicization of religion happens in the context of a
crisis of cultural modernity and its project of secularization, once viewed by Max
Weber as a 'disenchantment of the world' (*Entzauberung der Welt*), as well as
in a crisis of development in the new states that have emerged from incomplete
de-colonization.

In short, any accusation that Islam is being singled out in an expression of
Islamophobia is baseless and does not hold.

To turn to the search for an answer to the question of why some Western scholars and opinion leaders succumb to the claims of Islamism, fail to resist the intimidation and accept the imposition of a narrative, I will begin with a reference to a
remarkable book by Paul Berman. This writer accuses the intellectuals of a 'flight'

that provides Islamists with an intellectual safe haven to disseminate their ideology. The narrative criticized in this chapter fulfils this function. The providers of this narrative 'have turned out to be enduring and influential . . . [they] are bound to go on shaping the ways that a great many people in Western countries look on the Islamist movement, and how they look on the Muslim liberals, too, who are the Islamist movement's greatest enemies.'[24]

It did not take long to make Paul Berman pay for *The Flight of the Intellectuals*. He paid dearly for publishing this study that was critical of Islamism. Meanwhile, in a war of ideas, there has been a deplorable upgrading of Islamism at the expense of civil Islam.[25] The practices of some liberal pro-Islamist Western intellectuals in this war makes one indignant. The public debates are characterized by a lack of civility and fairness. People who think differently to them are defamed. Those who criticize the politicization of Islam, for instance, must also argue against the prevailing narrative that upgrades the Islamist *shari'a* state to an Islamic 'democracy'. To silence critics by accusing them of Islamophobia is conduct calculated to undermine free debate. As discussed in this chapter, such conduct is also applied to critical assessment of the Arab Spring. True liberalism, by contrast, would honour the debating culture for which John Stuart Mill established the rules in *On Liberty*. According to the Kantian imperative one should 'do unto others as you would have them do unto you', that is, treat them 'with courtesy and respect', even if you disagree with them. A prominent Arab-Muslim philosopher, Ali Oumlil, maintains that Arabs need the acceptance of a *haq al-ikhtilaf*, that is the right to dissent and discord, to go beyond ideologies of unity. In his view, submission to forced coherence in the name of unity could never be helpful for dealing properly with the problems of development and democracy.[26] Westerners need to emulate this kind of thinking.

Features of the prevailing narrative in Islamic studies in the West

The attentive reader will be well aware that this theme was addressed at length in Chapter 1, and might ask: Why this resumption in the concluding chapter? This is why. The ideas of the Harvard law professor Noah Feldman, discussed earlier, are characterized by a basic feature shared with the prevailing narrative in Islamic studies, namely a failure to understand the *shari'a*tization of polity and society in contemporary Islamic civilization.[27] I want here to relate this feature to the basic findings of the analysis conducted in the preceding chapters.

In general, Islamists engage in a reshaping of traditional *shari'a* in an action identified as an invention of tradition. This action takes place in a fight for a *shari'a* state, not for democracy. The narrative of the post-modern, post-Enlightenment approach employed in the bulk of books and articles for the study of Islamism is shocking when it is confronted with the reality on the ground. At times, this narrative is obsessed with the mindset of third-worldism.[28] Of course, there are exceptions, but these mostly reflect a minority among the opinion leaders. To this minority belongs the already quoted writer Paul Berman. In his controversy with

Ian Buruma and Timothy Garton Ash he argues against the upgrading of Islamism and of the work of al-Banna's grandson Tariq Ramadan. I am proud to quote a passage from Berman that invokes my work in the controversy. In Berman's view the criticized narrative:

> could not distinguish between Islam and Islamism: between the religion and the modern totalitarian ideology. Tibi was indignant that Buruma had ceded to Tariq Ramadan the right to speak for Islam. And Tibi was indignant that Buruma could not see the possibility of a genuinely new kind of Islam arising, something not at all like Tariq Ramadan's salafi reformism but, instead, an Islam in a genuinely attractive and European style – a 'Euro-Islam' in Tibi's phrase, which modern Muslim liberals like himself have championed, even if non-Muslim liberals have declined to offer much support.[29]

Instead of supporting the 'enlightened Muslim thought' that underpins a civil Islam, one faces an upgrading of Islamism by those Westerners who view this ideology in terms of 'multiple modernities'. In reality, *al-Islamiyyah*/Islamism is a vision for a remaking of the world along a *shari'a* order, and thus is not any kind of 'other modernity'. The remaking envisioned is a process that is supposed to happen on three levels: first in the world of Islam itself, then in the Islamic diaspora in Europe – at present consisting of some 25 to 30 million people of Islamic background – and finally in the world at large, with regard to world order itself.[30] It follows that the prevailing narrative about Islamism completely bypasses the reality on the ground.

In short, the basic contentions of the dominating narrative in Western Islamic studies on Islamism not only overlook the two branches of Islamism (one of them non-violent, the other jihadist[31]), they also ignore what Islamism is all about. The Arab Spring demonstrates the trend in which jihadism has been declining in the past years in favour of institutional Islamism. As I showed in the Introduction to this book, this change has been viewed by some as a sign of moderation. Some of these scholars go even further and speak of the decline of Islamism, or of post-Islamism. It is indeed a change, but it is not in any sense post-Islamism. The flaw in these scholars' understanding is that they reduce the Islamist movement to terrorism, overlooking the fact that Islamism is about the order of the world and remaking it, not about violence. The terror subsides, but the drive to remake the political order is still very much alive. So, there is no post-Islamism. Both branches of political Islam share the concept of Islamic governance and fight for the *shari'a* state. The difference between institutional and jihadist Islamists is not one between 'reformers or revolutionaries'.[32] The distinction between what is moderate and what is violent is a product of the well-known obsession with terrorism. Muslims themselves worry about the '*malédiction*'/'curse' of Islamism that plagues their civilization in this crisis-ridden situation.[33]

Beyond the obsession with Islamophobia: Islamology as a study of Islamism and global conflict

There is a traditional wisdom on constructive criticism that prescribes that, when one takes issue with a flawed approach, one is expected to suggest an alternative. In pursuance of this, I took pains in the past decades to establish a social-scientific international relations and comparative politics based study of Islam and conflict in global politics. To distinguish my effort from traditional Islamic studies, I identify my work by the term 'Islamology'.[32] There are a few political scientists and sociologists in the US and European community of Islamic studies on whose work I draw and whose insights I make use of. In religious studies and in historical studies, scripture and the archives matter most; but a political scientist who engages in the study of Islam needs to go beyond this style of Islamic studies, and also beyond the cultural-narrative approach of anthropology, which appears unsatisfactory to the present study. In addition to these methodological thoughts, what matters most is to go beyond ideological extra-scientific considerations – considerations external to the pursuit of knowledge – such as those often used to impose limits on scholarly inquiry, as will be discussed below with reference to insights put forward by Chris Mooney (see notes 14 and 54).

In pursuit of the study of Islam and global conflict in the outlined context of Islamology as a social science-based inquiry, I look at realities in the Islamicate and in Islamdom, driven not only by the motivation to promote a better alternative, but also by the desire for conflict resolution. In a way, Islamology resembles the old Sovietology, with the very basic difference that it replaces the latter's Cold-War mentality with a spirit of an inter-civilizational bridging of existing divides. We live in an age identified by Mark Juergensmeyer as a 'new cold war'[35] being fought in a war of ideas. Applied to the case under discussion, the conflict is one between the secular concept of order and the *shari'a* state for which Islamist movements are fighting in their religionized politics. The Arab Spring opened a window of opportunity for them to implement their *shari'a*, as discussed in Chapter 5.

In my view the approach of Islamology, presented in my book *Islam's Predicament with Modernity*, provides a narrative of conflict that reveals reality, Thus, it presents an alternative to the dominating narrative that instead conceals. The relations between Islamic civilization and the West are conflictual and they matter generally to the world at large. Of course, my intention is to bridge, but how can one accomplish this in a situation where tensions grow to conflict without a conflict resolution?

Islamology is the study of the pattern of post-bipolar politics as it is generated by the politicization of Islam in the course of a global return of religion to the public square. The conflict involves non-Muslims as well as Muslims. As a political inquiry, Islamology studies Islamism, not Islam as a faith; it is also a discipline for studying how political–religious tensions develop into conflicts. The intra-Islamic civil war becomes a geopolitical one, as John Brenkman contends.[36] Islamology is a political science discipline that studies these conflicts and engages in policy recommendations in the understanding of conflict resolution.

The proposed new field of study, Islamology, inquires into the phenomenon of Islamism and into its agenda of a *shari'a* state without a drive towards profiling and ostracization. The concern of Islamology is the tensions between secularism and an Islamist political religion that leads to conflict, and its search is for a democratic peace for the twenty-first century. In this search no one can ignore the power and the appeal of Islamism, and for this reason a democratic policy cannot escape engaging with Islamists – but it is possible to avoid risk-taking. Risk-taking happens when engagement is confused with empowerment. Make no mistake: the lip service paid by Islamists towards democracy cannot be trusted.[37] This is not mere misgiving, but an insight based on fact and experience.

To express this caveat out loud – in today's environment of debate that is not just heated, but polluted – is to be exposed to unpleasant polemics and accusations. All this proves is that, in the academy as elsewhere, polarization often closes the door to rational debate. The critique of Islamism should not be confused with name calling. The sensitivity of this matter makes clear how an academic description, when it relates to deeply disputed political questions, becomes a source of tension among scholars. Contemporary studies on Islamism largely reveal a deplorable polarization within the scholarly community. I therefore call on my colleagues to share the concern and practice of civility in the debate about narratives on Islamism. I keep repeating: the bottom line is that *we need to engage Islamists, but not to empower them.* Even if one does not agree with this insight, it must be kept possible to continue the debate without polemics, accusations and name calling.

A rational debate requires first that scholars and policy-makers take account of the Islamological distinction between the politics of Islamism and the religion of Islam. For sure, Islamism is not a passing phenomenon, as it – presumably – will be with us for decades to come. The core source of the binary world view of Islamism continues to be the work of Sayyid Qutb. The Islamist world's new polarization emerges from the idea of an imagined war between Islam and the West which is also an independent Islamist invention. The cold war of ideas, however, is a political reality.

The puzzle is that Islamists today – in particular since the Arab Spring – are supported in the West by both the left and the right. Why? Because, on the left, Qutb's anti-Westernism is reinterpreted as anti-capitalism; furthermore, the left supports Islamism on the grounds of the misperception that it is an ally against globalization. Meanwhile, the right, which by contrast demonizes Islam and Islamism altogether, has one thing in common with Islamism: antisemitism. Yet when the subject turns to 'the Jews', especially those who are believed to run Wall Street, one is astounded to see Islamists along with the European left and right united in a combination of antisemitism and anti-Americanism.[38] Despite his correct qualification of the Muslim Brotherhood as a 'spearhead of fundamentalist counterreformation and reactionary pan-Islamism', the British professor Gilbert Achcar seems to deny both truths, namely, Islamism and Islamist antisemitism, altogether. Instead, he adopts the Islamist propagandist slogan of Islamophobia, which combines with his denial in these words: 'Islamophobia has found a means of large-scale sublimation to what has come to be called Islamism.'[39] Therefore, he accuses even Muslim scholars – including myself – who unveil Islamism, in the mindset of 'enlightened Muslim thought' (see Introduction), to 'serve as warrant for Islamophobia'. Simultaneously, Achcar denies the existence of 'a new antisemitism in the Arab world' while simultaneously noting 'a huge increase in Islamophobia'. For him, the reality of the new antisemitism is nothing other than 'widespread anger . . . over the Arab-Israeli conflict' and also a 'reaction to the wave of Islamophobia'. These flawed views are an essential part of the dominating narrative. There is no need to comment, except to repeat the core idea of this chapter: namely, that Islamists themselves have invented the propaganda slogan of Islamophobia to outlaw criticism in their war of ideas. They also deny the distinction between Islamism and Islam and dismiss it as a 'Western conspiracy'[40] hatched by 'Jews' and 'Crusaders'.

Let us return to the academy and to the proposition of an Islamological approach to be employed in the study of 'the return of religion to the public square' and of the related conflicts. Islamology aims to provide a scholarly approach together with policy implications that facilitate 'democratic responses'[41] to Islamism. As already stated, these include a politics of engagement, but not of empowerment, of Islamism. This debate needs to include the thinking of Muslims who adhere to enlightened Muslim thought. One who appears to sympathize with enlightened Muslim thought, M. Zuhdi Jasser, recommends to Westerners that 'one should read the work of Hasan al-Banna . . . and . . . Sayyid Qutb . . . to understand the all encompassing transnational goals of Islamism. . . . Democracy is not only about the ballot box. It is about a system of law.'[42] This reading is exactly the requirement one needs to fulfil before making a judgement about Islamism. The dominating narrative of Islamic studies fails to do this. It puts the greatest obstacle in the way of an open, free debate on the confusion of the social and political reality of Islamism with an allegation that critics practise a 'violence of rhetoric'. The result is a 'hodgepodge' (Jasser) in the dominating narrative on Islamism. For some, Islamology is viewed as controversial, but it can fulfil an important task in illuminating the subject matter at issue. It can also help to move the discussion on to address the real issues on a basis of knowledge, beyond obsessions and wishful thinking, in scholarly civility, free from a culture of imposing limits and from defamatory accusations.

From one accusation to the next: the switch from 'Orientalism' to 'Islamophobia'

In the new century one gets the impression that the earlier accusing cry of 'Orientalism', generated by Said, is being replaced by another, much more serious cry: 'Islamophobia'. In contrast to this one is advised to look at what Muslims of the 'enlightened turn' themselves say. In an authoritative book on (and entitled) Islam and politics, *al-Islam wa al-Siyasa*, published in Arabic in 1977, an important Muslim thinker, Hussein F. al-Najjar, acknowledges some political implications in Islam, but then adds:

This does not mean a necessary binding of Islam to politics, not to speak about the [wrong] formula that Islam is *din-wa-dawla*/unity of state and religion. In fact, there is nothing in the authoritative Islamic *shari'a* that supports this view. The *shari'a* never provisions a system of government. . . . It is about *mu'amalat*/civil matters among Muslims on purely ethical grounds.[43]

Another enlightened Muslim author, Mohammed Said al-Ashmawi, provides in his authoritative book on the *usul al-shari'a*/principles of law, evidence for the fact that the notion of *shari'a* occurs only once in the Qur'an, and that it is not paired with a concept of order.[44] In Chapter 2 I mentioned the fact that in the Qur'an there is no mention of a '*shari'a* state'.

Muslims of the enlightened turn complain about sidelining and being denied the right to engage in a free debate in which it is prescribed 'to avoid calling Islamists what they are, namely Islamists, to keep us Muslims from having this debate at all'.[45] As earlier in the Introduction to this book, I prefer to speak of 'enlightened Muslim thought' rather than 'liberal Islam', and argue that this line of reasoning started with Ali Abdelraziq in his classic *al-Islam wa Usul al-Hukm/Islam and the Origins of Government*.[46] Earlier I joined Abdou Filali-Ansary in classifying the work of Abdelraziq as the cornerstone of modern enlightened Muslim thought. Abdelraziq's core argument is that the traditional Islamic caliphate is not provisioned by the divine scripture of Islam. I extend the application of this enlightened Muslim argument to invalidate the allegation of an 'Islamic *shari'a*-based state' as an item of Islamic faith. Dismantling this allegation is not an expression of Islamophobia, a new accusation that has replaced the earlier one of Orientalism.

Commitment to the academic rule that morality matters (e.g. the ethics of protecting Islam and Muslims against prejudice and demonization) ensures the necessary integrity, but not at the expense of factuality and of a sober analysis of realities. Distinctions (e.g. within Islam and Islamism) are an essential part of this venture, which has been practised in this book. Westerners are challenged to discern how Muslims (*al-Muslimun*) actually perceive themselves – which is not as Islamists (*al-Islamiyyun*). I cited as an example Hussein F. al-Najjar, who refers to Islam as faith and ethics, but not as a system of government. More such Islamic enlightened voices were cited in Chapters 1 to 3. One can relate Islam to politics in the positive terms of the political ethics of enjoining (or commanding) the good and forbidding the evil (*al-amr bi al-ma'ruf wa an-nahi an al-munkar*), as the Qur'an prescribes. What Islamists believe in, namely the unity of *din-wa-dawla*/state and religion is not an item of Islamic faith. Remember that the term *dawla*/state never occurs in the Qur'an. '*Shari'a*' occurs only once, and not then with the meaning of 'law'. This being so, why do Islamists confuse Islam with their construction of a *shari'a* state, and why do some Westerners preach respect for this ideology which is confused with the Islamic faith?

Now, in the turn to the end of the journey to seek acceptability for the critical study of Islamism without being called names, I argue for a bridging of the divides, without ignoring the reality or the security concerns. Therefore I repeat the need for a free debate that will include the distinction made between Islam as a faith and

Islamism as a political ideology. Today, this ideology is represented by a move-ment that subscribes to religionized politics. No one with integrity would deplore the fall of authoritarian regimes in the Arab part of Islamic civilization. What the Muslim Brothers promise is, however, not the *hall*/solution, as they proclaim; indeed, they themselves are the problem, not the solution. The fact that Mubarak's successor, Mohammed Morsi, is an Islamist does not validate the views of those Western scholars who argued in the pre-Arab Spring for 'the new Islamists' as the alternative for Egypt after the fall of Mubarak's regime.[47] True, some academics may afford themselves the luxury of denial and of reducing a serious reality to a 'violence of rhetoric' – making it a mere problem of language – but policy-makers, and scholars with a sense of responsibility, cannot afford to do so. They must know that Islamism, not Islam, is a challenge to the existing Westphalian world order of sovereign nation-states. After the 9/11 attacks, a prudent international rela-tions scholar published a remarkable article in *World Politics* that refers to this threat in its title – an article that I repeatedly quote (see note 10 to Chapter 3).

To go beyond the accusations of Orientalism and Islamophobia requires engag-ing in a combination of scholarly analysis and policy considerations. I want to launch such a discussion that pertains to both these fields. I start with policy and refer to Obama's ending the 'clash of civilizations', also discussing the views of the long-time Democrat senator Joseph Lieberman; I then move on to scholarship and refer to a contribution by Chris Mooney on a debate conducted at the Amer-ican Academy of Arts and Sciences on scholarly controversies and the related efforts at suppressing unwelcome views.

To start with the first matter, one can only be positive about Obama's ending on the US side of the polarization called the 'clash of civilizations', but some reservations concerning flaws are due. At the top of these is the absence of a distinction between Islamism and Islam. In Chapter 1 I quoted US senator Joe Lieberman acknowledging that Muslims in fact understand better than anyone else that their faith has to be dissociated from the terrorist political ideology of jihadism.[48] Deplorably, the Obama administration's national security strategy is reluctant to acknowledge these distinctions. In *Islamism and Islam* I took issue with Obama's security advisor on terrorism, John Brennan, who fails to grasp the challenge of the remaking of the world order, which is much greater than the one posed by jihadist terrorism.[49] In this sense, Lieberman is right in his criticism that Obama's policies ignore the basic issue, namely the 'broader political ideology', and also the 'ideological dimensions of the war [i.e. of ideas] that is taking place within Islam'. The popular slogan 'the West and Islam' distracts from our per-ceiving the tensions among Muslims themselves. Muslims of enlightened thought demand freedom on two fronts, first against authoritarian regimes, and second against impositions by Islamist movements. The latter do not allow dissent, and dismiss it as *kufr*/unbelief or heresy. Enlightenment is more promising than accu-sations of Orientalism and of Islamophobia.

Muslims who are aware of the distinctions between Islam and Islamism, as well as between institutional-peaceful and jihadist Islamism, are dismayed by the narrative that dominates US Islamic studies. It speaks paternalistically for all

Muslims and what they are supposed to do. In a free debate about Islamism one can go beyond the ideological struggle of a war of ideas to engage with an Islamic humanist mindset. If one honestly cares about bridging the divides related to the inter-civilizational conflict over values, then the alternative to the war of ideas waged by Islamism is a peace of ideas based on a civil Islam that is committed to a revival of Islamic humanism.[50] Argued from this standpoint, it is unfortunate to see a contribution to a major US policy journal such as *Foreign Affairs* upgrading non-violent Islamism without understanding its nature as an agenda for remaking the world using democracy as its instrument, while at the same time downgrading progressive liberal Islam with the derogatory qualification of Islamic liberals as a 'small slice of Muslim societies'.[51] The *Foreign Affairs* article, by the US political scientist Marc Lynch, recommends the embracing of non-violent, so-called moderate Islamism. I strongly contradict this belittling of 'enlightened Muslim thought' and refer to two major conferences in the world of Islam, one in Indonesia on 'Debating Progressive Islam: A Global Perspective', organized jointly by UIN Jakarta-McGill University Canada in July 2009, and the other in Morocco on 'Pluralism and Diversity in Islam'. The convening liberal Muslims of the enlightened thought were in both events not a 'small slice' as Lynch paternalistically portrays them (these 'other' Muslims), while at the same time confusing Islam and Islamism. It is outrageous to see how such pundits overlook the dark side of Islamism.[52] It would be better to address it, rather than to bypass it.

After the policy perspective just dealt with, which is situated under the impact of the assessment provided by the dominating narrative, I turn now to the scholarly perspective. The legitimacy of the present inquiry on the momentous distinction between Islam and Islamism has to be related to the question of why the scholars of the dominating narrative fail to understand such core issues as this distinction, and, moreover of why they suppress contradicting views. For scholars, the authority of the American Academy of Arts and Sciences (AAAS) not only matters, it matters a great deal: as an authority, it ranks high. This academy sponsored the Fundamentalism Project.[53] In this context it is pertinent to quote a report entitled 'Not blinded by science, but ideology', published in the *Washington Post* in 2010. The author of this report, Chris Mooney, writing about a long debate on a bizarre issue at the AAAS that lasted for over a year in 2009–2010, comments:

> Whenever controversies arise . . . a predictable dance seems to unfold. On the one hand, the nonscientists appear almost entirely impervious to scientific data that undermine their opinions and prone to arguing back with technical claims that are of dubious merit. In response, the scientists shake their heads and lament that if only the public weren't so ignorant, these kinds of misunderstandings wouldn't occur.[54]

The US debate on Islamism is such a case and demonstrates just such a dance. On the first page of the 'Outlook' section in which Mooney's coverage of the AAAS debate appears, the *Washington Post* announces the article thus: 'Political Science: Chris Mooney on why scientists should quit lecturing the public and start trying to understand.' The most pertinent passages of the article relate to controversies in which communication among scholars takes place neither with consent (including over terms, e.g. Islam, Islamism etc.), nor with mutual understanding. The recommendation by Chris Mooney that seems to emanate from the conclusions of the AAAS debate is this: 'Rather than simply crusading against ignorance the defenders of science should . . . determine how to defuse controversies by addressing their fundamental causes.' This recommendation is equally valid for how to address the issue with which I am concerned: it reflects the need for a change in the mindset of the dominating narrative in US Islamic studies. In the controversy about *shari'a*-related issues, the critics of the *shari'a* state are defamed, being called names and associated with evils (Orientalism, Islamophobia). This does not contribute to dealing with the 'fundamental causes' of the phenomenon in point; it merely engages in academic word games and in lashing others in a 'violence of rhetoric'.

Chris Mooney is also the author of a significant book in which he reminds scholars of the virtue that 'science should inform, but not dictate' and also warns of 'a politicized interference with science'.[55] These recommendations put one in mind of impositions regarding how one should think about Islamism and the *shari'a* state. Today, the earlier censorship practised in the name of political correctness seems to have been replaced by a reference to 'Muslim sensibilities' as a pretext and legitimation for forbidding critical thinking about Islamism and for accusing critics of Islamophobia. Mooney thinks, however, that referring to 'political sensibilities' to avert the publication of particular scientific results is an ideological, not a scholarly argument, often done 'for political, or ideological reasons'.[56] Earlier, I quoted Mooney's dismay about any interference that 'constitutes a fundamental assault on the integrity of science'. If Mooney and the scholars of the debate at the AAAS are right, then it is also right to question the practices of the representatives of the dominating US narrative on Islamism. In the name of the integrity of science and knowledge, politicized scholarship should be rejected, and with it the related binary polarization. Those who engage in impositions that create obstacles to the spirit of science – namely the search for the truth, free from any instructions – in a culture of limitations must be rejected. They justify their extra-scientific considerations with notions that are not acceptable to scholarly ethics. 'Respect for Islam' is honourable, but there is no one monolithic Islam. Enlightened Muslim thought, in diversity, is part of contemporary Islam as well.

The debate on: whither Islamic civilization? The legitimacy of criticism vs. accusations and prejudice

For a variety of reasons, the Arab part of Islamdom has culturally always been the core of the wider Islamic civilization. In terms of the post-bipolar global democratization, the Arab Spring was an Islamic–Arab attempt to join world history, as outlined in Chapter 4. Will this trend be lasting even after the Islamist empowerment? Whither Islamic civilization? The Islamicate of today consists of

57 states assembled in the Organization of the Islamic Conference under the influence of Wahhabi Saudi Arabia, a state that wrongly claims to speak for all Muslims.[57] This claim is underpinned by a religious legitimation only on the surface (the Saudi king's title as custodian of the holy shrines of Mecca and Medina); in reality it is underpinned by the power of the Saudi petro-dollar, which often operates under conditions of shameful corruption. Islamdom in the second decade of the twenty-first century accounts for approximately two billion people out of the seven billion world population. As demonstrated by the uprising of the Arab Spring, most Muslim people not only live in economic and social misery but are also denied basic rights – above all, freedom and dignity. That is why they rebel. The lucky ones among them flee the miserable conditions of life in the Islamicate and go as migrants to Europe and to the US. There, they get what their home countries in the Islamicate states deny them: better life and freedom.

Under these conditions not only Muslims, but also non-Muslims have the right to deal with the prevailing crisis phenomenon – because it affects us all. For the sake of integrity and in the name of freedom, one has to defend critical reasoning against accusations aimed at outlawing criticism. Four scholars address the phenomenon at issue in terms of 'the crisis of Islamic civilization'.[58] They – among others – look at Islam as a civilization, and do this in the Islamic tradition of Ibn Khaldun. In addition to these contributions, it is wise to draw in a complementary manner on the magnificent historical research of Hodgson, thus also considering other non-Muslim contributions.

In this book I catch up with this debate and relate the Arab Spring to the crisis referred to. The Arab Spring rebellion is not only a response to the denial of freedom to Arab Muslims, but also the outcome of a failure of development; both these features are embedded in the crisis of Islamic civilization. Therefore, it is justified to conclude this book with some reasoning on this issue and ask whether the Arab Spring, if it were to end with the empowerment of Islamism, could alleviate the crisis? Would the *shari'a* state be the solution to the civilizational crisis? Neither Wahhabi Saudi Arabia nor Islamist movements allow this question, and they smear the reasoning behind it with the accusation of Islamophobia. So, we are back to the problem of the freedom of critical reasoning and the culture of imposed limits in the name of respect.

After consulting and comparing the aforementioned four books on the crisis (see note 58) I decided to focus on the contribution of the Iraqi Ali Allawi, because it states the essentials.

In line with enlightened Muslim thought, Allawi thinks that the politicization of Islam into Islamism is not about religious faith, but rather about turning Islam 'into an ideology for achieving power' and 'some form of an Islamic state'.[59] Despite the fact that Islamism is not Islam, it is a fact that Islamist movements 'influenced the course of Muslim life and civilization . . . The introduction of *shari'a* becomes a mechanism . . . In power it is unlikely that Islamists will generate a new dynamic in Islamic civilization.' Why? Allawi believes that '*shari'a* rule . . . might remould the forms . . . but it will not necessarily produce a new Islamic civilizational force.' Allawi does not share the view that 'some form of

Islamic state' would be a solution. Instead he believes in the 'creative forces' of Islamic civilization and states a need for their 'nurturing'. Allawi does not think that 'establishing the primacy of political Islam' would fulfil the task of overcoming of the crisis. On the contrary, the 'Islamic awakening' heralded by Islamists would not contribute to 'regenerating an Islamic civilization'. He ends his book with the grim prospect that the Islamist *shari'a* state 'will not be a prelude to the rebirth of an Islamic civilization; it will be another episode in its decline'. This is a clear and equally strong Muslim voice that non-Muslims need to respect. Allawi's statement of a potential for 'decline' is not an expression of Islamophobia. The debate on Islamophobia predates the Arab Spring, but the Arab Spring has given it a new shape in providing protection against critics. No doubt, all democratic humanists have to join forces in combating Islamophobia when this evil is actually at work. However, one needs at first to clearly determine what Islamophobia is, and, second, having defined it, how to deal with it, which is certainly not through censorship and policing. Let us review some contributions to this debate.

In an *International Herald Tribune/New York Times* (*IHT/NYT*) column on 'The Wrong Way to Combat Islamophobia',[60] Paula Schriefer of Freedom House acknowledges the rise in prejudice against Islam and Muslims in the West, but she rightly argues that the related imposed pressure 'to enact laws that prohibit such forms of expression' reflects a 'campaign [that] is deeply flawed from a human rights perspective, both in its equation of religious discrimination . . . with the vague concept of defamation, as well as in the proposed remedy of imposing legal limits on freedom of expression.' This campaign takes place almost annually in the shape of UN resolutions orchestrated by the Saudi-Arabia-led Organization of the Islamic Conference. The problem is not only the unacceptable imposition of limitations on the freedom of speech, but also the hypocrisy involved – two states that carry and support the UN resolution are 'Pakistan and Saudi Arabia – countries with appalling records on religious freedom and broader human rights', as Schriefer rightly states. For an international standard of combating prejudice we need other ways than those the Saudi–Pakistani perspective tries to impose.

Besides the reference to hypocrisy, Paula Schriefer insightfully adds that 'governments should never be in the business of policing speech . . . Blasphemy laws don't work in any context and UN member states should reject them unconditionally'. Policing speech should never be advanced as a standard, because a humanist venture needs to be based on clear terms, nuances and distinctions, and above all to be free from ideologically blinkered views. No knowledgeable person could deny the statement that Islam has a bad image in the West that is highly charged with prejudice.[61] But is it therefore true that referring to this prejudice justifies making a highly consequential allegation such as this one made by James Carroll in an *IHT/NYT* editorial: 'The contempt toward the religion of Mohammad is a foundational pillar of Western civilization.'[62]

Islamists make this allegation too, and a quote like this could have been taken from an Islamist source, not from a *New York Times* editorial. But how correct is this allegation? In view of the real historical facts and records of the civilizational encounters between Islam, Christianity and the West[63] the allegation must be dismissed as baseless; more, it must be qualified as nonsense. Even more, it is not just wrong, but highly consequential. Although it is made with benign intent, it actually exceeds the negative effects of the Huntingtonian 'clash of civilizations'. It even resembles Islamist propaganda slogans designed to undergird anti-Western resentments in the pursuit of polarization. Islamists agree tactically to dialogue, but in their inner circles they propagate feeling against the '*gharb al-salibi*'/'Crusader West', believed to be by nature against Islam and with which therefore (they think) there can be no conciliation. It follows that civilizational prejudice exists also on the Islamic side. The mutuality of these prejudiced attitudes has to be stated for the sake of honesty and scholarly integrity. Those who read Arabic – Carroll presumably does not – know well how charged the notion of the '*gharb*'/'West' is in the Islamist literature. This final part of the present book is not the place to deal with mutual civilizational prejudice, as its focus is the legitimacy of criticism in an awareness that criticism is not an indication of Islamophobia. However, at issue is the future of Islamic civilization in the context of the Arab Spring. One cannot be silent about the use of this just rebellion by Islamists as a ladder to climb up to power through institutional participation. Their empowerment has changed everything, including the possible ways to look at the ongoing process critically. The spring has become an unpleasant winter.

Among the negative changes I see are the effects on academic freedom. The culture of accusation and defamation puts academic freedom in peril. This is the context in which scholars, journalists and policy-makers have been navigating the 'tumultuous effects of the Arab Spring. The choices are suddenly more complicated. Long-held assumptions have been upset'. These are the words of Scott Shane in a highly cogent *New York Times* news analysis that blames most Westerners for their inability to 'carefully distinguish between Islamists, who advocate a leading role for Islam in government, and violent jihadists, *who espouse the same good* but advocate terrorism to achieve it'.[64]

In my most recent book, *Islamism and Islam*, I present strong evidence for this distinction within Islamism, but was accused by a reviewer of 'lumping together' because I illuminate this subject matter precisely in identifying simultaneously a distinction (violence/non-violence) and the sharing of the same goal (in Shane's phrase, 'the same good').[65] My statement of the evidence is based on 30 years of research in twenty different Islamic countries. It is the contaminated environment of the study of Islamism and Islam that leads to fooleries such as this accusation of 'lumping together'. It is a fact proven with ample evidence that institutional and jihadist Islamists, very different as they are, 'espouse the same good', as also conceded by Shane: namely, the 'good' of the *shari'a* state.

Based on the analysis provided in Chapter 4 I argue that the 'role of government' envisioned by Islamists is not restricted to engagement in participatory democratic politics. What they want is to determine the order of the state itself. When it comes to engaging Islamist movements, no democrat would have any objection to this kind of inclusion. The problem is the Islamist goal, namely the imagined '*shari'a* state'. This is not about a simple participation. This order has never existed in Islamic history.

In the debate on the *shari'a* state presented as 'Islamic democracy' one faces critics who employ the accusation of Islamophobia as a weapon against free debate. To dismantle this accusation, I make an effort to base my thinking on an Islamic underpinning. This venture involves two tasks to fulfil the following related goals.

First, to make plain that the idea of a shari'a state lacks any roots in Islamic heritage. Those who cite Mawardi's *al-Ahkam al Sultaniyya*, or Ibn Taimiyya's *al-Siyasa al-Shar'iyya* to refute the position taken in this book are advised to do better homework with a careful reading of these sources. Even a superficial comparison of the writings of Mawardi and Ibn Taimiyya with those of al-Banna, Qutb and Qaradawi reveals how baseless any such a refutation is. I discussed my research on political thought in traditional Islam to support this argument with evidence in Chapter 4.

Second, to meet the insistence on an Islamic argumentation for democracy and democratization. In the Introduction I argued with Sohail Hashmi that Islamic heritage – though it includes a precious tradition of humanism (as witness the al-Jabri project) – lacks records of a democracy, which is a modern introduction to Islamdom. After all, democracy itself is a modern phenomenon. Nonetheless, there is an Islamic ethics compatible with democracy. The conclusion is then that arguing against the *shari'a* state must rest on an Islamic ethics of this sort to gain legitimacy among Muslims. In the past some – including myself – have used the term 'liberal Islam' to identify such a project. It is unfortunate that the label 'liberal' has been de-legitimated in its use with reference to Islamdom. It is not only the Islamists who have contributed to this de-legitimation through their highly derogatory use of the term 'liberal' to smear what they allege to be 'cultural treason' based on an 'import from the West'; a tremendously widely read Western reader entitled *Liberal Islam* has contributed to this outcome as well.[66] This so-called 'sourcebook' has given cause for replacing the contaminated term with another: I propose 'civil Islam', as used to describe the tolerant 'open Islam' that developed in Indonesia.[67] The Moroccan Muslim Abdou Filali-Ansary gives additional inspiration. He takes issue with the flawed Western reader cited above to make the point 'that the choice of terms can have surprisingly far-reaching effects: For example, the very expression "liberal Islam" would, within Muslim societies, greatly handicap the acceptance of the trends and approaches to which the phrase is meant to refer.'[68]

The alternative Filali-Ansary proposes is the notion 'enlightened Muslim thought', as represented in the trend identified as 'the enlightened turn' to which this book adheres. The assessment of the Arab Spring and the criticism of the Islamist *shari'a* state rest on this enlightened turn in Islamdom, and this inoculates my contribution against the accusation of Orientalism and Islamophobia. The major source of this enlightened turn is the medieval tradition of Islamic humanism. One of the great minds of this turn, the late Mohammed Abed al-Jabri, devoted his life to reviving this Islamic humanism (the al-Jabri project), in the firm belief that 'the survival of our philosophical tradition, i.e., what is likely to contribute to our time, can only be Averroist'.[69] I hasten to add that this could serve as a project of a democratization underpinned with authentic tenets of Islamic ethics. I am among the supporters of this al-Jabri project and therefore share with Ali Allawi, whom I quote above, the assessment that 'al-Jabri is probably the most significant Muslim thinker of the age'.[70] Ahead of al-Jabri, Ali Abdelraziq laid the grounds. His work marks the beginning of enlightened Muslim thought. This thought provides a better answer to the question 'Whither Islamic civilization?' than does Islamism.

When Islamists today cry 'Islamophobia!' in a propagandist manner, one often fails to find any supporting evidence to this accusation. For instance it is not Islamophobic to take issue with 'hatred of Christians in the Muslim World'. John Eibner, who wrote a telling editorial opinion piece under this title in the *New York Times*, condemns 'the scene of anti-Christian mob violence . . . in Cairo, against a background of churches in flames' and provides a powerful reminder of a 'grim reality':

> non-Muslim communities have become endangered species throughout much of the Islamic world . . . The effects of religious supremacy have been devastating, especially for non-Muslims in the Islamic Middle East. . . . The laudable goal of winning hearts and minds of Muslims must not be pursued at the expense of non-Muslim communities . . . Peace, pluralism and stability cannot be based on religious bigotry.[71]

Is this powerful reminder an expression of Islamophobia? No, it is not, and this caveat has to be an essential part of the debate on the question 'Whither Islamic civilization?' The *shari'a* state is a hegemonic order that negatively affects non-Muslims – as well as enlightened Muslims – both at home and in the international environment of a secular international system.

With the accusation of Islamophobia, Islamists and their Western supporters curb free debate of the issues and even silence humanist thinking. Some Muslims, mostly Islamists, also use the weapon of self-victimization, making unfounded allegations of a 'new Holocaust' against Islam to target free debate about what Islamists do to others, be they non-Muslims or non-Islamist Muslims. In this war of ideas, great limits are imposed on any critique of the agenda of Islamism, namely the *shari'a* state. In terms of diversity it has to be acknowledged that there are not only Islamists and Salafi-oriented Muslims, but also Muslims who adhere to a civil Islam of the 'enlightened turn'. Muslims of this trend should be allowed to speak out. One of the champions of this turn, Abdou Filali-Ansary, deplores existing confusions in the Islamicate, whether in the past or in the present, between what is religious and what is political. If an order is not 'a religious . . . but a political one', he argues, then it is 'amenable to critical scrutiny in the same way as any normal human institution'.[72] Based on this premise I ask with Filali-Insary in all honesty: why did this criticism not occur and flourish among Muslims? The answer is that 'this trend' enjoys little coverage and 'its influence has also been restricted by the educational policies of modern states and by intimidation on the part of the fundamentalists'. I agree with his answer and remind the reader of the description of critical Muslims by the Islamist sheykh Yusuf al-Qaradawi (cited in the Introduction) as 'disbelievers, wrong-doers and truly wicked'. This culture of a *shari'a* state reflects a political order, not a religious one. If one subjects it to critical scrutiny, democratic reasoning, not Islamophobia, is at work. One can only hope that non-Muslims and Muslims alike will follow the reasoning of Filali-Ansary adopted here.

Operating on the assumption that the Arab Spring matters to everyone, including non-Muslims, leads to the insight that a political reordering of the Islamicate matters to everyone as well. The issues involved have moved to the fore in public debates in politics and international affairs, and rational and well-founded criticism needs to be allowed. In this regard, the cogent argument against politically opportune thinking presented by the *New York Times* editorialist Roger Cohen is worth quoting in full:

> From Egypt to Pakistan, it must be understood that Islam cannot at once be a political force and above criticism. Once you enter the democratic platform, your beliefs are no longer a private matter but up for legitimate attack. . . . blasphemy laws are an affront to this principle.[73]

In a time of sound-bites and a culture where skimming replaces careful reading, it seems to me important to conclude by repeating that taking issue with the accusation of Islamophobia does not absolve one from fighting against prejudice of all kinds – not only against Islam and Muslims, but also against what John Eibner identified as 'hatred of Christians in the Muslim world'. The notion of Islamophobia singles out Muslims in an entirely inappropriate application of the Holocaust to the Muslim case; this is a mindset of self-victimization. In contrast to this, what is needed today is a humanist approach against prejudice, which is to combat prejudice in general to protect everyone, not just a single community.

In the context of the Arab Spring and its unpleasant aftermath there is a need for a debate based on freedom of speech and criticism. While arguing that critical reasoning is not an expression of prejudice, I need to add in a balanced way that criticism is a requirement to avoid prejudice. For this reason I dissociate my critical analysis from the highly prejudiced work of some Israeli scholars. Just as it is in no way an expression of Islamophobia to subject Islamism to reasonable criticism, it is similarly in no way antisemitic to dismiss the anti-Islamic work of Israeli scholars such as Efraim Karsh's *Islamic Imperialism* or Dan Diner's *Lost in the Sacred*.[74] One may, as I myself do, criticize the Islamist project of 'remaking the world'. However, it is not an indication of balanced criticism to employ such phrases for this vision as the 'quest for Allah's Empire' – quite apart from the absent distinction between Islamism and Islam. Muslims have the right to dismiss this racist offence. Similar profiling is included in the work of an Israeli political theorist who, unbelievably – over a short period of time – turned into an 'expert on Islam'. This is Dan Diner, who blames Islam and Muslims for having overslept the changed world. I view his book as an offence as well. Throughout the present book I speak of a crisis of Islamic civilization, and also end this section with this theme, but the crisis I speak of is something other than what Dan Diner writes about in a book based on poor knowledge and imbued with prejudice. Although I reject the unrestricted use of the notion of Islamophobia, as elaborated upon in this chapter, I am compelled to admit it when it comes to the work of some Israeli scholars such as those I have alluded to. I leave it open to debate whether this work is exceptional or exemplary, but for sure it is imbued with prejudice. My scholarly and political credentials include uncompromising criticism of Islamist antisemitism.[75] I add here the Islamophobia of some Israelis, which I reject in the same line of reasoning based on humanism. Last but not least, I dissociate my criticism of the US community of Islamic studies from the attacks on this community by the Israeli Martin Kramer.[76] In contrast to Kramer, my concern is not an obsession with 'security' and alerts against 'terror', but rather a humanism shared by Muslims and non-Muslims alike. This is the basis of my rejection of the hegemonic *shari'a* state.

Conclusions: the Arab Spring and its aftermath. Between the fragmentation of humanity and the 'violence of false unity and forced coherence'

At the end of the journey undertaken in this inquiry into the interrelation between the Arab Spring and democratization in the shadow of the empowerment of Islamism and the implementation of its agenda for a *shari'a* state, and in the light of the analysis provided in the preceding chapters, some conclusions are to be drawn. Above all is the insight that the blindspots of the dominating US narrative about Islam and Islamism not only have consequences for scholarship and public policy, but they also are a burden to the honest efforts made at cross-civilizational bridging in a conflict-ridden situation. At all levels the Islamist *shari'a* state runs, not just contrary to democratization in the world of Islam, but also contrary to the hoped-for global post-bipolar democratic peace. It thus generates fragmentation throughout humanity, since Islam is now present everywhere on the globe. Having said that, what more can I say? But I will add this question: Is engaging in this critical reasoning an expression of Islamophobia? This chapter defends the legitimacy of critical reasoning in scholarship and pursues this task on the grounds of enlightened Muslim thought. This critical perspective is imperative, unless one agrees to letting the Islamists go unquestioned in the name of respect. They have hijacked the Arab Spring in a process of empowerment that is confused by some with engagement. The ethics of free scholarship, and the mindset of enlightened Muslim thought, admit the debate that is needed. Urgently needed.

I referred in the Preface to my article on 'Islamic Humanism vs. Islamism', published in autumn 2012, around the time the manuscript of the present book was completed. There I wrote of two congenial mindsets, one mine, the other of the journal *Soundings* of the Society for Values in Higher Education. The values of this society rest on humanism, which is also the mindset of the enlightened Muslim thought to which this book adheres. The article published in *Soundings* reflects the findings of the present book, and therefore I want to quote the journal's editor, Professor John Kelsay, who in his editorial addresses the issues touched upon in my article as follows:

Tibi argues the case for the historical and contemporary utility of an intellectual tradition he (and some others) describe as 'Islamic humanism'. . . . Tibi's goal is to provide a kind of therapy for some of the more virulent behaviors associated with both inter- and intra-civilizational conflict. Looking at the remarkable developments associated with the Arab Spring, he worries that the triumph of Islamist parties will undermine hopes for democratic reform, and suggests that a lack of recognition of the possibilities presented by Islamic humanism may lead European and North American policy makers to overestimate the strength of popular support for Islamists. To put it another way, a lack of effort in ascertaining the contours of the social environment in, say Egypt, may well lead to failures of practical wisdom.[77]

Every author can hope for an empathy such as Kelsay's, that facilitates such an accurate identification of the spirit of my inquiry and of its substance. Professor Kelsay has not yet seen the present book, but the article he published in *Soundings* reflects both the spirit and the substance of the analysis of the Arab Spring provided here. But there is a still more important issue to address that relates to the theme of this concluding chapter and to its conclusions. Professor Kelsay expresses the values of the society that stands behind his journal, and these values are most pertinent to the writing of these conclusions. As mentioned in the Preface, on its inside cover page *Soundings* sets itself, as part of its introduction to the journal, the goal of establishing a balance between two opposing trends of our time. These are, first, 'the challenge of the fragmentation of modern intellectual life' and, second – which is 'worse', as the journal itself indicates – the opposing trend, namely 'the disguised violence of false unity and forced coherence'. In my conclusions I lean on this mindset to place the findings of the present book within this intellectual frame of reference. Let me elaborate.

In a section of Chapter 2 on the Islamist *shari'a* state I address the inter-civilizational tensions that are aroused by the claim of each civilization to have its own law. I end that section by quoting the Moroccan writer Abdou Filali-Ansary, who coined the formula 'enlightened Muslim thought' not only to substitute it for the contaminated label 'liberal Islam', but also to use it as a framework for the consolidation of Muslim contributions to enlightened Muslim thought since the publication of a major book by Ali Abdelraziq in 1925. The quotation I employed pertains to 'establishing social and political systems' based on 'a universal rule of law' to be shared across all civilizations – that is, also by Islamdom. This universality is intended to combat 'fragmentation' through commonalities in defining a 'framework' which is 'truly compatible with democratic ideals on the scale of humanity'.[78]

Among the findings of the present book is the insight that the envisioned Islamist *shari'a* state does not fulfil the compatibility stipulated by Filali-Ansary in the statement just quoted. It follows that, if the Arab Spring were to end up in the establishing of a *shari'a* state that rejects what Filali-Ansary identifies as 'a universal rule of law', the result would be further new sources of tensions that may lead, not only to conflict, but to a further 'fragmentation of modern intellectual life', to use the phrase of *Soundings*. If this analysis is correct – and I believe it is – then we do have a problem that relates to a prevailing of 'cultural particularisms' against some universality that is needed for a shared order of the world.[79] Do not mistake me: I am not arguing against diversity, but against fragmentation caused by the prevailing of cultural particularisms. In this context alone I endorse a right of veto for 'democracy vs. cultural difference'.[80] Again and again: diversity is not the same things as fragmentation and should not be equated with it. Such an equation would have disastrous consequences.

Let me now turn to the second trend opposed to 'fragmentation'. It is – as the *Soundings* phrase puts it – the 'disguised violence of false unity and forced coherence'. The spokesmen of Islamism, such as Qaradawi, speak of one *umma* characterized by 'unity and coherence'. As I have repeatedly quoted, Muslim dissidents are defamed as 'disbelievers, wrong-doers and truly wicked'. Are those Westerners who follow the prevailing narrative that outlaws criticism much better? No, for Muslims of the 'enlightened Muslim thought' they are not. These Westerners, whether they malign or exonerate, speak of 'Islam' and of 'Muslims', ignoring the great diversity on all levels within the Islamic *umma* community, called in Hodgson's terminology 'Islamdom'. Muslims of the enlightened thought – among whom I count myself – insist on their Islamic identity while at the same time refusing vehemently to submit to the violence of 'false unity and forced coherence' and to its associated mindset, whether this be of Islamist or of Western political correctness.

I wrote this book to enlighten, but I apprehend it may erupt a controversy with the prevailing narrative in the West, together with a dismissal of its conclusions. Some in our age prefer to live in a world of unity and coherence. The US journal *Soundings* aptly qualifies this unity and coherence more closely, speaking of 'the disguised violence of false unity and forced coherence'. This is a just description of a mindset that approves the *shari'a* state as an 'Islamic democracy' – an imposed outlook of unity and coherence. This mindset, which I criticize, views Islamist *shari'a* law as compatible with law in general and with international law as well. Discrepancies that really exist are whitewashed, belittled and palliated as a result of 'cultural misunderstanding'. Those who fail to comply with this 'forced coherence' and support its rejection with a reference to real fragmentation face being exposed to the mindset of 'violence' that prescribes the 'false unity and forced coherence'.

In this concluding chapter I have dealt with heavier weapons of silencing. Chief among them is the defamation based on the accusation of Islamophobia. This book suggests an alternative: an acknowledgement of conflict coupled with an effort at cross-civilizational bridging in the framework of conflict resolution. Isn't this more promising than the contentions of 'false unity and forced coherence'? Let us work together in this mindset to make the promise of the Arab Spring a real one! Let us stop hurling stones at one another. Rational criticism is not 'ranting', as one reviewer called it. Nor is it a hurling of stones. Communication is an effort at understanding the other, even if one disagrees!

Notes

Abbreviations in notes

IHT, International Herald Tribune (global edition of the *New York Times*)
NYT, New York Times

Introduction: will the *shari'a* state be the outcome? The Arab Spring and the hope for democratization

1　This is why I have chosen Egypt as a representative case study for testing and illustrating the approach employed in my earlier book, *Islam's Predicament with Modernity: Religious Reform and Cultural Change* (London and New York: Routledge, 2009), chapter 9: 'The Failed Transformation of Egypt', pp. 265–89.

2　Fernando Perez, 'The Key to Securing Religious Freedom in Post-Arab Spring Nations', *International Journal for Religious Freedom* 4, 2 (2011), pp. 7–9.

3　See Mary Habeck, *Knowing the Enemy: Jihadist Ideology and the War on Terror* (New Haven, CT: Yale University Press, 2006) and Marc Sageman, *Leaderless Jihad: Terror Networks in the Twenty-First Century* (Philadelphia, PA: University of Pennsylvania Press, 2008).

4　On these distinctions and the related nuances see B. Tibi, *Islamism and Islam* (New Haven, CT: Yale University Press, 2012).

5　Malise Ruthven's hostile review, 'Reason and Religion', of my book *Islamism and Islam* (and of myself) was published in: *Literary Review* (June 1, 2012), pp. 32–3 (accessed through Durants).

6　This view permeates all al-Banna essays collected in one volume in the ultimate book: Hasan al-Banna, *Majmu'at Rasa'il al-Imam al-Shahid/Collected Writings of the Martyr-Imam*, new legal edition (Cairo: Dar al-Dawa, 1990). See pp. 209–51 on the *nizam islami*/Islamic system. There is a classic publication on this theme by Richard Mitchell, *The Society of the Muslim Brothers* (London: Oxford University Press, 1969), chapter 9 of which discusses in detail the new notion of *nizam islami* presented by Islamists as the solution based on *shari'a*.

7　Yusuf al-Qaradawi, *Islamic Law in the Modern World* (Riad, Saudi Arabia: King Faisal Center, 2000). The following quotes are from pp. 17, 48, 49.

8　Qaradawi appears among those authors selected as 'liberal' in the highly flawed reader edited by Charles Kurzman, *Liberal Islam* (New York: Oxford University Press, 1998). For a criticism of this reader see Abdou Filali-Ansary, 'The Sources of Enlightened Muslim Thought', in: *Islam and Democracy in the Middle East* (Baltimore, MD: Johns Hopkins University Press, 2003), pp. 237–51, in particular pp. 241–4. The contamination caused by Kurzman compels Filali-Ansary to propose that the notion of 'liberal Islam' be abandoned.

9 Sayyid Qutb, *Ma'alim fi al-Tariq/Signposts along the Road*, legal edition (Cairo: Dar al-Shuruq, 13th printing, 1989), pp. 5 and 111.

10 *Hatmiyyat al-Hall al-Islami/The Islamic Solution*, 3 volumes (Beirut: Mu'assasat al-Risala, and Cairo: Dar Wahba, several editions); here volume 2, pp. 88–94. This is the most powerful articulation of the contemporary Islamist agenda.

11 B. Tibi, *The Challenge of Fundamentalism: Political Islam and the New World Disorder* (Berkeley, CA: University of California Press, 1998, updated 2002); *Political Islam, World Politics and Europe* (New York: Routledge, 2008); and *Islamism and Islam* (New Haven, CT: Yale University Press, 2012).

12 *IHT* February 3, 2012, p. 8.

13 See the chapter on Islam and knowledge in B. Tibi, *Islam's Predicament with Modernity* (see note 1 above), pp. 65–94.

14 The 'al-Jabri project' is the term used in the Arabic sources to refer to the efforts made by the late Islamic rationalist Mohammed Abed al-Jabri to revive, in an 'enlightened turn', the heritage of Islamic rationalism and humanism in medieval Islam. See his book *al-Turath wa al-Hadatha/Cultural Heritage and Modernity* (Beirut: al-Markaz al-Thaqafi al-Arabi, 1991), pp. 241–360. On al-Jabri's work as the major source of the revival of this medieval tradition in contemporary Islam, see the Preface and B. Tibi, 'Islamic Humanism vs. Islamism', *Soundings* 95, 3 (2012), pp. 230–54.

15 *Building a Knowledge Society*. United Nations Development Programme report on the Arab world (New York: UNDP, Arab Fund for Economic and Scoial Development, 2003).

16 Sohail Hashmi, 'Islamic Ethics in International Society', chapter 8 in: Sohail Hashmi, ed., *Islamic Political Ethics* (Princeton, NJ: Princeton University Press, 2002), here pp. 165–6.

17 Noah Feldman, *After Jihad: America and the Struggle for Islamic Democracy* (New York: Farrar, Straus and Giroux, 2004), pp. 24–5. The heading of the cited chapter, 'Islamic Democracy, not Islamist Democracy', makes no sense given Feldman's constant confusion of Islam with Islamism. See note 23 below.

18 Abdou Filali-Ansary, 'The Sources of Enlightened Muslim Thought' (see note 8 above), here p. 250. See also al-Jabri, *al-Turath wa al-Hadatha* (note 14 above).

19 See the 'culturalism-free' contributions to the Culture Matters Research Project, Lawrence Harrison chairperson and ed., *Developing Cultures*, 2 volumes (New York: Routledge, 2006).

20 Alan Richards and John Waterbury, *A Political Economy of the Middle East* (Boulder, CO: Westview, 2nd edn, 1990), p. 365.

21 *'Azmat al-Dimuqratiyya fi al-Watan al-Arabi*, Centre for Arab Unity Studies, Beirut, 1984. See the discussion of this Arabic debate in Chapter 4 of the present book.

22 B. Tibi, *'al-Bin'a al-Iqtisadi al-Ijtima'i lil-Dimuqratiyya'/*'The economic and social underpinning of democracy', paper presented at the congress *'Azmat al-Dimuqratiyya fi al-Watan al-Arabi/*The Crisis of Democracy in the Arab World and published in the proceedings volume of the same title (see note 21 above), pp. 73–87.

23 Noah Feldman, *The Fall and Rise of the Islamic State* (Princeton, NJ: Princeton University Press, 2008). On his earlier book see also note 17 above and my earlier criticism of Feldman's work in my book on Islamism (note 4 above), pp. 203–4. On Feldman see also below, note 41 to Chapter 4.

24 On Islamology see *Islam's Predicament* (note 1 above), pp. 7–15, and the discussion in the final chapter of the present book, pp. 195–7.

25 See 'Challenges Shift for Egypt's New Leader', *IHT*, June 26, 2012, pp. 1, 4. On 'Islamist democracy' as a contradiction in terms see *Islamism and Islam* (see note 4 above), chapter 4. On the totalitarian organization of Islamist movements, see the same book, chapter 8.

26 Eric Trager,'The Unbreakable Muslim Brotherhood: Grim Perspectives for a Liberal Egypt', *Foreign Affairs* (September/October 2011), pp. 114–26.

27 John Stuart Mill, *On Liberty and other Essays* (1859), ed. John Gray (London: Oxford University Press, 1998), p. 9.

28 Ali Allawi, *The Crisis of Islamic Civilization* (New Haven, CT: Yale University Press, 2009); the quotes are from pp. 104 and 273. Allawi's book is discussed in more detail in the concluding section of Chapter 6 of the present book.

29 See the contributions to the Harvard/MIT research project chaired by Philip Khoury and Joseph Kostiner, eds., *Tribes and State Formation in the Middle East* (Berkeley, CA: University of California Press, 1990), and B. Tibi, *Arab Nationalism: Between Islam and the Nation-State* (New York: Macmillan, 3rd edn, 1997).

30 Jens-Martin Eriksen and Frederik Stjernfeld, *The Democratic Contradictions of Multiculturalism* (New York: Telos, 2012), pp. 243–4. This debate is resumed in Chapter 6 of the present book.

31 Ali Oumlil, *Fi Shari'yyat al-Ikhtilaf/On the Legitimacy of Dissent* (Rabat: al-Majlis al-Qaumi, 1991).

32 Jillian Schwedler, 'Can Islamists Become Moderate?' *World Politics*, 63, 2 (April 2011), pp. 347–76, here p. 358.

33 Paul Berman, *The Flight of the Intellectuals* (New York: Melville House, 2nd edn, 2011), p. 285.

1 The *shari'a* state and Western scholarship: the reality of the Islamist *shari'a*tization of politics that seeks a name

1 Marshall G.S. Hodgson, *The Venture of Islam: Conscience and History in a World Civilization* (Chicago, IL: University of Chicago Press, 1977), 3 volumes. All of the following quotations are from volume 1, pp. 30–95: in succession, pp. 57, 30, 33, 37, 95.

2 I quote here from three contributions by Abdou Filali-Ansary that are all included in the volume edited by Larry Diamond, Marc Plattner and Daniel Blumenberg, *Islam and Democracy in the Middle East* (Baltimore, MD: Johns Hopkins University Press, 2003). The following quotations are from pp. 198, 243, 235, 236.

3 Charles Kurzman, ed., *Liberal Islam* (New York: Oxford University Press, 1998).

4 For a useful survey see Norman Daniel, *Islam and the West: The Making of an Image* (Oxford: Oneworld, 1960, new printing, 1993); by contrast, for a negative example see the ideologically obsessed book by Stephen Sheehi, *Islamophobia* (Atlanta, GA: Clarity Press, 2011).

5 B. Tibi, *Islam in Global Politics: Conflict and Cross-Civilizational Bridging* (London and New York: Routledge, 2012). For *Islamism and Islam*, see Introduction, note 4.

6 These three authoritative sources are: Mahmud Shaltut, *al-Islam Aqida wa Shari'a* (Cairo: Dar al-Shuruq, 10th edn, 1980), chapter 'Shari'a', pp. 78–197; Subhi al-Salih, *Ma'alim al Shari'a al-Islamiyya* (Beirut: Dar al-Ilm lil-Malayin, 1975); Ali Abdelraziq, *al-Islam was Usul al-Hukm* (1925, Beirut: Maktabat al-Hayat, reprint, 1966).

7 Mohammed Said al-Ashmawi, *Usul al-Shari'a* (Cairo: Madbuli, 1983).

8 Fazlur Rahman, *Islam and Modernity* (Chicago, IL: University of Chicago Press, 1982). The following quotations are from pp. 29, 32, 31, 30.

9 Hamilton A. R. Gibb, *Studies on the Civilization of Islam* (Princeton, NJ: Princeton University Press, 1962, reprinted, 1982); the quotations are from pp. 162 and 154.

10 Hamid Enayat, *Modern Islamic Political Thought* (Austin, TX: University of Texas Press, 1982), p. 67; the next quotation is from p. 131.

11 Ali M. Jarisha and Mohammed S. Zaibaq, *Asalib al-Ghazu al-Fikri lil Alam al-Islami* (Cairo: Dar al-I'tisam, 1978).

12 Daniel Varisco, 'Inventing Islamism: The Violence of Rhetoric' (as in note 21 below), p. 45.

13 Larry Diamond, *The Spirit of Democracy: The Struggle to Build Free Societies Throughout the World* (New York: New York Times Books, 2008), pp. 263–87; quotations are from pp. 286, 284, 287.

14 See the reference on Hodgson in note 1 above. These distinctions are elaborated upon in B. Tibi, *Islamism and Islam* (New Haven, CT: Yale University Press, 2012), in particular in the chapter 'Why Islamism Is Not Islam', pp. 1–30. This book is the third of a trilogy by the same author on political Islam. The earlier two books are *The Challenge of Fundamentalism: Political Islam and the New World Disorder* (Berkeley, CA: University of California Press, 1998, updated, 2002) and *Political Islam, World Politics and Europe* (New York: Routledge, 2008).

15 Hasan al-Banna, *Majmu'at Rasa'il al-Imam al-Shahid* (Cairo: Dar al-Da'wa, 1990). The quotations are from pp. 23 and 233. On al-Banna see the book by Dharif referenced in note 26 below, pp. 40–7, 251–2, 253–5, 269–74.

16 See John Kelsay's outstanding book, *Arguing the Just War in Islam* (Cambridge, MA: Harvard University Press, 2007), p. 166.

17 On 'Islamology' as a new discipline see my book *Islam's Predicament with Modernity: Religious Reform and Cultural Change* (New York: Routledge, 2009), in particular the introduction, here pp. 7–15.

18 See the section on AKP in B. Tibi, *Islamism and Islam* (referenced in note 14 above), pp. 98–105, and the sources referenced there, in addition to the valuable contributions in the new book edited by Briol Yeşilada and Barry Rubin, *Islamization of Turkey under the AKP Rule* (London: Routledge, 2011).

19 A statement by the Turkish AKP prime minister Recep Tayyip Erdogan, quoted by Andrew McCarthy, *The Grand Jihad* (New York: Encounter Books, 2010), here p. 39.

20 This is what Andrew McCarthy states as his conclusion, *The Grand Jihad*, p. 39, after quoting Erdogan (see preceding note).

21 Richard C. Martin and Abbas Barzegar, eds, *Islamism: Contested Perspectives on Political Islam* (Stanford, CA: Stanford University Press, 2010). This volume includes two lead essays, one by Donald K. Emmerson, 'Inclusive Islamism: The Utility of Diversity', and the other by Daniel Varisco, 'Inventing Islamism: The Violence of Rhetoric'.

22 Both quotations are from the editors' preface to *Islamism* (see preceding note), p. viii.

23 Daniel Varisco, 'Inventing Islamism: The Violence of Rhetoric' (see note 21). The quotations are from pp. 47, 34, 43 and 33.

24 Donald Emmerson, 'Inclusive Islamism: The Utility of Diversity' (see note 21), pp. 17–32. The quotations are from pp. 22, 27, 23 and 29.

25 Hasan Hanafi, 'Islamism: Whose Debate Is It?', in Martin and Barzegar, eds, *Islamism* (see note 21), pp. 63–6; the quotations are from pp. 64 and 66. I recommend looking at the controversy between the Islamist Hasan Hanafi and the late Muslim Mohammed Abed al-Jabri (of 'enlightened Muslim thought'). The controversy was published in the book *Hiwar al-Maghreb wa al-Mashreq* (Casablanca: Topical, 1990).

26 See the authoritative Arabic book by Mohammed Said al-Ashmawi, *al-Islam al-Siyasi/Political Islam* (Cairo: Madbuli, 1989) and Mohammed Dharif, *al Islam al-Siyasi fi al-Watan al-Arabi/Political Islam in the Arab World* (Casablanca: al-Majalla al-Maghribiyya, 1992).

27 Hasan al-Hanafi, *al-Usuliyya al-Islamiyya/Islamic Fundamentalism* (Cairo: Madbuli, 1989).

28 See the chapter by M. Zuhdi Jasser, 'Americanism versus Islamism', pp. 175–91, in: Zeyno Baran, ed., *The Other Muslims: Moderate and Secular* (New York: Palgrave Macmillan, 2010).

29 M. Zuhdi Jasser, 'Political Islam, Liberalism and the Diagnosis of a Problem', in: Martin and Barzegar, eds, *Islamism* (see note 21), pp.104–9; the quotations are from pp. 104, 104–5, 108, 106 and 108–9.

30 Richard C. Martin and Abbas Barzegar, in: Martin and Barzegar, eds, *Islamism* (see note 21), Preface, p. viii.

31 Abdelazim Ramadan, *Jama'at al-Takfir fi Misr* (Cairo: al Haya al-Misriyya, 1995).
32 On this ideological current of a third-worldism see B. Tibi, 'The Political Legacy of Max Horkheimer and Islamism', *Telos*, issue 148 (Fall 2009), pp. 7–15, and chapter 6 on the Western third-worldist romanticization of Islamism in: B. Tibi, *Islam in Global Politics: Conflict and Cross-Civilizational Bridging* (London and New York: Routledge, 2012), pp. 140–60.
33 Ziba Mir Hasseini and Richard Tapper, 'Islamism – Ism or Wasm', in: Martin and Barzegar, eds, *Islamism* (see note 21), pp. 81–92, here p. 82.
34 For a critical debate see the chapter on Islamism and violence in B. Tibi, *Islamism and Islam* (referenced in note 14 above), pp. 134–57.
35 Joseph I. Lieberman, 'Who's the Enemy in the War on Terror', *Wall Street Journal*, June 15, 2010, p. A17. All quotations are from this article.
36 On the conflict in the past between *fiqh* orthodoxy and the rational philosophy of Islamic humanism in medieval Islam, see my extensive chapter in *Pipers Handbuch der politischen Ideen* (5 volumes), here volume 2 (Munich: Piper, 1987), pp. 87–140, and the recent study by Robert R. Reilly, *The Closing of the Muslim Mind: How Intellectual Suicide Created the Modern Islamist Crisis* (Wilmington, DE: Intercollegiate Studies Institute, 2010). On the present, see the chapter 'Civil Islam as an Alternative to Islamism' in: B. Tibi, *Islamism and Islam* (reference in note 14), pp. 225–42.
37 Paul Berman, *The Flight of the Intellectuals: The Controversy over Islamism and the Press* (New York: Melville House, 2011), p. 285. Berman's book provoked a heated debate with varying responses. While it was praised in a positive review by Anthony Julius in *NYT* ('The Pretender', May 16, 2010, p. BR 26), it was polemically scorned by Marc Lynch in *Foreign Affairs* ('Veiled Truths', July/August issue, 2010).
38 In this book and in my trilogy on political Islam I keep arguing that Islamism is just one variety of global religious fundamentalism. On this subject matter see the five volumes of the Fundamentalism Project of the American Academy of Arts and Sciences, published between 1991 and 1995 by the University of Chicago Press (Martin Marty and Scott Appleby, eds). They are the authoritative source for the study of this phenomenon. It is deplorable to see this research ideologically dismissed in a wholesale manner in Martin and Barzegar, eds, *Islamism* (referenced in note 21), in particular on pp. 37–41. For a clarification of the issue, see the two articles by B. Tibi, 'Political Islam as a Forum of Religious Fundamentalism and the Religionization of Politics: Islamism and the Quest for a Remaking of the World', and 'Islamism and Democracy: On the Compatibility of Institutional Islamism and the Political Culture of Democracy', both published in: *Totalitarian Movements and Political Religions*, 10, 2 (2009), pp. 97–120 and 135–64.
39 Subtitle of volume 3 of the Fundamentalism Project, *Fundamentalism and the State* (referenced in the preceding note).
40 For a powerful example of this misperception see Noah Feldman, *The Fall and Rise of the Islamic State* (Princeton, NJ: Princeton University Press, 2008).
41 Abdou Filali-Ansary, 'The Sources of Enlightened Muslim Thought' (see note 2 above) and B. Tibi, 'Islamic Humanism vs. Islamism', *Soundings* 95, 3 (2012), pp. 230–54.
42 See Mohammed Abed al-Jabri, *al Turath wa al-Hadatha* (Beirut: al-Markaz al-Thaqafi, 1991); for the al-Jabri project see the appendix on pp. 241–360. See also B. Tibi, 'Bridging the Heterogeneity of Civilizations: Reviving the Grammar of Islamic Humanism', *Theoria: A Journal of Social and Political Theory*, 56, 120 (September 2009), pp. 65–80, and also the references in notes 36 and 41 above.
43 See note 41 above and Zeev Sternhall, *The Anti-Enlightenment Tradition* (New Haven, CT: Yale University Press, 2009). Sternhall's scope is Eurocentric and ignores the tradition of Islamic Enlightenment. Muslim medieval philosophers established an Enlightenment of *falsafa* rationalism against *fiqh* orthodoxy. On this issue see the chapter by B. Tibi in *Pipers Handbuch der politischen Ideen* (referenced in note 36 above). This medieval conflict is continued in our present as an intra-Islamic rivalry between civil

and *shari'a* Islam. See B. Tibi, 'Islamic Humanism vs Islamism: Cross-Civilizational Bridging' (referenced in note 41 above).

2 The *shari'a* state is not the faith of Islam: *shari'a* and politics

1 Muhammed Said al-Ashmawi, *Usul al-Shari'a/The Origins of the Shari'a* (Cairo: Madbuli, 1983), p. 31.
2 Joseph Schacht, *An Introduction to Islamic Law* (Oxford: Clarendon, 1979), p. 1.
3 John Kelsay, *Arguing the Just War in Islam* (Cambridge, MA: Harvard University Press, 2007), chapter 2. For a debate and a dialogue with Kelsay see B. Tibi. 'John Kelsay and Shari'a Reasoning,' *Journal of Church and State*, 53, 1 (2011), pp. 4–26, and Chapter 5 of the present book.
4 Nasr Hamed Abu-Zaid, *al-Tafkir fi Asr al-Takfir/Reasoning in the Age of Excommunication from the Religious Community* (Cairo: Madbuli, 1995), in particular pp. 41–54.
5 Hussain F. al-Najjar, *al-Islam wa al-Siyasa/Islam and Politics* (Cairo: Dar al-Sha'b, 1977), p. 66.
6 Schacht, *Introduction to Islamic Law* (referenced in note 2 above), p. 54.
7 The following quotes are adopted from Hasan al-Banna, *Majmu'at Rasa'il al-Imam al-Shahid/Collected Writings of the Martyr Imam* (Cairo: Dar al-Da'wa, 1990), pp. 163, 190, 223 and 291.
8 I draw on this debate generated by Daniel Bell, *The Winding Passage* (New York: Basic Books, 1980) in his collection of essays that includes on pp. 324–54 his 1977 essay 'The Return of the Sacred', based on a London School of Economics lecture. After the 9/11 attacks this debate was continued with rich references in Chapter 11, added to the second edition of B. Tibi, *Islam between Culture and Politics* (New York: Palgrave, 2005), pp. 234–72. For the ideas of Max Weber, see his collected writings, *Soziologie – Weltgeschichtliche Analysen – Politik* (Stuttgart: Kröner, 1964); on disenchantment of the world, see p. 317. The greatest challenge to secularism is posed by Islamism, as analysed by B. Tibi, 'Islam and Secularization, Religion and the Functional Differentiation of the Social System', *Archives for Philosophy of Law and Social Philosophy*, 66 (1980), pp. 207–22. This line of reasoning, first voiced in Cairo, was continued two decades later by the same author in the article 'Secularization and De-secularization in Modern Islam', *Religion–Staat–Gesellschaft* 1, 1 (2000), pp. 95–117.
9 See B. Tibi, *Islam in Global Politics: Conflict and Cross-Civilizational Bridging* (New York: Routledge, 2012), chapter 1.
10 Hedley Bull, *The Anarchical Society* (New York: Columbia University Press, 1977), p. 13.
11 For a defence of secularism against this fundamentalist 'remaking', see Paul Cliteur, *The Secular Outlook: In Defense of Moral and Political Secularism* (Oxford: Wiley-Blackwell, 2010). On the fundamentalist vision of a 'remaking of the world', see Martin Marty and Scott Appleby, eds, *Fundamentalisms and the State* (Chicago, IL: University of Chicago Press, 1993), part 3, 'Remaking the World Through Militancy'. This is volume 3 of the five volumes of the Fundamentalism Project of the American Academy of Arts and Sciences (referenced in note 38 to Chapter 1 above). On the claim to remake world order see also Daniel Philpott, 'The Challenge of September 11 to Secularism in International Relations', *World Politics*, 55, 1 (October 2002), pp. 66–95, and the chapter 'Islamism and the Political Order' in: B. Tibi, *Islamism and Islam* (New Haven: Yale University Press, 2012), pp. 31–53. This chapter continues my earlier reasoning on the matter in point, developed in the following earlier publications on Islamic *shari'a*: 'Islamic Law/Shari'a, Human Rights, Universal Morality and International Relations', *Human Rights Quarterly* 16, 2 (May 1994), pp. 277–99; chapter 7 on *shari'a* in *Islam between Culture and Politics* (referenced in note 8 above), pp. 148–66; see also B. Tibi, 'Islamic Shari'a as Constitutional Law?' in: The Japanese Association of Comparative Constitutional Law (ed.), *Church and State Towards*

Protection for Freedom of Religion (Tokyo: Nihon University, 2006), pp. 126–70; also 'Rechtsuniversalismus und kultureller Pluralismus des Rechts, dargestellt am Beispiel der Shari'atisierung des Islam', *Nihon University Comparative Law*, 24 (2007), pp. 131–47; and, finally, 'The Return of the Sacred to Politics as Constitutional Law: The Case of Shari'atization of Politics in Islamic Civilization', *Theoria: A Journal of Social and Political Theory*, 55, 115 (April 2008), pp. 91–119.

12 Abdullahi An-Na'im, *Toward an Islamic Reformation. Civil Liberties, Human Rights and International Law* (Syracuse, NY: Syracuse University Press, 1990), p. 100; the subsequent quotation is from p. 99. In that book An-Na'im argues against *shari'a*, but in a sea change 18 years later, in a new book, *Islam and the Secular State: Negotiating the Future of Shari'a* (Harvard, MA: Harvard University Press, 2008) he approves it uncritically. These two books document a change from an enlightened critique of *shari'a* to an apologetics of it. In the chapter on secularization and de-secularization in my book *Islam's Predicament with Modernity* (referenced in note 17 to Chapter 1 above), chapter 6, pp. 178–208, I take issue with An-Na'im's new thinking, which I view as regressive.

13 The major book on this subject matter is Niyazi Berkes, *The Development of Secularism in Turkey* (New York: Routledge, new edn, 1998; first published Montreal: McGill University Press, 1964).

14 For an update see Zeyno Baran, *Torn Country: Turkey between Secularism and Islamism* (Stanford, CA: Hoover Press, 2010).

15 Mark Juergensmeyer, *The New Cold War? Religious Nationalism Confronts the Secular State* (Berkeley, CA: University of California Press, 1993) and Eric Patterson and John Gallagher, eds, *Debating the War of Ideas* (New York: Palgrave, 2009).

16 On anti-colonial *jihad* see Nikki Keddie, ed., *An Islamic Response to Imperialism* (Berkeley, CA: University of California Press, new edn, 1983), and on the Islamist political internationalism poised for a remaking of the world see B. Tibi, *Political Islam, World Politics and Europe: Democratic Peace and Euro-Islam versus Global Jihad* (New York: Routledge, 2008), parts 1 and 2.

17 Sayyid Qutb, *Ma'alim fi al-Tariq* (Cairo: Dar al-Sharuq, 13th legal edn, 1989), pp. 5–7.

18 Sayyid Qutb, *al-Salam al-Alami wa al-Islam* (Cairo: Dar al-Sharuq, 10th legal edn, 1992).

19 Raymond Aron, *Paix et guerre entre les nations* (Paris: Calmann-Lévy, 1962).

20 Jürgen Habermas, *Glauben und Wissen* (Frankfurt: Suhrkamp, 2001); for a critique see: B. Tibi, 'Habermas and the Return of the Sacred', *Religion–Staat–Gesellschaft*, 3 (2002), pp. 267–96. See also Charles Taylor, *The Secular Age* (Cambridge, MA: Belknap Press of Harvard University Press, 2007). See also the references in note 8 above.

21 John Kelsay, *Islam and War* (Louisville, KY: John Knox Press, 1993), p. 117, see also the new book by Kelsay, *Arguing the Just War in Islam* (referenced in note 3 above).

22 The classical works on *shari'a* are: Joseph Schacht, *Introduction to Islamic Law* (references in note 1 above) (here p. 1), and N. J. Coulson, *A History of Islamic Law* (Edinburgh: Edinburgh University Press, 3rd printing, 1978). For Islamic sources see notes 6–10 to Chapter 1 above.

23 The classical work by Ibn Taimiyya, *al-Siyasa al-Shari'yya*, exists in many reprints; on Ibn Taimiyya and Mawardi see chapter 5 in B. Tibi, *Der wahre Imam: Der Islam von Mohammed bis zur Gegenwart* (Munich: Piper, 1996).

24 See the related two books by Nasr H. Abu Zaid, *al-Nas, al-Sulta, al-Haqiqa/The Scripture, the Power and the Truth* (Casablanca: al-Markaz al-Thaqafi, 1995) and *Naqd al-Khitab al-Dini/Critique of Religious Discourse* (Cairo: Madbuli, 1995).

25 A full reference to the published version of this Tokyo paper is given in note 11 above.

26 In addition to B. Tibi, 'Islamic Law/Shari'a, Human Rights, Universal Morality and International Relations' (referenced in note 11 above), see B. Tibi, 'The European Tradition of Human Rights and the Culture of Islam', included as chapter 5 in: Francis

Deng and Abdullahi An-Na'im, eds, *Human Rights: Cross-Cultural Perspectives* (Washington/DC: Brookings Institution, 1990), pp. 104–32.

27 On this theme see the results of the University of California, Berkeley project 'Islam and the Changing Identity of Europe', published as Nezar AlSayyad and Manuel Castells, eds, *Muslim Europe or Euro-Islam* (Lanham and New York: Lexington Books, 2002), and herein B. Tibi's chapter on Euro-Islam, pp. 31–52. See also B. Tibi, 'Europeanizing Islam or the Islamization of Europe', in: Timothy Byrnes and Peter Katzenstein, eds, *Religion in an Expanding Europe* (Cambridge: Cambridge University Press, 2006), pp. 204–24. Here, I argue, as the subtitle of the contribution indicates, that there is a choice of 'political democracy vs. cultural difference', and stand for a veto against particularisms as rights. This argument is elaborated upon in the chapter 'Euro-Islam as a Vision for Bridging' in my recent book *Islam in Global Politics: Conflict and Cross-Civilizational Bridging* (New York: Routledge, 2012), pp. 111–39.

28 On this subject see in particular B. Tibi, *Islam's Predicament with Modernity: Religious Reform and Cultural Change* (New York: Routledge, 2009), chapter 3 on law, pp. 95–129.

29 For pertinent examples see the books by two late sheykhs of al-Azhar, Mahmud Schaltut, *al-Islam, Aqida wa Shari'a/Islam Is a Religious Doctrine and Law* (Cairo: al-Shuruq, 10th edn, 1980) and, later, Jadulhaq Ali Jadulhaq, who edited the authoritative al-Azhar textbook, *Bayan li al-Nas/Declaration to Humanity*, in two volumes (Cairo: al-Azhar, 1984 and 1988). In these books *tashri'*/legislation is equated with *wahi*/revelation. Allah is viewed as the supreme legislator. The *faqih*s are supposed to know best what God legislates. This thinking leads to the confusion of *shari'a* and *fiqh*.

30 See Najib al-Armanazi, *al-Shar' al-Duwali fi al-Islam*/International Law in Islam (London: Riad El-Rayyes, new printing, 1990; based on a Sorbonne doctoral thesis, first published Damascus, 1930), and Ashmawi referenced in note 1 above.

31 See the references in note 29 and Subhi al-Salih, *Ma'alim al-Shari'a al-Islamiyya/Essential Characteristics of Islamic Law* (Beirut: Dar al-Ilm Lilmalayin, 1975), pp. 122ff.

32 For an early but powerful contribution in this direction see the constitutional study by Mohammed D. al-Rayyes, *al-Nazariyyat al-Siyasiyya al-Islamiyya/Islamic Political Theories* (Cairo, 1953).

33 On *post eventum* legal thinking in Islam see Sir Hamilton A. R. Gibb, *Studies in the Civilization of Islam* (Princeton, NJ: Princeton University Press, 1962), part 2, in particular pp. 154–62.

34 The origin of the term is Terence Ranger and Eric Hobsbawm, eds, *The Invention of Tradition* (Cambridge: Cambridge University Press, 1983), here the introduction, pp. 1–14 by Hobsbawm. The evidence for the assessment of Islamism as an invention of tradition is provided by B. Tibi, *Islamism and Islam* (New Haven, CT: Yale University Press, 2012).

35 The idea of *hakimiyyat Allah* can be traced back to Sayyid Qutb, *Ma'alim fi al-Tariq/Signposts along the Road* (Cairo: al-Shuruq, 13th legal printing, 1989).

36 For a case study on the cultural sources of tensions that develop into conflict see B. Tibi, 'Islam between Religious-Cultural Practice and Identity Politics', completed for the project led by Helmut Anheier and Y. Raj Isar, eds, *Conflicts and Tensions* (Los Angeles: Sage, 2007), pp. 221–31; see also chapter 5 in B. Tibi, *Islam's Predicament with Modernity*, pp. 147–77.

37 H. L. A. Hart, *The Concept of Law* (Oxford: Clarendon Press, 2nd printing, 1970), p. 221. See also on international law Michael Akehurst, *A Modern Introduction to International Law* (London: Unwin Hyman, 6th edn, 1987), pp. 21f. The classic work by F. S. C. Northrop, *The Taming of the Nations: A Study of the Cultural Basis of International Policy*, is fortunately reprinted in a 2nd edition (Woodbridge, CT: Ox Bow Press, 1987). The basic issues of international law are discussed by Terry Nardin, *Law, Morality and the Relations of States* (Princeton, NJ: Princeton University Press, 1983).

38 Abdou Filali-Ansary, 'Muslims and Democracy', in: Larry Diamond, Marc F. Plattner and Daniel Brumberg, eds, *Islam and Democracy in the Middle East* (Baltimore, MD: Johns Hopkins University Press, 2003), pp. 193–207, here pp. 205–6.

39 This issue was discussed earlier in contributions to the volume edited by Tore Lindholm and Kari Vogt, *Islamic Law Reform and Human Rights: Challengers and Rejoinders* (Copenhagen and Oslo: Nordic Human Rights Publications, 1993). In addition to the chapter by An-Na'im and Mohammed Arkoun, this volume also contains my own on this subject, pp. 75–96. This reformist Muslim reasoning is not shared by Tariq Ramadan; he claims to present 'radical reform', but the reader fails to find any reform beyond neo-Salafism in Tariq Ramadan, *Radical Reform: Islamic Ethics and Liberation* (Oxford: Oxford University Press, 2008). For a dispute with Ramadan, see my chapter in Zeyno Baran, ed., *The Other Muslims: Moderate and Secular* (New York: Palgrave: 2010). The best exit in this situation is offered by Mohammed Said al-Ashmawi, *al-Shari'a al-Islamiyya wa al-Qanun al Misri/Islamic Shari'a and Egyptian Law* (Cairo: Madbuli, 1996), pp. 17–27. For an Islamic debate on this issue see Salah al-Sawi, *al-Muhawara: Musajala Fikriyya haul Qadiyyata Tatbiq al Shari'a/The Dialogue: An Intellectual Debate on the Problems of the Implementation of Shari'a* (Cairo: Dar al-Islam, 1992).

40 For an interesting interpretation see W. M. Watt, *Islamic Revelation in the Modern World* (Edinburgh: Edinburgh University Press, 1969). See also W. M. Watt, *Islamic Political Thought: The Basic Concepts* (Edinburgh: Edinburgh University Press, 1969), p. 91, and B. Tibi, 'War and Peace in Islam', in: Terry Nardin, ed., *The Ethics of War and Peace: Religious and Secular Perspectives* (Princeton, NJ: Princeton University Press, 1996), pp. 128–45.

41 Mohammed Abed al-Jabri, *Arab Islamic Philosophy* (Austin, TX: University of Texas Press, 1999). See the references to al-Jabri in note 14 to Chapter 5. This project revives the tradition of Islamic rationalism; for more details see W. M. Watt, *Islamic Philosophy and Theology* (Edinburgh: Edinburgh University Press, 5th printing, 1979), pp. 37ff. and 91ff. See also note 41 to Chapter 1 above. On Islamic humanism see B. Tibi, *Islam in Global Politics*, pp. 85–110, and also, by the same author, 'Bridging the Heterogenity of Civilizations: Reviving the Grammar of Islamic Humanism', *Theoria: A Journal of Political and Social Theory*, 56, 120, (2009), pp. 65–80.

42 Josef Esser, *Vorverständnis und Methodenwahl in der Rechtsfindung* (Frankfurt am Main: Athenäum Verlag, 1970), p. 32.

43 Hart, *The Concept of Law* (referenced in note 37), p. 102.

44 See the chapter on law in B. Tibi, *Islam and the Cultural Accommodation of Social Change* (Boulder, CO: Westview Press, 1990), pp. 59–75.

45 See Charles C. Adams, *Islam and Modernism in Egypt: A Study of the Modern Reform Movement* (London, 2nd printing, 1968; first published 1933), and also Norman Anderson, *Law Reform in the Muslim World* (London: Athlone Press, 1976).

46 See, for example, Sabir Tuaima, *al-Shari'a al-Islamiyya fi Asr al-Ilm/Islamic Law in the Age of Science* (Beirut: Dar al-Jil, 1979), pp. 208ff.

47 See the reference to the late Nasr Hamed Abu-Zaid, *al Tafkir fi Asr al-Takfir* in note 4 above.

48 Malcolm Kerr, *Islamic Reform: The Political and Legal Theories of Muhammad Abduh and Rashid Rida* (Berkeley and Los Angeles, CA: University of California Press, 1966).

49 Muhammad Muslehuddin, *Philosophy in Islamic Law and the Orientalists: A Comparative Study of Islamic Legal System* (Pakistan: Lahore, no date). The quotes are from pp. 247 and 242.

50 See the general references in note 36 above and, more specifically, N. J. Coulson, *Conflicts and Tensions in Islamic Jurisprudence* (Chicago, IL: University of Chicago Press, 1969), p. 2; see also N. J. Coulson, 'The Concept of Progress and Islamic Law', in: Robert N. Bellah, ed., *Religion and Progress in Modern Asia* (New York: Free Press, 1965), pp. 74–92; as well as N. J. Coulson and Norman Anderson, 'Modernization: Islamic Law', in: Michael Brett, ed., *Northern Africa: Islam and Modernization* (London: Cass, 1973), pp. 73–83.

51 See my contributions on these issues to both volumes of Lawrence Harrison and others, eds, *Developing Cultures* (New York: Routledge, 2006, in two volumes). Volume 1 consists of essays on cultural change, volume 2 of case studies.

52 Ernst Bloch, *Avicenna und die Aristotelische Linke* (Frankfurt am Main: Suhrkamp, 1963). Avicenna's (Ibn Sina's) rationalism is one of the sources of 'enlightened Muslim thought'.

3 The challenge of the Islamist *shari'a* state to international order: torn between the Westphalian synthesis, *Pax Americana* and *Pax Islamica*

1 The author of this news analysis is Scott Shane, 'Gains by Islamists Force US to Reassess Its Views about Friends and Foes', *IHT*, July 10, 2012, front page.

2 The contributions of Abdou Filali-Ansary, 'The Sources of Enlightened Muslim Thought' and 'Muslims and Democracy', are included in: Larry Diamond and others, eds, *Islam and Democracy in the Middle East* (Baltimore, MD: Johns Hopkins University Press, 2003), pp. 193–207 and 237–51. The quotations are from pp. 246, 247 and 207. The reference is to Ali Abdelraziq, *al-Islam wa Usul al-Hukm/Islam and the Patterns of Government* (Beirut: reprinted Matabat al-Hayat, 1966, first published, 1925). For more details, see chapter 8 in B. Tibi, *Arab Nationalism* (New York: Macmillan, 3rd edn, 1997), pp. 170–7, on Abdelraziq and on Afghani's pan-Islamism. In this context see also the insightful book by the Egyptian Supreme Court judge Mohammed Said al-Ashmawi, *al-Khilafa al-Islamiyya/The Islamic Caliphate* (Cairo: Dar Sina, 1990). On the pivotal place of governance in *shari'a* reasoning see John Kelsay, *Arguing the Just War in Islam* (Cambridge, MA: Harvard University Press, 2007), p. 166.

3 B. Tibi, *Der wahre Imam: Der Islam von Mohammed bis zur Gegenwart* (Munich: Piper, 1996), part 2 (chapters 4–6) on medieval Islamic thought.

4 Hodgson's work is among the sources of inspiration for defying the Islamist contention that the *shari'a* state is based in the Islamic faith. The distinctions that I adopt from Marshall G. S. Hodgson, *The Venture of Islam: Conscience and History in a World Civilization*, 3 volumes (Chicago, IL: University of Chicago Press, 1977) have already been discussed in Chapter 1 above. My admiration of Hodgson's work also applies to his placing of Islamic history in world history; see his book *Rethinking World History: Essays on Europe, Islam and World History* (New York: Cambridge University Press, 1995). I also share Hodgson views about *shari'a* in the understanding of law as a historical product, not as the religious faith of Islam.

5 On this distinction see Joseph Schacht, *An Introduction To Islamic Law* (Oxford: Clarendon Press, 1979), pp. 54–5.

6 The source of this slogan is Yusuf al-Qaradawi, *Hatmiyyat al-Hall al-Islami/The Necessity of the Islamic Solution* (in 3 volumes), volume 1, *al-Hulul al-Mustawrada/ The Imported Solutions* (Beirut: al-Risalah, 1980, reprint). The idea of an 'Islamic *shari'a* state' is elaborated upon by Qaradawi in volume 2 (Beirut: al-Risalah, 1974), pp. 87–94 and 240–2. All six basic features of Islamism are dealt with in chapters 2–8 in B. Tibi, *Islamism and Islam* (New Haven, CT: Yale University Press, 2012). The existence of these features is demonstrated in the work of al-Qaradawi, who is close to the new Egyptian president Mohammed Morsi. They appeared jointly as speakers on Tahrir Square.

7 There are four major books on this internal crisis, three of them by Muslim scholars. The Muslim contributions were published successively in this order: B. Tibi, *The Crisis of Modern Islam* (Salt Lake City, UT: Utah University Press, 1988); Ali A. Allawi, *The Crisis of Islamic Civilization* (New Haven, CT: Yale University Press, 2009); Hichem Djait, *Islamic Culture in Crisis* (New Brunswick, NJ: Transaction, 2010). The fourth book is by Bernard Lewis, *The Crisis of Islam* (London: Weidenfeld and Nicolson, 2003). Underlying this civilizational crisis is a predicament analysed by B. Tibi, *Islam's*

Predicament with Modernity: Religious Reform and Cultural Change (New York: Routledge, 2009). This understanding of cultural modernity rests on Jürgen Habermas, *The Philosphical Discourse of Modernity* (Cambridge, MA: MIT Press, 1986).

8 The problem of minorities in Islam is not a new one, nor is it restricted to the *shari'a* state. See Bat Ye'or, *Islam and Dhimmitude: When Civilizations Collide* (Cranbury, NJ: Associated Universities Press, 2002). What is claimed to be Islamic tolerance in treating minorities does not fulfil current standards of international human rights. Even classical *shari'a* is in conflict with modern standards of human rights. See Yohanan Friedman, *Tolerance and Coercion in Islam: Interfaith Relations in the Muslim Tradition* (New York: Cambridge University Press, 2003); B. Tibi, 'Islamic Law/*Shari'a*, Human Rights, Universal Morality and International Relations', in: *Human Rights Quarterly*, 16, 2 (1994), pp. 277–99; and B. Tibi, 'The Return of the Sacred to Politics: The Case of Shari'atization of Politics in Islamic Civilization', in: *Theoria: A Journal for Political and Social Theory*, 55, 115 (April 2008), pp. 91–119.

9 See Hannah Arendt, *The Origins of Totalitarianism* (New York: Harcourt Inc., 1951, reprinted, 1976) and the chapter 'Islamism and Totalitarianism' in B. Tibi, *Islamism and Islam* (referenced in note 6 above), pp. 201–41, which draws on Arendt's theory. These views are also shared by Paul Berman; see his *The Flight of the Intellectuals: The Controversy over Islamism and the Press* (New York: Melville House, new edn, 2011).

10 See Hedley Bull (note 33) and in this tradition Daniel Philpott, 'The Challenge of September 11 to Secularism in International Relations', in: *World Politics*, 55, 1 (2002), pp. 66–95, who defends the Westphalian world order. In contrast to Philpott, the Turkish Muslim scholar Turan Kayaoglu accuses the Westphalian synthesis of Eurocentrism; see his 'Westphalian Eurocentrism in International Relations Theory', in: *International Studies Review*, 12, 2 (2010), pp. 193–217.

11 This issue was addressed in the debate on Islamist parties and democracy that consists of eight contributions published in: *Journal of Democracy*, 19, 3 (July 2008), pp. 5–54. Among these contributions is B. Tibi, 'Islamist Parties: Why They Can't Be Democratic', pp. 43–8. See also the chapter on Islamism and democracy in B. Tibi, *Political Islam, World Politics and Europe: Democratic Peace and Euro-Islam Versus Global Jihad* (New York: Routledge, 2008), pp. 216–34.

12 Hasan Hanafi, *al-Usuliyya al-Islamiyya/Islamic Fundamentalism* (Cairo: Madbuli, 1989). See also note 66 below.

13 See the classic by Richard P. Mitchell, *The Society of the Muslim Brothers* (London: Oxford University Press, 1969), a seminal work also available in a new reprint.

14 Mohammed Imara, *al-Sahwa al-Islamiyya wa al-Tahddi al-Hadari/The Islamic Awakening and the Civilizational Challenge* (Cairo: Dar al-Shuruq, 1991). In this line, Tariq Ramadan wrongly states in his questionable book, *Aux Sources du renouveau musulman. D'al-Afghani à Hassan al-Banna. Un Siècle de réformisme islamique* (Paris: Bayard Édition, 1998), that there is a historical and intellectual continuity of an awakening between the nineteenth-century revivalist al-Afghani and his grandfather al-Banna. In fact, al-Banna was by no means a revivalist, but truly – in an invention of tradition – the founder of jihadist Islamism.

15 For an example of such naive and simplistic as well as highly confused articles, see the contribution by Ermin Sinanovic, 'Islamic Revival as Development', in: *Politics, Religion and Ideology*, 13, 1 (2012), pp. 3–24.

16 On the politics of Islamist recruitment in the West see Lorenzo Vidino, *Al-Qaeda in Europe: The New Battleground of International Jihad* (Amherst, NY: Prometheus, 2006), as well as his more recent book *The New Muslim Brotherhood in the West* (New York: Columbia University Press, 2010). In general on the Islamic diaspora in Western Europe see B. Tibi, 'Muslim Migrants in Europe: Between Euro-Islam and Ghettoization', in: N. Alsayyad and M. Castells, eds, *Muslim Europe or Euro-Islam* (New York: Lexington Books, 2002), pp. 31–52, and B. Tibi, 'The Return of Ethnicity to Europe

via Islamic Migration?' in: Roland Hsu, ed., *Ethnic Europe* (Stanford, CA: Stanford University Press, 2010), pp. 127–56.

17 Sayyid Qutb, *al-Salam al-Alami wa al-Islam/World Peace and Islam* (Cairo: Dar al-Shuruq, 1992, reprint), pp. 172–3, not only argues for a new *jihad* as an 'Islamic world revolution', but also for a remaking of world order in line with Islamist tenets. This view is shared by the contemporary moderate Islamist Hasan Hanafi, expressed in these words: 'In the past, Islam found its way between two falling empires, the Persian and the Roman. Both were exhausted by wars. Both suffered moral and spiritual crises. Islam, as a new world order, was able to expand as a substitute to the old regime. Nowadays, Islam finds itself again a new power, making its way between the two superpowers in crises. Islam is regenerating, the two superpowers are degenerating. Islam is the power of the future, inheriting the two superpowers in the present.' Quoted by Martin Kramer, *Arab Awakening and Muslim Revival* (New Brunswick, NJ: Transaction Publishers, 1996), pp. 155–6.

18 John Kelsay, *Arguing the Just War in Islam* (referenced in note 2 above), pp. 165–6.

19 On these distinctions see B. Tibi, 'War and Peace in Islam', in: Terry Nardin, ed., *The Ethics of War and Peace* (Princeton, NJ: Princeton University Press, 1996, reprinted, 1998), pp. 128–45. For a general view see Jean Bethke Elshtain, *Just War Against Terror* (New York: Basic Books, 2003).

20 For more details on the AKP and the Movement of the Muslim Brothers, see B. Tibi, *Islamism and Islam* (referenced in note 6 above), pp. 98–105 and 124–33. The background of Islamism in Turkey is covered by Marvine Howe, *Turkey Today: A Nation Divided under Islam's Revival* (Boulder, CO: Westview Press, 2000); see also B. Tibi, 'Turkey's Islamist Danger: Islamists Approach Europe', in: *Middle East Quarterly*, 16, 1 (2009), pp. 47–54. There are two new insightful books on Turkey under AKP rule: Zeyno Baran, *Torn Country: Turkey Between Secularism and Islamism* (Stanford, CA: Hoover Institution, 2010), and Birol Yesilada and Barry Rubin, eds, *The Islamization of Turkey under AKP Rule* (New York: Routledge, 2011).

21 On internationalist jihadism see Peter Bergen, *Holy War, Inc. Inside the Secret World of Osama Bin Laden* (New York: Free Press, 2001). On the need for distinctions in dealing with the Islamist challenge to national and international security see B. Tibi, 'Religious Extremism or Religionization of Politics? The Ideological Foundations of Political Islam', pp. 11–37, in: Hillel Frisch and Efraim Inbar, eds, *Radical Islam and International Security* (New York: Routledge, 2008). Unfortunately, the security community fails to grasp these distinctions, as a review article published in *Terrorism and Political Violence* (2012) reveals.

22 On this peculiar assessment by a British politician see the report by James Slack, 'Terrorism? We'll Call It Anti-Islamic', in: *Daily Mail*, January 18, 2008, p. 8.

23 See B. Tibi, *Islam between Culture and Politics* (New York: Palgrave in association with Harvard's Weatherhead Center for International Affairs, 2001, new expanded edn, 2005), chapter 2. On this subject matter see also my contribution to the Fundamentalism Project referenced in note 66 below.

24 The work of Qutb is referenced in notes 17 and 29. The work of Hasan al-Banna is collected in the volume *Majmu'at Rasa'il al-Imam al-Shahid/Collected Essays of the Martyr Imam* (Cairo: Dar al-Da'wa, 1990). This collection includes the fundamental essay on the new Islamist interpretation of *jihad*, pp. 271–92.

25 On the Six-Day War and its effects see B. Tibi, *Conflict and War in the Middle East: From Interstate War to New Security* (New York: St. Martin's Press, 1993; 2nd edn, 1998), chapters 3 and 4. The earlier book by Fouad Ajami, *The Arab Predicament: Arab Political Thought and Practice since 1967* (Cambridge: Cambridge University Press, 1981), is relevant for the understanding of the aftermath of 1967. In contrast to Ajami's later work, this book continues to be a useful resource on the repercussions of the Six-Day War. See also note 34 below.

26 On the case of Egypt see Carry Rosefsky Wickham, *Mobilizing Islam* (New York:

Columbia University Press, 2003) as well as B. Tibi, 'Egypt as a Model of Development for the World of Islam', in: Larry Harrison and Peter L. Berger, eds, *Developing Cultures: Case Studies* (New York: Routledge, 2006), pp. 163–80. This volume grew from the Culture Matters Research Project. See also the chapter on Egypt in B. Tibi, *Islam's Predicament with Modernity* (referenced in note 7 above), pp. 265–89.

27 Hedley Bull, 'Revolt against the West', in: Hedley Bull and A. Watson, eds, *The Expansion of International Society* (Oxford: Clarendon Press, 1984), pp. 217–28. The revolt is also against the secular order; on this issue see B. Tibi, 'Secularization and Desecularization in Islam', in: *Religion–Staat–Gesellschaft*, 1, 1 (2000), pp. 95–117, and B. Tibi, *Islam's Predicament with Modernity* (referenced in note 7 above), chapter 6, pp. 178–208.

28 See the contributions in Eric Patterson and John Gallagher, eds, *Debating the War of Ideas* (New York: Palgrave, 2009).

29 Sayyid Qutb, *Ma'alim fi al-Tariq/Signposts along the Road* (Cairo: Dar al-Shuruq, legal edition, reprinted, 1989), pp. 5–10 and 201–2. See also the references in note 17 above.

30 Roxanne Euben, *Enemy in the Mirror: Islamic Fundamentalism and the Limits of Modern Rationalism* (Princeton, NJ: Princeton University Press, 1999), pp. 54–5.

31 David Cook, *Understanding Jihad* (Berkeley, CA: University of California Press, 2005), p. 102.

32 The Qutb quotations are from *Ma'alim fi al-Tariq*, pp. 150–1. See also Albert J. Bergesen, ed., *The Sayyid Qutb Reader: Selected Writings on Politics, Religion and Society* (New York: Routledge, 2008). On the Islamic conformism of al-Nasiri, see B. Tibi, 'War and Peace in Islam' (see note 19 above), pp. 134–5.

33 See the reference in note 10 above and the major work by Hedley Bull, *The Anarchical Society: A Study of Order in World Politics* (New York: Columbia Press, 1977), pp. 20–2, 276–81.

34 The book by Charles Hill, *Trial of a Thousand Years: World Order and Islamism* (Stanford, CA: Hoover Institution Press, 2011) – prefaced by Fouad Ajami – is a disappointing, West-centered contribution, in contrast to the sound criticism of the Turkish-Muslim scholar Turan Kayaoglu (see note 10 above). I find Ajami's preface to Hill distasteful. I admired the early work of Ajami, in particular his fascinating book *The Arab Predicament* (see note 25 above). At that time I even sided with Ajami against Edward Said. However, with Ajami's disappointing development – in an apologetics in defence of US wars and of the Bush presidency – my admiration has, sadly, turned to strong criticism.

35 See Jürgen Habermas, *The Philosophical Discourse of Modernity*, p. 2, and B. Tibi, *Islam's Predicament with Modernity* (both referenced in note 7 above).

36 Richard Haas, *Wars of Necessity, Wars of Choice* (New York: Simon and Schuster, 2009), p. 278.

37 My chapter, 'International Morality and Cross-Cultural Bridging', is included in the volume by Roman Herzog, the former president of Germany, *et al.*, *Preventing the Clash of Civilizations* (New York: St. Martin's Press, 1999), pp. 107–26.

38 See note 33 above, especially the reference to Bull.

39 This interpretation of history has been admitted to the *Encyclopedia of Global Studies*, Hellmut K. Anheier and Mark Juergensmeyer, eds (Los Angeles and London: Sage, 2012), 4 volumes, here volume 1, pp. 967–71; it stands in contrast to Hill (referenced in note 34 above). See also the historical survey of the inter-civilizational history of Islam, Christianity and the West as backstory: B. Tibi, *Kreuzzug und Djihad: Der Islam und die christliche Welt* (Munich: Bertelsmann, 1999). At issue is a competition between two models for mapping the globe. On the European dimension of expansion see Geoffrey Parker, *The Military Revolution and the Rise of the West 1500–1800* (Cambridge: Cambridge University Press, 1988) and Philip Curtin, *The World and the West: The European Challenge* (Cambridge: Cambridge University Press, 2000).

40 In my view the work of the late Mohammed al-Jabri constitutes an essential part of this turn; it is a true Islamic revivalism, referred to as 'the al-Jabri project'. On this project see the appendix in al-Jabri, *al-Turath wa al-Hadatha* (Beirut: al-Markaz al-Thaqafi, 1991), pp. 241–360. On the overall historical context of this issue in which the al-Jabri project is placed, see B. Tibi, 'Islamic Humanism vs. Islamism', in: *Soundings* 95, 3 (2012), pp. 230–54.

41 See the documentation on this issue in *Harvard Human Rights Journal* 5 (Spring 1992). The issue includes a review article by B. Tibi on the universality of human rights versus authenticity on pp. 221–6.

42 Samuel P. Huntington, *The Third Wave of Democratization in the Twentieth Century* (Norman and London: University of Oklahoma Press, 1991), p. 13.

43 Charles Tilly, ed., *The Formation of the National States in Western Europe* (Princeton, NJ: Princeton University Press, 1975), p. 45.

44 Charles Tilly, *Coercion, Capital and European States* (Cambridge, MA: Basil Blackwell, 1990), p. 191.

45 See Robert Jackson, *Quasi-States: Sovereignty, International Relations and the Third World* (Cambridge: Cambridge University Press, 1990). On these 'nominal states' in the Arab world see B. Tibi, 'The Simultaneity of the Unsimultaneous: Tribes and Imposed Nation-States', in: Philip S. Khoury and Joseph Kostiner, eds, *Tribes and State Formation in the Middle East* (Berkeley, CA: University of California Press, 1990), pp. 127–52.

46 See the survey by Efraim Karsh, *Islamic Imperialism: A History* (New Haven, CT: Yale University Press, 2006), pp. 207–19, which lacks differentiations and nuances and ends up in prejudice. Disturbingly, Karsh confuses *Pax Islamica* with the insulting notion of 'Allah's Empire'. See also the survey by Alan Jamieson, *Faith and Sword: A Short History of Christian-Muslim Conflict* (London: Reaktion Books, 2006). This kind of literature is criticized in Chapter 6 (see Chapter 6, note 74).

47 On the Six-Day War of 1967 and its epochal repercussions see the references in note 25 above and the new part added to the third edition of B. Tibi, *Arab Nationalism: Between Islam and the Nation State* (New York: St. Martin's Press, 3rd edn, 1997), pp. 199–233.

48 Francis Fukuyama, *The End of History* (New York: Avon Books, 1992). As early as 1995 in *Der Krieg der Zivilisationen* (Hamburg: Hoffmann & Campe, 1995), I argued that, rather than Fukuyama's alleged end of history, there are signs of 'a return of history' occurring, in the shape of an Islamist nostalgia that revives the historical competition between civilizational models. More than a decade later, in *Political Islam: World Politics and Europe*, I took issue with Fukuyama's triumphalism, in the Introduction, in particular pp. 2–9, and in chapter 5, pp. 161–87.

49 See the references in note 45 above.

50 On authenticity, see B. Tibi, *Islamism and Islam*, chapter 7, pp. 177–200.

51 Alan Richards and John Waterbury, *A Political Economy of the Middle East* (Boulder, CO: Westview Press, 2nd edn, 1990), pp. 355 and 347.

52 On the Sunni–Shi'ite rift see B. Tibi, *Political Islam, World Politics and Europe* (New York: Routledge, 2008), part 2.

53 See Alireza Jafarzadeh, *The Iran Threat. President Ahmadinejad and the Coming Nuclear Crisis* (New York: Palgrave, 2007).

54 François Burgat and William Dowell, *The Islamic Movement in North Africa* (Austin, TX: University of Texas Press, 1993), p. 185.

55 John Kelsay, *Islam and War* (Louisville, KY: John Knox Press, 1993), pp. 115–18.

56 For references see Eric R. Wolfe, *Europe and the People Without History* (Berkeley, CA: University of California Press, new edn, 1997) and Bull, 'Revolt Against the West' (see note 27 above).

57 See B. Tibi, *Islamism and Islam* (referenced in note 6 above), chapter 3: 'Islamism and Antisemitism', pp. 54–93.

58 The quotations are from Charles Hill, *Trial of a Thousand Years* (referenced in note 34 above), pp. 65, 25–6, 27, 121, and from Ajami's preface to that book, pp. ix, xv. Hill's book makes large allegations, but has no supporting footnotes at all.

59 On this Islamic humanism see B. Tibi, *Islam in Global Politics, Conflict and Cross-Civilizational Bridging* (New York: Routledge, 2012), chapter 4.

60 Ernest Gellner, *Religion and Postmodernism* (London: Routledge, 1992), p. 84, and Franz Rosenthal, *The Classical Heritage of Islam* (London: Routledge, 1975).

61 See Immanuel Kant, *Zum ewigen Frieden* included in: *Friedensutopien* (Frankfurt am Main: Suhrkamp, 1978, reprint), revived by Bruce Russet, *Grasping Democratic Peace* (Princeton, NJ: Princeton University Press, 1993).

62 For more details see B. Tibi, *Islam in Global Politics* (referenced in note 59 above), chapter 1, and, same author, *Islamism and Islam*, chapter 1.

63 This ideology of Islam as a political order is reflected in the major works of the influential Islamists Mustafa Abu Zaid Fahmi, *Fan al-Hukm fi al-Islam/The Art of Government in Islam* (Cairo: al-Maktab al-Masri al-Hadith, 1981), and Salim al-Awwa, *Fi al-Nizam al-Siyyasi lil-Dawla al-Islamiyya/On the Political System of the Islamic State* (Cairo: al-Maktab al-Misri al-Hadith, 1981, reprinted, 1983).

64 See the published papers of the Culture Matters Research Project edited by Larry Harrison, *Developing Cultures*, 2 volumes, referenced in note 26 above; see also B. Tibi, *Islam's Predicament with Modernity* (referenced in note 7 above), subtitled: *Religious Reform and Cultural Change*.

65 Robert Hefner, *Civil Islam* (Princeton, NJ: Princeton University Press, 2000).

66 See above, Chapter 1, note 38, and Chapter 2, note 11, on the published work of the Fundamentalism Project, conducted at the American Academy of Arts and Sciences, in particular volume 3, *Fundamentalisms and the State: Remaking Polities, Economies, and Militance* (1993). The project was conducted in the years 1989–1993 and published in five volumes by the University of Chicago Press with the project chairpersons, Martin Marty and Scott Appleby, as editors. Volume 2 is *Fundamentalisms and Society: Reclaiming the Sciences, the Family, and Education* (1993); it includes B. Tibi, 'The Worldview of Sunni-Arab Fundamentalists', pp. 73–102.

4 *Shari'a* and Islamism in the 'Arab Spring': from the promise of a blossoming spring to a frosty and lethal winter

1 David D. Kirkpatrick, 'Libyan Democracy Clashes with Fervor for Jihad', *New York Times Supplement to Süddeutsche Zeitung*, July 2, 2012, p. 3.

2 The source of this approach is Charles Tilly, *Big Structures, Large Processes, Huge Comparisons* (New York: Russell Sage Foundation, 1984).

3 For more details on the leading role and exemplary place of Egypt in the MENA region see the case study provided in chapter 9 on Egypt in B. Tibi, *Islam's Predicament with Modernity* (New York: Routledge, 2009), pp. 265–89.

4 Kareem Fahim, 'Morsi Forces Key Military Leaders to Step Down', *IHT*, August 13, 2012, front page.

5 For an overview on the literature on the moderation thesis see the review article by Jillian Schwedler, 'Can Islamists Become Moderate?', *World Politics* 63, 2 (April 2011), pp. 347–76. For a critical position on these views see the references below in notes 38 and 39.

6 On this feature (one of six) that characterizes a general Islamist mindset see chapter 3 in B. Tibi, *Islamism and Islam* (New Haven, CT: Yale University Press, 2012), pp. 54–93, and on its occurrence in particular in the Arab Spring, p. 93; see also the article by Raymond Stock on this feature (referenced in note 39 below).

7 Robert Worth, 'The Unwavering Arab Spring', *IHT*, February 3, 2012, front page, continued p. 6.

8 Editorial, 'If Assad Falls in Syria', *IHT*, August 8, 2012, p. 6.

9 Neil Macfarquhar, 'Iran Begins Fervent Courtship', *IHT*, May 25, 2012, front page.

10 On the Ba'th dictatorship see the books of Middle East Watch on Syria and Iraq, *Syria Unmasked: The Suppression of Human Rights by the Assad Regime* (New Haven, CT: Yale University Press, 1991) and *Human Rights in Iraq* (New Haven, CT: Yale University Press, 1990). In particular on oppression in Iraq under Saddam Hussein see Samir al-Khalil (alias Kanan Makiyya), *Republic of Fear* (Berkeley, CA: University of California Press, 1987). Syria is also a 'republic of fear' in which Saddam's slaughtering practices are exceeded by far.

11 Daniel Byman, 'Terrorism after the Revolutions', *Foreign Affairs* (May/June 2011), pp. 48–54, here p. 51.

12 I refer repeatedly to these two fundamental, unsurpassable books by John Waterbury. The first is *The Egypt of Nasser and Sadat: The Political Economy of Two Regimes* (Princeton, NJ: Princeton University Press, 1983), see in particular p. 100. The second is Alan Richards and John Waterbury, *A Political Economy of the Middle East* (Boulder, CO: Westview Press, 2nd edn, 1990). These books are extraordinary in their quality, and continue even to be the best on this matter. See also the reference to Egypt in note 3 above.

13 Barak Barfi, 'Washington's Myopic View of Egypt', *IHT*, August 8, 2012, p. 6.

14 Daniel Lerner, *The Passing of Traditional Society: Modernizing the Middle East* (New York: Free Press of Glencoe, 1962). Instead of this transition from traditional to modern society, authoritarian regimes evolved. These too were – before the Arab Spring – not well understood in the Western academic literature. On change under these so-called 'authoritarian regimes' see the overview provided in B. Tibi, 'Reform, Change and Democratization in the Middle East in Postbipolarity', *International Studies Review*, 12, 2 (June 2010), pp. 309–15. Some people fail to learn, and this seems to be repeated in the current illusion about 'transition to civilian rule' in the context of the Arab Spring.

15 Paul Berman, *The Flight of the Intellectuals: The Controversy over Islamism and the Press* (New York: Melville House, 2011).

16 Abdou Filali-Ansary, 'The Sources of Enlightened Muslim Thought', in: Larry Diamond, Marc F. Plattner and Daniel Brumberg, eds, *Islam and Democracy in the Middle East*, pp. 237–51; the quotations are from pp. 250 and 234. See also the section on Filali-Ansary's 'enlightened turn' in Chapter 3 of the present book.

17 The proceedings of this earlier meeting in Tunis in October 1980 were published under the title *Les Arabes face à leur destin* (Tunis: Centre D'Etudes et de Recherche Economiques Sociales, 1980) with the publisher acting as editor.

18 Centre for Arab Unity Studies, ed., *Azmat al-Dimuqratiyya fi al-Watan al-Arabi/ Crisis of Democracy in the Arab World* (Beirut: Markaz Dirasat al-Wihda al-Arabiyya, 1983).

19 For the papers presented by these Arab democrats in Istanbul, see Elisabeth Özdalga and Sune Persson, eds, *Civil Society, Democracy and the Muslim World* (Istanbul: Swedish Research Institute, 1997).

20 Ali Oumlil, *Fi Shari'yyat al-Ikhtilaf/The Legitimacy of Dissent* (Rabat: al-Majlis al-Qaumi, 1991).

21 The book by Fouad Ajami, *The Dream Palace of the Arabs*, gives a distasteful image of 'the Arabs' that seeks Western favour. This book is also shamefully regressive compared with Ajami's earlier admirable book, *The Arab Predicament* (see note 25 to Chapter 3 above).

22 'Männer mit Knüppeln', *Der Spiegel*, issue 25, June 18, 2012, p. 84.

23 'Syrian Leader Claims Broad Support', *IHT*, July 10, 2012, p. 5.

24 See the chapter on 'Western Third-Worldism' (chapter 6), and the one on 'Islamic humanism' (chapter 4), both in B. Tibi, *Islam in Global Politics* (New York: Routledge, 2012).

25 See the editorial 'Syria's Cease-Fire of the Grave', *Wall Street Journal*, June 15, 2012, p. 16.

26 B. Tibi, *Islamism and Islam* (referenced in note 6 above), p. xv.

27 The editorial article by Thomas Friedman, 'Hama Rules', *IHT*, February 16, 2012, p. 7, is an unsurpassable example of first-class journalism.

28 All quotes are from Neil Macfarquhar, 'Assad's Response', *IHT*, June 11, 2012, front page, continued p. 5. The same issue includes on p. 5 the report: 'Syria Shells Rebel Area'. For accuracy 'Syria' should be changed to 'Alawi forces'.

29 Lydia Palgreen, 'Arab Uprisings Reveal Court's Flaws', *IHT*, July 9, 2012, p. 4.

30 'Al-Qaeda Slips into Syria!' *IHT*, July 26, 2012, front page, continued p. 8.

31 David Kirkpatrick, 'Egypt Dissolves Parliament', *IHT*, June 15, 2012, front page, continued p. 6.

32 David Kirkpatrick, 'A Revolution Foiled by Naiveté', *IHT*, June 16–17, 2012, p. 4; on the same page 'Security Forces in Cairo Surrounded Dissolved Parliament'; and by the same reporter 'Dissolution of the Parliament Challenges Shift for Egypt's New Leader', *IHT*, June 26, 2012, front page and p. 4.

33 Cited in the report: 'Egyptian Confrontation Heats Up', *IHT*, July 10, 2012, p. 5.

34 The first report is 'Islamists' Role Fuels a Debate Among Libyans', by Rod Nordland and David Kirkpatrick, *IHT*, September 15, 2011, front page and p. 4; the second report is by David Kirkpatrick, 'Libya Militias Turn to Politics', *IHT*, April 4, 2012, p. 5.

35 The notion 'imam' covers in Islam two meanings: (1) the religious leader of collective prayer, (2) the political leader of the *umma*. For a history of Islamic political thought as a framework for the search for the rightful imam see B. Tibi, *Der wahre Imam: Der Islam von Mohammed bis zur Gegenwart* (Munich: Piper, 1996).

36 Scott Shane, 'Gains by Islamists Force US to Reassess its Views about Friends and Foes', *IHT*, July 10, front page and p. 5, and David Kirkpatrick, 'Islamists Fall Behind in Early Libya Vote Count', *IHT*, July 9, 2012, front page and p. 5.

37 Robert Kaplan, *The Coming Anarchy* (New York: Random House, 2000). The following quotations are from pp. 59, 61, 64, 61, 69 and 71.

38 Eric Trager, 'The Unbreakable Muslim Brotherhood: Grim Prospects for a Liberal Egypt', *Foreign Affairs*, 90, 5 (2011), pp. 14–126, and, by the same author, 'The Muslim Brotherhood's Long Game: Egypt's Ruling Party Plots Its Path to Power', *Foreign Affairs*, July 6, 2012.

39 Raymond Stock, 'The Donkey, the Camel and the Facebook Scam: How the Muslim Brotherhood Conquered Egypt and Conned the World', *Foreign Policy Research Institute e-notes*, July 2012. Available at http://www.fpri.org/articles/2012/07/donkey-camel-and-facebook-scam-how-muslim-brotherhood-conquered-egypt-and-conned.

40 Emad E. Shahin, 'The Egyptian Revolution', *Journal of the Middle East and Africa*, 3, 1 (2012), pp. 46–69. The quotations are from p. 58.

41 Noah Feldman, *After Jihad: America and the Struggle for Islamic Democracy* (New York: Farrar, Strauss and Giroux, 2003, paperback 2004). The quotes are from pp. xvi, 20 and 172–3. It is shocking to see this naive trust in the 'sincerity' based on 'truth' of the Islamist Muslim Brotherhood expressed on the grounds of taking at face value what Islamists publicly state. One of the Western experts who knows Egypt best, Raymond Stock, writes in 'The Donkey, the Camel and the Facebook Scam: How the Muslim Brotherhood Conquered Egypt' (referenced in note 39 above): 'The record of their dishonesty is so indisputable that it shocks the ear to hear the voices that still trust them.' Lorenzo Vidino, too, presents in his research based on insider knowledge 'ample evidence showing that the aims of the Muslim Brothers do not . . . correspond to those publicly stated'; see his *The New Muslim Brotherhood in the West* (New York: Columbia University Press, 2010), p. 223. I also quote the French expert Caroline Fourest, who tells us that double-speak 'is a basic feature of Islamism'. Why do Islamists behave in this manner? The answer is that double-speak takes 'advantage of speaking with two voices . . . speaking with one voice to people outside [the] community and with another to people within it'. Why do they they lie? Fourest's answer is: 'to avoid exposure . . . [and] simply as a means of pursuing their ends while remaining disguised'

(pp. 24–5). They disguise themselves as Muslim democrats fighting authoritarianism in the pursuit of an 'Islamic democracy'. Islamists promise, then con the world, as Stock puts it. See Caroline Fourest, *Brother Tariq: The Doublespeak of Tariq Ramadan* (London: Encounter Books, 2008). The central figure in Fourest's book is Tariq Ramadan. He is the grandson of Hasan al-Banna, who was the founder of the Muslim Brotherhood. Some Westerners either swallow or simply overlook the facts related to Islamist double-speak in the name of respect for Islam, taking at face value everything that Islamists say. Here is a representative example, from a review of my book *Islamism and Islam* – published online for *The New Republic* – in which the reviewer, a young PhD candidate, rejects my analysis of *shari'a* based on three decades of research in twenty Islamic countries: in evidence he cites a US imam of New York who says that US democratic values 'and the US constitution are the embodiment of Islamic values and the Sharia. Therefore . . . America is a Sharia compliant state' (Samuel Helfont, 'Term Warfare', *The New Republic*, July 11, 2012). I leave it to the intelligence of my readers to make a judgement about the allegation that the US is an example of a 'Sharia compliant state'. See the references to Eric Trager and Filali-Ansary on this subject of Islamists playing games with non-Islamists, both in Islamdom and in the West.

42 Noah Feldman, *The Fall and the Rise of the Islamic State* (Princeton, NJ: Princeton University Press, 2008), pp. 148–9.

43 See the books by Sohail Hashmi, ed., *Political Ethics: Civil Society, Pluralism* (Princeton, NJ: Princeton University Press, 2002) and Michèle Schmiegelow, ed., *Democracy in Asia* (New York: Campus, 1997). Both books include chapters by me and both argue for the ethical compatibility of Islam (not of Islamism) with democracy.

44 Sayyid Qutb, *Ma'alim fi al-Tariq/Signposts along the Road* (Cairo: Dar al-Shuruq, 13th legal edition, 1989), p. 5.

45 See Anthony Reid and Michael Gilsenan, eds, *Islamic Legitimacy in a Plural Asia* (London: Routledge, 2007); my chapter is on pp. 28–52.

46 B. Tibi, *Islam between Culture and Politics* (New York: Palgrave Macmillan in association with the Weatherhead Center for International Affairs, 2nd edn, 2005), preface to the second edition, p. xix.

47 Editorial, 'Iraq's Latest Battle', *IHT*, December 23, 2011, p. 6.

48 Ali Allawi *et al.*, 'How to Save Iraq', *IHT*, December 29, 2011, p. 8.

49 Thomas Friedman, 'Looking for Luck in Libya', *IHT*, March 23, 2011, p. 9.

50 More nuances are included in the chapter 'Can the Middle East Democratize?' by Larry Diamond, *The Spirit of Democracy: The Struggle to Build Free Societies Throughout the World* (New York: Times Books/Henry Holt, 2008). For more details on democracy in Islamdom see chapter 7 on democracy in B. Tibi, *Political Islam, World Politics and Europe* (London: Routledge, 2008), pp. 216–34.

51 Thomas Friedman, 'Pay Attention', *IHT*, May 30, 2011, p. 9.

52 Michael Slackman, 'To Egypt's Better Organized Go the Spoils', *IHT*, March 25, 2011, front page.

53 David Kirckpatrick, 'The Brotherhood Flexes its Muscles', *IHT*, November 30, 2011, p. 4.

54 Anthony Shadid, 'Arab Spring Turns to Blazing Summer', *IHT*, August 26, 2011, p. 5.

55 Nicholas D. Kristof, 'Democracy is Messy', *IHT*, April 1, 2011, p. 7.

56 Abdou Filali-Ansary, discussed in Chapter 3 above.

57 Khairi Abaza, 'Is Egypt Flying Apart at the Seams', *IHT*, December 24–25, 2011, p. 6.

58 This theme dominated the social science based development studies in the 1960s. The related debates are extensively covered in B. Tibi, *Militär und Sozialismus in der Dritten Welt* (Frankfurt am Main: Suhrkamp, 1973).

59 Lorenzo Vidino, *The New Muslim Brotherhood in the West* (referenced in note 41 above).

60 See the country case study by Robert Hefner, *Civil Islam* (Princeton, NJ: Princeton University Press, 2000).

61 'Islamists' Role Fuels a Debate', referenced in note 34 above.

62 Associated Press, 'Erdogan in Cairo Touts Turkey as Model for All Arab Nations', *Haaretz* supplement to *IHT*, September 15, 2011, p. 2.

63 Nabil Abdel Fattah, quoted in the report 'Erdogan in Cairo', *Jerusalem Post*, September 14, 2011. On this AKP orientation see B. Tibi, *Islamism and Islam* (referenced in note 6 above), pp. 98–103.

64 Quoted in Anthony Shadid, 'Arab World Turns to Defining Islam after Revolt', *IHT*, September 30, 2011, front page, continued p. 7.

65 John Stuart Mill, *On Liberty* (originally 1859; quoted from the Oxford University Press edn, 1998), p. 9. On 'Political Islam and Democracy's Decline to a Voting Procedure' see the chapter entitled thus in B. Tibi, *Political Islam, World Politics and Europe* (referenced in note 50 above), pp. 216–34.

66 Amitai Etzioni, 'Tunisia: The First Arab Islamocracy', in: *The National Interest*, October 26, 2011. Available online at http://nationalinterest.org/commentary/tunisia-the-first-arab-islamocracy-6084.

67 On these two pertinent issues see, first, B. Tibi, 'Islamic Law, Shari'a, Human Rights and Universal Morality', *Human Rights Quarterly*, 16, 2 (1994), pp. 277–99; and, second, B. Tibi, 'Global Communication and Cultural Particularisms', in: Robert Fortner and Mark Fackler, eds, *Handbook of Global Communication*, in 2 volumes (Oxford: Wiley Blackwell, 2010), here volume 1, pp. 54–78.

68 Reza Afshari, 'An Essay on Islamic Cultural Relativism in the Discourse of Human Rights', *Human Rights Quarterly*, 16, 2 (1994), pp. 235–76.

69 Abdou Filali-Ansary, 'Muslims and Democracy', in: Diamond *et al. Islam and Democracy in the Middle East*, note 16 above, here p. 206.

70 On these themes see the contributions included in Roman Herzog *et al., Preventing the Clash of Civilizations* (New York: Palgrave, 1999) and the assembled essays in B. Tibi, *Islam in Global Politics: Conflict and Cross-Civilizational Bridging* (London and New York: Routledge, 2012).

71 Abdou Filali-Ansary (as in note 69 above), p. 207.

5 From traditional *shari'a* reasoning to Islamist *shari'a*tization of politics in the post-Arab Spring

1 Emad E. Shahin, 'The Egyptian Revolution: The Power of Mass Mobilization and the Spirit of Tahrir Square', *Journal of the Middle East and Africa*, 3, 2 (2012), pp. 46–69, here p. 58.

2 Hamid Enayat, *Modern Islamic Political Thought* (Austin, TX: University of Texas Press, 1982), p. 67.

3 Editorial, 'Morsi and his Critics', *IHT*, August 27, 2012, p. 8.

4 For more details see Bernard Lewis, *The Emergence of Modern Turkey* (London: Oxford University Press, 1961, 2nd edn, 1979), pp. 271–4 and chapter 8, pp. 239–93, as well as chapter 12, pp. 401–42. See also Niyazi Berkes, *The Development of Secularism in Turkey* (London: Routledge, 1998; first pub. 1964), pp. 467–78.

5 Abdou Filali-Ansary, 'Sources of Enlightened Muslim Thought', in: Larry Diamond, Marc F. Plattner and Daniel Brumberg, eds, *Islam and Democracy in the Middle East* (Baltimore, MD: Johns Hopkins University Press, 2003), pp. 237–51.

6 Ali Abdelraziq, *al-Islam wa Usul al-Hukm* (Beirut: Maktabat al-Hayat, 1966; first pub. 1925), p. 201. Abdelraziq emphasizes the spirituality of the Islamic faith. The contrast to Abdelraziq's enlightenment is the Islamist *shari'a*tization as an invention of tradition. For more details see B. Tibi, *Islamism and Islam* (New Haven, CT: Yale University Press, 2012), pp. 158–76.

7 John Kelsay, *Arguing the Just War in Islam* (Cambridge, MA: Harvard University Press, 2007). The following quotations are from pp. 125 and 137, and further to pp. 126, 141–3, 166–97, 165–6, 167. For a dialogue with Kelsay focusing on the book, see B. Tibi, 'John Kelsay and "Shari'a Reasoning" in Just War in Islam', *Journal of Church and State*, 53, 1 (2011), pp. 4–26.

8 For a criticism on Sachedina and his inconsistencies regarding Islam and pluralism see B. Tibi, 'The Predicament of Islam with Democratic Pluralism', *Religion–Staat–Gesellschaft*, 7, 1 (2006), pp. 83–117.

9 The new book by Abdullahi An-Na'im, *Islam and the Secular State: Negotiating the Future of Shari'a* (Cambridge, MA: Harvard University Press, 2008), in particular p. 290, is a step backwards in comparison with his earlier accomplishments. See Chapter 2, note 12, above.

10 Ahmed bin Khalid al-Nasiri, *al-Istiqsa' fi Akhbar Duwal al-Maghreb*, 9 volumes, published in a reprint by Dar al-Kitab (Casablanca, 1955); on al-Nasiri, see the monograph devoted to al-Nasiri's work by Abdullatif Husni, *al-Islam wa al-Alaqat al-Duwaliyya* (Casablanca: Ifriqiya al-Sharq, 1991) and chapter 1 in B. Tibi, *Political Islam, World Politics and Europe* (New York: Routledge, 2008), in particular pp. 53–8.

11 Jadulhaq Ali Jadulhaq on behalf of al-Azhar, *Bayan lil Nas*, 2 volumes (Cairo: al-Azhar, 1984, 1988). By then Jadulhaq was the sheykh/rector of al-Azhar in Cairo.

12 See Yusuf al-Qaradawi, *Hatmiyyat al-Hall al-Islami*, 3 volumes (exists in numerous reprints, published in Cairo and Beirut) and Daniel Philpott, 'The Challenge of September 11 to Secularism in International Relations', *World Politics*, 55, 1 (2002), pp. 66–95. The article by Turan Kayaoglu, 'Westphalian Eurocentrism in International Relations Theory', *International Studies Review*, 12 (2010), pp. 193–217 is honest, but it obviously overlooks the congeniality to the Islamist rejection of the Westphalian synthesis. On this debate see Chapter 3 of the present book.

13 On the competition carried out as a kind of a war of ideas between *falsafa* and *fiqh* in medieval Islam see B. Tibi, 'Politisches Denken im klassischen und mittelalterlichen Islam zwischen Fiqh und Falsafa', chapter 3 in: Iring Fetscher, ed. *Pipers Handbuch der Politischen Ideen*, 5 volumes, here volume 2 (Munich: Piper, 1993), pp. 87–174.

14 Mohammed Abed al-Jabri, *Takwin al-Aql al-Arabi* (Beirut: Dar al-Tali'a, 1984) and also on the al-Jabri project see the appendix to al-Jabri, *al-Turath wa al-Hadatha* (Beirut: al-Markaz al-Thaqali, 1991).

15 Here I draw methodologically on the historical sociology of Charles Tilly, *Big Structures, Large Processes, Huge Comparisons* (New York: Russell Sage Foundation, 1984). In this orientation I completed my two books on overall Islamic history: *Der wahre Imam. Der Islam von Mohammed bis zur Gegenwart* (Munich: Piper, 1996) and *Kreuzzug und Djihad* (Munich: Bertelsmann, 1999).

16 For detailed references see note 13 above and also B. Tibi, *Der wahre Imam* (referenced in note 15 above), chapter 4 on Farabi, chapter 5 on Mawardi and Ibn Taimiyya, and chapter 6 on Ibn Khaldun. For a recent work on this subject see Peter Adamson and Richard C. Taylor, eds, *Cambridge Companion to Arabic Philosophy* (Cambridge: Cambridge University Press, 2005).

17 Mohammed Abed al-Jabri, *Arab Islamic Philosophy* (Austin, TX: CMES – University of Texas, 1999), p. 124, see also note 14 above and also the book by al-Jabri, *al-Turath wa al-Hadatha* referenced there.

18 On this Hellenization see W. M. Watt, *Islamic Philosophy and Theology* (Edinburgh: Edinburgh University Press, 1962, reprint, 1979), parts 2 and 3. See also Franz Rosenthal, *The Classical Heritage of Islam* (London: Routledge, 1975, reprint, 1992). On the Islamic tradition of humanism see chapter 4, pp. 85–110 in B. Tibi, *Islam in Global Politics: Conflict and Cross-Civilizational Bridging* (New York: Routledge, 2012).

19 Anke von Kügelgen, *Averroes und die arabische Moderne* (Leiden: Brill, 1994).

20 On Arab intellectuals after 1967 see the survey by B. Tibi, 'Intellektuelle als verhinderte

Aufklärer: Das Scheitern der Intellektuellen im Islam', in: Walter Reese-Schäfer and Harald Bluhm, eds, *Die Intellektuellen und der Weltenlauf* (Baden-Baden: Nomos, 2006), pp. 97–125. The chapter argues that *shari'a* reasoning dominated twice against rationalism: in medieval Islam and in the post-1967 developments. Arabic-secular thought also existed in the liberal age; see Albert Hourani, *Arabic Thought in the Liberal Age 1798–1939* (London: Oxford University Press, 1962). In both periods secular Muslims failed to establish their new tradition.

21 For instance Rifa'a R. al-Tahtawi, *Takhlis al-Ibriz fi Talkhis Paris* (Beirut: Dar Ibn Zaidun, reprint, no date). Tahtawi was the first Muslim to study in France, between 1826 and 1832.

22 B. Tibi, *Arab Nationalism: Between Islam and the Nation-State* (New York: Macmillan, 3rd edn, 1997).

23 B. Tibi, 'The Return of the Sacred to Politics as Constitutional Law: The Case of Shari'atization of Politics in Islamic Civilization', *Theoria*, 55 (issue 115, April 2008), pp. 91–119.

24 See Abdulahi Abdul-Rahman, *Sultat al-Nas/The Authority of the Scripture* (Beirut: al-Markaz al-Thaqafi, 1993); Mohammed Said al-Ashmawi, *Usul al-Shari'a/The Origins of the Shari'a* (Cairo: Madbuli, 1983), pp. 93–8; and also al-Ashmawi, *al-Islam al-Siyasi/Political Islam* (Cairo: Madbuli, 1989), pp. 73–91.

25 For a comparison of these Sunni and Shi'ite varieties see B. Tibi, *Political Islam, World Politics and Europe: Democratic Peace and Euro-Islam vs. Global Jihad* (New York: Routledge, 2008), chapters 3 and 4.

26 On the AKP see Zeyno Baran's book, *Torn Country: Turkey between Secularism and Islamism* (Stanford, CA: Hoover Institution Press, Stanford University, 2010), and her earlier article 'Turkey Divided', *Journal of Democracy*, 19, 1 (2008), pp. 55–69; also B. Tibi, 'Turkey's Islamist Danger: Islamists Approach to Europe', *Middle East Quarterly*, 16, 1 (Winter 2009), pp. 47–54. On the relationship between the AKP and the Muslim Brothers see B. Tibi, *Islamism and Islam* (New Haven, CT and London: Yale University Press, 2012), pp. 98–105.

27 Eric Hobsbawm, 'Introduction', in: Eric Hobsbawm and Terence Ranger, eds, *The Invention of Tradition* (New York: Cambridge University Press, reprint 1996), p. 4.

28 Noah Feldman, *The Fall and the Rise of the Islamic State* (Princeton, NJ: Princeton University Press, 2008) does not agree with this interpretation, elaborated upon in B. Tibi, 'The Return of the Sacred to Politics: The Case of the Shari'atization of Politics' (referenced in note 23 above), an article which appeared in advance of Feldman's book.

29 See B. Tibi, *Islamism and Islam* (New Haven, CT: Yale University Press, 2012), chapter 8 'Islamism and Totalitarianism', pp. 201–25.

30 Tariq Ramadan, *Aux Sources de Renouveau Musulman: D'al-Afghani à Hasan al-Banna* (Paris: Bayard, 1998).

31 This quotation and the next are from Joseph Schacht, *An Introduction to Islamic Law* (Oxford: Clarendon Press, reprinted, 1979), p. 54–5.

32 John Kelsay, *Arguing the Just War in Islam* (referenced in note 7 above), pp. 75 and 121–2.

33 H. L. A. Hart, *The Concept of Law* (Oxford: Clarendon Press, 1970), p. 221.

34 The best book on this theme continues to be Myron Weiner, *The Global Migration Crisis* (New York: Harper Collins, 1995). It is – in contrast to the hopeless and misleading book by Jonathan Laurence and Justin Vaisse, *Integrating Islam: Political and Religious Challenges in Contemporary France* (Washington, DC: Brookings, 2006) – a great contribution. There is no integation, but rather an ethnicization in parallel societies; on the ethnicized Islamic diaspora in Europe see Roland Hsu, ed., *Ethnic Europe* (Stanford, CA: Stanford University Press, 2010), pp. 127–56.

35 John Kelsay, *Islam and War* (Louisville, KY: John Knox Press, 1993). The first quotation is from p. 5, the second from pp. 117–18. The result is an ethnicization process. See my chapter to the book edited by Roland Hsu cited in note 34 above.

36 John Kelsay, *Arguing the Just War in Islam*, p. 23. On Islam and migration see B. Tibi, 'A Migration Story: From Muslim Immigrants to European Citizens of the Heart', in: *The Fletcher Forum of World Affairs*, 31 (2007), pp. 147–68.

37 Paul Berman, *The Flight of the Intellectuals: The Controversy over Islamism and the Press* (New York: Melville House, 2011), p. 150.

38 Michael Emerson, ed., *Democratization in the European Neighbourhood* (Brussels: Centre for European Policy Studies, 2005). The Centre for European Policy Studies is a European Union think tank.

39 B. Tibi, 'Europeanizing Islam or the Islamization of Europe', in: Timothy Byrnes and Peter Katzenstein, eds, *Religion in an Expanding Europe* (New York: Cambridge University Press, 2006), pp. 204–24, and also my chapter on Islam in Roland Hsu, ed., *Ethnic Europe* (referenced in note 34 above).

40 John Brenkman, *The Cultural Contradictions of Democracy: Political Thought Since September 11* (Princeton, NJ: Princeton University Press, 2007), p. 165.

41 See the references in note 18 above, and also B. Tibi, 'Intercivilizational Conflict between Value Systems and Concepts of Order: Exploring the Islamic Humanist Potential for a Peace of Ideas', in: Eric Patterson and John Gallagher, eds, *Debating the War of Ideas* (New York: Palgrave, 2009), pp. 157–74, and B. Tibi, 'Islamic Humanism vs. Islamism', in: *Soundings*, 95, 3 (2012), pp. 230–54.

42 B. Tibi, *Islam's Predicament with Modernity: Religious Reform and Cultural Change* (New York: Routledge, 2009), chapters 2–4 and 7.

43 Anthony Reid and Michael Gilseman, eds, *Islamic Legitimacy in Plural Asia* (New York: Routledge, 2007). The volume includes my research paper 'Islam and Cultural Modernity: In Pursuit of Democratic Pluralism', pp. 28–52. This concept contradicts the *dhimmi* and Islamic tolerance concepts analyzed by Bat Ye'or, *Islam and Dhimmitude* (Cransbury, NJ: Associated University Presses, 2002), and Yohanan Friedman, *Tolerance and Coercion in Islam* (New York: Cambridge University Press, 2003).

44 B. Tibi, *Islam in Global Politics* (referenced in note 18 above), chapter 1.

45 Moataz El-Fegiery, 'A Tyranny of the Majority? Islamists' Ambivalence about Human Rights' (FRIDE Working Paper no. 113, Madrid, October 2012; available at http://www.fride.org/publication/1067/islamists'-ambivalence-about-human-rights, accessed February 27, 2013).

6 Torn between combating prejudice and the accusation of Islamophobia: the *shari'a* state and policing speech in the debate 'Whither Islamic civilization?'

1 Published as: Stephen Schwartz, 'Georgetown and the Islamist Money Changers', *The American Thinker*, June 24, 2011. Available at: http://www.americanthinker.com/2011/06/georgetown_and_the_islamist_money_changers.html (accessed February 27, 2013).

2 Pascal Bruck.ner, 'The Invention of Islamophobia', published online January 3, 2011, http://www.signandsight.com/features/2123.html. Originally published as: 'L'invention de l'"islamophobie"', *La Libération*, November 23, 2010.

3 Nicolas Sarkozy, quoted in the report 'Turkey Hits Back', *IHT*, December 24–25, 2011, p. 3.

4 Paul Berman, *The Flight of the Intellectuals* (Brooklyn New York: Melville House, 2010, new edition, 2011), p. 285. Paul Berman's book provoked a heated debate with varying responses. While it was praised in a positive review by Anthony Julius, 'The Pretender', in the *New York Times* Sunday Book Review, May 16, 2010, p. BR 26, it was polemically scorned by Marc Lynch, 'Unveiled Truth', in *Foreign Affairs* (July/August 2010), and by Malise Ruthven in his article 'Righteous & Wrong', in the *New York Review of Books*, August 19, 2010.

5 These Sayyid Qutb quotations (my translation) are taken from the major books by Qutb, *Ma'alim fi al-tariq/Signposts along the Road* (Cairo: al-Shuruq, reprint, 1989),

pp. 150–1, and *al-Salam al-Alami wa al-Islam/World Peace and Islam* (Cairo: al-Shuruq, reprint, 1992), pp. 171–3.

6 John Brenkman, *The Cultural Contradictions of Democracy: Political Thought Since September 11* (Princeton, NJ: Princeton University Press, 2007), pp. 165–9.

7 The book by Edward Said, *Orientalism* (London: Routledge and Kegan Paul, 1978) kindled an awkward controversy. While it was criticized by Sadik J. al-Azm, '*al-Istishraq wa al-Istishraq Ma'kusan*'/'Orientalism and Orientalism in Reverse', included as a chapter in al-Azm's book *Dhihniyyat al-Tahrim/Mentality of Taboos* (London and Limassol: Riad El-Rayyes, 1992), pp. 17–85, it became the bible of the US Islamic studies community. The notions 'Orientalism' and 'Orientalism in reverse' inspire, by analogy, the reversing of racism into 'racism in reverse'. On this reversal see Frantz Fanon, *Les damnés de la terre* (Paris: Maspero, 1964) and therein the preface by Jean-Paul Sartre, who speaks of a 'racist anti-racism'. Fanon criticizes the ideology of '*négritude*' that highlights blackness against whiteness as a case in point. This 'anti-racist racism' is a thinking that remains entangled in the logic of racism. On this debate see B. Tibi, *Internationale Politik und Entwicklungsländer-Forschung* (Frankfurt am Main: Suhrkamp, 1979), pp. 33–51.

8 Sadik J. al-Azm and B. Tibi are among the contributors to Edward Said, ed., *The Arabs Today: Alternatives for Tomorrow* (Columbia, OH: Forum Associates, 1973). The three of us were then very close friends.

9 Eric Patterson and John Gallagher, eds, *Debating the War of Ideas* (New York: Palgrave, 2010).

10 Stephen Sheehi, *Islamophobia: The Ideological Campaign against Muslims* (Atlanta, GA: Clarity Press, 2011).

11 John Stuart Mill, *On Liberty* (Oxford: Oxford University Press, 1998; originally published, 1859), p. 9.

12 Islam is conceptualized as an Islamic civilization partly – but not exclusively – by reference to the 3 volumes by Marshall G. S. Hodgson, *The Venture of Islam: Conscience and History in a World Civilization* (Chicago, IL: University of Chicago Press, 1974, reprinted, 1977). For more details on this conceptualization see Chapter 1 of the present book.

13 See Daniel Varisco, 'Inventing Islamism: The Violence of Rhetoric', lead chapter in: Richard Martin and Abbas Barzegar, eds, *Islamism: Contested Perspectives on Political Islam* (Stanford, CA: Stanford University Press, 2010), pp. 33–50, here pp. 34 and 45. I do not follow Varisco's suggestion. As a native speaker and writer of Arabic I am somewhat intrigued by Varisco's views on the Arabic language.

14 See Chris Mooney, *The Republican War on Science* (New York: Basic Books, 2005).

15 On this Islamist threat to this legitimacy of world order see: Daniel Philpott, 'The Challenge of September 11 to Secularism in International Relations', *World Politics* 55, 1 (October 2002), pp. 66–95, and also the reference in note 6 above.

16 B. Tibi, 'Bridging the Heterogeneity of Civilizations: Reviving the Grammar of Islamic Humanism', *Theoria: A Journal of Social and Political Theory*, 56, 120 (September 2009), pp. 65–80 (see also the reference in note 34 below), and, more recently by the same author, 'Islamic Humanism vs Islamism: Cross-Civilizational Bridging', *Soundings* 95, 3 (2012), pp. 230–54.

17 See Richard C. Martin and Abbas Barzegar, *Islamism: Contested Perspectives on Political Islam* (referenced in note 13 above), p. 7.

18 See the major four books on this crisis referenced above, note 7 to Chapter 3.

19 See the reference to Alan Richards and John Waterbury, *A Political Economy of the Middle East*, above, note 20 to the Introduction.

20 Zeyno Baran, ed., *The Other Muslims: Secular and Moderate* (New York: Palgrave, 2010). The volume includes my chapter 'Euro-Islam' on pp. 157–74, in which I take issue with Tariq Ramadan.

21 On the al-Jabri project see above, note 14 to the Introduction.

22 I acknowledge the existence of differences and nuances within Islamism (e.g. between institutional Islamism and jihadist Islamism) in chapters 4 and 5 of my book *Islamism and Islam* (New Haven, CT: Yale University Press, 2012).

23 See the authoritative five volumes of the Fundamentalism Project, edited by Martin Marty and Scott Appleby and published by Chicago University Press. Volume 2: *Fundamentalisms and Society* (1993) includes as chapter 4 my study on the world view of Islamic fundamentalists, pp. 73–102.

24 Paul Berman, *The Flight of the Intellectuals* (referenced above, note 4), p. 26.

25 Eric Patterson and John Gallagher, eds, *Debating the War of Ideas* (referenced in note 9 above) includes my chapter on Islamism and the Islamic humanist alternative to it on pp. 157–73.

26 Ali Oumlil, *Fi Shar'iyyat al-Ikhtilaf* (Rabat: al-Majlis al-Qaumi, 1991).

27 See Noah Feldman, *The Fall and Rise of the Islamic State* (Princeton, NJ: Princeton University Press, 2008). For a contrast see B. Tibi, 'The Return of the Sacred to Politics as Constitutional Law: The Case of Shari'atization of Politics in Islamic Civilization', *Theoria: A Journal of Social and Political Theory* 55, 115 (2008), pp. 91–119.

28 For more details on this see B. Tibi, 'The Political Legacy of Max Horkheimer and Islamism', *Telos*, issue 148 (Fall 2009), pp. 7–15, and the chapter on Islamism/third-worldism in B. Tibi, *Islam in Global Politics* (referenced in note 34 below).

29 Paul Berman, *The Flight of the Intellectuals* (referenced in note 2 above), p. 275. On Ramadan see Caroline Fourest, *Frère Tariq: Discours, stratégie et méthode de Tariq Ramadan* (Paris: Grasset, 2004), English translation: *Brother Tariq: The Double-Speak of Tariq Ramadan* (New York: Encounter Books, 2008). In *The Flight of the Intellectuals*, Berman focuses on Ramadan.

30 On the Islamist assaults on the nation-state and world order see B. Tibi, *The Challenge of Fundamentalism: Political Islam and the New World Disorder* (Berkeley, CA: University of California Press, 1998, updated, 2002) and on the Islamic diaspora in Europe see B. Tibi, 'Europeanizing Islam or the Islamization of Europe', in: Peter Katzenstein and Timothy Byrnes, eds, *Religion in an Expanding Europe* (New York: Cambridge University Press, 2006), pp. 204–24, as well as the book by Roland Hsu, ed., *Ethnic Europe* (Stanford, CA: Stanford University Press, 2010).

31 See note 22 above and for more details see the two articles by B. Tibi, 'Political Islam as a Forum of Religious Fundamentalism and the Religionization of Politics: Islamism and the Quest for a Remaking of the World', pp. 97–120, and 'Islamism and Democracy: On the Compatibility of Institutional Islamism and the Political Culture of Democracy', pp. 135–164, both published in the special issue on Islamism of the journal *Totalitarian Movements and Political Religions*, 10, 2, 2009.

32 Barry Rubin, ed., *Revolutionaries and Reformers* (Albany, NY: State University of New York Press, 2003).

33 The concern is expressed by Abdelwahab Meddeb, *Sortir de la Malédiction: L'Islam entre civilisation et barberie* (Paris: Seuil, 2008).

34 On 'Islamology' as a new field of study see B. Tibi, *Islam's Predicament with Modernity* (New York: Routledge 2009), in particular the introduction. An example of this approach is provided in B. Tibi, *Islam in Global Politics: Conflict and Cross-Civilizational Bridging* (London and New York: Routledge, 2012). The latter book includes a chapter on Islamic humanism.

35 Mark Juergensmeyer, *The New Cold War? Religious Nationalism Confronts the Secular State* (Berkeley, CA: University of California Press, 1994).

36 See the book by John Brenkman referenced in note 6 above, pp. 165–9.

37 In its July 2008 issue the *Journal of Democracy* published eight contributions on Islamism and gave me the floor to ask the question about Islamist movements: 'Why Can't They be Democratic?', pp. 43–8.

38 See B. Tibi, 'Public Policy and the Combination of Anti-Americanism and Antisemitism in Contemporary Islamist Ideology', *The Current* (Cornell University), 12 (Winter

2008), pp. 123–46 and also the chapter on antisemitism in B. Tibi, *Islamism and Islam* (New Haven, CT: Yale University Press, 2012), pp. 54–93.

39 Gilbert Achcar, *The Arabs and the Holocaust* (New York: Metropolitan Books, 2010), p. 268 and, worse, p. 296, in a most disturbing confusion of criticism and Islamophobia.

40 On this with more details see B. Tibi, *Die Verschwörung: Das Trauma arabischer Politik* (Hamburg: Hoffmann & Campe, 1994), with a focus on the conspiracy-driven Arab ideologies.

41 See the contributions to Leonard Weinberg, ed., *Democratic Responses to Terrorism* (New York: Routledge, 2008), including my chapter on 'Islamism and Democracy', pp. 41–62.

42 M. Zuhdi Jasser, 'Political Islam, Liberalism and the Diagnosis of a Problem', in: Richard Martin and Abbas Barzegar (referenced in note 13 above), pp. 104–9, here p. 106, and the chapter by Jasser in: Zeyno Baran, ed., *The Other Muslims* (referenced in note 20 above), pp. 175–91. See also the essays by Hasan al-Banna, *Majmu'at Rasail al-Imam al-Shahid* (Cairo: Dar al-Da'wa, 1990), p. 23. See the classic by Richard Mitchell, *The Society of the Muslim Brothers* (London: Oxford University Press, 1969).

43 Hussain F. al-Najjar, *al Islam wa al-Siyasah/Islam and Politics* (Cairo: Dar al-Sha'b, 1977), p. 66. The translation of the quotation is mine.

44 Mohammed Said Ashmawi, *Usul al-Shari'a* (Cairo: Madbuli, 1983), p. 30.

45 Jasser (see note 42 above), p. 109. In a submission to a journal the editor and one of his reviewers requested me to omit the quotation of Jasser. I withdrew the submission.

46 Ali Abdul-Raziq, *al-Islam wa Usul al-Hukm/Islam and the Origins of Government* (1925; reprint Beirut, 1966).

47 Among these misguided books are Raymond Baker, *Islam without Fear: Egypt and the New Islamists* (Cambridge, MA: Harvard University Press, 2003), and Bruce Rutherford, *Egypt after Mubarak* (Princeton, NJ: Princeton University Press, 2008).

48 Joseph I. Lieberman, 'Who's the Enemy in the War on Terror', *Wall Street Journal*, June 15, 2010, p. A17.

49 B. Tibi, *Islamism and Islam* (referenced in note 22 above), chapter 5, in particular pp. 135–7.

50 On an inter-civilizational peace based on Islamic humanism see the references in notes 16 and 21 above and my chapter in Eric Patterson and Eric Gallagher (referenced in note 9 above).

51 Marc Lynch, 'Veiled Truths' (referenced in note 4 above).

52 This dark side (Islamist cooperation with Nazi Germany) is meticulously documented by the historian Jeffrey Herf, *Nazi Propaganda for the Arab World* (New Haven, CT: Yale University Press, 2009). The collaboration between Islamism and Nazi Germany during World War Two is the subject matter of Herf's book, which is attacked by Lynch (see note 4 above).

53 See the reference to this project in note 23 above, in particular volume 2: *Fundamentalisms and Society* (1993).

54 Chris Mooney, 'Not Blinded by Science, but Ideology', *Washington Post*, June 27, 2010, p. B3.

55 Chris Mooney, *The Republican War on Science* (referenced in note 14 above).

56 Mooney, *Republican War on Science*, pp. 17 and 18.

57 See Stephen Schwartz, *The Two Faces of Islam: The House of Sa'ud from Tradition to Terror* (New York: Doubleday, 2002).

58 See above, note 7 to Chapter 3.

59 Ali Allawi, *The Crisis of Islamic Civilization* (New Haven, CT: Yale University Press, 2009). The quotes are adopted in succession from pp. 252–3, 256, 268, 108, 273.

60 Paula Schriefer, 'The Wrong Way to Combat Islamophobia', *IHT*, November 10, 2010, p. 8.

61 A major book on this theme is Norman Daniel, *Islam and the West: The Making of an Image* (Oxford: Oxford University Press, 1993; first published, 1960).

62 This nonsense is from James Carroll, 'Bigotry in America', *IHT*, April 5, 2011, p. 6.

63 On this see the basic books by William M. Watt, *Muslim-Christian Encounters* (London: Routledge, 1991), and Maxime Rodinson, *La Fascination de l'Islam* (Paris, Maspero, 1981).

64 Scott Shane, 'Gains by Islamists Force US to Reassess Its Views about Friends and Foes', *IHT*, July 10, 2012, p. 5. The emphasis in the quotation is mine.

65 See above, note 41 to Chapter 4.

66 For *Liberal Islam*, see above, note 8 to the Introduction.

67 Robert Hefner, *Civil Islam: Muslims and Democratization in Indonesia* (Princeton, NJ: Princeton University Press, 2000).

68 Abdou Filali-Ansary, 'Muslims and Democracy', in: Larry Diamond, Marc F. Plattner and Daniel Brumberg, eds., *Islam and Democracy in the Middle East* (Baltimore, MD: Johns Hopkins University Press, 2003), pp. 194–207, here p. 204.

69 Mohammed Abed al-Jabri, *Arab-Islamic Philosophy* (Austin, TX: University of Texas, 1999; translated from the French by Aziz Abbassi), p. 124.

70 Ali Allawi, *The Crisis of Islamic Civilization* (see note 59 above), p. 104.

71 John Eibner, 'Hatred of Christians in the Muslim World', *IHT*, May 12, 2011, p. 6. On this theme see also the book by Eliza Griswald, *The Tenth Parallel: Dispatches from the Faultline Between Islam and Christianity* (New York: Farrar, Straus and Giroux, 2010).

72 Abdou Filali-Ansary, 'Muslims and Democracy' (see note 68 above), p. 204.

73 Roger Cohen, 'Religion Does Its Worst', *IHT*, April 5, 2011, p. 6.

74 Efraim Karsh, *Islamic Imperialism* (New Haven, CT: Yale University Press, 2006) and Dan Diner, *Lost in the Sacred* (Princeton, NJ: Princeton University Press, 2009).

75 My book *Islamism and Islam* (note 22) was completed at the Yale Interdisciplinary Initiative for the Study of Antisemitism (YIISA); it includes as chapter 3 'Islamism and Antisemitism'. The book was finalized at the Center for Advanced Holocaust Studies where I served as the first Muslim as the Resnick Scholar for the study of antisemitism.

76 Martin Kramer, *Ivory Towers on Sand: The Failure of Middle Eastern Studies in America* (Washington, DC: The Washington Institute for Near East Policy, 2001).

77 John Kelsay, editorial, *Soundings* 95, 3 (2012), pp. 227–8.

78 Abdou Filali-Ansary, 'Muslims and Democracy' (see note 68 above).

79 See B. Tibi, 'Global Communication and Cultural Particularisms', in: Robert Fortner and Mark Fackler, eds, *Handbook of Global Communication and Media Ethics*, 2 volumes (Oxford: Wiley Blackwell, 2011), here volume 1, pp. 54–78.

80 See B. Tibi, 'Europeanizing Islam or the Islamization of Europe? Democracy vs. Cultural Difference', in: Timothy Byrnes and Peter Katzenstein, eds, *Religion in an Expanding Europe* (New York: Cambridge University Press, 2006), pp. 204–24.

Index